Mastering Excel 365

An All-in-One Tutorial Resource

Nathan George

Mastering Excel 365: An All-in-One Tutorial Resource

2024 Edition.

Published by GTech Publishing.

ISBN: 978-1-915476-11-1

https://www.excelbytes.com

Contents

Chapter 2: Lookup and Reference Functions...........................381

Introduction

Welcome to *Mastering Excel 365*, your all-in-one guide to the latest and most powerful version of Excel from Microsoft 365. This book contains everything you need to know to master the basics of Excel and a selection of advanced topics relevant to real-world productivity tasks. This guide has been designed to be a resource for you whether you're an Excel beginner, an intermediate user, or a power user.

This book is concise and to the point, using clear and practical examples that you can adapt to your own needs. The aim is to show you how to perform tasks in Excel as quickly as possible without getting bogged down with unnecessary verbosity and filler text that you may find in other Excel books. This book shows you how to use specific features and in what context those features need to be used. Mastering Excel 365 is made up of three books brought together and organized as an all-in-one guide.

How This Book Is Organized

Book 1: Excel Basics

This book starts with the very basics. You first get to familiarize yourself with the Excel user interface and ribbon. You learn to create, edit, format, organize, and print your worksheets. You learn how to enter formulas and perform different types of calculations in Excel. You learn how to use named ranges, Excel tables, charts, and dropdown lists. You learn how to sort and filter your data in different ways. This book provides you with most of what you would need for everyday Excel tasks, including all the fundamentals you need to proceed to topics in Books 2 and 3, like functions and pivot tables.

Book 2: Excel Advanced Topics

This book covers a selection of topics that will enable you to take advantage of more powerful tools in Excel to perform tasks more geared for the power user. In this book, you'll learn how to transform data with various data tools, import data from external sources like CSV files and Access, troubleshoot and fix formula errors, automate repetitive tasks with macros, create and analyze projections with What-If Analysis, analyze large sets of data with Pivot Tables and Pivot Charts, and protect workbooks, worksheets, or ranges.

Book 3: Excel Functions

This book is a deep dive into Excel functions and covers over 80 of the most useful and powerful functions in Excel from different categories. The functions covered include lookup and reference functions like XLOOKUP and XMATCH; math and statistical functions like SUMIF and MAXIFS; logical functions like IF and IFS; date functions like DATEDIF and NETWORKDAYS; text functions like TEXTSPLIT and TEXTJOIN; and financial functions like PV, FV, and NPV.

The functions covered in this book have been carefully selected based on how often they're used in common Excel tasks and specialized work. Important new functions introduced recently have also been included. Each function is covered in detail, including the syntax, description of arguments, and practical examples to demonstrate its use. You also learn how to combine different functions to solve more complex problems.

How to Use This Book

Mastering Excel 365 can be used as a step-by-step training guide or a reference manual that you come back to from time to time. If you're a beginner, you ideally want to read all the chapters in Book 1 in sequential order. Book 1 provides all the fundamentals to proceed to selected topics in Books 2 and 3. You also want to cover commonly used functions in Book 3, like SUM, IF, IFS, and XLOOKUP, as these will come in handy for everyday Excel use.

If you're already familiar with Excel, you can read this book cover to cover or skip to specific chapters. Although the topics have been organized logically, as much as possible, each topic has been designed as a standalone tutorial on how to perform a specific task. Book 3, in particular, has been designed as a resource guide for Excel functions, so the chapters are as self-contained as possible.

There are many ways to carry out the same task in Excel, so, for brevity, I have focused on the most efficient way of performing a task. However, I provided alternative ways to perform a task on some occasions.

As much as possible, the menu items and commands mentioned are bolded to distinguish them from the other text. This book contains many screenshots to illustrate the discussed features and tasks.

Assumptions

The software assumptions made when writing this book are that you already have Microsoft 365 or Excel 2021 (the latest standalone version of Excel) installed on your computer and that you're working on the Windows 11 (or Windows 10) platform.

If you run an earlier version of Excel, you can still use this book (as long as you're aware that some of the dialog boxes shown may look slightly different). Many of the core features covered are present in previous versions of Excel.

If you use Excel 365 on a Mac, simply substitute any Windows keyboard commands mentioned in the book for the Mac equivalent. All the features within Excel remain the same for both platforms.

If you're using Excel on a tablet or touchscreen device, substitute any keyboard commands mentioned in the book with the equivalent on your touchscreen device.

Practice Files

Downloadable Excel files have been provided to save you time if you want to practice in Excel as you follow the examples in the book. All examples are fully detailed in the book, so the sample files are optional. These files can save you time in recreating the sample data.

You can practice by changing the data to view different results. Please note that practice files have only been included for chapters where the examples use a sizable amount of sample data. You can download the files from the following link:

https://www.excelbytes.com/mastering-excel-365-download

Notes:

- Type the URL in your Internet browser's address bar, and press Enter to go to the download page. If you encounter an error, double-check that you have correctly entered all the URL characters.

- The files have been zipped into one download. Windows 11 (or Windows 10) has the functionality to unzip files. If your OS does not have this functionality, you'll need software like WinZip or WinRAR to unzip the file.

- The files are Excel for Windows 365 files, so you will need to have Excel installed on your computer to open and use these files (preferably Excel 2013 and above).

- If you encounter any problems downloading these files, please contact me at **support@excelbytes.com**. Include the title of this book in your email, and the practice files will be emailed directly to you.

Book 1

Excel Basics

Chapter 1

Getting Started with Excel

This chapter covers the following:

- ■ Creating, saving, and closing a new Excel workbook.

- ■ Opening an existing workbook.

- ■ Best way to use Autosave.

- ■ Restoring a previous version of your workbook.

- ■ Customizing the ribbon.

- ■ The Quick Access Toolbar.

- ■ Accessing Help in Excel.

To start Excel, click the Windows Start icon and enter "Excel" in the search bar. Windows displays the Excel app in the results below. Click Excel to start the application.

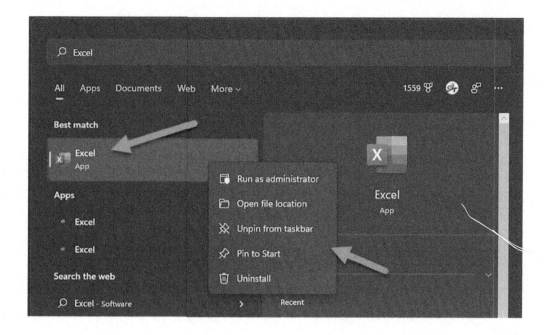

To access Excel faster next time, you can pin it to the **Start menu, taskbar**, or place a shortcut on your **desktop**.

Do the following to pin Excel to your **Start menu**:

1. Click the Windows **Start** icon.
2. On the Start menu, enter "Excel" in the search bar.
3. On the results list below, right-click **Excel** and select **Pin to Start**.

Do the following to pin Excel to your **taskbar:**

1. Click the Windows **Start** icon.
2. On the Start menu, enter "Excel" in the search bar.
3. Right-click **Excel** and select **Pin to taskbar**.

To place a copy of Excel's shortcut on your **desktop**, do the following:

1.   Click the Windows **Start** icon.

2.   On the Start menu, enter "Excel" in the search bar.

3.   Right-click **Excel** and select **Open file location** on the shortcut menu.

     Windows will open the shortcut folder location of Excel in Windows Explorer.

4.   In the folder, right-click **Excel**, and select **Copy** on the shortcut menu.

5.   On your desktop, right-click any area and select **Paste**.

Creating a New Excel Workbook

Launch Excel from the Start menu or the shortcut you have created on your taskbar or desktop.

Excel will open and display the **Home** screen. The Excel start screen enables you to create a new blank workbook or open one of your recently opened workbooks. You also have a selection of predefined templates that you can use as the basis of your workbook.

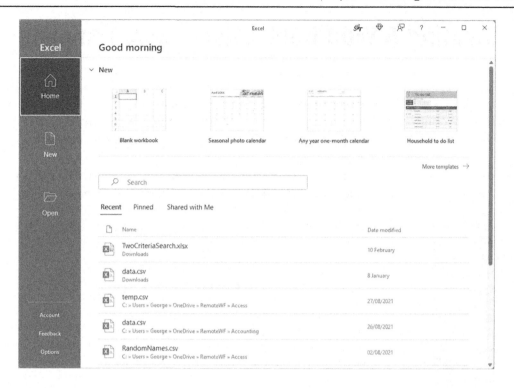

To create a new workbook, click **Blank workbook**. Excel creates a new workbook with a worksheet named **Sheet1**.

Tip To quickly create a new workbook when you already have a workbook open, press **Ctrl + N** on your keyboard.

Creating A Workbook Based on A Template

To create a new workbook based on one of Excel's predefined templates, open Excel and click the **New** button on the left navigation pane to display the New screen. The categories of available templates are listed under the search bar next to **Suggested searches**.

You can narrow down the displayed templates by clicking one of the listed categories: Business, Personal, Planners and Trackers, Lists, Budgets, Charts, or Calendars.

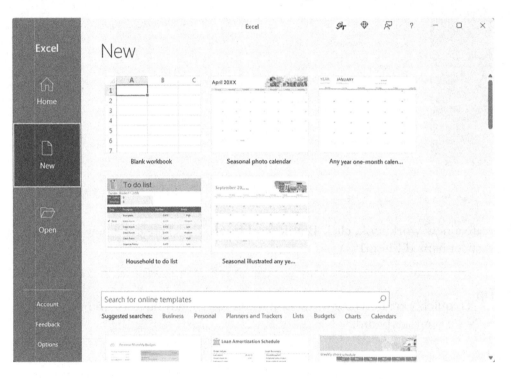

Once you identify the template you want to use, double-click the thumbnail to create a new worksheet based on it.

Saving Your Excel Workbook

To save your workbook for the first time:

1. Click the **File** tab to go to the Backstage view.

2. In the Backstage view, click **Save As** (you'll see **Save a Copy** if your file has been previously saved to OneDrive).

3. On the next screen, click **OneDrive – Personal** (if you're using OneDrive) or **This PC** (if you're not saving it to OneDrive).

4. You get a text box to enter the file name on the right side of the window. Enter the name of your worksheet here.

5. To save the file to an existing folder, navigate to the folder using the list displayed below on the lower-right of the screen. Double-click a folder name to navigate to that folder.

   You can also create a new folder by clicking the **New Folder** button.

6. Click the **Save** button to save the workbook.

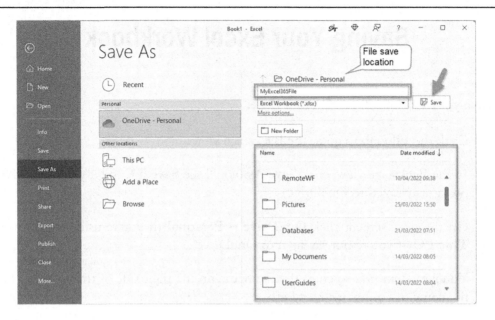

Excel returns you to the **Home** tab after it saves the file.

Note If your workbook has been previously saved to OneDrive or SharePoint, and **AutoSave** is set to on, you'll have **Save a Copy** in place of **Save As**. You can use Save a Copy to save your workbook as a different file.

When you save a file, you overwrite the previous version of the file. If you want to keep an old version of the file while working on it, you need to use **Save As** (or **Save a Copy**). Excel saves the workbook you're working on as a new file while the old version remains unchanged.

Tip To save your workbook quicker, you can use the **Ctrl+S** shortcut after the first save. For a list of the most frequently used shortcuts in Excel, see the Appendix in this book.

Opening an Existing Workbook

Click the **File** menu button to display the Backstage view, and then click **Open** or press **Ctrl+O**.

On the **Open** screen of the Backstage view, you'll see the following options:

- **Recent**: To open a recent workbook, select **Recent** and click the workbook you want to open on the right.

- **Shared with me**: Select this tab to see the files that others have shared with you. Files can be shared through outlook email attachments, a link in an email, a link in Teams, or other methods.

- **OneDrive - Personal**: To open a workbook saved on OneDrive, click OneDrive - Personal and select your file from the right.

> **Note** If you're not in the root folder of OneDrive, you can use the blue up-arrow to navigate to the folder that contains your workbook.

- **This PC**: To open a workbook from the Documents local folder on your PC, click **This PC** to display the Documents folder. Navigate to the folder containing your workbook. Click the file to open it.

- **Browse**: To browse for a file on your computer, click the **Browse** button and use the Open dialog box to locate the file you want to open. Then, select the file and click the **Open** button.

Closing a Workbook

Ensure you've saved the workbook (if you want to keep the changes).

Click **File** to display the Backstage view, and then click **Close**.

Or

Press the **Ctrl+W** shortcut keys to close the workbook.

The Excel User Interface

This section provides an overview of the Excel user interface to familiarize you with the names of various parts of the interface mentioned throughout the book.

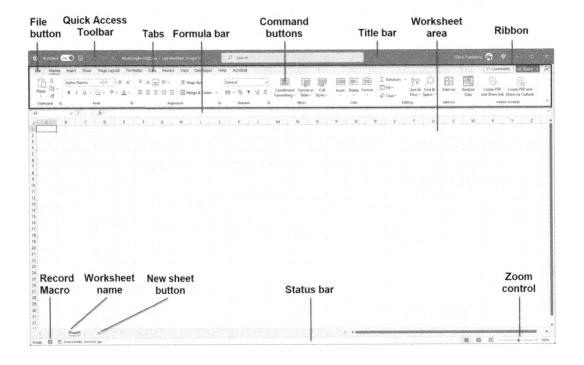

The **Ribbon** contains the bulk of the commands in Excel arranged into a series of tabs from Home to Help.

The **File** button/tab opens the Backstage view when clicked. The Backstage view has several menu options, including Home, New, Open, Info, Save, Save As, Print, Share, Export, Publish, and Close. You have the Account menu option at the bottom of the list to view your user information. You also have Options where you can change many of Excel's default settings.

Note that if your Excel workbook is saved on OneDrive and **AutoSave** is set to **On**, you'll not see the **Save As** menu option. Instead, you'll have **Save a Copy** in its place.

To exit the Backstage view, click the back button (the left-pointing arrow at the top-left of the page).

The **Home** tab provides the most used set of commands. The other tabs provide command buttons for specific tasks like inserting objects into your spreadsheet, formatting the page layout, working with formulas, working with datasets, reviewing your spreadsheet, etc.

The **Worksheet area** contains the cells that will hold your data. The row headings are numbered, while the column headings have letters. Each cell is identified by the combination of the column letter and row number. For example, the first cell on the sheet is A1, the second cell in the first row is B1, and the second cell in the first column is A2. You use these references to identify the cells on the worksheet.

A **workbook** is the Excel document itself. A **worksheet** is a sheet inside a workbook. Each workbook can have several worksheets. You can use the tabs at the bottom of the screen to name, move, copy, and delete worksheets. The plus (+) button next to the name tab enables you to add a new worksheet.

The **Formula bar** displays the contents of the active cell, including any formula.

The **Status bar** provides information on the current display mode. You can zoom in and out of your spreadsheet by clicking the plus (+) and minus (-) signs at the bottom-right of the status bar.

The **Dialog Box Launcher** is a button with a diagonal arrow in the lower-right corner of some groups. When clicked, Excel opens a dialog box containing additional command options related to that group. So, if you cannot see a command on the Ribbon for a task you want to perform, click the small dialog box launcher to display more options for that group.

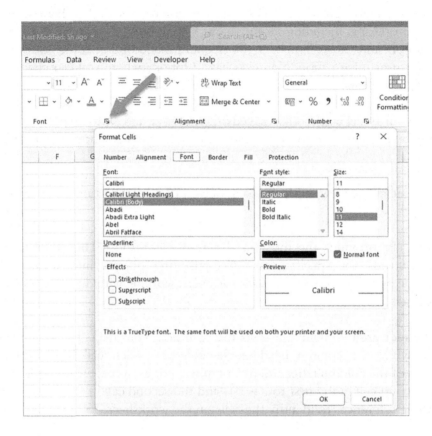

Using AutoSave

AutoSave is a feature on the top-left of the title bar that is enabled when a file is stored on OneDrive or SharePoint. It automatically saves your changes every few seconds as you are working. The main advantage of AutoSave is that if your PC were to crash for any reason, your changes right up to the point it crashed would have been saved to disk. So, you'll hardly lose any work.

With AutoSave on, the **Save As** menu option in the Backstage view is replaced by **Save a Copy**. If you're making changes to your workbook and you normally use **File** > **Save As** to avoid changing the original file, it is recommended that you use **File** > **Save a Copy** before making your changes. That way, AutoSave will not overwrite the original file with the changes but the copy.

If like me, you're in the habit of just closing a workbook without saving it, if you do not want to keep the changes, then AutoSave becomes an issue. In such a case, you can turn off AutoSave before you make any changes and then save your workbook manually if you want to keep the changes.

With **AutoSave** set to On, if you make a mistake that you want to undo, ensure you use the **Undo** button on the **Home** tab to undo the changes before closing the workbook.

Turning off AutoSave

Switching off AutoSave is not recommended. However, if you want to be able to just close Excel and discard all changes whenever you wish, you could turn off AutoSave for that particular file and manually save your workbook.

The default setting for AutoSave is On for files on the cloud (OneDrive or SharePoint). However, if you set AutoSave to Off for a particular workbook, Excel will remember the setting and keep it off every time you reopen it. If you switch it back to On, it will remember to keep it on for that workbook.

Restoring a Previous Version of your Workbook

You can also restore a previous version of your workbook from the Version History.

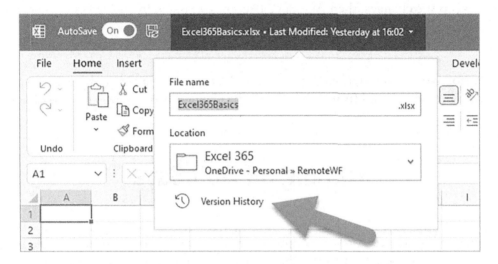

To restore an older version from the Version History list, do the following:

1. Click the file name on the title bar.

2. Click **Version History**.

    Excel displays the **Version History** pane on the right side of the window. The Version History pane shows you the different versions of your document, including the date and time they were saved. The versions are grouped under the date the file was saved. Look at the dates and times to find the version you want to restore.

3. Double click the version you want to restore, and Excel will open the workbook in a second window.

4. Click the **Restore** button displayed just under the Ribbon to revert to this version.

Renaming Your Workbook

You can rename a previously saved workbook from the pop-up menu displayed when you click the file name on the title bar. In the **File Name** box, you can enter a new name for the workbook and press Enter to rename the workbook.

Customizing the Ribbon

The area of the window containing the tabs and command buttons is called the **Ribbon**. You can customize the Ribbon to your liking by adding or removing tabs and command buttons.

To customize the Ribbon, right-click anywhere on the Ribbon, below the tabs, and select **Customize the Ribbon** from the pop-up menu.

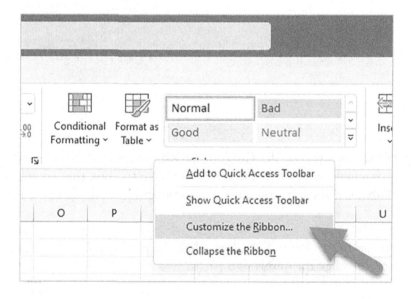

Excel opens the **Excel Options** window.

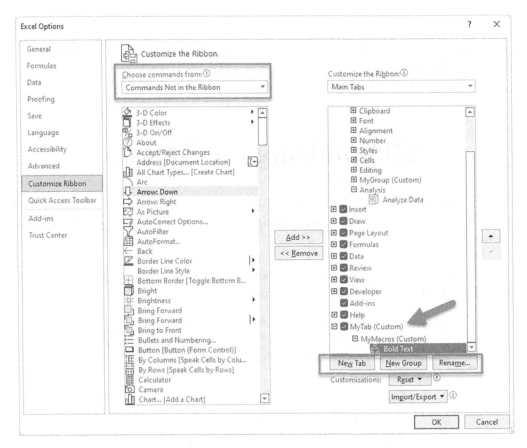

In the **Excel Options** window, the **Customize Ribbon** tab will be selected, and on that tab, you have two main boxes. On the right, you have the box that shows your current tabs - **Main Tabs**. On the left, you have the command buttons that you can add to the Ribbon.

To expand a group in the **Main Tabs** box, click the plus sign (+) to the left of an item. To collapse a group, click the minus sign (-).

To find commands not currently on your Ribbon, click the drop-down arrow on the left box (**Choose commands from**) and select **Commands Not in the Ribbon** from the drop-down list.

You will see a list of commands not on your Ribbon, which is useful as it filters out the commands already on your Ribbon.

Note You can't add or remove the default commands on the Ribbon, but you can uncheck them on the list to prevent them from being displayed. Also, you can't add command buttons to the default groups. You must create a new group (called a custom group) to add a new command button.

To create a new tab, do the following:

Click the **New Tab** button to create a new tab. Inside the tab, you must create at least one group before you can add a command button from the list of commands in the box on the left side of the Excel Options dialog box.

To create a custom group, do the following:

1. Select the tab in which you want to create the group. It could be one of the default tabs or the new one you've created.

2. Click the **New Group** button (located at the bottom of the dialog box, under the Main Tabs list). Excel will create a new group within the currently selected tab.

3. Select the new group and click **Rename** to give the group your preferred name.

You now have a custom group in which you can add commands.

To add commands to your custom group, do the following:

1. Select your custom group in the box on the right side of the screen.

2. Select the new command you want to add from the box on the left side of the screen and click the **Add** button to add it to your custom group.

   To remove a command from your custom group, select the command in the right box and click the **Remove** button.

3. Click **OK** to confirm the change.

When you view the customized tab on the Ribbon, you'll see your new group and your added command buttons.

The Quick Access Toolbar

The Quick Access Toolbar has been restored to the title bar by default in the current iteration of Excel 365. The Quick Access Toolbar is a customizable toolbar with commands independent of the active tab on the ribbon. Hence, it makes regularly used commands available to you at any point for easy access, regardless of which tab is currently displayed.

Displaying the Quick Access Toolbar

By default, the Quick Access Toolbar is displayed in a standard installation of Excel on the top left corner of the Excel window above the ribbon. However, if it is not displayed in your installation, right-click any blank area of the Excel ribbon and select **Show Quick Access Toolbar** from the pop-up menu.

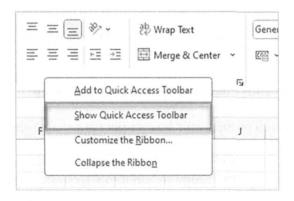

To hide the quick access toolbar, right-click any blank area of the Excel ribbon and select **Hide Quick Access Toolbar** from the pop-up menu.

Changing the Location of the Quick Access Toolbar

If you prefer to display the Quick Access Toolbar below the ribbon, you can switch it below the ribbon by right-clicking anywhere on the toolbar and selecting **Show Quick Access Toolbar Below the Ribbon**.

Likewise, if your Quick Access Toolbar is below the ribbon, and you want to switch it above the ribbon, right-click anywhere on the toolbar and select **Show Quick Access Toolbar Above the Ribbon**.

Note If you hide and redisplay the Quick Access Toolbar, Excel remembers where it was last positioned and displays it there again.

Customizing the Quick Access Toolbar

The Quick Access Toolbar allows you to add commands you often use in Excel. To customize the Quick Access Toolbar, select its drop-down arrow to display a drop-down menu.

On the menu, select the items you want to add to the Quick Access Toolbar and clear the items you want to remove.

To add commands to the Quick Access Toolbar that are not available on the menu, follow the steps below:

1. On the Quick Access Toolbar menu (shown in the image above), select **More Commands**. Excel opens the Quick Access Toolbar pane in **Excel Options**.

2. In the drop-down list named **Choose commands from**, select **All Commands**.

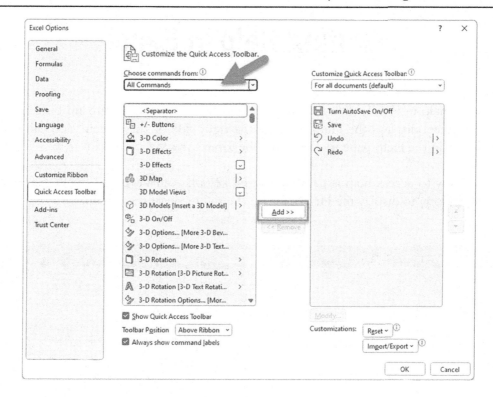

3. From the list of commands on the left, select a command you would like to add to the Quick Access Toolbar and click the **Add** button to add it to the list on the right. Do this for every command you want to add to the list.

4. To change the order of commands on the Quick Access Toolbar, select an item on the list on the right and use the up and down arrows to change its position.

Click **OK** when you are done.

Getting Help in Excel

To access help in Excel, click the Help tab and then the Help command button on the Ribbon. Excel displays the Help pane on the right side of the screen. You can use the search box in the Help pane to search for the topic for which you want help.

A quick way to access help is to press the **F1** key on your keyboard (while Excel is the active window) to display the Help pane on the right side of the screen.

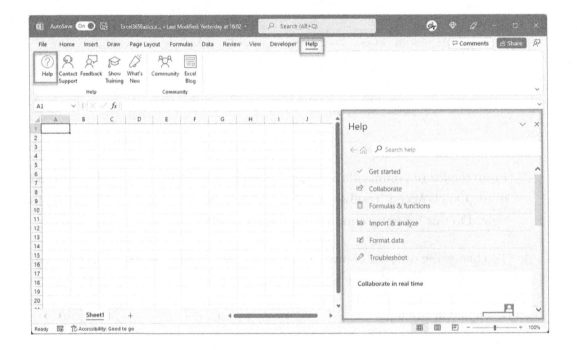

Using Search

Another way to get help in Excel is to use the Search box on the title bar. Click the Search box or press **ALT+Q** to activate the search box.

Before you type anything, the search box will display a drop-down list of help topics related to your recent actions and other suggestions based on what you appear to be doing. If any of the suggestions is related to the topic for which you're seeking help, select it from the list. Otherwise, you can enter words or phrases regarding actions you want to perform or a topic for which you want further information.

Depending on the topic or how direct your question is, Excel will either list the steps needed to complete the task, take you to the appropriate dialog box, or display information related to the topic in the Help pane.

Chapter 2

Entering and Editing Data

This chapter covers the following:

- ■ Manually entering and editing data

- ■ Using Autofill

- ■ Using Flash Fill

There are several ways to enter and edit data in Excel, including using features that automate data entry. By the end of this chapter, you'll be familiar with manually entering data into your worksheet and using automated features to make data entry faster.

Entering and Editing Data Manually

Entering data:

Click a cell in the worksheet area, and a rectangular box will appear around the cell. This box is the **cell pointer** or the active cell. You can move the cell pointer with the left, right, up, or down arrow keys on your keyboard.

To enter data, simply type it directly into the cell, or you can click in the formula bar and type the data in there. To enter a formula, you need to prefix your entry with the equal sign (=). We will cover this later in the chapter on formulas.

Editing data:

When typing in the worksheet area, use the BACKSPACE key to go back and not the left arrow key if you want to make a correction. The arrow keys move the cell pointer from cell to cell. To use the arrow keys when editing data, select the cell, then click in the formula bar to edit the data there.

To overwrite data, click the cell to make it the active cell and just type in the new value. Your entry will overwrite the previous value.

If you only want to edit parts of the data in a cell, for example, a piece of text, then select the cell and click in the formula bar to edit the contents there.

Deleting data:

Select the data and hit the Delete key to delete data from your worksheet.

Default content alignment:

In Excel, numbers and formulas are right-aligned in the cell by default. Everything else is left-aligned by default. So, you can tell if Excel recognizes an entry as a number or text value.

Using AutoFill

The Autofill feature in Excel lets you fill cells with a series of sequential dates and numbers. It enables you to automate repetitive tasks as it is smart enough to figure out what data goes in a cell (based on another cell) when you drag the fill handle across cells.

Entering Dates with AutoFill

You may have a worksheet where you need to enter dates. You can enter *January* in one cell and use the AutoFill feature to automatically enter the rest of the months.

The **Fill Handle** is the small black square at the lower right of the cell pointer. When you hover over the lower right corner of the active cell, a black plus sign (+) appears. This change is an indication that when you drag the selection down (or to the right), Excel will either copy the contents of the first cell to the selected cells or use it as the first entry in a consecutive series.

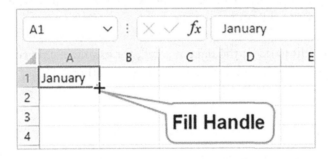

So, you first need to click the cell to select it and then hover over the bottom right corner to display the small plus sign (+).

To AutoFill dates, enter *January* or any other starting month in one cell, then grab the small fill handle and drag it across the other cells.

AutoFill also works with abbreviations, but they must be three letters. For example, if you enter Jan and then drag down, Excel will fill the cells with Feb, Mar, Apr, May, etc.

Let's say you want to enter the seven days of the week as your row headings. In the first cell of your range, enter *Monday* or *Mon*. Then drag the autofill handle down over the remaining six cells. Excel will AutoFill the remaining cells with Tuesday to Sunday.

Excel keeps the filled days selected, giving you a chance to drag the handle back if you went too far or to drag it further if you didn't go far enough.

You can also use the **AutoFill Options** drop-down menu to refine your fill options further. To access the AutoFill options, you will see a drop-down button that appears on the last cell with the cells still selected. When you click it, Excel displays a list of options that enable you to choose whether you want to copy the data across the cells, fill the series, copy formatting only, ignore the formatting, flash fill, etc.

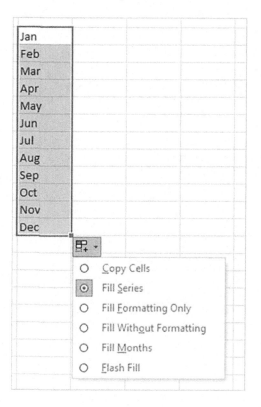

Note If you don't see a button that enables you to access the AutoFill Options drop-down menu (shown in the image above) after an autofill, it is most likely because the option hasn't been enabled in Excel Options.

To enable AutoFill Options, do the following:

1. On the Ribbon, click **File** > **Options** > **Advanced**.

2. Under the **Cut, copy, and paste** section, select the checkbox for **Show Paste Options button when content is pasted**.

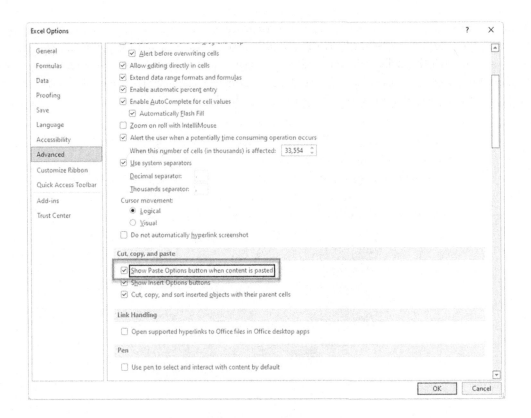

AutoFill Incremental Values

To AutoFill other incremental values, you need to first let Excel know the difference. Thus, you would need to enter values in at least two cells before dragging the fill handle across the other cells.

For example, let's say you want to enter dates that increment by seven days, i.e., a weekly interval. You would need to enter two dates (for example, 01/10/22 and 01/17/22). Then you select <u>both</u> cells and drag across the empty cells to autofill the other cells with dates having an interval of seven days.

You can do the same with other numbers. If you enter number 1 and drag down the fill handle, the number 1 will just be copied to the other cells. However, if you enter numbers 1 and 2 in two cells and then select both cells and drag the fill handle down (or to the right), you will get 3, 4, 5, 6, etc.

AutoFill Formulas

To AutoFill a formula across several cells, enter the formula in the first cell and drag the fill handle over the other cells in the range. If the cell references are relative, then the references will also change to match the position of the active cell.

For example, if the first cell of your formula is $= A1 + B1$, when you drag this formula down to the other cells, the formula in the other cells will be, $=A2+B2$, $=A3+B3$, $=A4+B4$, and so on.

Another way to use AutoFill is to click the **Fill** button in the **Editing** group on the **Home** tab.

Note If the cell references in your formula are absolute, then the cell references will not change when you use AutoFill to copy it to other cells. See the difference between relative and absolute cell references in chapter 6 in this book.

AutoFill the Same Values

To AutoFill the same value across a series of cells, enter the value in the first cell, then hold down the **Ctrl** key while dragging the fill handle across the other cells.

For example, if you want to fill a range of cells with January:

1. Enter **January** in the first cell.

2. Hold down the **Ctrl** key.

3. Hover over the fill handle (small square in the lower-right of the cell pointer), click and then drag it across the other cells.

   Excel will enter January in all the selected cells.

Using Flash Fill

Flash Fill is a feature introduced in Excel 2013 that enables you to split and rearrange data automatically. In the past, you would need to combine several Excel text functions like LEFT and MID to get the same results that you can now get with the Flash Fill command.

Example 1

In this example, we have a name field (made up of the first name and last name) that we want to sort by **Last Name**. To sort by Last Name, we need to re-enter the names in another column with the last name first. This change is required because Excel starts sorting with the field's first character, then the next, etc.

With Flash Fill, you can insert a new column next to the name column and enter the first value starting with the last name. When you enter the second value, Excel will figure out what you're trying to do and automatically Flash Fill the other cells in the format it predicts you want to enter the data. This automation will save you a lot of time as you only need to enter two cells to have the rest automatically completed for you.

	A	B	C	D
	B3		fx	West, Peter
1	Employee		Month1	Month2
2	Jane Smith	Smith, Jane	$1,453.00	$1,946.00
3	Peter West	West, Peter	$1,713.00	$1,251.00
4	Derek Brown	Brown, Derek	$1,467.00	$1,582.00
5	Jason Fields	Fields, Jason	$1,356.00	$1,097.00
6	Mark Powell	Powell, Mark	$1,919.00	$1,118.00
7	Julie Rush	Rush, Julie	$1,282.00	$1,437.00
8				
9				

Steps in Flash Fill:

1. Enter the value in the first cell in the new format.

2. Start entering the second value in the next cell.

3. You'll see a preview of the rest of the column displaying the suggested entries.

4. Press **Enter** to accept the suggestions.

Excel populates the other cells in the column with the data in the new format.

Another way to use Flash Fill is to use the **Flash Fill** command button in the **Data Tools** group on the **Data** tab.

To use the Flash Fill command button for the same example above, do the following:

1. Enter the value the way you want it in an adjacent cell and press enter.

2. On the **Data** tab, in the **Data Tools** group, click the **Flash Fill** button.

Excel automatically enters the rest of the values in the same format as the first cell.

Example 2

To quickly split a full name field up into first name and last name fields, do the following:

1. Assuming the full name is in column A2, enter the first name in B2 and press enter.

2. On the **Data** tab, in the **Data Tools** group, click **Flash Fill**.

   Excel populates the other rows in column B with the first name from column A.

3. Enter the last name from A2 in C2 and apply the Flash Fill command.

   Excel populates the other rows with the last name from column A.

| C2 | ⋮ | ✕ ✓ *fx* | Smith |

◢	A	B	C	D
1	**Name**	**First name**	**Last name**	
2	Jane Smith	Jane	Smith	
3	Peter West	Peter	West	
4	Derek Brown	Derek	Brown	
5	Jason Fields	Jason	Fields	
6	Mark Powell	Mark	Powell	
7	Julie Rush	Julie	Rush	
8				

Chapter 3

Design and Organize Workbooks

In this chapter, we will cover the following:

- Adding and removing worksheets.

- Moving, copying, hiding, and deleting worksheets.

- Freezing rows and columns.

- Applying themes to your worksheets.

This chapter focuses on managing and organizing your workbook. Each workbook can have one or more worksheets. Hence, learning how to keep your workbooks organized is an essential part of building your Excel skills.

Adding New Worksheets

We covered creating a new workbook in Chapter 1. When you first create a workbook, you'll have one worksheet named **Sheet1**.

To add a new sheet to your workbook, click the plus sign (+) at the bottom of the worksheet area, to the right of Sheet1, and it will create a new worksheet named Sheet2. You can add more worksheets to your workbook this way.

The number of worksheets you can have in a workbook is unlimited. You're only limited by your computer resources like RAM and hard disk space. However, try not to have too many sheets in one workbook as the file can become very large, and taking longer to open.

Naming a Worksheet

To name your worksheet, double-click the name tab at the bottom of the screen, and the name will become editable. For example, if you double-click *Sheet1,* the name will be selected with the cursor blinking, allowing you to type in the new name.

Moving and Copying Worksheets

You can move and reorder your worksheets by clicking the name and dragging it to the left or right. You can also move a sheet by right-clicking the name and selecting **Move or Copy** from the pop-up menu.

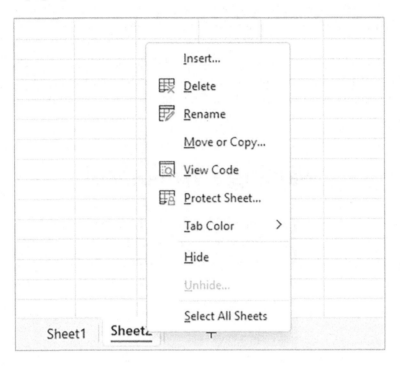

On the **Move or Copy** screen, select a name from the list and click OK. The selected worksheet will be moved to the front of the sheet selected.

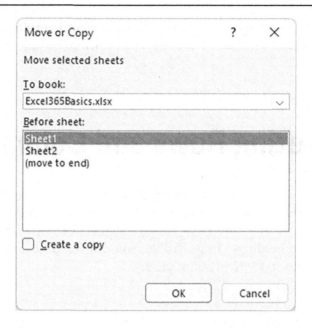

If you want the worksheet copied instead of moved, select the **Create a copy** checkbox before clicking OK. A copy will be placed in front of the selected sheet.

Removing a Worksheet

On the Sheet tab, right-click the sheet you want to remove and click **Delete**.

If the sheet is empty, it will be deleted right away. If the sheet has data, Excel will prompt you with a message asking you to confirm the deletion. Click **Delete** to confirm the deletion.

Hiding and Unhiding Worksheets

To **hide** a worksheet, right-click the name tab of the sheet you want to hide and select **Hide** on the pop-up menu.

To **unhide** a worksheet, right-click any of the sheet name tabs. The **Unhide** option will be enabled on the pop-up menu if a sheet is hidden. Select **Unhide** to display a window listing the hidden sheets. You can select any sheet on the list and click **OK** to show it again.

Freezing Rows and Columns

When you have a large worksheet with lots of data, you may want your data headers (row and/or column) to remain visible as you scroll down or to the right of the page.

To make your column headings always visible, you can freeze them on the page so that scrolling down does not take them out of view.

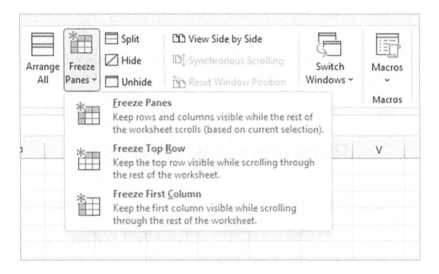

To quickly freeze the top row of your worksheet:

1. Click the **View** tab on the Ribbon.

2. In the Window group, click **Freeze Panes** and select **Freeze Top Row.**

When you now scroll down the page, the top row will always remain visible.

To quickly freeze the first column of your worksheet:

1. Click the **View** tab on the Ribbon.

2. In the Window group, click **Freeze Panes** and select **Freeze First Column**.

When you now scroll to the right of the page, the first column will always remain visible.

On some occasions, you may want to freeze rows and columns other than the first ones.

To freeze any row of your choosing:

1. Place the cell pointer directly under the row you want to freeze to make it the active cell.

2. Click the **View** tab.

3. In the Window group, click **Freeze Panes** and select **Freeze Panes** from the pop-up list.

To freeze any column of your choosing:

1. Select a cell on the first row of the column that's to the right of the one you want to freeze. For example, if you want to freeze **column B**, then you would select cell **C1**.

2. Click the **View** tab.

3. In the Window group, click **Freeze Panes** and select **Freeze Panes** from the pop-up list.

Other examples:

- If you want to freeze the first row and first column of your worksheet, select cell **B2** and then select **View > Freeze Panes > Freeze Panes**.

- If you want to freeze only rows 1 and 2, select cell **A3** and select **View > Freeze Panes > Freeze Panes**.

- If you want to freeze only columns A and B, click cell **C1** and select **View > Freeze Panes > Freeze Panes**.

Unfreeze panes:

To unfreeze any frozen row or columns, click **View** > **Freeze Panes** and select **Unfreeze Panes** from the pop-up menu.

Applying Themes to Your Worksheet

A theme is a predefined formatting package that you can apply to your worksheet that may include colors for headers, text fonts, the size of cells, etc.

There are several themes in Excel that you can apply to your whole worksheet.

To change the look and feel of your worksheet with themes, do the following:

1. Click the **Page Layout** tab on the Ribbon.

2. In the Themes group, click the **Themes** button to display a drop-down list with many themes you can apply to your worksheet.

3. You can hover over a theme on the list to get an instant preview of how your worksheet would look with that theme without selecting it.

4. When you find a theme you want, click it to apply it to your worksheet.

Removing a Theme

If you apply a theme, you don't like, simply click the **Undo** button on the **Home** tab to undo the changes and return your worksheet to its previous state.

Chapter 4

Organizing Your Data

This chapter covers:

- Copying and pasting data.

- Moving data.

- Inserting/deleting rows and columns.

- Finding and replacing data.

- Sorting data.

- Filtering data.

In this chapter, we will cover some essential tasks to do with organizing your data in Excel.

Copying, Moving, and Deleting Data

Selecting a Group of Cells

Method 1

1. Click the first cell of the area.

2. Ensure your mouse pointer is a white plus sign.

3. Click and drag over the other cells in the range you want to include in the selection.

Method 2

1. Click the top-left cell in the range, for example, A2.

2. Hold down the Shift key and click the bottom-right cell in the range, for example, D10.

Excel selects range A1:D10.

Deselecting Cells

Sometimes, you might accidentally select more cells than you intended when selecting several cells or ranges. With the deselect feature, you can deselect any extra cells within the selected range.

To deselect cells within a selection, hold down the **Ctrl** key, then click (or click and drag) to deselect any cells or ranges within the selection.

If you need to reselect any cells, hold down the **Ctrl** key and click the cells to select them again.

Copying and Pasting Data

Quick Copy and Paste

To quickly copy and paste values in a range, do the following:

1. Select the range that you want to copy.

2. On the **Home** tab, in the **Clipboard** group, click **Copy**.

   You will see a dotted rectangle around the area, which is called a bounding outline.

3. Click the first cell of the area where you want to paste the contents.

4. Click **Paste**.

   The bounding outline remains active to let you know that you can carry on pasting the copied content if you wish to paste it in multiple areas. To get rid of the bounding outline, hit the **ESC** key.

Using the Shortcut Menu

Another way to copy or move data is to use commands on the shortcut menu:

1. Select the source range.

2. Right-click the source range and select Copy (or Cut) from the shortcut menu.

3. Right-click the first cell of the destination range and select the Paste icon (the first icon under Paste Options) on the shortcut menu.

Other Pasting Options

To access other pasting options, after copying data, click the drop-down arrow on the **Paste** command button to display a drop-down menu with several paste options.

You can hover over each icon on the menu for a tip on what each one does. You'll also see a preview of the paste action on your worksheet.

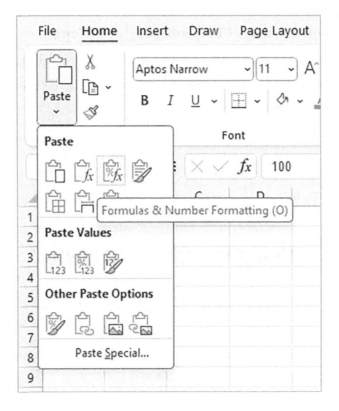

Hover over an icon for a description of what it does

For example, to copy and paste a range while maintaining the column widths, do the following:

1. Select and copy the source range.

2. In the destination worksheet, click the down-arrow on the **Paste** button and select the option that says **Keep Source Column Widths (W)**. This icon is on the second row of the menu.

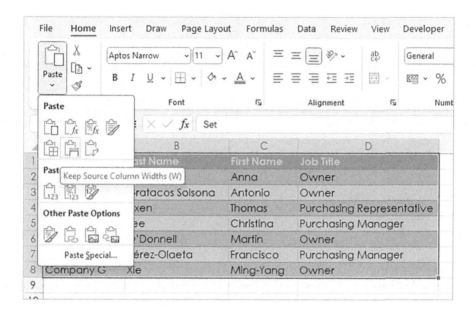

3. Select that option to paste the data and the cell formatting and column width.

4. Once done, remove the bounding outline around the source range by hitting the ESC key. Pressing ESC tells Excel you've completed the copying action.

Using Paste Special

Another way to copy and paste values is to use the **Paste Special** command. Paste Special provides more paste options, including basic calculations like addition, subtraction, and multiplication with the paste operation.

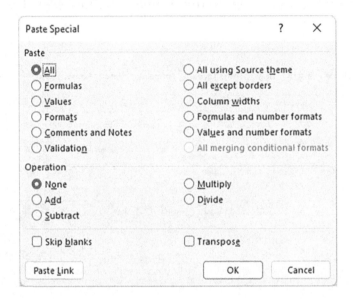

In the following example, we want to convert a list of negative values to positive values. We can use the **Multiply** operation in the Paste Special dialog box to help us perform this action.

To convert a range of negative numbers to positive values, do the following:

1. In any cell in your worksheet, enter **-1**.

2. Copy the value to the clipboard.

3. Select the range of cells with the negative numbers you want to convert.

4. On the Home tab, in the Clipboard group, select **Paste** > **Paste Special**.

   Excel displays the Paste Special dialog box.

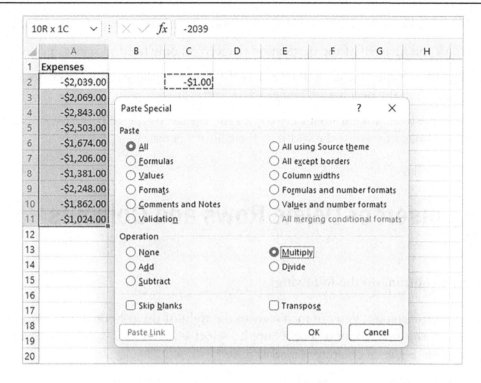

5. In the Paste Special dialog box, select **All** and **Multiply**.

6. Click **OK**.

Excel converts the values in the range to positive numbers by multiplying them by -1 during the paste action.

Moving Data

To move content, you follow a similar set of actions as we did with copying, but you would **Cut** the data instead of **Copy** it.

To move content, do the following:

1. Select the range you want to move.

2. On the Home tab, click the **Cut** button (this is the command with the scissors

icon). A bounding outline will appear around the area you've chosen to cut.

3. Click the first cell of the destination range. You only need to select one cell.

4. On the Home tab, click **Paste**. Excel will move the content from its current location to the destination range.

The copy & paste action automatically copies the format of the cells across, but not the width. So, you need to adjust the width of the cells if necessary.

Insert or Delete Rows and Columns

To insert a column, do the following:

1. Click the column letter immediately to the right of the column where you want to insert the new column. For example, select column B if you want to insert a column between columns A and B.

2. On the **Home** tab, in the **Cells** group, click the **Insert** button.

Excel will insert a new column to the left of the column you selected, and the new column will now be B.

Inserting a new column by using the pop-up menu:

1. Click the column letter to the right of the insertion point to select the whole column.

2. Right-click and select **Insert** from the pop-up menu to insert the new column.

Inserting a new row by using the pop-up menu:

1. Click the row number directly below the insertion point to select the whole row.

2. Right-click and select **Insert** from the pop-up menu to insert a new row directly above the selected row.

You could also insert new rows and columns with the **Insert** command button on the

Home tab.

Inserting multiple rows or columns:

1. Hold down the Ctrl key.

2. One by one, select the rows up to the number you want to insert. For example, if you want to insert four rows, select four rows directly under the insertion point.

3. Click **Home** > **Insert** (or right-click and select **Insert**).

Excel will insert four new rows above the insertion point.

Finding and Replacing Data

A worksheet can have over a million rows of data, so it may be difficult to locate specific information in a large worksheet. Excel provides a Find and Replace feature to quickly find and replace data in your worksheet if required. If you have used the Find feature in other Microsoft 365 applications, you should be familiar with this feature.

To find text or numbers in your worksheet, do the following:

1. On the **Home** tab, in the **Editing** group, click **Find & Select** > **Find**. Alternatively, press **Ctrl+F**.

   Excel displays the Find tab of the **Find and Replace** dialog box.

📝**Note** By default, Excel displays a dialog box with Options hidden (if it wasn't expended when previously used). Click the **Options >>** button to expand the dialog box, as shown below.

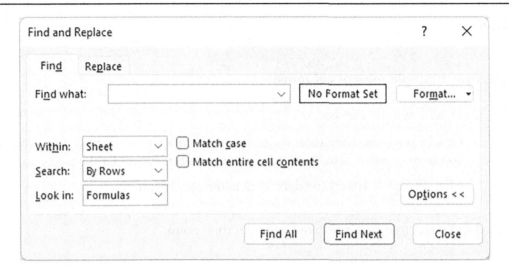

2. In the **Find what** box, enter the text or number you want to find.

You can also click the down-arrow on the **Find what** box and select a recent item you've searched for.

Click **Find All** (to find all instances of your criteria) or **Find Next** (to find them one by one).

Note When you click **Find All**, Excel lists every instance of your criteria. Click a column heading to sort the results by that column. Click an item on the list to select its cell in the worksheet.

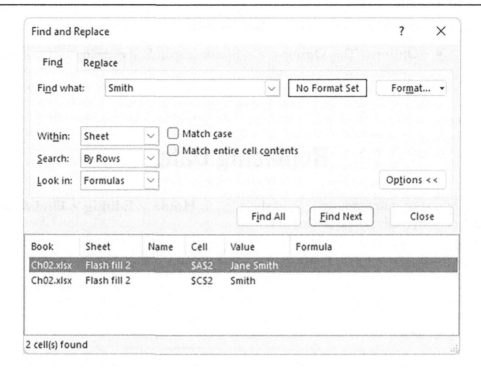

3. The expanded dialog box (when you click **Options >>**) gives you the following additional search options:

- **Format:** This option allows you to select the data format you're searching for.

- **Within:** Allows you to search the current worksheet or the whole workbook.

- **Search:** Allows you to search by rows (default) or columns.

- **Look in:** Enables you to search for Formulas, Values, Notes, or Comments. The default is Formulas.

  Select **Values** here if the search area has formulas, but you want to find the values derived from those formulas. Otherwise, leave this setting as the default.

- **Match case:** This option enables you to only find values that match the case of the entry in the **Find what** box.

- **Match entire cell contents:** Select this option to only find values that match the exact value in the **Find what** box.

- **Options**: The **Options >>** button expands the dialog box with more options to refine your search.

Replacing Data

To replace text or number in your worksheet, go to **Home** > **Editing** > **Find & Select** > **Replace**. Alternatively, press **Ctrl+H**.

If the Find dialog box is already open, click the **Replace** tab.

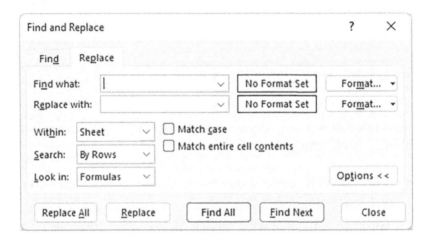

In addition to the options on the Find tab (described above), the Replace tab has the following options:

- **Replace with**: Use this box to specify an alternative value to replace any values found in your worksheet that match the criteria specified in **Find what**.

- **Replace All**: Automatically replaces all instances found with the value in **Replace with**.

- **Replace**: Replaces only the next one found.

All the other options on the dialog box remain the same on this tab as described for Find.

Tip If you use **Replace/Replace All** to change data by mistake, use the **Undo** button on the Home tab to reverse your changes.

Sorting Data

Excel offers various methods to sort your data, from a quick and basic sort to more complex sorts using your own custom list. We will be covering the popular methods in this section.

Quick Sort

To quickly sort data in Excel, do the following:

1. Select any single cell in the column you want to sort.

2. Right-click the cell. From the pop-up menu, select **Sort A to Z** (for ascending) or **Sort Z to A** (for descending).

    If your column is a number field, you'll have **Sort Smallest to Largest** (for ascending) and **Sort Largest to Smallest** (for descending).

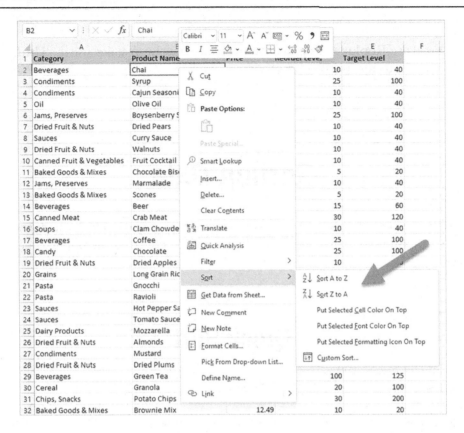

The Sort action does not change your data in any way. It simply reorders your rows according to your chosen sort order and column.

Custom Sort

In the example above, we sorted using just one column. However, you can sort using multiple columns. For example, in the data shown below, we may want to sort by *Category* and *Product Name*. We would use the Custom Sort command on the Ribbon in this case.

	A	B	C
1	Category	Product Name	Price
2	Beverages	Chai	18.00
3	Condiments	Syrup	10.00
4	Condiments	Cajun Seasoning	22.00
5	Cereal	Granola	4.00
6	Chips, Snacks	Potato Chips	1.80
7	Baked Goods & Mixes	Brownie Mix	12.49
8	Baked Goods & Mixes	Cake Mix	15.99
9	Beverages	Tea	4.00
10	Canned Fruit & Vegetables	Pears	1.30
11	Canned Fruit & Vegetables	Peaches	1.50
12	Canned Fruit & Vegetables	Pineapple	1.80
13	Canned Fruit & Vegetables	Cherry Pie Filling	2.00
14	Canned Fruit & Vegetables	Green Beans	1.20
15	Canned Fruit & Vegetables	Corn	1.20
16	Canned Fruit & Vegetables	Peas	1.50
17	Canned Meat	Tuna Fish	2.00
18	Canned Meat	Smoked Salmon	4.00
19	Cereal	Hot Cereal	5.00
20	Soups	Vegetable Soup	1.89
21	Soups	Chicken Soup	1.95
22			

To apply a Custom Sort, do the following:

1. Select a single cell anywhere in the data.

2. On the **Home** tab, in the **Editing** group, click **Sort & Filter**, then select **Custom Sort** from the pop-up menu.

   Excel displays the **Sort** dialog box.

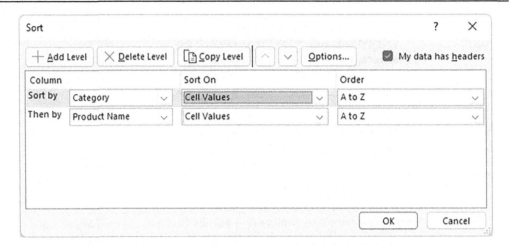

3. In the **Sort by** list, select the first column you want to sort.

4. In the **Sort On** box, you can select Cell Values, Cell Color, Font Color, or Conditional Formatting Icon. If you're sorting by value, select **Cell Value**.

5. In the **Order** list, select the order for the sort. For a text column, you can choose **A to Z** (ascending order) or **Z to A** (descending order).

   For a number column, you can choose **Smallest to Largest** or **Largest to Smallest**.

6. Click **OK** when you're done.

Your data will now be sorted according to the criteria you've entered.

Sorting with a Custom List

In the Sort dialog box, the **Order** drop-down list has an option named **Custom List**, which enables you to sort data by days of the week or months.

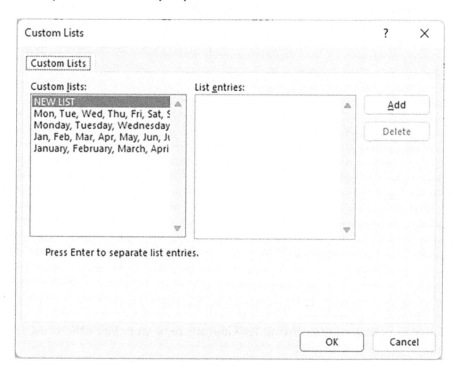

You can add a custom list if none of the pre-defined custom lists meet your needs. Creating your custom list is useful for sorting with an order different from the standard ascending or descending.

For example, if we wanted to sort our data by *employee grade,* we could enter the grades in our list in the order we want the data sorted.

To add a new custom list, do the following:

1. Select NEW LIST in the **Custom lists** box.

2. In the **List entries** box (on the right), enter your list items, one item per line. Press Enter to go to the next line.

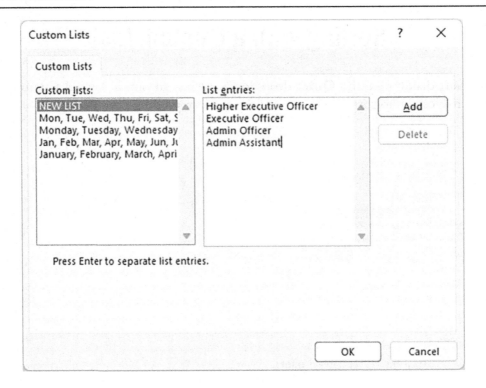

3. When you're done, click the **Add** button to add the list.

4. You can now select the list under **Custom lists** and click **OK** to use it for your sort.

Your custom list will now be available to all Excel workbooks on the PC.

Filtering Data

Excel worksheets can hold a lot of data, and you might not want to work with all the data at the same time. For example, you might want to only display a category of products or products within a certain price range.

Excel provides several ways to filter your data so that you can view only the data you want to see. Filters provide a quick way to work with a subset of data in a range or table. When you apply a filter, you temporarily hide some of the data so that you can focus on the data you need to work with.

Excel tables have column headings by default, but if your data is just a range, ensure you have column headings like Category, Product Name, Price, etc. Column headings makes filtering and sorting much easier.

Category	Product Name	Price	Reorder Level	Target Level
Beverages	Chai	18.00	10	40
Condiments	Syrup	10.00	25	100
Condiments	Cajun Seasoning	22.00	10	40
Oil	Olive Oil	21.35	10	40
Jams, Preserves	Boysenberry Spread	25.00	25	100
Dried Fruit & Nuts	Dried Pears	30.00	10	40
Sauces	Curry Sauce	40.00	10	40

Column headings

You can add column headings to your data by inserting a new row at the top of your worksheet and entering the headings. Column headings are important because Excel will use the first row for the filter arrows.

Quick Filter

To filter data, do the following:

1. Select any cell within the data that you want to filter.

2. Select **Home** > **Editing** > **Sort & Filter** > **Filter**.

    Alternatively, select **Data** > **Sort & Filter** > **Filter**.

    You will get a **filter arrow** at the top of each column, also called an **AutoFilter**. Note that in Excel tables, filter arrows are turned on by default.

3. Click the AutoFilter of the column you want to filter. For example, Price.

4. Uncheck **Select All** and check the values you want to use for the filter.

5. Click **OK**.

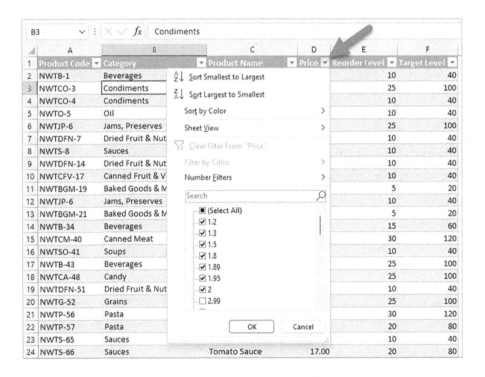

The AutoFilter changes to a funnel icon to show that the column is filtered. If you look at the row heading numbers, you'll see that they're now blue, indicating which rows are included in the filtered data.

Custom Filter

You can create a custom filter if the default options do not meet your needs. To access the **Custom Filter** command, click the **AutoFilter** of the column you want to use to filter the data.

You'll get the following options depending on the data type of the selected column:

- **Text Filters**: Available when the column is a text field or has a mixture of text and numbers. The filter options available include, Equals, Does Not Equal, Begins With, Ends With, or Contains.

- **Number Filters**: This option is available when the column contains only numbers. The filter options available include, Equals, Does Not Equal, Greater Than, Less Than, or Between.

- **Date Filters**: This option is available when the column contains only dates. The filter options available include, Last Week, Next Month, This Month, and Last Month.

- **Clear Filter from [Column name]:** This option is only available if the column already has a filter. Select this option to clear the filter.

When you select an option related to any of the three options above, Excel displays the **Custom AutoFilter** dialog box, where you can specify your custom filter criteria.

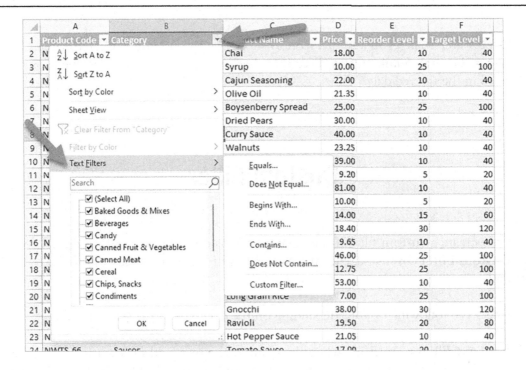

Example

Let's say we wanted to display only data with a price range between $2 and $10.

Follow the steps below to filter the data for the chosen criteria:

1. Click the AutoFilter on the **Price** column, and on the dropdown menu, select **Number Filters > Between**.

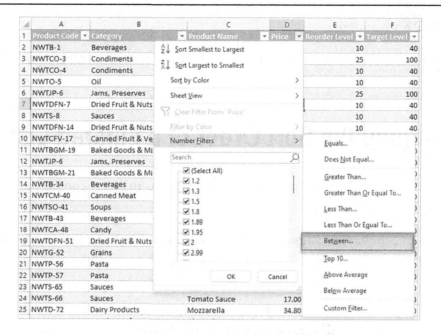

The **Custom AutoFilter** dialog box allows you to enter the criteria and specify the condition.

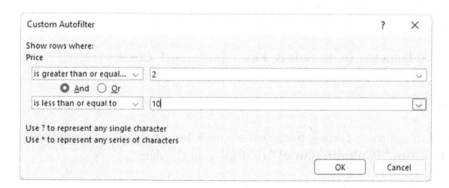

2. Enter the values you want to use for the filter. In our example, the values would be 2 and 10.

3. Select the logical operator. In this case, we will need **And**, as both conditions must be true.

Price >= 2 And <= 10.

If only one of the conditions needs to be true, select **Or**.

4. Click **OK** when done.

Excel filters the data to only show records where the Price is between $2 and $10.

Changing the Sort Order of a Filtered List

To change the sort order of the filtered results, click the **AutoFilter** icon on the column used for the filter.

Select either **Sort Smallest to Largest** or **Sort Largest to Smallest**. For a text column, it would be **Sort A to Z** or **Sort Z to A.**

Removing a Filter

To remove a filter, do the following:

1. Select any cell in the range or table.

2. On the **Data** tab, in the **Sort & Filter** group, click **Clear**.

Excel removes the filter and displays all the data.

Another way to remove a filter is to click the AutoFilter of the filtered column and select **Clear Filter From "[Column name]"** to display all the data.

Chapter 5

Formatting Cells

This chapter covers:

- Resizing cells, rows, and columns.

- Hiding and unhide rows and columns.

- Merging cells and aligning data.

- Hiding and unhiding worksheets.

- Applying predefined cell styles.

- Applying different types of number formats to cells.

- Creating and applying custom cell formats.

- Applying conditional formatting to add visual representations to your data.

In this chapter, we will cover various methods to format and resize cells in your worksheet to present your data in your desired format.

Arrange Cells, Rows, and Columns

Resizing Rows and Columns

You can resize rows and columns with your mouse or use the **Format** command on the toolbar.

To resize a **column**, do the following:

1. Click any cell in the column.

2. Click the right edge of the column letter and drag it to the right to widen the column.

To resize a **row**, do the following:

1. Click any cell in the row.

2. Click the bottom edge of the row number, then drag it down to increase the row's height.

Resizing Cells with the Cells Format Command

You can increase the column width and row height of a range of cells simultaneously by using the **Format** command on the **Home** tab of the Ribbon.

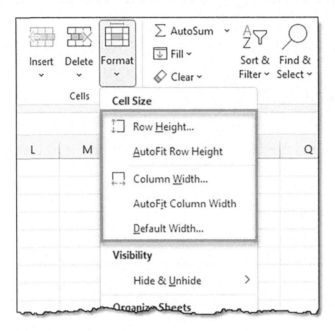

For example, to increase the widths of columns A to E, do the following:

1. Hover over the header for column A until you see a downward pointing arrow.

2. Click **A** to select the column and drag to column **E** to select columns A to E.

> ⭑Tip Another way to select a range of columns is to select the first column, hold down the **Shift** key, and select the last column.

3. Click **Home** > **Format** > **Column Width**.

4. Enter the **Column width** in the box.

5. Click **OK**.

To increase the height of rows 1 to 14, do the following:

1. Hover over the header of row 1 until you get an arrow pointing right.

2. Click to select the whole row.

3. Hold down the Shift key and click the header of row 14.

4. Go to **Home** > **Cells** > **Format** > **Row Height...**

5. The default row height is 15. Thus, you can enter any number higher than 15 to increase the height of the selected rows.

6. Click **OK**.

Automatically adjust columns to fit your data using AutoFit:

1. Select the columns you want to adjust.

2. On the **Home** tab, in the **Cells** group, select **Format** > **AutoFit Column Width**.

Excel adjusts each column to fit the length of all entries.

Automatically adjust row heights to fit your data using AutoFit:

1. Select the rows to which you want to apply AutoFit.

2. On the **Home** tab, in the **Cells** group, select **Format** > **AutoFit Row Height**.

Excel adjusts each column to fit the height of all entries. This setting is particularly useful if you have **Wrap Text** enabled, and some cells have more than one line of text.

Set the default column width for the whole workbook:

1. On the **Home** tab, in the **Cells** group, select **Format** > **Default Width**.

2. Enter the new default value in the **Standard column width** box.

Hide Rows and Columns

Sometimes, with very large worksheets, you may want to hide some rows or columns to make it easier to access the data with which you want to work.

To hide rows:

1. Select the rows you want to hide.

2. Go to **Home** > **Cells** > **Format**.

3. On the pop-up menu, under **Visibility**, select **Hide & Unhide**, and then click **Hide Rows**.

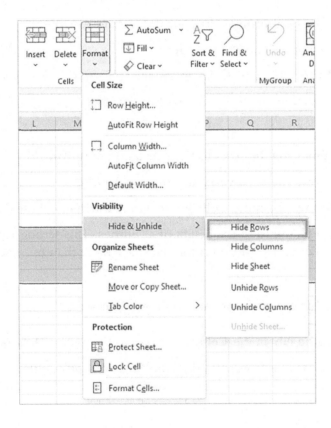

To hide columns:

1. Select the target columns

2. Go to **Home** > **Cells** > **Format**.

3. On the pop-up menu, under **Visibility**, select **Hide & Unhide** and then click **Hide Columns**.

To unhide rows and columns:

Go to **Home** > **Cells** > **Format** > **Hide & Unhide** and then select **Unhide Columns** to display hidden columns (or **Unhide Rows** to display hidden rows).

Hide and Unhide a Worksheet

You can use two methods to Hide a worksheet:

- **Method 1:** Right-click the worksheet's name tab and select **Hide** from the pop-up menu.

- **Method 2:** Ensure the worksheet you want to hide is the active one, then on the Ribbon, select **Home** > **Cells** > **Format** > **Hide & Unhide** > **Hide Sheet**.

To hide multiple worksheets simultaneously, do the following:

1. Select the first worksheet's name tab.

2. Hold down the **Ctrl** key and click any additional worksheet tabs you want to hide.

3. Right-click any of the worksheet tabs and select **Hide** on the shortcut menu.

There are two ways to Unhide a worksheet:

- **Method 1**:

  1. Right-click any of the tabs at the bottom of the workbook and select **Unhide** on the shortcut menu.

  2. Select the worksheet name in the **Unhide** dialog box and click **OK**.

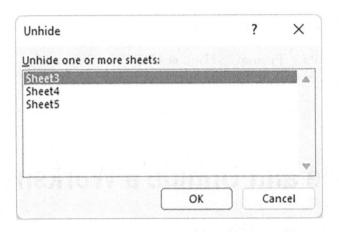

- **Method 2**:

  1. On the Ribbon, go to **Home** > **Cells** > **Format** > **Hide & Unhide** > **Unhide Sheet**.

  2. Select the worksheet name in the **Unhide** dialog box and click **OK**.

Note To unhide more than one worksheet, hold down the **Ctrl** key and select any additional worksheets you want to unhide in the Unhide dialog box.

Applying Cell Styles

You can select a predefined color format for your cells from a wide selection of styles from the **Styles** group on the **Home** tab.

To format a cell or range with a different style:

1. Select the cell or range that you want to format.

2. On the **Home** tab, in the **Styles** group, click the **More** dropdown arrow to expand the style gallery.

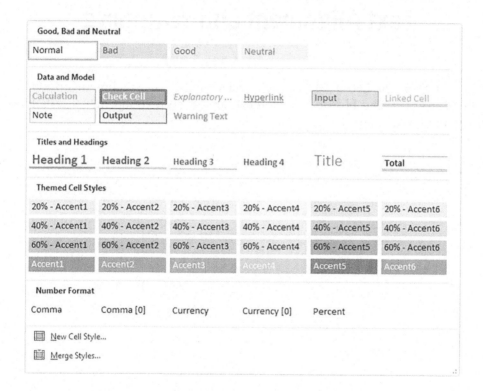

You can hover over the different styles for a preview on your worksheet before selecting one.

3. Select a style on the gallery to apply it to your worksheet.

Merging Cells and Aligning Data

To **merge** cells on your worksheet, select the cells you want to merge. On the **Home** tab, click **Merge & Center**. Alternatively, you can click the drop-down button for Merge & Center and choose other merge options from the drop-down menu.

To **unmerge** cells, select the merged cells, then on the **Home** tab, click the drop-down button for **Merge & Center**. Select **Unmerge Cells** from the drop-down menu.

Text Alignment and Wrapping

To align text in a cell, select the cell and click one of the alignment options in the **Alignment** group on the **Home** tab. You can also wrap text and merge cells from the command options available.

Shrink to Fit and Text Direction

The **Format Cells** dialog box provides additional formatting options like **Shrink to fit** and **Text direction**. To open the dialog box, click the dialog box launcher on the bottom-right of the **Alignment** group.

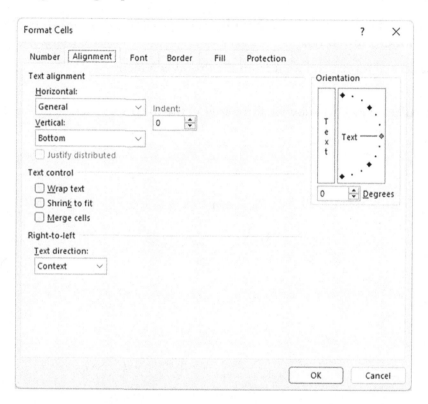

On the Alignment tab, you can:

- Align text in your cells vertically and horizontally.
- Wrap text to go to a new line in a cell instead of continuing into other cells to the right.
- Shrink text to fit one cell.
- Merge cells.

Applying Number Formats

To quickly set the format for a range of cells:

1. Select the range of cells that you want to format.

2. On the **Home** tab, in the **Number** group, click the dropdown arrow on the **Number Format** box.

3. Select the format you want from the dropdown menu.

The selected cell/range will now be formatted in the format you selected.

Number Format dropdown menu.

Accessing More Formats

To access formats not available on the **Number Format** dropdown menu, open the **Format Cells** dialog box.

For example, if you're in the US and you want to change currency formats in your worksheet to UK pounds, do the following:

1. Select the range of cells that you want to format.

2. On the **Home** tab, in the **Number** group, click the dropdown arrow on the **Number Format** box, and select **More Number Formats**.

    Excel displays the **Number** tab of the **Format Cells** dialog box.

> 🔅**Tip** Another way to display the Format Cells dialog box is to click the dialog box launcher in the Number group on the Home tab.

3. On the left side of the dialog box, under **Category**, select **Currency**.

4. Click the **Symbol** field to display a dropdown list. Select the British pound sign (£) from the list.

    You can also set the number of decimal places and the format you want for negative numbers on this tab. The **Sample** box displays how the selected format will look on your worksheet.

5. Click **OK** to confirm your changes when done.

Creating Custom Numeric Formats

Excel has many predefined number formats you can select and then amend to create your own custom format if none of the predefined formats meets your needs.

For example, imagine that you have a column in your worksheet that you use to record a set of numbers. It could be product serial numbers, unique product IDs, or even telephone numbers. You may want the numbers to appear in a certain format regardless of how they've been entered.

In some applications like Microsoft Access, this would be called a *format mask*.

In Excel, you can create a custom format for a group of cells so that every entry is automatically formatted with your default format.

To create a custom format, follow the steps below:

1. Select the range of cells to be formatted.

2. Right-click any area in your selection and select **Format Cells** from the pop-up menu.

Alternatively, on the **Home** tab, in the **Number** group, click the dialog box launcher to open the **Format Cells** dialog box.

3. Under **Category,** select **Custom**.

4. In the **Type** box, select an existing format close to the one you would like to create.

Note If you find a format on the list that meets your needs, you can select that one and click OK.

---

5. In the **Type** box, enter the format you want to create. For example, *0000-00000.*

6. Click **OK.**

	A	B	C
1	Serial Number		
2	234401107	2344-01107	
3	234434589	2344-34589	
4	234466123	2344-66123	
5	234455692	2344-55692	
6	234234500	2342-34500	
7	234410976	2344-10976	
8	232310978	2323-10978	
9	234093419	2340-93419	
10	230923100	2309-23100	
11	234109035	2341-09035	
12	234102345	2341-02345	
13	234109093	2341-09093	
14			

In the image above, column A has a set of numbers. Column B shows the same numbers with a custom format (*0000-00000*) now applied to them.

Copy Cell Formatting

A quick way to format a cell or group of cells based on another cell in your worksheet is to use the **Format Painter** in the **Clipboard** group on the **Home** tab. The Format Painter can be a time saver as you only create the format once and copy it to other cells in your worksheet.

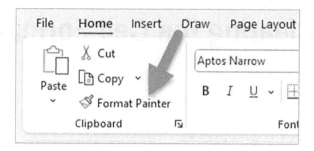

To copy cell formatting with the **Format Painter**, do the following:

1. Select the cell with the format you want to copy.

2. On the **Home** tab, in the **Clipboard** group, click **Format Painter**. The mouse pointer will turn into a plus sign (+) and a brush icon.

3. Click and drag over the cells to which you're applying the format.

The destination cells will now have the same format as the source cell.

Tip When clicked once, the **Format Painter** is enabled for only one use and then turned off. If you want to apply the same format to multiple ranges, double-click the Format Painter to turn it on for multiple uses. It remains enabled until you click it again to turn it off.

Example:

In the following example, we want to copy the **Currency** format in cell **A2** and apply it to range **A3:A14**.

Follow the steps below to copy the format using the Format Painter:

1. Click cell *A2* to select it.

2. Select **Home** > **Clipboard** > **Format Painter**.

3. In the worksheet area, click *A3* and drag to *A14*.

Excel applies the currency format in *A2* to the range A3:A14.

Clearing the Cell Format

To remove formatting from a cell or range, do the following:

1. Select the cells you want to clear.

2. Select **Home** > **Editing** > **Clear**.

3. Excel displays a dropdown menu with several options - Clear All, Clear Formats, Clear Contents, Clear Comments and Notes, and Clear Hyperlinks.

4. To clear just the format and not the values, click **Clear Formats**.

Excel returns the format of the selected cells to **General,** which is the default.

Conditional Formatting

You can format your data based on certain criteria to display a visual representation that helps to spot critical issues and identify patterns and trends. For example, you can use visual representations to clearly show the highs and lows in your data and the trend. This type of formatting is called conditional formatting in Excel.

In the example below, we can quickly see the trend in sales and how they compare to each other.

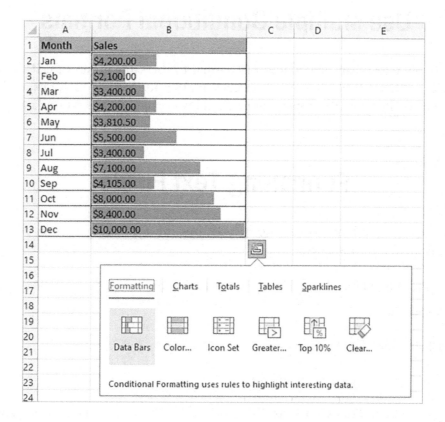

To quickly apply a conditional format:

1. Select the range of cells you want to format. The quick analysis button will be displayed at the bottom-right of the selection.

2. Click the Quick Analysis button, and use the default **Formatting** tab.

3. Hover over the formatting options on the Formatting tab to see a live preview of what your data will look like when applied.

4. Click **Data Bars** to apply the formatting to your data.

You now have a visual representation of the data that's easier to analyze.

Use Multiple Conditional Formats

You can apply more than one conditional format to the same group of cells. Select the cells, click the Quick Analysis button, and click another format option, for example, **Icon Set**. The arrows illustrate the upper, middle, and lower values in the set of data.

Formatting Text Fields

You can apply conditional formatting to text, but the formatting options for text are different from that of numbers.

For example, to highlight all the rows with "Sauce" in the name, do the following:

1. Select the range.

2. Click the Quick Analysis button.

3. Select **Text** on the Formatting tab.

4. In the **Text That Contains** dialog box, enter "Sauce" in the first box and select the type of formatting from the drop-down list.

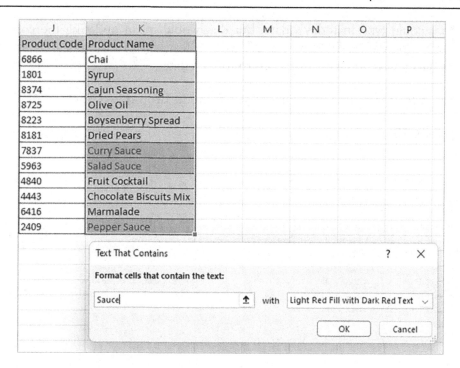

You can explore the formatting options for different data types by selecting the data to be formatted and clicking the Quick Analysis button.

Conditionally Formatting Time

Let's say we had a list of projects, and we wanted to see which projects are overdue, that is, the ones with a due date before today.

To highlight the overdue projects, do the following:

1. Select the cells in the *Due date* column.

2. Click the Quick Analysis button, and then click Less Than.

3. Type in **=TODAY()**

You could type in today's date, but that would mean updating the conditional formatting daily, which would get tedious fast and even introduce errors! The TODAY function will always return today's date.

4.   Select the formatting you'll like to use from the drop-down list.

5.   Click **OK**.

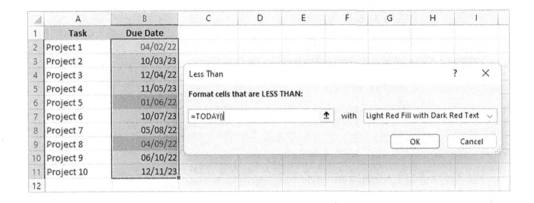

The overdue projects now stand out on the list and are easy to identify immediately. The date format used here is **mm/dd/yy**.

Note You can also sort the data in this example to figure out the overdue projects, but depending on your data, sorting is not always an available option.

Creating Conditional Formatting Rules

An alternative way to create conditional formatting is by creating **Rules** in Excel.

To launch the **New Formatting Rule** dialog box:

1. Select the range to which you want to apply the conditional formatting.
2. On the Ribbon, go to **Home** > **Styles** > **Conditional Formatting** > **New Rule**.

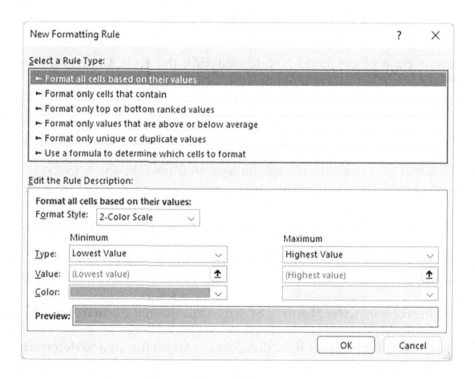

You can use the New Formatting Rule dialog box to create more complex rules using a series of conditions and criteria.

You can select a rule type from the following options:

- Format all cells based on their values.

- Format only cells that contain.

- Format only top or bottom ranked values.

- Format only values that are above or below average.

- Format only unique or duplicate values.

- Use a formula to determine which cells to format.

The bottom section of the dialog box, labeled **Edit the Rule Description**, gives you different fields to define your rule for each rule type.

Example:

Let's say you had a list of products, and you want to format the whole row grey if one of the fields, the product Stock, fell below 10.

Follow the steps below to create a conditional formatting rule for the above scenario:

1. Select the range you want to conditionally format, that is, A2:C18. Note that A2 is the active cell.

2. On the Ribbon, select **Home > Styles >Conditional Formatting > New Rule**.

3. In the **New Formatting Rule** dialog, select **Use a formula to determine which cells to format**.

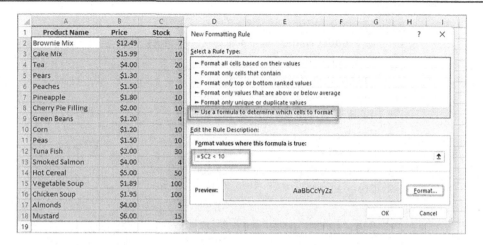

Since A2 is the active cell, you need to enter a formula that is valid for row 2 and will apply to all the other rows.

4. Type in the formula **=$C2 < 10**.

The dollar sign before the C means it is an **absolute reference** for column C ($C). The value in column C for each row is evaluated and used to determine if the format should be applied.

Note The difference between an absolute reference and a relative reference is covered in chapter 6.

---

5. For the fill color, click the **Format** button, select the fill color you want, and click **OK**, and **OK** again to apply the rule.

The rows with Stock below 10 will now be filled with grey.

	A	B	C
1	**Product Name**	**Price**	**Stock**
2	Brownie Mix	$12.49	7
3	Cake Mix	$15.99	10
4	Tea	$4.00	20
5	Pears	$1.30	5
6	Peaches	$1.50	10
7	Pineapple	$1.80	10
8	Cherry Pie Filling	$2.00	10
9	Green Beans	$1.20	4
10	Corn	$1.20	10
11	Peas	$1.50	10
12	Tuna Fish	$2.00	30
13	Smoked Salmon	$4.00	4
14	Hot Cereal	$5.00	50
15	Vegetable Soup	$1.89	100
16	Chicken Soup	$1.95	100
17	Almonds	$4.00	5
18	Mustard	$6.00	15
19			

Chapter 6

Carrying out Calculations with Formulas

This chapter covers:

- Operator precedence in Excel and its effect on calculations.
- How to enter formulas in Excel.
- How to calculate percentages, dates, and time.
- How to use the AutoSum feature for automated calculations.
- The difference between relative and absolute cell references.
- How to access data in other worksheets in your formulas.

Formulas enable you to perform different types of calculations, from basic arithmetic to complex engineering calculations. This chapter discusses the operators used in Excel before we delve into creating formulas for various types of calculations.

Operators in Excel

Arithmetic Operators

The following arithmetic operators are used to perform basic mathematical operations such as addition, subtraction, multiplication, or division.

Arithmetic operator	Meaning	Example
+ (plus sign)	Addition	=4+4
– (minus sign)	Subtraction	=4-4
	Negation	=-4
* (asterisk)	Multiplication	=4*4
/ (forward slash)	Division	=4/4
% (percent sign)	Percent	40%
^ (caret)	Exponentiation	=4^4

Comparison Operators

Comparison operators allow you to compare two values and produce a logical result, that is, TRUE or FALSE.

Comparison operator	Meaning	Example
=	Equal to	=A1=B1
>	Greater than	=A1>B1
<	Less than	=A1<B1
>=	Greater than or equal to	=A1>=B1
<=	Less than or equal to	=A1<=B1
<>	Not equal to	=A1<>B1

Operator Precedence

If you combine several operators in a single formula, Excel performs the operations in the following order.

Operator	Description
: (colon) (single space) ,(comma)	Reference operators
–	Negation (as in –1)
%	Percent
^	Exponentiation
* and /	Multiplication and division
+ and –	Addition and subtraction
&	Connects two strings of text (concatenation)
= <> <= >= <>	Comparison

At a basic level, you just need to remember that Excel performs multiplication and division before addition and subtraction. If a formula contains operators with the same precedence, for instance, multiplication and division, Excel will evaluate the operators from left to right.

Parentheses and Operator Precedence

You can change the order of evaluation by enclosing parts of your formula in parentheses (). The part of the formula in parentheses will be calculated first.

For example, the following formula produces 75 because Excel calculates multiplication before addition. So, Excel multiplies 7 by 10 first before adding 5 to the result.

=5+7*10

Answer = 75

In contrast, if we enclose 5+7 in parentheses, Excel will calculate 5 + 7 first before multiplying the result by 7 to produce 120.

=(5+7)*10

Answer = 120

In another example, we want to add 20% to 300. The parentheses around the second part of the formula ensure Excel calculates the addition first before the multiplication to produce 360.

=300 * (1 + 0.2)

Answer = 360

Entering a Formula

To enter a formula in a cell, always start your entry with an equal sign (=) in the formula bar. The equal sign tells Excel that your entry is a formula, not a static value.

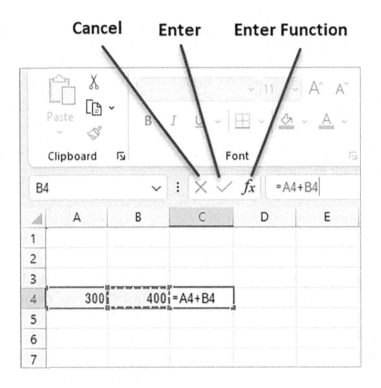

Next to the formula bar, you have the **Enter** command (checkmark) that you use to confirm your formula. You enter your formula in the formula bar and click **Enter** to confirm the entry. If you wish to cancel your entry, click **Cancel** to discard it.

For example, if you wanted to add two numbers, 300 + 400, you would do the following:

1. Enter 300 in cell **A4**.

2. Enter 400 in cell **B4**.

3. In cell C4, enter **= A4 + B4**.

4. Click **Enter**.

5. C4 will now have the sum of the two figures, 700.

Tip To minimize errors, avoid typing cell references directly into the formula bar as much as possible. After you type in the leading equal sign (=) in the formula bar, you can add cell references to your formula by selecting them on the worksheet with your mouse. Select the cell on the worksheet with your mouse to automatically enter its reference in the formula bar whenever you want to reference a cell.

Thus, for the basic calculation we performed above, the way you would enter it in the formula bar is as follows:

1. Enter 300 in cell **A4**, and 400 in cell **B4**.

2. Select **C4**.

3. Type "=" in the formula bar.

4. Select **A4**.

5. Type "+" in the formula bar.

6. Select **B4**.

7. Click **Enter**.

Excel displays the sum of the two cells, 700, in cell C4.

Calculating Percentages

In this example, we want to calculate 20% of a value and then add it to the total, the way sales tax is calculated in invoices.

The product price is $2,900, and the sales tax is 20%.

Note 100 percent is 1 in Excel. Anything less than 100 percent will be less than 1. Hence, 20 percent will be 0.2. Always enter a percent as a decimal place number unless it is 100% or greater.

For the **Sales tax,** we then enter 0.2 in cell B3.

We can format the cell as a **Percentage** data type (although this is not compulsory when calculating percentages in Excel). On the **Home** tab, in the **Numbers** group, click the **%** sign. Excel changes the 0.2 you entered in the cell to 20%.

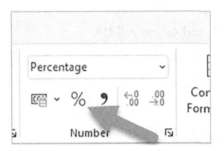

For the **Price**, enter $2,900.

For the Sales Tax formula, enter *=A6*B3* to calculate 20% of $2,900, which is $580.00.

For the **Total**, you can use the AutoSum tool to generate the sum, or you can enter the formula directly *=SUM(A6:B6)* to produce the total figure of $3,480.00.

B6		⌄	⁝	✕ ✓ *fx*	=A6*B3	

	A	B	C	D
1	**Calculating percentages**			
2				
3	**Sales tax rate:**	20%		
4				
5	**Price**	**Sales Tax**	**Total**	
6	$2,900.00	$580.00	$3,480.00	
7				
8				

You can use the same method above to subtract percentages. For example, to subtract the Sales Tax from the Price, enter *=A6-B6* in cell c6.

Using AutoSum

The AutoSum tool can be found on the **Home** tab, in the **Editing** group. It is the Greek Sigma symbol. AutoSum allows you to insert functions in your worksheet. The tool automatically selects the range to be used as your argument. You can use AutoSum with the SUM, AVERAGE, COUNT, MAX, and MIN functions.

AutoSum will default to the SUM function when clicked, but you can use a different function with AutoSum. Click the AutoSum drop-down button to display a pop-up menu of the other functions you can use. Select another function on the menu, for example, **Average**, to insert it as the function used with AutoSum.

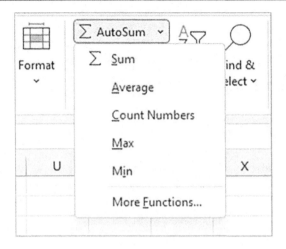

A *range* in Excel is a collection of two or more cells that contain the data with which you're working. See chapter 8 for more on ranges.

A function *argument* is a piece of data that a function needs to run. The SUM function, for example, can have one or more arguments for the input ranges to be summed.

=SUM(A2:A10)

=SUM(A2:A10, C2:C10)

The great thing about AutoSum is that it selects the most likely range of cells in the current column or row that you want to use. It then automatically enters them in the function's argument.

For the most part, it selects the correct range of cells and marks the selection with a moving dotted line called a bounding outline. For non-continuous data, AutoSum may not automatically select everything. In those cases, you can manually correct the range by dragging the selection (bounding outline) over the other cells you want in the formula.

Example

In the following example, we have figures in B2 to B14 that we want to sum up, and we can do this quickly with the AutoSum command.

Follow the steps below to apply AutoSum to a range of continuous data:

1. Click the cell where you want the total displayed. For this example, this would be **B14**.

2. Click the **AutoSum** command button (**Home** > **Editing** > **AutoSum**).

3. AutoSum will automatically select the range of cells with continuous data (above or to the side of the cell with the formula). In this case, it selects B2 to B13.

4. Click **Enter** (the checkmark button next to the formula bar) or hit the **Enter** key.

Cell B14 will now show the sum of the numbers.

SUM		∨ ⋮ ✕ ✓ *fx*	=SUM(B2:B13)	
	A	B	C	D
1	Month	Expenses		
2	Jan	$950.00		
3	Feb	$716.00		
4	Mar	$981.00		
5	Apr	$903.00		
6	May	$625.00		
7	Jun	$825.00		
8	Jul	$930.00		
9	Aug	$983.00		
10	Sep	$745.00		
11	Oct	$768.00		
12	Nov	$950.00		
13	Dec	$824.00		
14	Sum	=SUM(B2:B13)		
15		SUM(number1, [number2], ...)		
16				

Using AutoSum with Non-contiguous Data

A non-contiguous range has blank rows or columns in the data. AutoSum will only select the contiguous range next to the cell with the formula. So, you must manually drag the selection over the rest of the data.

To use AutoSum with non-contiguous data, do the following:

1. Click the cell where you want the total to be displayed.

2. Click the **AutoSum** command button.

3. AutoSum will automatically select the range of cells next to the cell with the formula.

4. Hover your mouse pointer over the right edge of the selection until it turns into a double-headed arrow. Then drag over the rest of the cells in your range.

5. Click the **Enter** button or hit the **Enter** key on your keyboard.

The formula cell will now show the sum of the numbers.

B17	⌄ ⋮ ✕ ✓ _fx_	=SUM(B2:B16)	
	A	B	C	D
1	Month	Expenses		
2	Jan	$950.00	Drag up	
3	Feb	$716.00		
4	Mar	$981.00		
5				
6	Apr	$903.00		
7	May	$625.00		
8	Jun	$825.00		
9				
10	Jul	$930.00		
11	Aug	$983.00		
12	Sep	$745.00		
13				
14	Oct	$768.00		
15	Nov	$950.00		
16	Dec	$824.00		
17	Sum	=SUM(B2:B16)		
18		SUM(number1, [number2], ...)		

Using AutoSum with Different Ranges

Sometimes the data you want to calculate may be in different parts of your worksheet or even on different sheets in the workbook. With AutoSum, you can have arguments for individual values, cell references, ranges, or a mix of all three. To calculate different ranges, you add different ranges to the AutoSum calculation.

To sum values in different ranges, do the following:

1. Click the cell where you want the formula, and then click **AutoSum**.

2. If AutoSum does not select the first range for you, then select it by clicking the first cell and dragging to the last cell of the range.

3. Hold down the **Ctrl** key and select any additional ranges you want to add to the calculation.

4. Click **Enter**.

B4	∨ ⋮ ✕ ✓ *fx*	=SUM(D4:D13,B4:B13)		
◢	A	B	C	D	E
1					
2					
3		Month 1		Month 2	
4	Hugo	$1,848.00		$1,190.00	
5	Felipe	$1,897.00		$1,642.00	
6	Wayne	$1,267.00		$1,639.00	
7	Mae	$1,149.00		$1,421.00	
8	Lee	$1,571.00		$1,061.00	
9	Oscar	$1,659.00		$1,791.00	
10	Fannie	$1,509.00		$1,043.00	
11	Terrance	$1,307.00		$1,680.00	
12	Sylvester	$1,589.00		$1,884.00	
13	Elijah	$1,426.00		$1,768.00	
14					
15	Total (all months)			=SUM(D4:D13,B4:B13)	
16				SUM(number1, [number2], ...)	
17					

The sum of both ranges will now be entered. You can include up to 255 ranges as arguments in the SUM function.

Using AutoSum for Other Aggregate Functions

Despite its name, you can also use the AutoSum feature to calculate the **Average**, **Count**, **Max**, and **Min**. To select these other functions, click the drop-down arrow on the AutoSum command button and select an option on the menu.

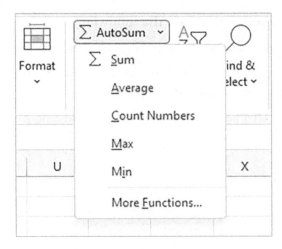

For example, to calculate the average of a row of numbers in cells B4 to G4, you would do the following:

1. Place the cell pointer in the cell where you want to display the average, which is H4 for this example (see image below).

2. On the **Home** tab, click **AutoSum** > **Average**.

    AutoSum will automatically select the cells with numbers next to the formula cell. In this example, AutoSum selects the range B4:G4.

3. Click **Enter** (or press the **Enter** key) to accept the selection.

    Excel calculates the average of the selection using the AVERAGE function in cell H4.

| YEAR | | ⌄ | : | ✕ | ✓ | *fx* | =AVERAGE(B4:G4) | | | |

⯾	A	B	C	D	E	F	G	H	I	J
1	**Exam Marks**									
2										
3	**Students**	**Math**	**English**	**Physics**	**Chemistry**	**Biology**	**Computer Sci**	**Average**		
4	Barbara	44	69	25	83	78	35	=AVERAGE(B4:G4)		
5	Michelle	69	85	57	28	26	56	AVERAGE(number1, [number2], ...)		
6	Pamela	79	57	73	34	74	48			
7	Mildred	88	71	90	73	97	88			
8	Kathy	66	94	85	61	81	92			
9	Bruce	41	25	76	42	87	25			
10	Kathleen	90	77	31	43	61	63			
11	Joshua	92	84	64	78	82	56			
12	Andrew	91	73	42	87	90	88			
13	Todd	33	56	79	76	40	85			
14	Kathryn	55	33	30	33	69	43			
15	Irene	38	72	59	32	87	32			
16										
17										

Quick Sum with the Status Bar

If you want to quickly see the sum of a range of cells, select the range and view the information on the Status Bar.

To select a range of cells, click the first cell in the range, hold down the **Shift** key, and click the last cell in the range.

Once you have selected the range, look at the lower right-hand side of the Excel **Status Bar**. You'll see the **Average**, **Count**, and **Sum** for the selected cells.

	Month 1	Month 2
Hugo	$1,848.00	$1,190.00
Felipe	$1,897.00	$1,642.00
Wayne	$1,267.00	$1,639.00
Mae	$1,149.00	$1,421.00
Lee	$1,571.00	$1,061.00
Oscar	$1,659.00	$1,791.00
Fannie	$1,509.00	$1,043.00
Terrance	$1,307.00	$1,680.00
Sylvester	$1,589.00	$1,884.00
Elijah	$1,426.00	$1,768.00

Average: $1,517.05   Count: 20   Sum: $30,341.00

This feature provides a way of quickly viewing aggregate data for a range of values in a worksheet without entering a formula.

Calculating Date and Time

Native support for date and time calculations has vastly improved in Excel over previous editions. You can now perform many date and time calculations in the worksheet area using arithmetic operators where functions were previously needed. The trick is to apply the right data format to the cells to get the right results. This section will cover some of the common date and time calculations.

Adding Time

When you enter two numbers separated by a colon, for example, 8:45, Excel recognizes the value as time and will treat it as such when you perform calculations based on that cell.

In the following example, we calculate how many hours and minutes it took to complete two trips. The first trip took 8 hours and 45 minutes, and the second one took 6 hours and 30 minutes.

B4	⌄	⋮	✕ ✓ fx	=SUM(B2:B3)	
◢	A		B	C	D
1	**Trip**		**Time**		
2	Trip 1		08:45		
3	Trip 2		06:30		
4	Total		15:15		
5					

We enter **08:45** in B2 and **06:30** in B3.

The values are added in cell B4 with the formula **=SUM(B2:B3)**, and it returns an answer of **15:15** (15 hours and 15 minutes).

As you can see from the example above, when we sum the two values, Excel uses hours and minutes to perform the calculation rather than hundreds.

Note that Excel only recognizes time up to 24 hours by default. If you want to calculate time greater than 24 hours, you'll need to format the cell to accept time over 24 hours.

To format a cell to display values over 24 hours, do the following:

1. Click the dialog box launcher in the **Number** group on the Home tab.

2. In the **Format Cells** dialog box, click **Custom**.

3. In the **Type** box, enter **[h]:mm**. This custom format tells Excel to display values beyond 24 hours.

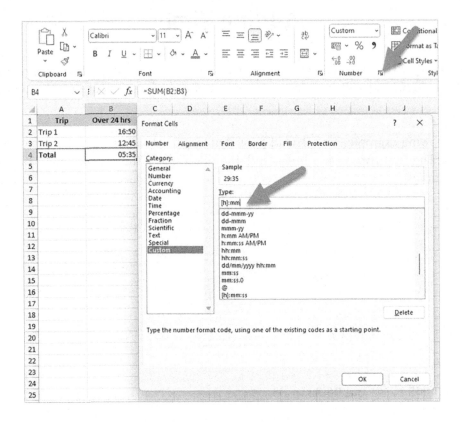

After this change to the cell format, when you add 16:50 + 12:45, you now get **29:35** instead of 05:35.

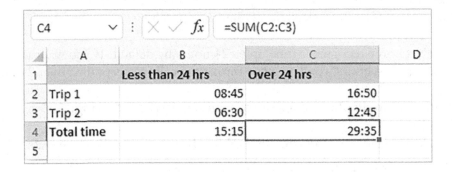

Subtracting Time

You can calculate the number of hours between two times by subtracting one from another, like in a work timesheet.

E4		fx	=(D4-B4)-C4		
	A	B	C	D	E	F
1	**Timesheet**					
2						
3		**Start time**	**Break (hrs:min)**	**End time**	**Total (hrs:min)**	
4	Mon	9:30 AM	1:00	7:30 PM	9:00	
5	Tue	9:00 AM	0:40	5:00 PM	7:20	
6	Wed	8:10 AM	0:50	4:30 PM	7:30	
7	Thu	7:50 AM	1:30	4:30 PM	7:10	
8	Fri	8:00 AM	0:30	4:30 PM	8:00	
9						

If you enter the time with a colon between the hours and minutes, a simple subtraction can be used to calculate the difference between two times.

In the example above, the simple formula we need to calculate the total time worked per day is:

=(D4-B4)-C4

This formula first subtracts the **Start time** (B4) from the **End time** (D4), then subtracts the **Break** (C4) from the difference to create the total time worked for the day.

Just a few years back, you would need a series of nested IF statements to create the same solution we have achieved above. You would have to perform all the calculations in hundredths and then use logical tests to derive the minutes. So, Excel (and spreadsheet technology in general) has come a long way since then!

> **Note** To ensure the elapsed time is displayed correctly, format the cells showing hours and minutes rather than AM/PM (in this case, C4:C8 and E4:E8) with a custom time format **[h]:mm**. On the other hand, the cells showing AM/PM time (in this case, B4:B8 and D4:D8) have been given the custom format **h:mm AM/PM**.

Calculating Time Across Days

You can use the same method above to calculate the time elapsed across days.

In the following example, we have two times:

Time1: *11/24/22 12:30*

Time2: *11/25/22 14:40*

If **Time1** is in cell **A2** and **Time2** is in cell **B2**, the formula **=B2-A2** will produce the result **26:10** (26 hours and 10 minutes).

Note that the cell containing the result has to be formatted as **[h]:mm** to display the result accurately.

C2	∨ ⋮ ✕ ✓ *fx*	=B2-A2	

	A	B	C	D
1	Time1	Time2	Result	
2	11/24/2022 12:30	11/25/2022 14:40	26:10	
3				
4				
5				
6				

Using the TIME Function

You can use the TIME function to properly convert values to hours, minutes, and seconds if directly entered in the formula bar.

Syntax:

=TIME(hour, minute, second)

The following example subtracts 1 hour 40 minutes from 8:20 AM. We want to subtract the value in the formula bar rather than enter it in a cell. If the time is in cell A4, we could use the following formula to subtract 1 hour 40 minutes from it:

=A4 - TIME(1,40,0)

B4	⌄ : ✕ ✓ fx	=A4-TIME(1,40,0)		
	A	B	C	D	E
1	Subtract 1 hour 40 minutes				
2					
3	Source	Result			
4	8:20 AM	6:40 AM			
5					
6					

For more on date functions, see Book 3 – Excel Functions.

Adding and Subtracting Dates

Excel now has improved native functionality for handling dates. For example, in the past, if you wanted to add several days to a date, you would need to use a specific function to make the calculation. You can now just use basic addition and subtraction, and Excel handles all the complexity behind the scenes.

Example 1

Add 40 days to 12/17/2023

1. Enter *12/17/2023* in cell A2 and *40* in cell B2.
2. Enter the formula *=A2+B2* in cell C2
3. Click Enter.

   The result will be *01/26/2024*.

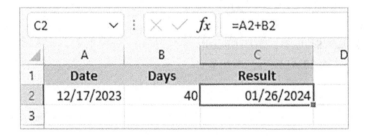

Example 2

Subtract 30 days from 12/14/2022

1. Enter *12/14/2022* in cell A2 and *30* in cell B2.
2. Enter the formula *=A2-B2* in cell C2
3. Click Enter.

The result will be *11/14/2022*.

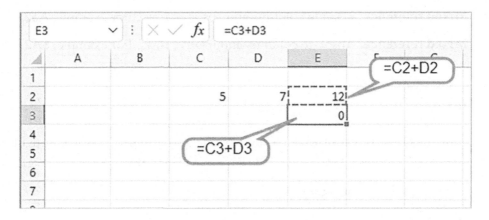

For more on calculating dates, see Book 3 – Excel Functions.

Relative and Absolute Cell Reference

Relative Cell Reference

By default, a cell reference in Excel is relative. When you refer to cell **B2** from cell **E3**, you are pointing to a cell that is three columns to the left (E minus B) and one row above (3-2). A formula with a relative cell reference changes as you copy it from one cell to another.

For example, if you copy the formula **=C2+D2** from cell E2 to E3, the formula changes to **=C3+D3**. The relative positions of the cells in the formula remain on the same columns but are one row down. When copying a formula with relative cell references, you need to be aware that the formula will change.

Examples of relative references:

=D2+E2

=A3*B3

Absolute Cell Reference

Suppose you want to maintain the original cell reference when copying a formula. In that case, you need to make the cell reference *absolute* by inserting a dollar sign (**$**) before the column letter and row number, for example, **=$C$2 + $D$2**. The dollar sign before the column and row tells Excel that the cell reference does not change when the formula is copied to other cells. When you copy the formula **=$C$2 + $D$2** from E2 to E3, the formula stays the same.

To convert a cell reference to an absolute reference, select the reference in the formula bar (or place the cursor between the column letter and row number) and press the **F4** key.

For example, if you have =C2 + D2 in the formula bar and want to make C2 an absolute reference, select C2 in the formula bar and press F4. Excel converts it to **$C$2**.

If you keep pressing F4, Excel cycles through the different types of cell references available as listed below:

- **Relative reference** (default): Relative columns and rows. For example, **A2**.

- **Absolute reference**: Absolute columns and rows. For example, **$A$2**.

- **Mixed reference**: Relative columns and absolute rows. For example, **A$2**.

- **Mixed reference**: Absolute columns and relative rows. For example, **$A2**.

Example

In the example below, we calculate the Sales Tax on various items. The Tax Rate of **20%** has been entered in cell B3. The cell format of B3 is **Percentage**.

The formula in cell C6 is **=B6*$B$3**.

As you can see, cell B3 in the formula has been set to an absolute reference. Thus, when we copy the formula (using autofill) to the rest of the cells under Tax (column C), the reference to cell B3 remains the same.

If the Tax Rate were to change in the future, we would only change the value in cell B3. The Tax for all the items will automatically be updated.

C6	⌄ ⋮ ✕ ✓ fx	=B6*$B$3

◢	A	B	C
1	Sales Tax Calculation		
2			
3	Tax Rate:	20%	
4			
5	Product	Price (excl. tax)	Tax
6	Item 1	$40.00	$8.00
7	Item 2	$58.00	$11.60
8	Item 3	$85.00	$17.00
9	Item 4	$47.00	$9.40
10	Item 5	$56.00	$11.20
11	Item 6	$28.00	$5.60
12	Item 7	$31.00	$6.20
13	Item 8	$65.00	$13.00
14	Item 9	$25.90	$5.18
15	Item 10	$78.30	$15.66
16	Item 11	$69.30	$13.86
17	Item 12	$56.80	$11.36
18			

Mixed Cell Reference

In some cases, you may want to use a "mixed" cell reference. You prefix either the column letter or row number with a dollar sign to lock it as an absolute reference, but allow the other to be a relative reference.

For example, **=$B2 + $C2**

This formula says the columns in cell references (B and C) are locked down as absolute, but row (2) is left free to be relative.

When this formula is copied from E4 to F5 (one column to the right and one row down), it will change to **=$B3 + $C3**. The columns remain the same, but the row changed because the formula moved down one row. You can also lock down the row and leave the column as relative, for example, **=B$2**.

Examples of mixed references:

=$D2+$E2

=A$3*$B3

Using Data from Other Worksheets

On some occasions, you may be working on one worksheet, and you want to access data on another worksheet in your formula. Or perhaps you may decide to separate your summary reports from your data using different worksheets. For example, you may want to have the raw data on **Sheet2** and the summary calculations on **Sheet1**.

Example 1

The following example has a formula in cell **A6** on **Sheet1** and grabs a value from cell **A1** on **Sheet2**.

1. Place the cell pointer in A6 on Sheet1.

2. Enter *=Sheet2!A1* in the formula bar.

3. Click **Enter**.

Excel will now reference cell A1 from Sheet2 as part of your formula in A6 on Sheet1.

Another way to reference a cell on another sheet in your formula is to select it with your mouse. Follow the steps below to reference a cell on another sheet:

1. Select **A6** on **Sheet1**.

2. Type the equal sign (=) in the formula bar.

3. Click the **Sheet2** tab (at the bottom of the window).

4. Select cell **A1** on **Sheet2**.

5. Click **Enter**.

Excel enters the reference **Sheet2!A1** automatically in cell A6 in Sheet1.

The same method applies when your reference is a range. Sometimes you may want your data on one sheet, and your summary calculations on another sheet.

If you want to reference more than one cell, like a range, click Sheet2 and select the range of cells. For example, A1:A10. The reference **Sheet2!A1:A10** will now be added to the formula bar in Sheet1. If you have a named range, you can use the range's name in place of the cell reference, for example, **Sheet2!MyRange**.

Example 2

In the following example, we have our raw data on Sheet2, and we're calculating the totals for each Quarter on Sheet1.

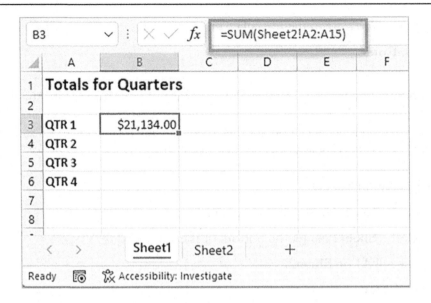

1. On **Sheet1**, select B3, and in the formula bar, enter *=SUM(*.

2. Click the **Sheet2** tab at the bottom of the window.

3. On Sheet 2, select cells **A2:A15** by selecting A2 and dragging down to A15.

   Excel adds **Sheet2!A2:A15** in the formula bar. Your syntax should now look like this **=SUM(Sheet2!A2:A15**.

4. Click in the formula bar and enter the closing bracket. Your formula should now look like this **=SUM(Sheet2!A2:A15)**.

5. Click **Enter** to confirm the entry.

The sum of the figures from A2 to B15 on Sheet2 will now be shown in sheet1.

Chapter 7

Drop-down Lists and Validation Rules

In this chapter, we will cover:

- Creating and using a dropdown list.
- Creating data validation rules for cells.

A drop-down list enables you to restrict the values users can enter in a cell to a subset of predefined values. Having a predefined list of values can help streamline workflow and minimize errors. A validation rule allows you to restrict the type of data, or the range of values users can enter into a cell. You can insert validation rules in cells to ensure the entered data meets a certain set of criteria.

Entering Data with a Drop-down List

There are occasions when you can make your worksheet more efficient by using drop-down lists in cells. Drop-down lists enable users to select an item from a list you create instead of entering their own values. On occasions where you have a defined set of values from a lookup list or column, being able to select the value directly from the source data saves time and reduces errors.

You can use a comma-delimited list or a range in your worksheet for the data source of your drop-down list.

Using a Comma-Delimited List as the Source

In the following example, we'll use a comma-delimited list for a drop-down list used to populate the grades for students. The grades we'll use as our source are - Merit, Credit, Pass, and Fail.

	A	B
1	**Student**	**Grade**
2	Judith	
3	Paul	
4	David	
5	Randy	
6	Mary	
7	Dorothy	
8	Kimberly	
9	Raymond	
10	Shirley	

Follow the steps below to create a drop-down list with comma-delimited values:

1. Select all the cells for which you want to add a drop-down list. For our example, we'll select B2:B10.

2. On the Ribbon, click the **Data** tab. Then click the **Data Validation** command.

3. In the Data Validation dialog box, set **Allow** to **List**.

4. Click in the **Source** box and enter your values separated by commas.

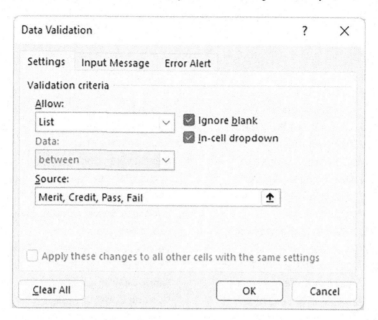

5. Click **OK**.

The selected cells now have a drop-down list.

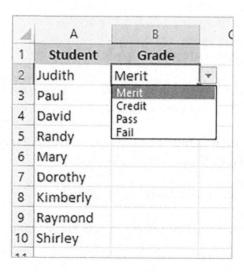

Using a Range as the Source

In the following example, the source for our drop-down list will be from a worksheet named **SalesData** in a different worksheet in the same workbook. Our drop-down list will be pulling data from the Product column (C4:C51).

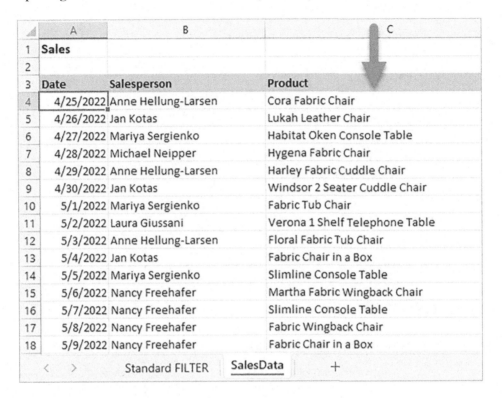

Follow the steps below to create the drop-down list:

1. On a blank worksheet, select the cell where you want to create the drop-down list. For example, cell B3 in a blank worksheet.

2. On the **Data** tab, in the **Data Tools** group, click the **Data Validation** command. Excel opens the **Data Validation** dialog box.

3. On the **Settings** tab, in the **Allow** box, select **List**.

4. Click in the **Source** box, then select the data range you want to display in your list.

For our example, we're selecting range C4:C51 on the SalesData worksheet. Excel will automatically enter the selected range in the Source box.

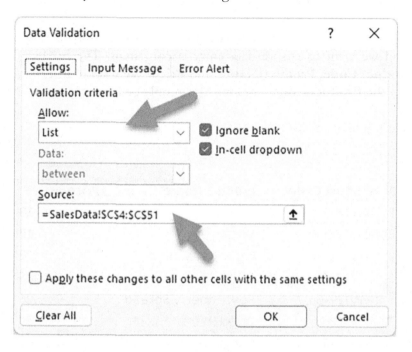

5. Click **OK** to finish creating the drop-down list.

When done, the drop-down list will display a list of values from the selected source when you click the drop-down arrow.

Creating Data Validation Rules

In the following example, let's say we have a product list that is updated by different staff members, and we want to ensure data entry is consistent. The list has the following columns: **Product Code**, **Product Name**, and **Price**. We want to insert a validation rule to ensure that the **Product Code** (column A) can only be between 5 and 10 characters.

Below is an example of the list.

	A	B	C
1	Product Code	Product Name	Price
2	NWTB-1	Chai	18
3	NWTCO-3	Syrup	10
4	NWTCO-4	Cajun Seasoning	22
5	NWTO-5	Olive Oil	21.35
6	NWTJP-6	Boysenberry Spread	25
7	NWTDFN-7	Dried Pears	30
8	NWTS-8	Curry Sauce	40
9	NWTDFN-14	Walnuts	23.25
10	NWTCFV-17	Fruit Cocktail	39
11	NWTBGM-19	Chocolate Biscuits Mix	9.2
12	NWTJP-6	Marmalade	81
13	NWTBGM-21	Scones	10

To add a validation rule for the Product Code, do the following:

1. Select the cells for which you want to apply the rule. For our example, we select column A.

2. On the **Data** tab, in the **Data Tools** group, click the **Data Validation** command.

   Excel opens the Data Validation dialog box.

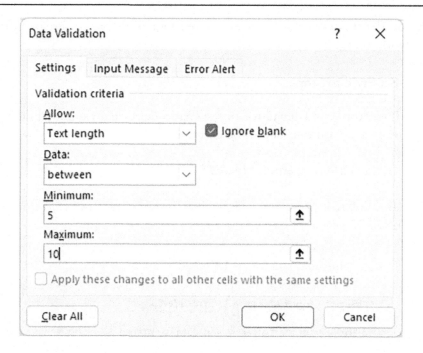

3. On the **Settings** tab, enter the following settings:

   - **Allow:** Text length
   - **Data:** between
   - **Minimum:** 5
   - **Maximum:** 10

4. On the **Input Message** tab, add a **Title** and the **Input message**.

   Excel displays this message as a small pop-up when the user clicks on a cell with the validation rule.

   For this example, we can add a message like:

   "The Product Code can be alphanumeric, and it should be between 5 and 10 characters."

5. On the **Error Alert** tab, we define the message to display when an entry fails the validation rule.

- Set **Style** to **Stop**.

  The Stop icon is ideal for this scenario because a value that does not meet the validation rule cannot be entered.

- In the **Title** box, enter: "*Invalid Entry.*"

- In the **Error Message** box, enter: "*Invalid entry. Please enter a value between 5 and 10 characters in length.*"

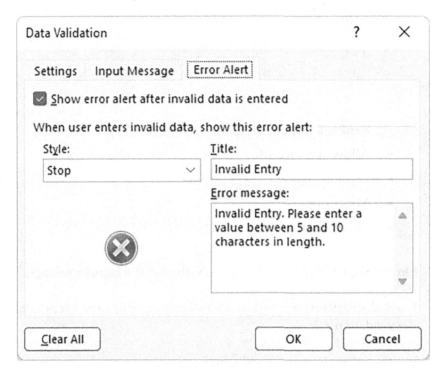

6. Once you have completed all the tabs, click **OK.**

Data validation will now be applied to the selected cells.

Editing or Removing Data Validation Rules

Occasionally you may want to change or remove data validation. To remove data validation, do the following:

1. Select the cells where data validation has been applied.

2. On the **Data** tab, in the **Data Tools** group, click the **Data Validation** command to open the Data Validation dialog box.

3. To change the validation rule, simply edit the various entries and click OK when done.

4. To remove the validation rule, click **Clear All**.

5. Click **OK**.

Chapter 8

Named Ranges

This chapter covers:

- Defining a named range.
- Editing and renaming a named range.
- Removing a named range.
- How to use named ranges in your formulas.

When working with a lot of data, it is sometimes useful to identify your data as a group with one name to make it easier to reference in your formulas. A named range is a group of cells in Excel selected and given one name. After you specify a name for the selection, the range can now be referenced as one unit using that name in Excel formulas and functions. A named range is similar to a table with a name but different from Excel tables.

Creating a Named Range

In the following example, we have a list of contacts we would like to use in formulas. We could either use A1:G17 to identify the range of data, or we could name the range "Contacts" and then use that name to reference the data throughout our worksheet.

One of the benefits of using a named range is that Excel makes it an absolute reference by default. When you create a formula with that name, you can copy and paste the formula anywhere in your workbook, including different worksheets in the workbook, and the name will always point to the same group of cells.

There are two ways you can create a named range:

Method 1

1. Select the cells you want to include in the named range.

2. Click in the **Name** box (the box on the left side of the window, just above the worksheet area) and enter the name for your named range.

3. Press **Enter** on your keyboard to save the name.

The example below has A1:G17 defined as a named range called "Contacts" in the Name box. You can now use Contacts in place of A1:G17 in all formulas and functions in the workbook. When you create a named range using this method, the name will be available across all worksheets in your workbook.

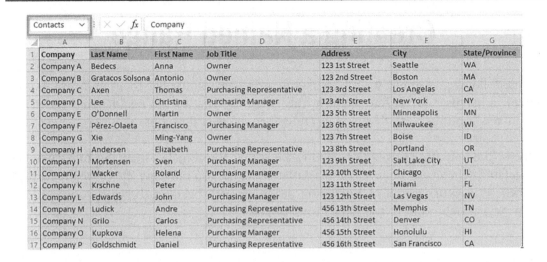

Contacts | | × ✓ *fx* | Company

	A	B	C	D	E	F	G
1	Company	Last Name	First Name	Job Title	Address	City	State/Province
2	Company A	Bedecs	Anna	Owner	123 1st Street	Seattle	WA
3	Company B	Gratacos Solsona	Antonio	Owner	123 2nd Street	Boston	MA
4	Company C	Axen	Thomas	Purchasing Representative	123 3rd Street	Los Angelas	CA
5	Company D	Lee	Christina	Purchasing Manager	123 4th Street	New York	NY
6	Company E	O'Donnell	Martin	Owner	123 5th Street	Minneapolis	MN
7	Company F	Pérez-Olaeta	Francisco	Purchasing Manager	123 6th Street	Milwaukee	WI
8	Company G	Xie	Ming-Yang	Owner	123 7th Street	Boise	ID
9	Company H	Andersen	Elizabeth	Purchasing Representative	123 8th Street	Portland	OR
10	Company I	Mortensen	Sven	Purchasing Manager	123 9th Street	Salt Lake City	UT
11	Company J	Wacker	Roland	Purchasing Manager	123 10th Street	Chicago	IL
12	Company K	Krschne	Peter	Purchasing Manager	123 11th Street	Miami	FL
13	Company L	Edwards	John	Purchasing Manager	123 12th Street	Las Vegas	NV
14	Company M	Ludick	Andre	Purchasing Representative	456 13th Street	Memphis	TN
15	Company N	Grilo	Carlos	Purchasing Representative	456 14th Street	Denver	CO
16	Company O	Kupkova	Helena	Purchasing Manager	456 15th Street	Honolulu	HI
17	Company P	Goldschmidt	Daniel	Purchasing Representative	456 16th Street	San Francisco	CA

Method 2

This method enables you to specify more settings as you create the named range:

1. Select the cells you want to include in the named range.

2. On the Ribbon, click the **Formulas** tab, and in the **Defined Names** group, click **Define Name**.

   Excel displays the **New Name** dialog box.

3. In the **New Name** dialog box, specify the following settings:

   - In the **Name** box, enter the name of your range.

   - Leave the **Scope** box as **Workbook** (the default) unless you want to restrict the name to the current worksheet.

   - In the **Refers to** box, check the reference that it matches your selection. You can use the up-arrow on the box to reselect the range if necessary.

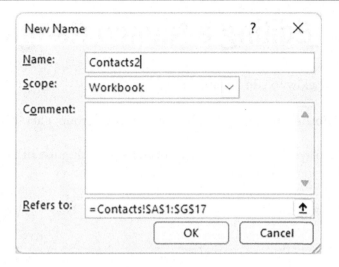

4. Click **OK** when done.

Note If you set the scope of a named range to **Workbook**, the name will be available in all worksheets in the workbook. You can't create another named range using the same name in that workbook. If the scope is set to a particular sheet, then the name can be used within the sheet only. Also, you'll be able to use that name for named ranges within the scope of other sheets.

Note Excel creates a named range that is an absolute reference by default. If you want a relative named range, remove the $ sign from the reference in the **Refers to** box. See chapter 6 for more on relative and absolute references.

Editing a Named Range

Follow the steps below to edit a named range:

1. On the **Formulas** tab, in the **Defined Names** group, click **Name Manager**.

   Excel displays the Name Manager dialog box with a list of all the named ranges and tables in the workbook.

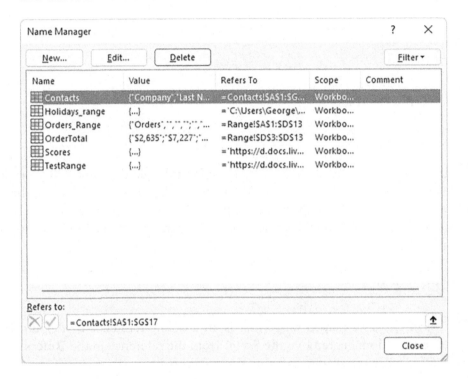

2. In the Name Manager dialog box, select the name you want to edit and click the **Edit** button.

3. In the Edit Name dialog box, enter the name in the **Name** box.

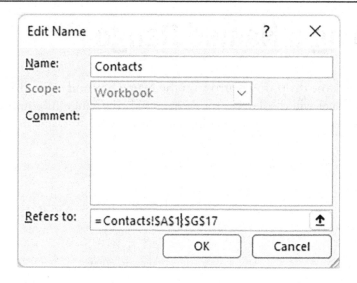

4. To change the reference, click in the **Refers to** box.

    Excel selects the current range on the worksheet, allowing you to resize it if necessary. You can adjust the current selection by holding down the **Shift** key and resizing it with your mouse.

5. Click **OK** on the Edit Name box.

6. Click **Close**.

Using a Named Range

To select a named range, click the drop-down arrow on the Name box and select the name from the drop-down list. Excel will display the worksheet with the range (if you're on a different worksheet) and select all the rows and columns in the range.

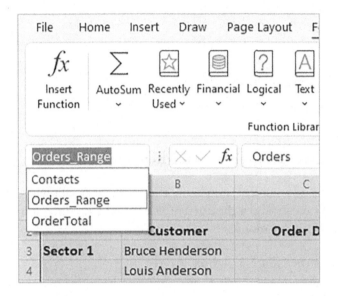

Example

The following example shows the use of two named ranges, *Orders_Range and OrderTotal,* in place of the cell references, A1:D13 and D3:D13. The formulas below use the named ranges as arguments in place of cell references.

=COUNT(Orders_Range)

=COUNTBLANK(Orders_Range)

=SUM(OrderTotal)

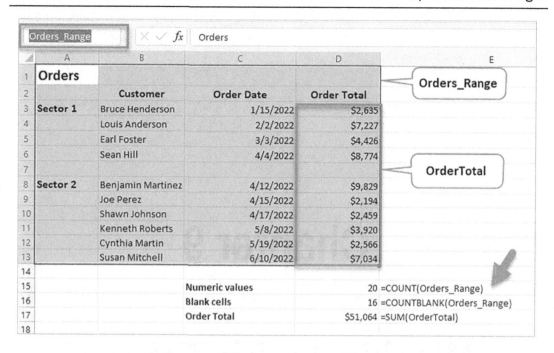

Deleting a Named Range

You may need to delete names as you tidy up your workbook on some occasions. Also, a name can only be used once in a workbook, so deleting a name frees that name for reuse. Deleting a name does not delete the data. It simply removes that name as a reference from the worksheet.

Follow the steps below to delete a named range:

1. On the **Formulas** tab, click **Name Manager**.

2. Select the named range you want to delete from the list.

3. Click the **Delete** button.

4. Click **Close** when done.

Chapter 9

Working with Tables

In this chapter, we will cover how to:

- Convert a range to an Excel table.

- Apply different styles to a table.

- Sort and filter data in a table.

- Add a totals row to a table.

- Remove table attributes (if you want to convert your list back to a range).

- Use a table name in a formula.

You can turn your Excel data into a table. Creating a table in Excel makes managing and analyzing your data easier. You also get built-in sorting, filtering, Banded Rows, and you can add a Total Row.

Preparing Your Data

Before creating a table, ensure there are no empty columns or rows in the data.

In the next example, we will convert the following range of data into a table.

	A	B	C	D	E
1	Last Name	First Name	Company	Job Title	Address
2	Bedecs	Anna	Company A	Owner	123 1st Street
3	Gratacos Solsona	Antonio	Company B	Owner	123 2nd Stree
4	Axen	Thomas	Company C	Purchasing Represen	123 3rd Street
5	Lee	Christina	Company D	Purchasing Manager	123 4th Street
6	O'Donnell	Martin	Company E	Owner	123 5th Street
7	Pérez-Olaeta	Francisco	Company F	Purchasing Manager	123 6th Stree
8	Xie	Ming-Yang	Company G	Owner	123 7th Street
9	Andersen	Elizabeth	Company H	Purchasing Represen	123 8th Stree
10	Mortensen	Sven	Company I	Purchasing Manager	123 9th Street
11	Wacker	Roland	Company J	Purchasing Manager	123 10th Street
12	Krschne	Peter	Company K	Purchasing Manager	123 11th Stree
13	Edwards	John	Company L	Purchasing Manager	123 12th Stre
14	Ludick	Andre	Company M	Purchasing Represen	456 13th Stree
15	Grilo	Carlos	Company N	Purchasing Represen	456 14th Street
16	Kupkova	Helena	Company O	Purchasing Manager	456 15th Stre

First, check that there are no empty columns or rows in your data:

1. Select any cell within the data and press **Ctrl** + **A**.

2. Then press **Ctrl** + **.** (period) a few times to move around the data.

Note **Ctrl** + **A** selects the data range in question. **Ctrl** + **.** moves around the four edges of the data so you can see where the data starts and ends.

Creating an Excel Table

To convert a range to a table, do the following:

1. Select any cell within the data.

2. Click the **Insert** tab, and in the **Tables** group, click **Table**.

3. Excel displays a dialog box showing you the range for the table. You can adjust the range here if necessary.

4. Select **My table has headers** to ensure that the first row of your table is used as the header.

Tip If your table has no column headers, create a new row on top and add column headers. Row headers make it easier to work with tables in Excel.

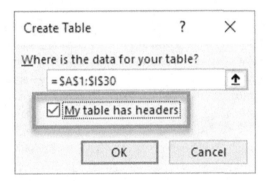

5. Click **OK**.

Excel creates the table with the first row used as column headers.

	A	B	C	D	E
1	Last Name ▼	First Name ▼	Company ▼	Job Title ▼	Address
2	Bedecs	Anna	Company A	Owner	123 1st Street
3	Gratacos Solsona	Antonio	Company B	Owner	123 2nd Street
4	Axen	Thomas	Company C	Purchasing Represen	123 3rd Street
5	Lee	Christina	Company D	Purchasing Manager	123 4th Street
6	O'Donnell	Martin	Company E	Owner	123 5th Street
7	Pérez-Olaeta	Francisco	Company F	Purchasing Manager	123 6th Street
8	Xie	Ming-Yang	Company G	Owner	123 7th Street
9	Andersen	Elizabeth	Company H	Purchasing Represen	123 8th Street
10	Mortensen	Sven	Company I	Purchasing Manager	123 9th Street
11	Wacker	Roland	Company J	Purchasing Manager	123 10th Street
12	Krschne	Peter	Company K	Purchasing Manager	123 11th Street
13	Edwards	John	Company L	Purchasing Manager	123 12th Street
14	Ludick	Andre	Company M	Purchasing Represen	456 13th Street
15	Grilo	Carlos	Company N	Purchasing Represen	456 14th Street
16	Kupkova	Helena	Company O	Purchasing Manager	456 15th Street

-ᗕ̣́-**Tip** Other ways to quickly create a table:

Select the cells in the range, and on the Ribbon, click **Home > Format as Table.**

Choosing a Table Style

When you convert a range to a table, Excel applies a style with alternating row colors to the table. You can change this style by selecting a new style from many options provided by Excel if you want.

When you select any cell in the table, Excel displays the **Table Design** contextual tab on the Ribbon. This tab includes the groups, **Table Style Options**, and **Table Styles**. Table Styles provides several predefined styles you can apply to your table, while Table Style Options provides further options to style your table.

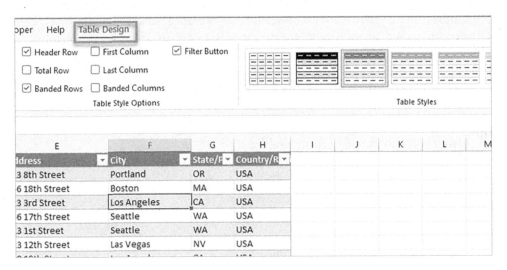

Applying a Table Style

To apply a predefined style to your table, do the following:

1. Select a cell within the table.

2. On the **Table Design** tab, locate the **Table Styles** group and click the drop-down button for the styles. A drop-down menu will show you more styles.

3. Hover over each style to preview how applying it would look on your worksheet.

4. When you find a style you want, click it to apply it to your table.

Applying Table Style Options

Here you have several options for configuring the style of your table.

For example, you can change your table from **Banded Rows** to **Banded Columns**. Banded rows are the alternating colors applied to your table rows. The Banded Rows setting is the default, but if you want banded columns instead, uncheck **Banded Rows** and check **Banded Columns** to have your columns alternate in color instead of your rows.

Note that if a new column or row is added to the table, it will inherit the current table style automatically. When you add a new row, any formulas applied to your table will also be copied to the new row.

Sorting Data in a Table

Before sorting data, ensure there are no blank rows and blank columns. Also, ensure your table header is a single row. If the header is more than one row, change it to a single row to make things easier.

Tip To check for blank rows or columns, select a cell within the data and press **Ctrl + A**. Then press **Ctrl + .** (period) a few times. This keystroke moves the cell pointer around the four corners of the range so that you can see the whole area.

Sort by One Column

To quickly sort your table using one column, do the following:

1. Select a cell in the column you want to use for the sorting. For example, **Last Name**.

2. On the **Data** tab, in the **Sort & Filter** group, click **AZ** (to sort the table in ascending order) or **ZA** (to sort the table in descending order).

That's it. Excel sorts your table in the order you've chosen.

Sort by Multiple Columns

There are often occasions when you want to sort a table using more than one column. A **Custom Sort** is required to sort a table by multiple columns.

To sort your data using several columns, follow these steps:

1. Select any cell within the data.

2. On the **Home** tab, in the **Editing** group, click **Sort & Filter**.

3. Select **Custom Sort** from the drop-down menu.

   Excel displays the **Sort** dialog box.

Tip: Another way to open the Custom Sort dialog box is to click **Data** > **Sort** (in the **Sort & Filter** group).

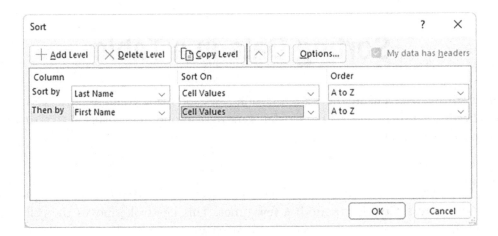

4. Click **Add Level**.

5. Under **Column**, select the column you want to **Sort by** from the drop-down list. Select the second column you want to include in the sort in the **Then by** field. For example, Sort by Last Name and First Name.

6. Under **Sort On**, select **Cell Values**.

7. Under **Order**, select the order you want to sort on, **A to Z** for ascending order, and **Z to A** for descending order.

8. Click **OK**.

You can add additional columns to your sort. Excel allows you to have up to 64 sort levels. For each additional column you want to sort by, repeat steps 4-7 above.

Filtering Table Data

Excel provides an array of options to filter your data so that you can view only the data you want to see. Filters provide a quick way to work with a subset of data in a range or table. When you apply the filter, you temporarily hide some of the data so that you can focus on the data you need to view.

Follow the steps below to filter data in an Excel table:

1. Select any cell in the table that you want to filter.
2. Click **Home** > **Sort & Filter** > **Filter** (or click **Data** > **Filter**).
3. You will get filter arrows at the top of each column.
4. Click the arrow in the column header. For example, **Price**. This arrow is also known as the AutoFilter.
5. Uncheck **Select All** and check the values you want to use for the filter.
6. Click **OK**.

	A	B	C	D	E
1	Product Code	Product Name	Price	Reorder Level	Category
16	NWTSO-41	Clam Chowder	$9.65	10	Soups
17	NWTB-43	Coffee	$46.00	25	Beverages
18	NWTCA-48	Chocolate	$12.75	25	Candy
19	NWTDFN-51	Dried Apples	$53.00	10	Dried Fruit & Nuts
20	NWTG-52	Long Grain Rice	$7.00	25	Grains
21	NWTP-56	Gnocchi	$38.00	30	Pasta
22	NWTP-57	Ravioli	$19.50	20	Pasta
23	NWTS-65	Hot Pepper Sauce	$21.05	10	Sauces
24	NWTS-66	Tomato Sauce	$17.00	20	Sauces
25	NWTD-72	Mozzarella	$34.80	10	Dairy Products
26	NWTDFN-74	Almonds	$10.00	5	Dried Fruit & Nuts
27	NWTCO-77	Mustard	$13.00	15	Condiments
28	NWTDFN-80	Dried Plums	$3.50	50	Dried Fruit & Nuts
29	NWTB-81	Green Tea	$2.99	100	Beverages
30	NWTC-82	Granola	$4.00	20	Cereal

The AutoFilter changes to a funnel icon to indicate that the column is filtered. If you look at the row heading numbers, you'll see that they're now blue, indicating which rows are included in the filtered data.

To remove the filter, on the **Data** tab, in the **Sort & Filter** group, click **Clear**. The filter will be removed, and all data will be displayed.

Applying a Custom Filter

A custom filter allows you to manually define your criteria for filtering the data.

To apply a custom filter to an Excel table, do the following:

1. Click the arrow (AutoFilter) on the column you want to filter.

2. Depending on the format of the column being filtered, you'll get one of the following options:

    - **Text Filters:** Available when the column has text values or has a mixture of text and numbers.

    - **Number Filters:** Available when the column contains only numbers

    - **Date Filters:** Available when the column contains only dates.

    - **Clear Filter from [Column name]:** Available when a filter has already been applied to the column. Select this option to clear the filter.

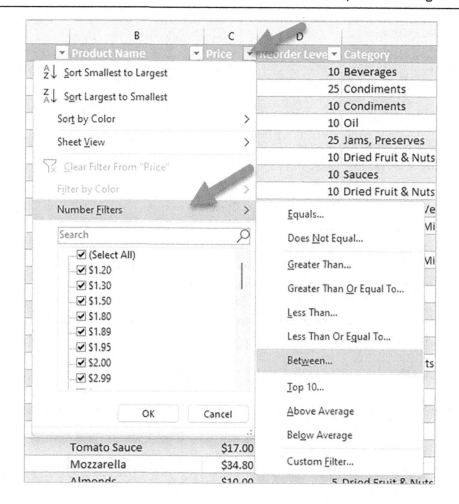

3. Select one of the first three options (Text Filters, Number Filters, or Date Filters) and then select a comparison. For this example, we've selected **Between**.

Excel opens the **Custom AutoFilter** dialog box.

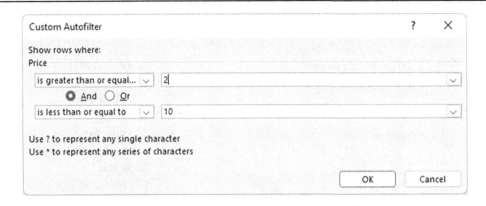

4. Enter the filter criteria.

    For the logical operator, select **And** if both conditions must be true, or select **Or** if only one of the conditions needs to be true.

    Our example filters the **Price** column so that only rows between $2 and $10 are displayed in the table.

5. Click **OK**.

The AutoFilter changes to a Filter icon. You can click this icon to change or clear the filter.

	A	B	C		E	
1	Product Code	Product Name	Price	Reorder Level	Category	
3	NWTCO-3	Syrup	$10.00	25	Condiments	
11	NWTBGM-19	Chocolate Biscuits Mix	$9.20	5	Baked Goods & Mixes	
13	NWTBGM-21	Scones	$10.00	5	Baked Goods & Mixes	
16	NWTSO-41	Clam Chowder	$9.65	10	Soups	
20	NWTG-52	Long Grain Rice	$7.00	25	Grains	
26	NWTDFN-74	Almonds	$10.00	5	Dried Fruit & Nuts	
28	NWTDFN-80	Dried Plums	$3.50	50	Dried Fruit & Nuts	
29	NWTB-81	Green Tea	$2.99	100	Beverages	
30	NWTC-82	Granola	$4.00	20	Cereal	
34	NWTB-87	Tea	$4.00	20	Beverages	
38	NWTCFV-91	Cherry Pie Filling	$2.00	10	Canned Fruit & Vegetables	
42	NWTCM-95	Tuna Fish	$2.00	30	Canned Meat	
43	NWTCM-96	Smoked Salmon	$4.00	30	Canned Meat	
44	NWTC-82	Hot Cereal	$5.00	50	Cereal	

Filtered results

Tip To change the order of the filtered results, click the filter icon and then select either **Sort Largest to Smallest** or **Sort Smallest to Largest**. For a text column, it would be **Sort A to Z** or **Sort Z to A.**

Adding a Totals Row to Your Table

You can add totals to a table by selecting the **Total Row** check box on the **Design** tab. Once added to your worksheet, the Total Row drop-down button allows you to add a function from a list of options.

To add totals to your table:

1. Select a cell in a table.
2. Select **Table Design** > **Total Row**. Excel adds a new row to the bottom of the table called the **Total Row**.
3. On the Total Row drop-down list, you have an array of functions you can select like **Average**, **Count**, **Count Numbers**, **Max**, **Min**, **Sum**, **StdDev**, **Var**, and more.

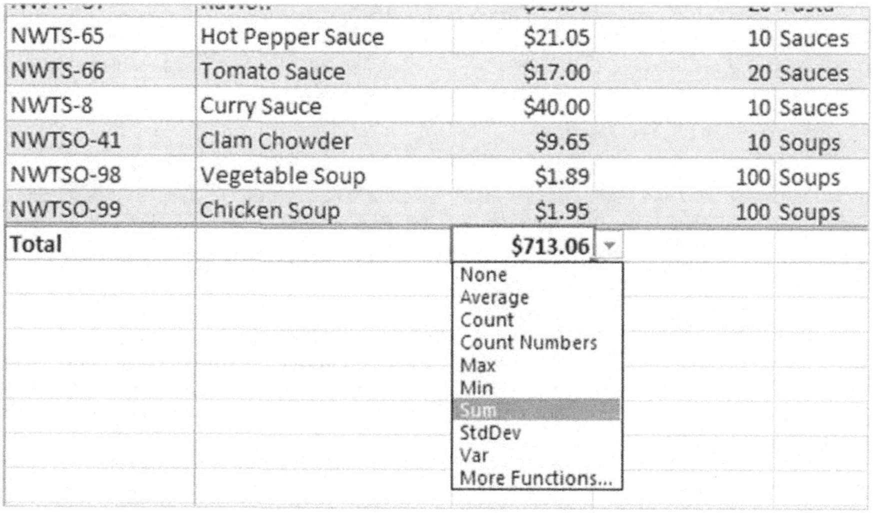
NWTS-65 Hot Pepper Sauce $21.05 10 Sauces
NWTS-66 Tomato Sauce $17.00 20 Sauces
NWTS-8 Curry Sauce $40.00 10 Sauces
NWTSO-41 Clam Chowder $9.65 10 Soups
NWTSO-98 Vegetable Soup $1.89 100 Soups
NWTSO-99 Chicken Soup $1.95 100 Soups
Total $713.06
None
Average
Count
Count Numbers
Max
Min
Sum
StdDev
Var
More Functions...

> **Tip** If you need to add a new row of data to your table at any point, deselect **Total Row** on the **Table Design** tab, add the new row, and then reselect **Total Row**.

Giving Your Table a Custom Name

After creation, Excel gives your table a default name like Table1, Table2, etc. However, you can give your table a custom name, especially if you want to use that name to reference data in the table in formulas.

Follow the steps below to give your table a custom name:

1. On the Ribbon, click the **Table Design** tab.

2. In the **Properties** group, type in your table name in the **Table Name** field (overwriting the default name).

3. Press **Enter**.

    You can now use to table name in formulas to reference data in the table.

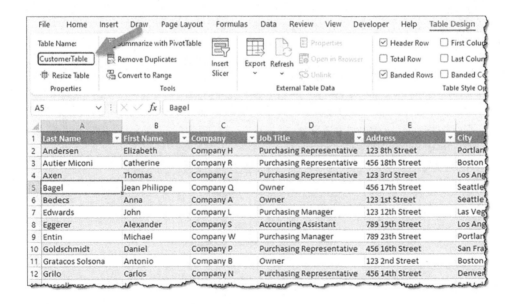

Using Table Names in Formulas

In the following example, instead of using the range **B2:B11**, the formulas use **Sales[Sales Amount]** to refer to that range. The table name is **Sales**, and the column name is **Sales Amount**.

This reference uses the combination of the table and column names to refer to the data range in the table. This type of reference is called a structured reference.

=SUM(Sales[Sales Amount])

=MAX(Sales[Sales Amount])

=AVERAGE(Sales[Sales Amount])

	E2		⌄	⁞	✕ ✓	*fx*	=SUM(Sales[Sales Amount])	
	A	B	C	D	E	F	G
1	Sales Person ▾	Sales Amount ▾				Formula Text	
2	Hugo	$1,848.00		Total sales	$23,222.00	=SUM(Sales[Sales Amount])	
3	Felipe	$3,897.00		Max sale	$5,509.00	=MAX(Sales[Sales Amount])	
4	Wayne	$1,267.00		Average	$2,322.20	=AVERAGE(Sales[Sales Amount])	
5	Mae	$1,149.00					
6	Lee	$2,571.00					
7	Oscar	$1,659.00					
8	Ming-Yang	$5,509.00					
9	Terrance	$2,307.00					
10	Sylvester	$1,589.00					
11	Elijah	$1,426.00					
12							

Structured references provide certain benefits, including the following:

- The name is an absolute reference, so you can copy the formula to any part of your workbook without the reference changing.

- You don't need to adjust the reference in your formulas when you add or remove rows from the table.

- You could find it easier to refer to ranges in your formulas. For example, it may be easier to enter the table and column name in your formula in a large workbook instead of identifying explicit cell references.

Removing Table Attributes

On some occasions, you may want to switch a table back to a normal range. Maybe you want to perform tasks where a table is unnecessary or transform the data before converting it to a table again.

You can convert an Excel table back to a range using one of the following methods.

Method 1

1. Click anywhere in the table so that the cell pointer is inside the table.
2. Click the **Table Design** tab, and in the Tools group, click **Convert to Range**.
3. Click **Yes** to confirm the action.

    The table will now be converted to a normal range of cells without Excel's table features.

Method 2

1. Right-click anywhere in the table.
2. On the pop-up menu, select **Table > Convert to Range**.
3. Click **Yes** at the confirmation prompt.

    Excel removes all table attributes and returns the data to a range.

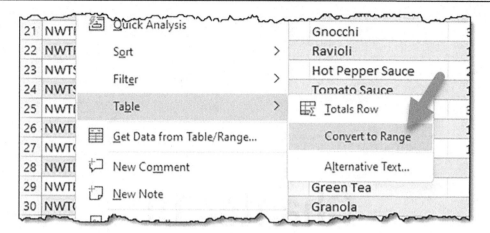

After converting a table back to a range, the range will still retain the style and formatting that was applied to the table, like banded rows, for example. However, the formatting does not affect the behavior of the range.

To clear all formatting, do the following:

1. Select the range.

2. Click the **Home** tab.

3. In the **Editing** group, click **Clear** > **Clear Formats**.

Chapter 10

Creating Charts

This chapter covers:

- ■ Creating a quick chart with the Quick Analysis tool.
- ■ Manually creating a chart.
- ■ Editing and customizing your chart with different styles and formats.
- ■ Creating a sparkline chart.

Excel charts provide a way to analyze and present your data visually. As the saying goes, *a picture is worth a thousand words*. Some of us don't absorb numbers as easily as others because we're more visual, and this is where charts come in. A visual representation may sometimes have more of an impact on your audience.

Preparing Your Data

To prepare your data for charting, you'll need to organize it in a list with only the items you want to report on. Leave out any extraneous data and grand totals you don't want on the chart. Ideally, you should have column headings. The example below has **Product Name** and **Total Sales** as column headings. Excel's charting tools will use the column headings when labeling your chart.

	A	B
1	**Product Name**	**Total Sales**
2	Chai	$1,800.00
3	Beer	$3,400.00
4	Coffee	$4,600.00
5	Green Tea	$200.00
6	Tea	$1,400.00
7	Chocolate Biscuits Mix	$900.20
8	Scones	$1,000.00
9	Brownie Mix	$1,200.49
10	Cake Mix	$1,500.99
11	Granola	$400.00
12	Hot Cereal	$500.00
13	Chocolate	$1,200.75
14	Fruit Cocktail	$3,900.00
15	Pears	$100.30
16	Peaches	$1,000.50

Creating a Chart with the Quick Analysis Tool

The Quick Analysis tool appears as a button on the bottom-right of your selection when selecting a range of data in Excel. The Quick Analysis button offers a host of features for quickly adding conditional formatting, totals, tables, charts, and Sparklines to your worksheet.

To generate a chart using the Quick Analysis tool:

1. Select the range you want to use for your chart. The Quick Analysis button is displayed at the bottom-right of the selection.

2. Click the Quick Analysis button and then click **Charts**. You'll get a list of recommended charts.

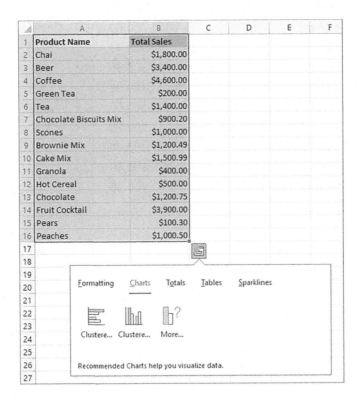

3. Click the second option to generate a column chart.

A floating chart will be created in the same worksheet as your data. You can click and drag this chart to another part of the worksheet if necessary.

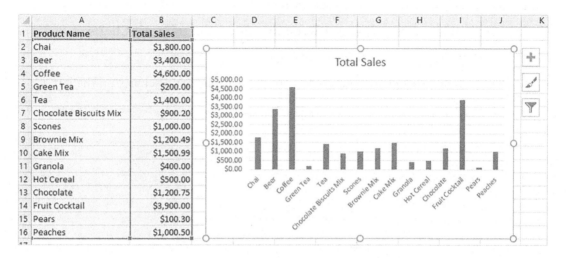

To create another type of chart, for example, a pie chart, you can click the **More** option on the Quick Analysis menu to show a list of all chart types.

-ᗰ-**Tip**   Another way to create a quick chart is to select the data and press the **F11** key to generate a chart of the default type on a new chart sheet. The default chart created would be the column chart unless you've changed the default chart. To create an embedded chart using this method (in the same worksheet as the data), press the **Alt + F1** keys together.

Creating a Chart Manually

The **Charts** group in the **Insert** tab has several commands to create different types of charts. You can click a chart type, for example, the pie chart icon, to display a list of chart options available for that chart type.

Alternatively, you can open the **Insert Chart** dialog box that shows a list of all the chart types you can create in Excel.

To create a chart from the Insert Chart dialog, do the following:

1. Select the range of data for your chart.

2. On the Ribbon, click **Insert** > **Recommended Charts** > **All Charts**.

   Excel displays the **Insert Chart** dialog box.

3. Select the type of chart you want to create from the list of charts on the left.

4. Click **OK**.

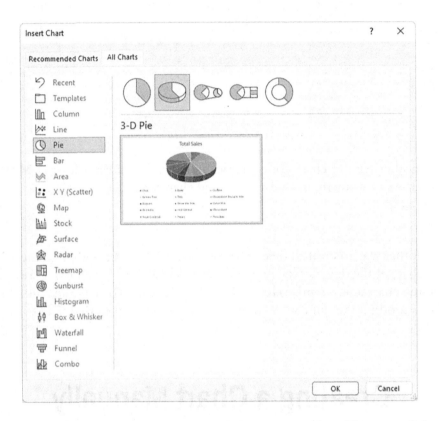

Excel creates a floating chart in the same worksheet as your data. You can click and drag this chart to another part of the screen if necessary.

To delete a chart, simply select the chart and press the **Delete** key.

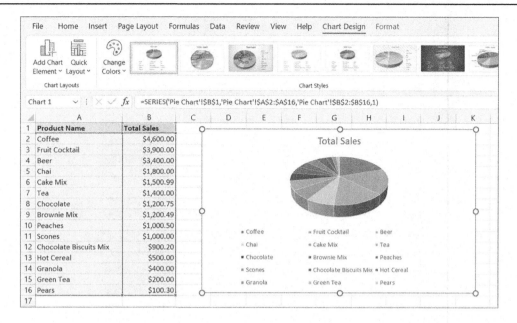

When you select a chart by clicking it, Excel displays the **Chart Design** tab on the Ribbon. This tab provides many options for editing and styling your chart. The next section will cover editing the chart axis labels and style.

Customizing Charts

After creating a chart, Excel provides several commands for customizing the chart to your liking. For example, you can swap the axis, change/adjust the data source, update the chart title, adjust the layout, apply a chart style, and apply a theme color to your chart.

To demonstrate some of these options, let's say we need to create a chart with four quarters of sales, as shown in the image below.

	A	B	C	D	E
1	Sales by Quarter				
2	Product	QTR1	QTR2	QTR3	QTR4
3	Chai	300	300	200	400
4	Beer	300	200	400	300
5	Coffee	350	400	500	500
6	Green Tea	250	150	100	300
7	Tea	100	400	100	500
8	Chocolate Biscu	320	200	100	300
9	Scones	250	500	200	100
10	Brownie Mix	350	400	550	200
11	Cake Mix	200	370	300	200
12	Granola	250	100	200	400
13	Hot Cereal	350	500	300	200
14	Chocolate	350	200	500	500
15	Fruit Cocktail	200	230	250	200
16	Pears	100	200	300	450
17	Peaches	200	300	200	600
18					

To create the chart:

1. Select the range with the data, including the column headers and row headers.

2. Select **Insert > Charts > Recommended Charts**.

   Excel displays the **Insert Chart** dialog with several chart recommendations for your data.

3. Select the **Clustered Column** option.

4. Click **OK**.

A chart will be created and added to your worksheet.

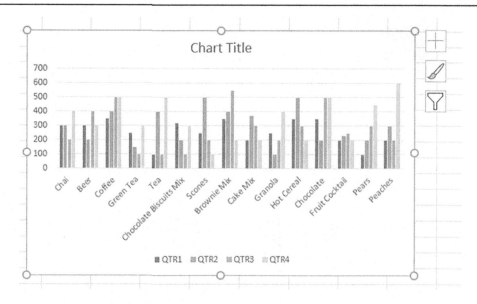

Switching the X and Y Axes

You can switch the values Excel applies to the vertical axis (also called the y-axis) and horizontal axis (also called the x-axis).

To switch the values applied to the axes:

1. Select the chart.
2. Click **Chart Design** > **Switch Row/Column**.

Excel swaps the values applied to the vertical and horizontal axes.

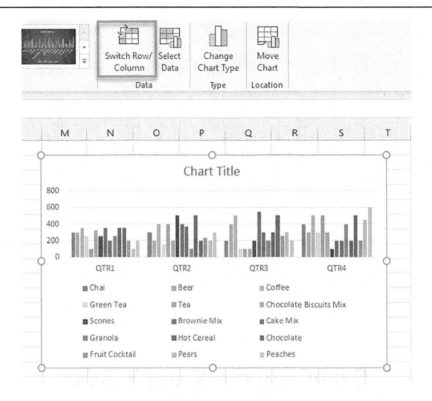

To swap the values back, simply click the **Switch Row/Column** button again.

Change the Data Source

To change the data used as the source of the chart, do the following:

1. Click the Chart to activate the **Chart Design** tab.

2. In the **Data** group, click **Select Data**.

   Excel displays the **Select Data Source** dialog.

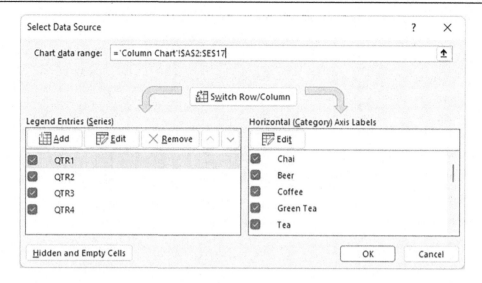

3. Click the Expand Dialog button (up-arrow) on the **Chart data range** field.

4. Select the cells you want in the worksheet area and click the Collapse Dialog button (down-pointing arrow) to return to the **Select Data Source** dialog box.

5. Click **OK** to confirm the change.

The new data source will now be used for the chart.

Adding Axis Titles

When you create a new chart, you'll see "Chart Title" as a placeholder that needs to be edited with the chart's title. There are also no labels at the axis, and we may want to add them to the chart.

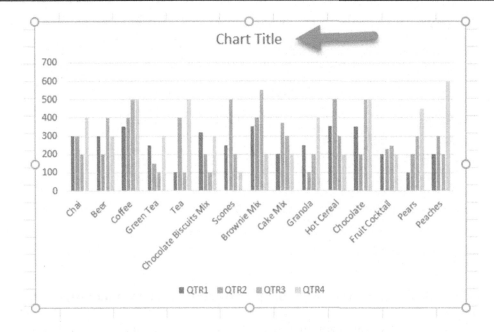

To change the **Chart Title**, you can simply click it and type in the title. Alternatively, you can select the name from a field on your worksheet. For example, to change the chart title to *Sales by quarter,* a value in cell **A1** of the worksheet, click the **Chart Title** label and enter "=A1" in the formula bar. Excel will use the value in cell A1 for our chart title.

We can also add titles down the left-hand side and at the bottom of the chart. These are called axis titles. The left side is the *y*-axis, while the bottom is the *x*-axis.

To change the layout of your chart, click **Chart Design** > **Quick Layout**.

You'll get a pop-up with several chart layouts. With the chart selected, you can hover over each layout to view more details and get a preview of how your chart will look with that layout. A few of the options provide axis titles and move the legend to the right of the chart. If you want a layout with both axis titles, then **Layout 9** is a good option.

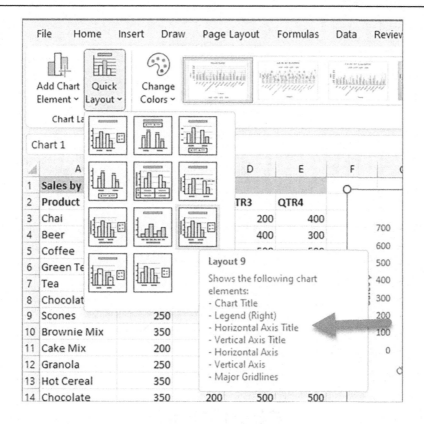

If we select **Layout 9**, we get a chart with labels that we can edit to add titles to the x-axis and y-axis.

You can edit the axis labels as described above. You can click the labels and type in the text directly or pull the text from your worksheet area by typing in a cell reference, for example, **=A1**, assuming cell A1 as the text you want for that label.

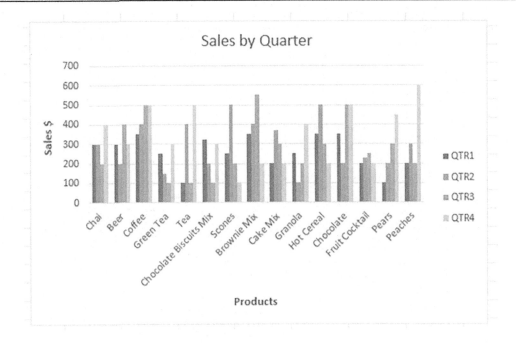

Chart Styles

The **Chart Design** tab shows up on the Ribbon when you click a chart. On this tab, you have various **Chart Styles** you can choose from to change your chart's overall look and color.

To change your Chart Style, do the following:

1. Click the chart to select it.

2. On the **Chart Design** tab, in the **Chart Styles** group, click the down arrow to expand the list of predefined styles.

3. You can hover over each style to preview how your graph will look with that style.

4. When you find the one you want to use, click it to apply it to your graph.

To change the color of the plot area:

1. Click the plot area to select it (this is the center of the chart).

2. On the Ribbon, click the **Format** tab, and in the **Shape Styles** group, click the drop-down button to expand the list of Theme Styles.

3. Hover over each style to see a preview of what your chart would look like if selected.

4. When you find the style you like, click it to apply it to your graph.

To change the colors of the bars on the graph, do the following:

1. Click the chart to select it.

2. On the **Chart Design** tab, in the **Chart Styles** group, click **Change Colors**.

3. Hover over the color combinations to see how your graph will look with an option. When you see the one you like, select it to apply it to your graph.

Creating Sparkline Charts

Sparklines are mini charts you can place in single cells to show the visual trend of your data. Excel allows you to quickly add Sparkline charts to your worksheet in a few steps. Sparklines are an excellent visual representation that can be viewed alongside the data. The following example uses the Quick Analysis tool to add sparklines to a dataset.

Adding a Sparkline:

1. Select the data you want to create a Sparkline chart for. You'll see the **Quick Analysis** tool on the lower-right edge of the selection.

2. Click the Quick Analysis tool to open a pop-up menu of Quick Analysis options - **Formatting**, **Charts**, **Totals**, **Tables**, and **Sparklines**.

3. Click **Sparklines** and select one option from **Line**, **Column**, or **Win/Loss**.

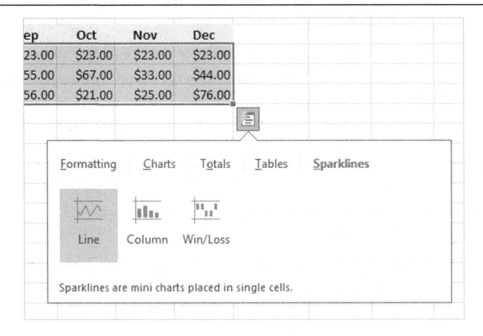

This example uses the **Line** option. The sparklines will be created in the cells immediately to the right of the selected values.

Notice how it's easier to see the data trend with the sparkline than with the figures.

	A	B	C	D	E	F	G	H	I	J	K	L	M	N
1	**Expenses**													
2		Jan	Feb	Mar	Apr	May	Jun	Jul	Aug	Sep	Oct	Nov	Dec	
3	Building 1	$45.00	$22.40	$33.70	$44.90	$21.90	$22.00	$10.00	$23.00	$23.00	$23.00	$23.00	$23.00	
4	Building 2	$31.00	$33.00	$32.00	$41.00	$31.00	$42.00	$11.00	$55.00	$55.00	$67.00	$33.00	$44.00	
5	Building 3	$34.00	$60.00	$21.00	$30.00	$55.00	$60.00	$23.00	$45.00	$56.00	$21.00	$25.00	$76.00	
6														
7														

Formatting a Sparkline Chart

Select the chart to display the **Sparkline** contextual tab on the Ribbon. The Sparkline tab provides various options to edit, format, and style your sparkline chart.

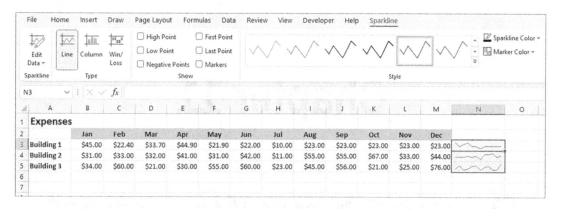

You can use the following options on the Sparkline tab to format and design your sparkline:

- In the **Type** group, you can use the **Line**, **Column**, or **Win/Loss** buttons to change the chart type.

- The **Show** group provides options to add Markers that highlight specific values in the Sparkline chart.

- You can select a different **Style** for the Sparkline.

- You can change the **Sparkline Color** and the **Marker Color**.

- Click **Sparkline Color** > **Weight** to change the width of the Sparkline.

- Click **Marker Color** to change the color of the markers.

- Click **Axis** to show the axis if the data has positive and negative values.

Chapter 11

Printing Your Worksheet

This chapter covers:

- Configuring your print settings in Page Setup.

- Setting the Print Area.

- Previewing and printing your document.

E ven though we live in an increasingly digital world, on some occasions, you may need to print your worksheet on paper as part of a report or present it to others. Excel provides several features that allow you to print your worksheet.

Page Setup

Before you print your document, you may need to change some settings to get the page layout the way you want it. The Page Setup dialog lets you configure several page layout settings in one area.

To open the Page Setup dialog box, click the **Page Layout** tab, and in the **Page Setup** group, click the dialog box launcher.

Excel displays the Page Setup dialog.

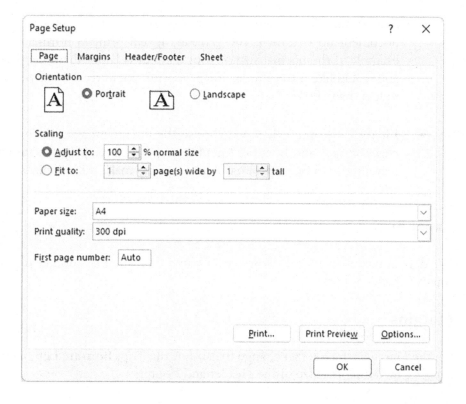

There are several settings on this page that you can configure to get the layout exactly how you want it for your printed document.

■ Orientation

On the **Page** tab, set the orientation to **Landscape**. Landscape is usually the best layout for printing worksheets unless you have specific reasons to use Portrait.

■ Scaling

Under scaling, you have two options:

- **Adjust to:** This option enables you to scale the font size of your document up or down. 100% means it will print in normal size. For example, if the normal size of your content is larger than one page, but you would like it to print as one page, you would reduce the percentage to less than 100%.

- **Fit to:** This option lets you choose the document's width (number of pages across) and how tall (number of pages down). For example, you may choose to fit the width on one page and make it more than one page tall.

■ Paper Size

The default paper size is A4. However, if you are printing to another paper size, you can change it here.

■ Margins

On the Margins tab, you can change the size of the Top, Bottom, Left, and Right margins, including the size of the Header and Footer.

■ Header/Footer

You can insert a header or footer on this tab. For example, you can insert a document header that'll appear on all pages and a page number in the footer. You can either select an option from the dropdown list or enter a custom header/footer by clicking the **Custom Header** or **Custom Footer** buttons.

Click **OK** to save your changes and close the Page Setup window when you're done.

Setting the Print Area

You need to set the Print Area so that unpopulated parts of the worksheet are not included in your print, as this could lead to blank pages. You can set the print area in the Page Setup dialog, but it is easier to use the **Print Area** command on the Ribbon.

To set the print area:

1. Select the area in the worksheet that contains the data you want to print.

2. On the **Page Layout** tab, click the **Print Area** button.

3. Select **Set Print Area**.

Note To clear the print area at any point, click the Print Area button and select **Clear Print Area**.

Preview and Print Your Worksheet

Click **File** to display the Backstage view, then click **Print** from the menu on the left.

Excel displays the Print page. You can adjust several settings here to change the page layout, many of which are also available in the Page Setup dialog.

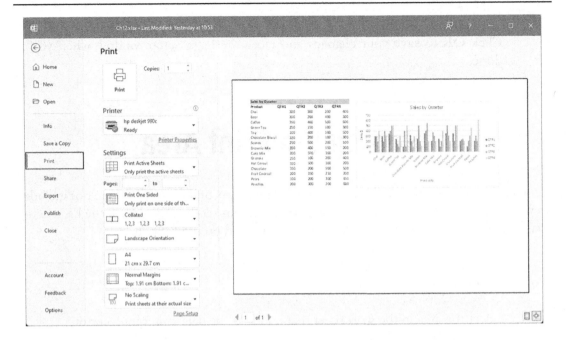

The options on this screen are self-explanatory and similar across Microsoft 365 applications. However, we'll touch on the ones you'll most likely need to set.

Printer

This option allows you to choose the printer to which you want to print. If your printer has been configured on the computer, it will be available for selection here. You also can print to an electronic document like PDF, OneNote, Microsoft XPS Document Writer, etc.

Settings

Print Active Sheets is the default. Leave this option selected if you want to print only the active worksheet. If your workbook has more than one worksheet and you want to print the entire workbook, then click the drop-down list and select **Print Entire Workbook** from the list. If you have selected a range and want to print only those cells, use the **Print Selection** option.

The last option on this page is **scaling**. If you have not set the scale in the Page Setup dialog box, there are four predefined scaling options to choose from here:

- **No Scaling**: The document will be printed as it is, with no scaling.

- **Fit Sheet on One Page**: All columns and rows in the print area will be scaled into one page.

- **Fit All Columns on One Page**: All the columns in the print area will be scaled down to fit one page, but the rows can carry on to other pages.

> **Tip** This is the recommended option if you have many rows of data but a few columns. Always try to scale the columns into one page, if possible, so that you can see a full record on one page.

- **Fit All Rows into One Page**: All rows in the print area will be scaled to fit one page, but the columns can carry on to other pages.

Previewing Your Document

The right side of the screen shows a preview of how your printed document would look. If you have more than one page, use the navigation buttons at the bottom of the screen to view the other pages.

> **Note** Always preview your document before printing to ensure you're happy with the layout. You'll save yourself a ton of ink and paper!

The other settings on the Print page are self-explanatory.

When you're happy with your settings and the preview, click the **Print** button to print your document.

Book 2

Excel Advanced Topics

Chapter 1

Working with Multiple Workbooks

In this chapter, we will cover how to:

- Switch between multiple open workbooks.

- View multiple workbooks side-by-side.

- Arrange all open workbooks on your screen.

- Split the screen of your worksheet.

- Move data between workbooks.

- Move worksheets between workbooks.

There are occasions when you need to work with several open workbooks, and Excel provides features that make it easier to work with multiple windows.

Managing Multiple Windows

To work with multiple workbooks, open the main workbook and all the others.

Switch Between Workbooks

To switch between workbooks, do the following:

1. On the **View** tab, in the **Window** group, click **Switch Windows**.

2. Select the workbook you want to switch to from the dropdown list.

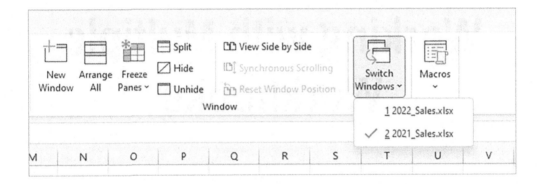

View Side-By-Side

To view worksheets from the different workbooks simultaneously, you can manually arrange them on your desktop or use an Excel command to tile them automatically.

To arrange two workbooks side by side, do the following:

1. In one of the workbooks, click the **View** tab. In the **Windows** group, click the **View Side by Side** button (if you have more than one workbook open, the **View Side by Side** command will be enabled).

If you have only two workbooks open, Excel will place the last one you opened above the earlier one.

If you have more than two workbooks open, Excel will display the **Compare Side by Side** dialog so that you can select which workbook to display alongside the active workbook.

2. Select the workbook you want to display alongside the active workbook and click **OK**.

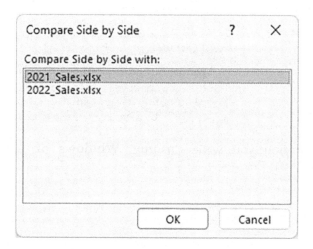

3. You can toggle the **View Side by Side** button to switch between a full screen of the active workbook and two workbooks.

Arrange All

The example above showed how to compare two workbooks side by side. Use the **Arrange All** command to compare more than two workbooks on your screen.

To view two or more workbooks on your desktop side by side, do the following:

1. Open the workbooks you want to view side by side.

2. On the **View** tab of one of the workbooks, click the **Arrange All** button.

    Excel displays the **Arrange Windows** dialog box, which has the options **Tiled**, **Horizontal**, **Vertical**, and **Cascade**.

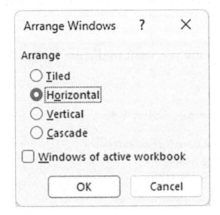

3. Select the option you want, ensuring **Windows of Active Workbook** is unchecked.

4. Click **OK**.

New Window

Sometimes, you may want to view and work with worksheets in the same workbook in different windows.

To open a worksheet in a new Excel window, do the following:

1. Select the worksheet you want to view in a different window (click the worksheet tab).

2. On the **View** tab, in the **Window** group, click the **New Window** button.

3. Excel opens a new window of the same workbook (note that a new file is not created).

4. On the **View** tab, in the **Window** group, click the **Arrange All** button.

Excel displays the **Arrange Windows** dialog box.

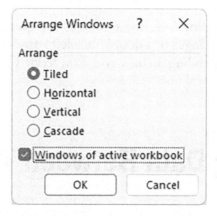

5. Under **Arrange**, select **Tiled** to tile the windows on your screen (or select your desired option).

6. Select the **Windows of active workbook** checkbox.

7. Click **OK**.

Excel arranges the windows of the same workbook side by side on your screen.

Split Screen

The split screen method allows you to split your worksheet so you can see different parts of the worksheet in the same window. This feature comes in handy when you have a large amount of data and want to see different parts of the worksheet while working on the data.

To split the screen of a worksheet, do the following:

1. On the **View** tab, in the **Window** group, click the **Split** button.

A horizontal and vertical dividing line will split the screen into four parts, with a scroll bar for each part. You can adjust the position of these dividers with your mouse pointer, depending on how you want the layout.

2. To move a dividing line, for example, the horizontal divider, hover over the divider until it changes to a double-headed arrow. You can now move the divider up or down, depending on how you want to view the split screen. You can do the same for the vertical line.

Moving Data Between Workbooks

There are two ways you can copy or move data between open workbooks.

Method 1

1. Arrange the workbooks so that the worksheets you want to work with are visible side-by-side on the screen.

2. Select the data you want to move or copy in the source worksheet.

3. On the **Home** tab, in the **Clipboard** group, click the **Copy** button (or select Ctrl+C on your keyboard) to copy the data. To move data, click the **Cut** button (or select Ctrl+X on your keyboard).

4. On the destination worksheet, click the top leftmost cell of the area where you want to paste the data.

5. On the **Home** tab, in the **Clipboard** group, click **Paste** (or select Ctrl+V on your keyboard) to paste the data.

Method 2

The second method to move or copy data between workbooks is to drag and drop the data from one workbook to the other.

Use the following steps to drag and drop data between workbooks:

1. Select the data in the source worksheet.

2. Hover over the edge of the selected range until the mouse pointer changes to a crosshair. This is the move pointer in Excel (see image below).

$10,227	$8,343	$5,467	$9,002
$13,263	$10,201	$6,199	$12,083
$13,680	$9,565	$14,089	$6,906
$5,610	$6,557	$5,756	$9,387
$11,335	$6,363	$5,980	$12,584
$10,214	$5,270	$11,708	$7,479
$5,746	$8,398	$6,390	$8,263
$5,594	$11,446	$7,794	$5,736
$14,537	$11,826	$8,848	$9,674
$9,118	$5,774	$7,533	$11,096
$13,417	$12,864	$13,032	$10,514
$6,573	$8,805	$13,254	$9,397

3. Once the pointer has changed to a move pointer, click and drag the selection to the other worksheet window.

4. You'll see a rectangle at the destination worksheet window representing the area containing the data to be pasted. Drag it to the left topmost cell of the range where you want to place the data and release the mouse button.

Note To copy the data, rather than move it, hold down the **Ctrl** key as you drag the data across to the other window.

---

5. After you release the mouse button, you may get a prompt that says: *"There's a problem with the clipboard, but you can still paste your content within this workbook."* Just click **OK** to dismiss the prompt and complete the action.

Moving Worksheets Between Workbooks

There are two ways you can copy or move worksheets between open workbooks. You can copy the worksheet using the Move and Copy command or drag and drop worksheets between workbooks.

Method 1

To use the Move or Copy command to copy sheets between workbooks, do the following:

1. Open the source workbook (that contains worksheets to be moved or copied) and the destination workbook where the worksheets will go. You must open the source and destination files to copy or move worksheets between them.

2. On the **View** tab, use the **Arrange All** command to arrange the windows side-by-side, preferably using the **Vertical** option.

3. Select the source workbook to make it the active window.

4. Select the source sheet by clicking its tab at the bottom of the window (to select more than one worksheet, hold down the **Ctrl** key and click additional sheets).

5. On the **Home** tab, in the **Cells** group, click the **Format** button and select **Move or Copy Sheet** on the menu.

    Excel displays the **Move or Copy** dialog box.

6. In the **Move or Copy** dialog box, select the destination workbook in the **To book** dropdown list box.

7. Under **Before sheet**, select where to place the worksheet inside the destination workbook.

    To create a copy of the worksheet, rather than move it, select the **Create a copy** checkbox.

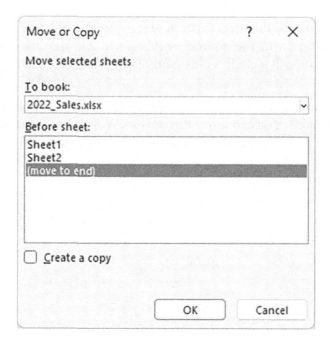

8. Click **OK** to complete the action.

Method 2

Just as you can copy data in a range between workbooks using drag-and-drop, you can also move or copy worksheets between workbooks using drag-and-drop.

To move or copy worksheets between workbooks using drag-and-drop, do the following:

1. Arrange the source and destination workbooks side-by-side to see both on the screen. You can do this manually or use the **Arrange All** command described above. Preferably you should arrange them vertically.

2. Click the sheet tab in the destination workbook to select the worksheet to be moved or copied (to select more than one sheet, hold down the **Ctrl** key and click additional sheets).

3. Drag the sheet from the source workbook to the destination workbook with your mouse. You'll see a little document icon representing the sheet you're moving.

Note To copy the sheet (instead of moving it), hold down the **Ctrl** key as you drag the sheet from the source workbook to the destination workbook. The document icon will include a plus symbol (+) to indicate the copy action.

4. You'll see a small arrow at the destination workbook indicating where the sheet would be placed. You can move this arrow left or right to choose where you want to place the sheet before releasing the mouse button to place the sheet there.

This method is a much faster way to move or copy worksheets between two open workbooks.

Chapter 2

Using External Data

This chapter covers the following:

- Importing data from a Microsoft Access database.

- Importing data from a delimited text file like a CSV file.

- Importing data from a website with constantly changing live data, for example, Forex data.

When working with Excel, you often have situations when you have to import data from other applications. The most common are comma-separated files (CSV) or some other form of delimitation.

Importing Data from Microsoft Access

Follow the steps below to import data from an Access Database:

1. Open the workbook in which you want to import the data.

2. On the **Data** tab, in the **Get & Transform Data** group, click **Get Data**. Then select **From Database** > **From Microsoft Access Database**.

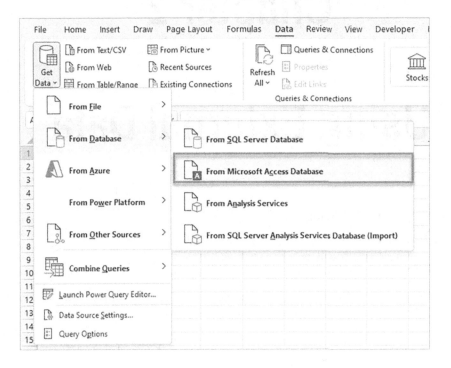

3. In the **Import Data** dialog box, navigate to the Access database (this will usually be an ACCDB or MDB file). Select the file and click the **Import** button. For this example, we're using the file **HighlandFurniture.accdb**.

    Excel displays the **Navigator** dialog box.

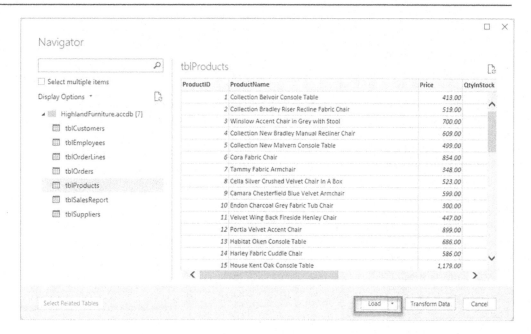

The Navigator dialog box is divided into two panes. The left pane displays a list of tables and queries from the data source. The right pane displays a preview of the fields and data in the selected item.

Note To import more than one table from the selected Access database, click the **Select Multiple Items** checkbox on the left pane. Excel will then display check boxes against each item on the list, which allows you to select more than one table from the list.

4. After selecting the table(s) to import, click the **Load** button.

Excel imports the data into a new worksheet as an Excel table (with table features).

	A	B	C	D	E	F	G	H	I
1	ProductID	ProductName	Price	QtyInStock	Discontinued	Category	SupplierID		
2	1	Collection Belvoir Console Table	413	9	FALSE		4		
3	2	Collection Bradley Riser Recline Fabric Chair	519	6	FALSE		4		
4	3	Winslow Accent Chair in Grey with Stool	700	5	FALSE		4		
5	4	Collection New Bradley Manual Recliner Chair	609	7	FALSE		4		
6	5	Collection New Malvern Console Table	499	10	FALSE		4		
7	6	Cora Fabric Chair	854	10	FALSE		7		
8	7	Tammy Fabric Armchair	348	5	FALSE		9		
9	8	Cella Silver Crushed Velvet Chair In A Box	523	4	FALSE		10		
10	9	Camara Chesterfield Blue Velvet Armchair	599	4	FALSE		13		
11	10	Endon Charcoal Grey Fabric Tub Chair	300	5	FALSE		15		
12	11	Velvet Wing Back Fireside Henley Chair	447	9	FALSE		4		
13	12	Portia Velvet Accent Chair	899	9	FALSE		13		
14	13	Habitat Oken Console Table	686	10	FALSE		8		
15	14	Harley Fabric Cuddle Chair	586	10	FALSE		9		
16	15	House Kent Oak Console Table	1179	10	FALSE		1		
17	16	Hygena Fabric Chair	898	5	FALSE		2		
18	17	Hygena Fabric Chair in a Box	1091	4	FALSE		3		
19	18	Hygena Lumina Console Table	1149	10	FALSE		1		
20	19	Hygena Zander Console Table	847	4	FALSE		7		
21	20	Leather Effect Tub Chair	512	7	TRUE		14		
22	21	Lukah Leather Chair	909	10	TRUE		14		
23	22	New Paolo Manual Recliner Chair	952	7	TRUE		14		
24	23	Premier Housewares Shoreditch Table	964	6	FALSE		15		
25	24	Shelf Solid Pine and Glass Top Telephone Table	716	10	TRUE		14		
26	25	Slimline Console Table	417	7	FALSE		10		
27	26	Slimline Console Table - Oak Effect	770	7	FALSE		13		

tblProducts   Sheet1   +

The Navigator dialog box also provides other options for uploading the Access data.

Transforming Data Before Importing

The **Transform Data** button is at the bottom of the Navigator dialog box. When you click this button, Excel opens the Excel **Power Query Editor**, which provides several tools to transform the data before it is imported. For example, you may want to import only some columns or only some of the rows.

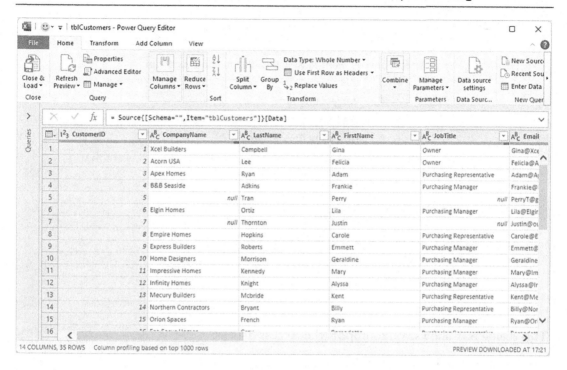

The Power Query Editor is covered in more detail in chapter 3 in this book – Transforming Data with Date Tools.

Other Load Options

For more load options, at the bottom of the **Navigator** dialog, click the dropdown arrow on the **Load** button, then select **Load To** from the menu to open the **Import Data** dialog box.

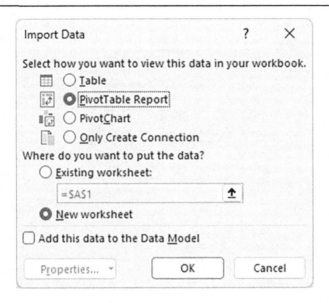

This dialog box allows you to import the Access data as:

- An Excel Table (default)

- A PivotTable

- A PivotChart

- Only a connection to the database.

You can also import the data into an **Existing worksheet** or a **New worksheet** (default).

Importing Text/CSV Files

As Excel stores data in cells, the text files you can import need to have a method of separating the values. The character that marks this separation is called a *delimiter* because it marks the "limit" of a value. The most common delimiter used for text files is the comma. For example, you may have a series of numbers [200, 400, 100, 900] representing data in four cells. The text files that use a comma as a delimiter are called comma-separated values (CSV) files.

Sometimes, text files use different delimiters when a comma might not be appropriate. For example, using a comma delimiter may present a problem for financial figures (like $100,000) because commas are part of the values. Hence, some financial data programs export their data by using the tab character as a delimiter, and these files are referred to as Tab-delimited files.

Follow the steps below to import a text data file into Excel:

1. Open the workbook in which you want to import the data.

2. On the **Data** tab, in the **Get & Transform Data** group, click the **From Text/CSV** button. Excel displays the **Import Data** dialog box.

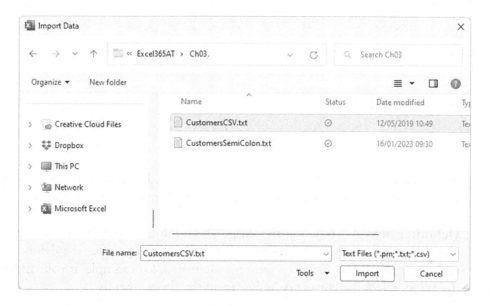

3. In the **Import Data** dialog box, navigate to the text or CSV file. Select the file and click the **Import** button. For this example, we're using **CustomersCSV.txt**.

Excel displays the Navigator dialog box.

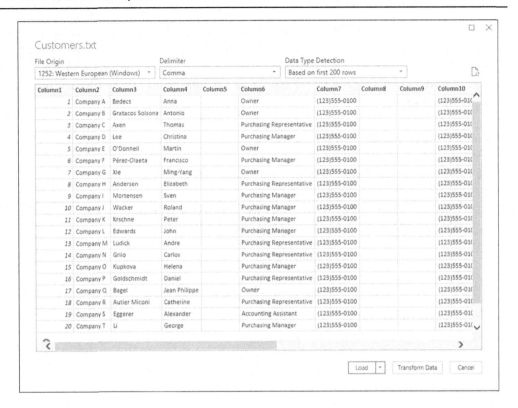

Excel examines the data in the text or CSV file and attempts to correctly split it into separate columns based on the delimiter it identifies as the separator.

4. **Delimiter box**: As shown in the image above, three boxes are at the top of the Navigator dialog box. The **Delimiter** dropdown list specifies the delimiter used in the text file. If this has been wrongly identified, for example, if your file is Tab delimited, select the correct delimiter from the dropdown list.

Leave **File Origin** and **Data Type Detection** at their default values for anything other than complex data imports requiring advanced knowledge.

5. **Load option**: If Excel correctly parsed the data in your text file as shown in the Navigator's preview, you can select one of the following options to import the data into your worksheet.

At the bottom of the dialog box, you have three options for uploading the data:

- The **Load** button imports the data, as seen in the Navigator preview, into your workbook (in a new worksheet).

- The **Load To** option (on the Load button's dropdown menu) gives you more options for how you want to import the data and where to place the data. The Load To dialog box is discussed above under importing data from Microsoft Access.

- The **Transform Data** button opens the data in the **Power Query Editor**. This enables you to query and transform the data before importing it. For example, you may want to import only a few columns in the data set or data that meet some criteria. Transform data allows you to remove the columns you don't want to import.

-ῷ-**Tip** If the source table is not too large, you can also import the full data into Excel and delete the columns you don't want.

Using the Convert Text to Columns Wizard

Occasionally, Excel cannot correctly parse the data into separate columns even after you change the Delimiter, File Origin, and Data Type Detection. If Excel insists on importing each row as a single column, you can import the data and then use the **Text to Columns** tool to split the values into separate columns.

After importing the data into Excel, follow the steps below to split the data into separate columns:

1. In your worksheet, select the range containing the data that needs to be separated. For this example, we're using the file **TextToColumnsWizard.xlsx**.

2. On the **Data** tab, in the **Data Tools** group, click the **Text to Columns** button.

    Excel opens the **Convert Text to Columns Wizard** dialog box.

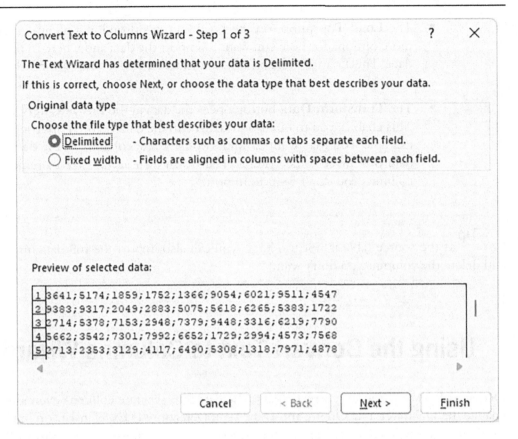

3. On step 1 of the wizard, choose between **Delimited** and **Fixed width**, depending on how your data is separated. Then click the **Next** button to go to step 2.

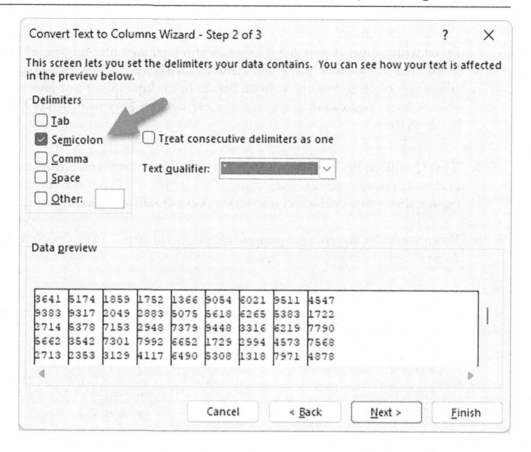

4. **Delimiters**: If you selected the Delimited option in Step 1 of the wizard, do one of the following in Step 2:

- Under the **Delimiters** section, select the delimiter for your text file. In our example above, the delimiter is a semicolon.

- Select **Other** if the delimiter in your text file is not one of the provided options. Then, enter the character in the text box next to Other.

- If your file uses more than one delimiter type, for example, a comma and a space, select all of them under Delimiters, including the **Treat Consecutive Delimiters As One** checkbox.

Fixed width files: If your file is a fixed-width separated file and you selected the Fixed width option in step 1 of the wizard, then in step 2, you'll see a preview that allows you to determine the column breaks by clicking in the text area to create column lines. You can drag and resize these column lines to match the column breaks in the text.

5. **Text Qualifier**: By default, the Convert Text to Columns Wizard treats characters enclosed in double quotes as text entries, not numbers. If your text file uses single quotes, then you would select it from the **Text Qualifier** dropdown list.

6. When you're happy with the preview of the text in step 2, click the **Next** button to go to step 3 of the wizard.

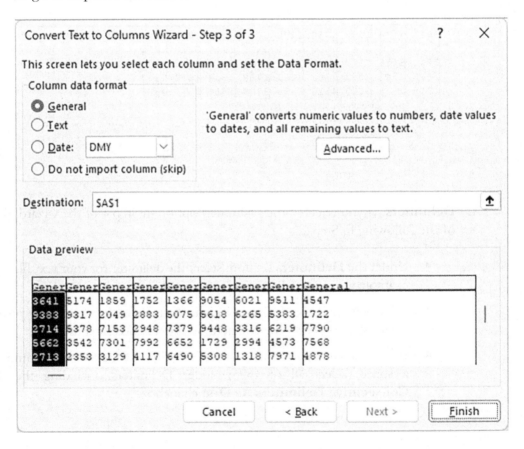

7. In step 3 of the process, you can click each column under **Data preview** and select different settings for importing the data in the top section (**Column data format)**.

    You can choose between General (default), Text, and Date data formats. Alternatively, you can select **Do not import column (skip)** to skip importing that column.

Tip On some occasions, it would be faster to import the data using the **General** data format and then change the data format for the columns you want to change within Excel.

---

8. The **Destination** box shows you the top-leftmost cell of the range where the text will be placed. If you want it in a different part of the worksheet, select a different destination by clicking the Expand Dialog button (up arrow) on the right of the field.

9. Once you're done, click **Finish** to convert the data.

Excel splits the imported text file entries into separate columns in place of the previous data. You can now set the data format (if you didn't do that during the conversion) and adjust column widths.

Tip You can directly open some CSV files in Excel and convert them to Excel workbooks. If CSV files are associated with Excel on your computer, you can double-click the file to open it in Excel. Alternatively, you can open the file from within Excel even if the CSV extension is not associated with Excel on your PC. Once the file is open in Excel and the data is displayed properly, you can then save the file as an Excel workbook.

Importing Data from a Website

To import data from the web, you must first identify the web address (URL) that contains the data you want to import. Then you can use the import tools in Excel to import the data directly from the webpage into your worksheet.

Let's say we want to import currency exchange rates from the web into our worksheet.

Below is how the data looks on the website after using our date criteria to select the records we want to see. We can now use this URL to import the data tables on the website.

https://www.xe.com/currencytables/?from=USD&date=2023-01-01#table-section

Currency Table: USD — US Dollar

All figures are mid-market rates, which are not available to consumers and are for informational purposes only.

Jan 1, 2023, 17:00 UTC

CURRENCY	NAME	UNITS PER USD	USD PER UNIT
USD	US Dollar	1	1
EUR	Euro	0.9343609460913234	1.0702502113163677
GBP	British Pound	0.82655869945566	1.2098354305127534
INR	Indian Rupee	82.7284215423729	0.012087744228116419
AUD	Australian Dollar	1.46760063390014427	0.6813842791424928
CAD	Canadian Dollar	1.353572833123755	0.7387855130722556

To import data from a website, do the following:

1. Identify the URL for the web page containing the table you want to import and copy it to the clipboard.

2. On the **Data** tab, in the **Get & Transform Data** group, click the **From Web** button. Alternatively, on the **Data** tab, select **Get Data** > **From Other Sources** > **From Web**.

Excel displays the **From Web** dialog box.

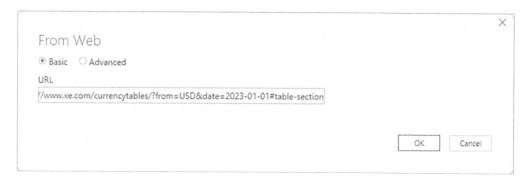

3. Paste the web address containing the data you want to import in the **URL** box.

4. Click **OK** to establish a connection to the website.

Note If this is the first time you've connected to the website, Excel may display an **Access Web-content** dialog box with different connection options. Connect with the default, which is **Anonymous**.

Once connected, Excel will display the **Navigator** dialog box, listing the data tables on the Selection pane on the left.

5. Select the required table on the left pane. You can preview the data on the right pane.

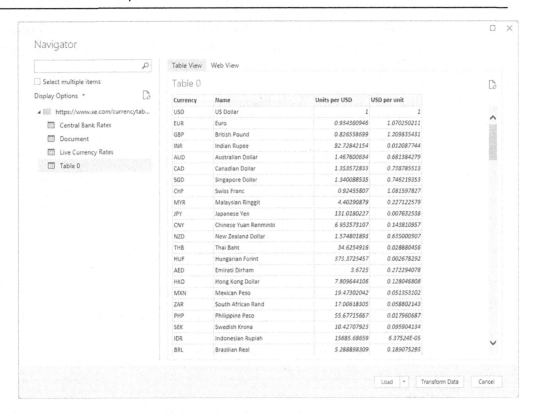

6. Click the **Load** button to import the data into a new worksheet in your workbook.

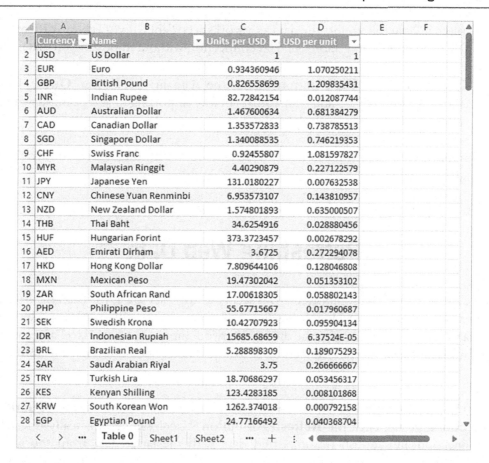

	A	B	C	D	E	F
1	Currency	Name	Units per USD	USD per unit		
2	USD	US Dollar	1	1		
3	EUR	Euro	0.934360946	1.070250211		
4	GBP	British Pound	0.826558699	1.209835431		
5	INR	Indian Rupee	82.72842154	0.012087744		
6	AUD	Australian Dollar	1.467600634	0.681384279		
7	CAD	Canadian Dollar	1.353572833	0.738785513		
8	SGD	Singapore Dollar	1.340088535	0.746219353		
9	CHF	Swiss Franc	0.92455807	1.081597827		
10	MYR	Malaysian Ringgit	4.40290879	0.227122579		
11	JPY	Japanese Yen	131.0180227	0.007632538		
12	CNY	Chinese Yuan Renminbi	6.953573107	0.143810957		
13	NZD	New Zealand Dollar	1.574801893	0.635000507		
14	THB	Thai Baht	34.6254916	0.028880456		
15	HUF	Hungarian Forint	373.3723457	0.002678292		
16	AED	Emirati Dirham	3.6725	0.272294078		
17	HKD	Hong Kong Dollar	7.809644106	0.128046808		
18	MXN	Mexican Peso	19.47302042	0.051353102		
19	ZAR	South African Rand	17.00618305	0.058802143		
20	PHP	Philippine Peso	55.67715667	0.017960687		
21	SEK	Swedish Krona	10.42707923	0.095904134		
22	IDR	Indonesian Rupiah	15685.68659	6.37524E-05		
23	BRL	Brazilian Real	5.288898309	0.189075293		
24	SAR	Saudi Arabian Riyal	3.75	0.266666667		
25	TRY	Turkish Lira	18.70686297	0.053456317		
26	KES	Kenyan Shilling	123.4283185	0.008101868		
27	KRW	South Korean Won	1262.374018	0.000792158		
28	EGP	Egyptian Pound	24.77166492	0.040368704		

‹ › ⋯ Table 0 Sheet1 Sheet2 ⋯ + ⋮

Other Import Options

To import more than one table of data from the web page, select the **Select Multiple Items** check box and then click the checkboxes against the table names you want to import.

Once you've selected the table(s) you want to import on the page, you have the following three import options:

- **Load:** This option imports the data, as seen in the Navigator preview pane, into a new worksheet (as shown above).

- The **Load To** option (on the Load button's dropdown menu) opens the **Import Data** dialog box, giving you more options for importing the data and where to place it. You can import the data as a worksheet Table, PivotTable, or PivotChart. You can choose to establish a data connection without importing the data.

- The **Transform Data** button opens the data in the **Power Query Editor**, allowing you to query and transform it before importing it. For example, you may want to import only a subset of the data.

After importing the data, you can manipulate and work with the data as you would with any other Excel table.

Refreshing Web Data

When working with tables imported from websites with live data, for example, financial websites like the Nasdaq or Dow Jones (while the markets are still open), you can refresh the data to reflect any changes in the data. When you import the data, Excel automatically stores information about the connection, so you just need one button click to refresh the data.

To refresh data imported from a website, on the **Data** tab, in the **Queries & Connections** group, click the **Refresh All** button. Excel will automatically re-establish the connection and refresh the imported data with the latest data from the website. Alternatively, you can refresh the data anytime by right-clicking the table name in the **Queries & Connections** pane and selecting **Refresh** from the shortcut menu.

In the case of dynamic values that are constantly changing, it comes in handy to be able to refresh the values regularly without having to re-import the data.

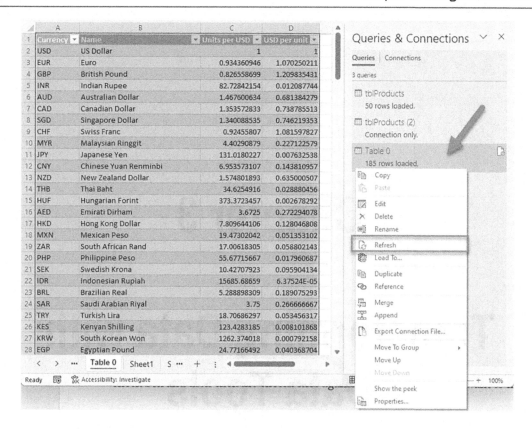

Other Database Sources

Apart from Microsoft Access, the **Get Data** command on the **Data** tab also enables you to import data from a variety of database sources, including:

- **From SQL Server Database:** This option enables you to import data from or create a connection to an SQL Server database.

- **From Analysis Services**: This option enables you to import data from an SQL Server Analysis cube.

- **From SQL Server Analysis Services Database (Import)**: This is to import data from an SQL Server database with the option to use an MDX or DAX query.

Chapter 3

Transforming Data with Data Tools

In this chapter we will cover how to:

- Find and remove duplicate rows in your data.
- Find and delete blank rows in your data.
- Convert text to columns.
- Consolidate data from different worksheets into one worksheet.
- Using the Power Query Editor to transform data.

There are several data tools provided in Excel for Microsoft 365 you can use to quickly perform data organizing tasks. We'll cover the most common tasks where these tools are utilized in this chapter.

Removing Duplicates

On some occasions, you may have a data set, for example, a list of customers you want to use for a mail merge. You want to make sure that you don't have duplicate records before you start the mail merge process so that you don't send the mail to the same customer more than once.

To remove duplicate entries in a list, do the following:

1. Click any cell in the range.

2. On the **Data** tab, in the **Data Tools** group, click the **Remove Duplicates** button.

    Excel displays the **Remove Duplicates** dialog box.

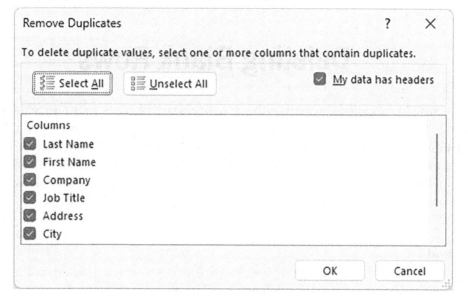

3. Leave all the columns selected (if you want the full row checked against one another) and click **OK**.

4. A message will be displayed telling you if any duplicates were found and how many records were deleted. Click **OK** to complete the process.

Note You may have cases where you only want to use a few columns to check for duplicate records. For example, you may have more than one person on your list from the same address, but you only want each address once for the mail merge. In cases like that, deselect all the other columns and only select the columns you want to use to check for duplicates.

Tip You can also use the Power Query Editor to remove duplicate rows. See the section **Delete Blank Rows** below for how to open and use the Power Query Editor to transform your data.

Deleting Blank Rows

There may be occasions when you have unnecessary blank rows in your data that you want to remove. If you have a large list with a lot of empty rows, it could be time-consuming to manually find and delete the empty rows. Fortunately, there are ways you can do this automatically. We will cover two methods for achieving this task here. The first method uses commands on the Excel ribbon and the second method involves using the Power Query Editor, which has a command for deleting blank rows.

Method 1

There is no direct command for deleting blank rows on the ribbon, but you can combine a couple of commands to achieve the task.

To delete blank rows, do the following:

1. Select the range that contains the blank rows.

2. On the **Home** tab, in the **Editing** group, click **Find & Select**.

3. Select **Go To Special** from the dropdown menu.

4. On the **Go To Special** dialog, select **Blanks** and click **OK**.

Excel will select the blank cells in the range.

	A	B	C	D	E
1	**Sales**				
2		New York	Los Angeles	London	Paris
3	Jan	$547.00	$934.00	$412.00	$447.00
4	Feb	$880.00	$590.00	$961.00	$605.00
5	Mar	$717.00	$961.00	$460.00	$652.00
6					
7	Apr	$540.00	$542.00	$574.00	$754.00
8	May	$620.00	$497.00	$531.00	$462.00
9	Jun	$423.00	$874.00	$799.00	$699.00
10	Jul	$937.00	$755.00	$877.00	$446.00
11					
12	Aug	$683.00	$715.00	$792.00	$742.00
13	Sep	$633.00	$421.00	$877.00	$576.00
14	Oct	$551.00	$941.00	$675.00	$598.00
15	Nov	$680.00	$520.00	$867.00	$916.00
16	Dec	$766.00	$524.00	$401.00	$707.00
17					

5. On the **Home** tab, in the **Cells** group, select **Delete** > **Delete Sheet Rows**.

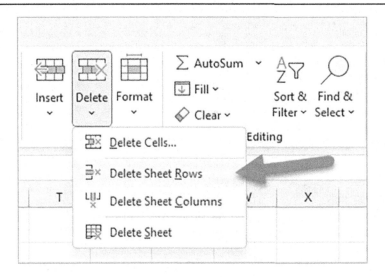

And that's it! Excel will delete all the rows that were identified and selected using the Go To Special command.

-💡-**Tip**   If you delete any rows in error, you can undo your changes by clicking the **Undo** button on the **Home** tab to reverse your changes.

Method 2

The second method involves using the Power Query Editor in Excel.

To delete blank rows using the Power Query Editor, do the following:

1. Select the data list for which you want to remove blank rows.

-💡-**Tip**   To quickly select a range, click the top-left cell of the range, hold down the **Shift** key, and click the bottom-right cell.

---

2. On the **Data** tab, in the **Get & Transform Data** group, click the **From Table/Range** command button.

Excel will open and display your data in the **Power Query Editor**, which is an add-on tool in Excel with a separate user interface and ribbon.

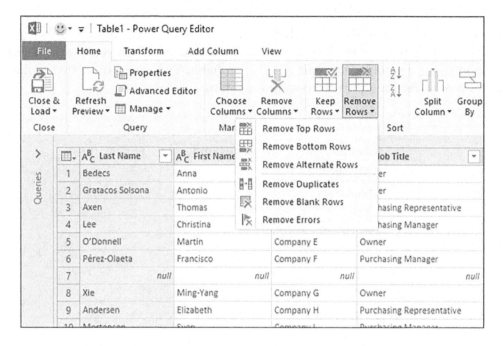

3. On the **Home** tab of the Power Query Editor, click the dropdown arrow on the **Remove Rows** command button, and select **Remove Blank Rows** from the dropdown menu.

   Excel deletes all the blank rows identified in the data list.

4. To save your transformed data, on the **Home** tab of the Power Query Editor, click the **Close & Load** command button to paste the transformed data in a new sheet in your workbook and close the Power Query Editor.

That's it! Your data list without the blank rows will now be in a new sheet with the original data list unchanged. Note that, among many other actions, you can also use the Power Query Editor to remove duplicate rows.

Converting Text to Columns

If you work with a lot of data from different sources, there could be occasions where you receive a text file with values that are separated by commas. When you copy and paste the values in Excel, it would place them all in one column. You can separate these values into different columns using the text to columns command.

	A	B	C
1	**Name**	**Last Name**	**First Name**
2	Henderson, Bruce		
3	Anderson, Louis		
4	Foster, Earl		
5	Hill, Sean		
6	Martinez, Benjamin		
7	Perez, Joe		
8	Johnson, Shawn		
9	Roberts, Kenneth		
10	Martin, Cynthia		
11	Mitchell, Susan		
12			
13			

To convert delimited text values into separate columns, do the following:

1. Select the range containing the text you want to split.

2. On the **Data** tab, in the **Data Tools** group, click the **Text to Columns** button.

3. In the Convert Text to Columns Wizard, select **Delimited** and click **Next**.

4. Select the **Delimiters** for your data. For our example (in the image above), the delimiters are **Comma** and **Space**. You also have the options of Tab, Semicolon, and Other, which allows you to specify the delimiter if it's not one of the default options.

   The **Data preview** portion of the screen shows you a preview of how your data would look after the conversion.

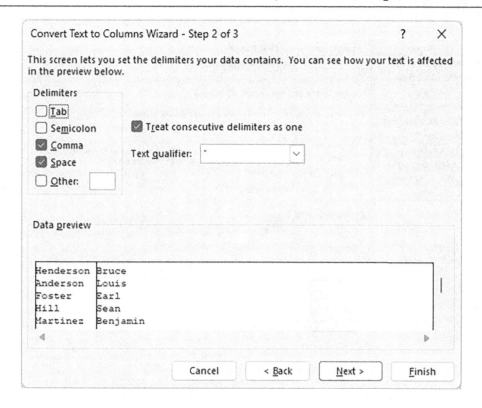

5. Click **Next**.

6. In Step 3 of the wizard, select the **Column data format** or use what Excel chooses for you.

7. In the **Destination** field, click the Expand Dialog button (up arrow), and on your worksheet, select the top leftmost cell where you want the split data to appear. The cell reference for the destination will be entered in the field.

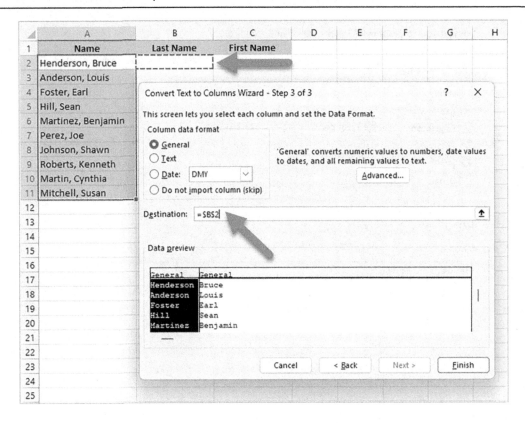

8. Click **Finish**.

The delimited text will now be split into different columns. You can delete the initial column with the original text from the worksheet or move it to another sheet if you intend to keep it.

◢	A	B	C	D
1	**Name**	**Last Name**	**First Name**	
2	Henderson, Bruce	Henderson	Bruce	
3	Anderson, Louis	Anderson	Louis	
4	Foster, Earl	Foster	Earl	
5	Hill, Sean	Hill	Sean	
6	Martinez, Benjamin	Martinez	Benjamin	
7	Perez, Joe	Perez	Joe	
8	Johnson, Shawn	Johnson	Shawn	
9	Roberts, Kenneth	Roberts	Kenneth	
10	Martin, Cynthia	Martin	Cynthia	
11	Mitchell, Susan	Mitchell	Susan	
12				
13				

Consolidating Data from Multiple Worksheets

Data consolidation provides an easy way to summarize data from multiple worksheets in a master worksheet. You can consolidate data from different worksheets in the same workbook, different workbooks, or a combination of both. The process allows you to select the ranges you want to add to the consolidation from different sources and Excel will aggregate the data in another workbook.

To consolidate data, all the ranges to be included in the consolidation must be of the same shape and size.

In the following example, we have sales data from 2020 to 2022 that we want to consolidate from three worksheets into one worksheet titled **Sales for 2020 - 2022**.

◢	A	B	C	D	E
1	**Sales for 2020 - 2022**				
2					
3		**New York**	**Los Angeles**	**London**	**Paris**
4	Jan				
5	Feb				
6	Mar				
7	Apr				
8	May				
9	Jun				
10	Jul				
11	Aug				
12	Sep				
13	Oct				
14	Nov				
15	Dec				

The three workbooks we will be consolidating the data from are:

- 2020_Sales.xlsx
- 2021_Sales.xlsx
- 2022_Sales.xlsx

To consolidate cell ranges from the three workbooks, do the following:

1. Open the destination workbook (the workbook into which you want to consolidate your data). In our example, it will be 2020_2022_Sales.xlsx.

2. Open the source workbooks (the workbooks with the data you want to consolidate). For this example, the source workbooks are the three workbooks listed above.

3. Switch back to the source workbook.

4. On the **Data** tab, in the **Data Tools** group, click the **Consolidate** button.

   Excel displays the **Consolidate** dialog box.

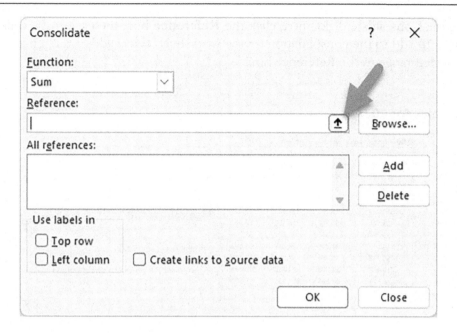

5. On the **View** tab, in the **Window** group, click **Switch Windows**. The menu has a list of all open workbooks.

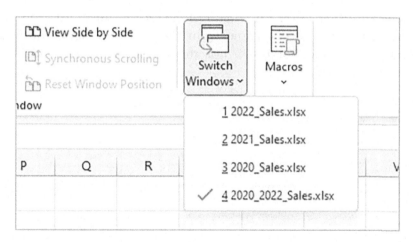

6. On the dropdown menu, select the first workbook containing data you want to consolidate. Excel makes this the active workbook. For our example, the first workbook is *2020_Sales.xlsx*.

7. In the Consolidate dialog box, click the **Reference** box, then select the cells you want to add to the consolidation on the worksheet. Excel adds a reference to the selected range to the Reference box.

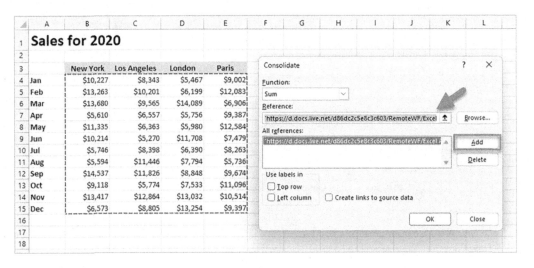

8. In the Consolidate dialog box, click the **Add** button to add the selected range to the **All references** box.

9. Repeat steps 5 to 8 above for any additional ranges containing data you want to consolidate. These ranges can come from different workbooks or different worksheets in the same workbook. For this example, these would be from *2021_Sales.xlsx* and *2022_Sales.xlsx*.

10. **Function**: The default function Excel uses to aggregate the data in the consolidated worksheet is **Sum**. You can select a different function from the **Function** dropdown list, like Count or Average.

11. Click **OK** when you've added all the ranges to be consolidated.

	A	B	C	D	E
1	**Sales for 2020 - 2022**				
2					
3		New York	Los Angeles	London	Paris
4	Jan	$37,112	$37,034	$33,116	$28,834
5	Feb	$26,928	$31,263	$21,982	$33,483
6	Mar	$36,511	$28,649	$33,158	$28,713
7	Apr	$26,144	$20,178	$22,248	$24,655
8	May	$32,717	$29,072	$25,157	$29,413
9	Jun	$38,505	$22,090	$29,286	$35,879
10	Jul	$30,452	$35,911	$27,040	$24,865
11	Aug	$22,207	$32,373	$22,887	$32,187
12	Sep	$31,925	$36,538	$28,356	$27,973
13	Oct	$38,797	$24,493	$22,909	$32,532
14	Nov	$33,490	$33,315	$39,205	$35,915
15	Dec	$27,475	$34,710	$26,777	$29,943
16					

Each cell in the consolidated data will now hold the sum for that cell from all the consolidated worksheets.

Transforming Data with the Power Query Editor

The Power Query Editor enables you to transform external data in different ways before importing the data into Excel. For example, you may want to import data from an SQL Server table with several columns and hundreds of thousands of records. However, you only want to import a subset of the columns and rows. You could attempt to bring the full table into Excel and then remove the unwanted data, but for very large datasets, Excel may not be able to handle all the records. Also, it may be too cumbersome to bring all the records into Excel. In cases like these, you can use the Power Query Editor to query and return only the data you need from the external data source.

You can also use the Power Query Editor for advanced queries involving multiple tables linked by relationships. However, that level of coverage is outside the scope of this book. For basic data-transforming tasks, the Power Query Editor should be familiar to you as its interface and ribbon are not that dissimilar to Excel.

Example

The following example details how to import a subset of data from an Access database, **tblProducts**. We only want some of the columns and records for products that are not discontinued.

> Open the destination workbook.

> On the **Data** tab, in the **Get & Transform Data** group, select **Get Data** > **From Database** > **From Microsoft Access Database**.

> On the **Import Data** dialog box, navigate to the Access database (this will usually be an ACCDB or MDB file). Select the file and click the **Import** button.

Excel displays the **Navigator** dialog box. The left pane of the dialog box has a list of tables and queries from the data source. On the right, there is a preview of the fields and values in the selected table.

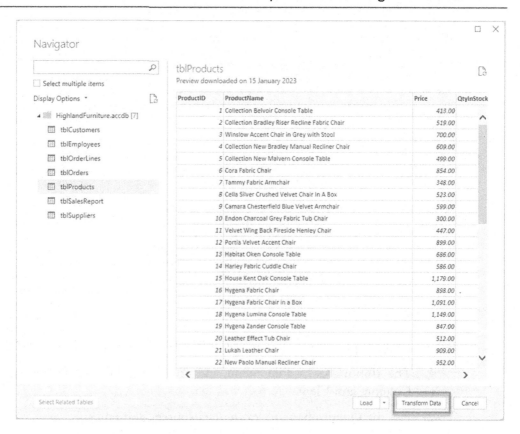

➤ Select the source table and then click the **Transform Data** button to open the data as a new query in the Power Query Editor. The source table in this case is tblProducts.

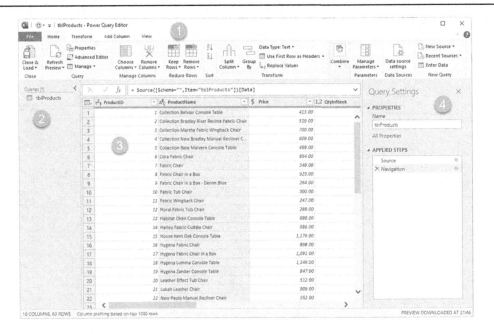

Below is a description of each part of the Power Query Editor user interface:

1. The ribbon has a File menu and four tabs: Home, Transform, Add Column, and View.

2. Use the Queries pane to locate data sources and tables.

3. The Data Preview displays the data, including any transformation performed on it.

4. The Query Settings pane has the query name under PROPERTIES, and APPLIED STEPS keeps a history of all the steps applied to the query.

Notice that the imported data has column headings with AutoFilter dropdown buttons. To remove a column from the query, select the column header (which selects the whole column) and click the **Remove Columns** button on the **Home** tab. We're removing the CategoryID, Notes, and SupplerID columns for our example.

➢ To filter the dataset, click the AutoFilter button of the column you want to use to filter the data and deselect the values you don't want to include in the query. You can also clear the **Select All** checkbox and individually select the values you want to include in the query.

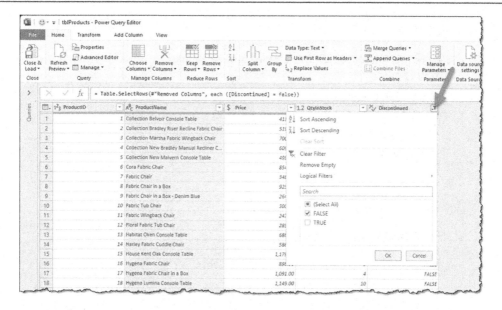

> ➤ To apply a custom filter, select **Logical Filters** and follow the steps to enter your criteria. This option will differ depending on the data type of the field. For a text column, you'll get **Text Filters**. For a number column, you'll get **Number Filters,** etc.

> ➤ When you have applied all the steps to transform the data as you would like to import it, you can now load the results to your Excel worksheet.

> ➤ On the ribbon, select **Home** > **Close & Load** > **Close & Load To**.

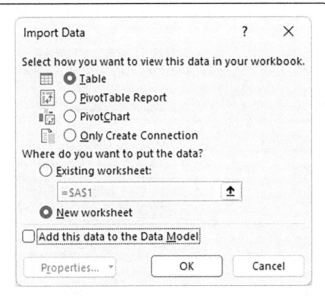

> ➤ In the **Import Data** dialog box, accept the default settings of **Table** and **New Worksheet**, and then click **OK**.

That's it! Excel places the data in the new worksheet in your workbook named after the query. You can perform any formatting changes using Excel's formatting commands here.

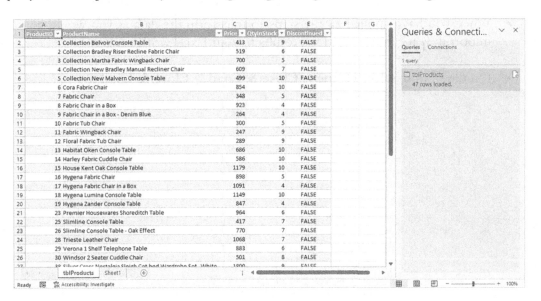

Modifying Your Query

Excel maintains a link to the original query for data generated using the Power Query Editor and displays this information in the **Queries and Connections** pane.

To edit the data using the Power Query Editor again, select any cell in the table in your worksheet, and click the **Edit** button in the **Edit** group on the **Query** tab. Note that the Query contextual tab is only available for data generated with a query and thus linked to a query in the Power Query Editor.

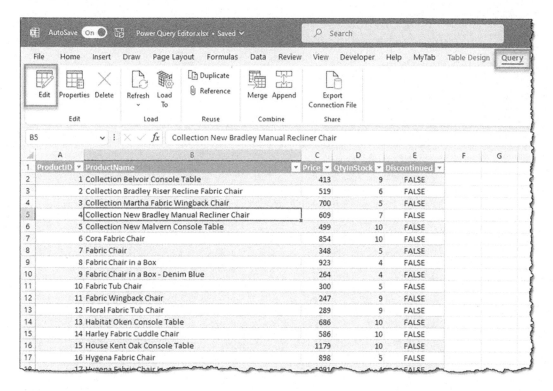

Excel opens the table in the Power Query Editor (see below), enabling you to further transform the data and load the results to your worksheet.

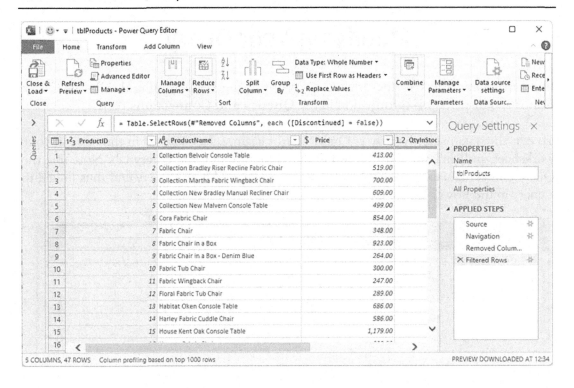

Chapter 4

Troubleshoot and Fix Formula Errors

In this chapter, we will cover how to:

- Use Trace commands to trace the precedents and dependents in your formulas to identify the relationships between the results and cell references.

- Step through a nested formula one level at a time to see results at each level.

- Use the Watch Window to display the value of a cell even when the cell is not in view.

Errors in simple Excel formulas are usually caused by syntax issues that are easily fixed by correcting the syntax. For example, Excel may generate an error because a formula is missing an opening or closing parenthesis. To fix the error, you simply add the parenthesis to the syntax. On the other hand, you may have a formula that doesn't generate an error, but it fails to return the expected result. This is called a logical error. These types of errors can be difficult to detect.

Programming tools tend to have debuggers that can be used to step through the code to identify and fix logical errors. Fortunately, Excel provides several tools that you can use to step through complex formulas to troubleshoot and fix logical errors.

Tracing Precedents and Dependents

To help with troubleshooting your formula, you can use the **Trace Precedents** and **Trace Dependents** commands to show the relationships between the formula and any precedent or dependent cells using tracer arrows.

The Trace commands on the Excel ribbon are enabled by default (see image below). However, if they are disabled on your system, you need to enable them in Excel Options.

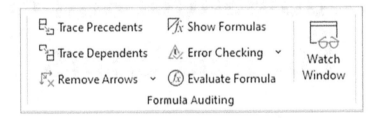

To enable Trace commands in **Excel Options**, do the following:

1. Select **File** > **Options** > **Advanced**.

2. Scroll down to the section labeled **Display options for this workbook** and select the workbook (if it is not already selected).

3. Select **All** under **For objects, show**.

Tracing Precedents

Precedents are cells that are referred to by a formula in another cell. For example, if cell C2 contains the formula =A2+B2, then cells A2 and B2 are precedents to cell C2.

To Trace Precedents, do the following:

1. Select the cell that contains the formula that you want to trace.

2. On the **Formulas** tab, in the **Formula Auditing** group, click the **Trace Precedents** command button. Excel displays a tracer arrow to each cell or range that directly provides data to the active cell (cell with the formula).

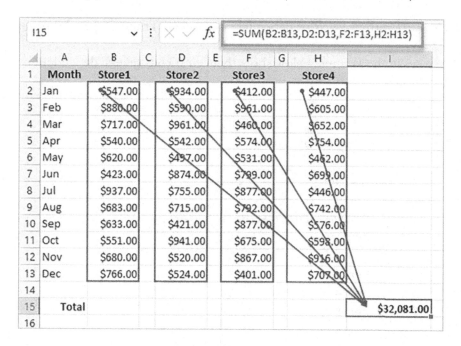

Blue arrows will show cells without errors, while red arrows will show cells that cause errors. If the formula references a cell in another worksheet or workbook, a black arrow will point from the formula cell to a worksheet icon. If cells are referenced in other workbooks, they must be open before Excel can trace those dependencies.

3. If more levels of cells provide data to the formula, click Trace Precedents again.

Tracing Dependents

Dependents are cells that contain formulas that refer to other cells. For example, if cell C2 contains the formula =A2+B2, then cell C2 is dependent on cells A2 and B2.

To Trace Dependents, follow these steps:

1. Select the cell that contains the formula for which you want to trace dependents.

2. On the **Formulas** tab, in the **Formula Auditing** group, click **Trace Dependents**. Excel displays a tracer arrow to each cell that is dependent on the active cell.

3. To identify further levels of dependent cells, click **Trace Dependents** again.

The tracer arrows in the example below show that cell B3 has several dependent cells with formulas in column C.

Removing Tracer Arrows

To remove all tracer arrows, on the **Formulas** tab, in the **Formula Auditing** group, click the arrow next to **Remove Arrows**.

To remove only the precedent or dependent arrows, click the down arrow next to **Remove Arrows** and select **Remove Precedent Arrows** or **Remove Dependent Arrows** from the drop-down list. If you have more than one level of tracer arrows, click the button again.

Evaluate a Formula

Sometimes formulas can be complex, for example, a nested formula with several nested levels. Knowing how the formula arrives at the final result may become difficult if there are several intermediate calculations and logical tests. Formulas that fail to produce the desired result may include logical errors that are difficult to spot at first glance.

The good news is that Excel has a tool called **Evaluate Formula**, which allows you to step through a complex formula. You can see how each level of the formula is evaluated, what the logical tests are doing, and the result at each level. Hence, you can more easily identify and resolve any logical errors in the syntax.

Example

In the following example, we'll use Evaluate Formula to evaluate the following nested formula:

=IF(D2 >= 10000,IF(E2 >= 15,D2*0.2,D2*0.15),IF(E2 >= 15,D2*0.15,D2*0.1))

The formula calculates the following:

- If a sales rep generates $10,000 in sales AND 15 signups, they earn a 20% commission on their sales amount.

- If a sales rep generates either $10,000 in sales OR 15 signups, they earn a 15% commission on their sales amount.

- If a sales rep generates less than $10,000 in sales and less than 15 signups, they earn a 10% commission on their sales amount.

The data being evaluated is shown in the image below.

fx	=IF(D2 >= 10000,IF(E2 >= 15,D2*0.2,D2*0.15),IF(E2 >= 15,D2*0.15,D2*0.1))				

C	D	E	F	G	H
Sales rep	**Sales**	**Signups**	**Commission**		
Gilbert Higgins	$12,500	20	$2,500		
Clinton Bradley	$14,300	25	$2,860		
Bob Nash	$9,000	10	$900		
Lee Powers	$8,050	5	$805		
Mae Stevens	$5,000	7	$500		
Inez Griffith	$8,900	10	$890		
Theresa Hawkins	$7,900	10	$790		
Felix Jacobs	$6,000	17	$900		
Erik Lane	$11,000	18	$2,200		
Jesse Garza	$12,676	12	$1,901		
Alberta Fletcher	$13,163	14	$1,975		
Melody Mendoza	$8,795	20	$1,319		
Abraham Graves	$12,875	26	$2,575		
Van Sims	$6,646	16	$997		

Follow the steps below to evaluate a formula:

1. Select the cell that you want to evaluate. In our example, it would be cell **F2**. Note that Excel can only evaluate one cell at a time.

2. On the **Formulas** tab, in the **Formula Auditing** group, click the **Evaluate Formula** button.

   Excel opens the **Evaluate Formula** dialog box. In the **Evaluation** box, Excel displays the evaluated formula and underlines the next statement to be evaluated.

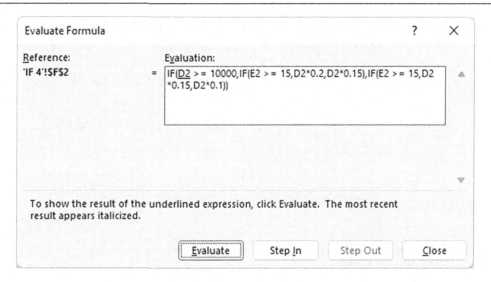

3. Click **Evaluate**. Excel evaluates the underlined statement and shows the result in italics. The next item to be evaluated is then underlined.

=IF(*12500 >= 1000*,IF(E2 >= 15,D2*0.2,D2*0.15),IF(E2 >= 15,D2*0.15,D2*0.1))

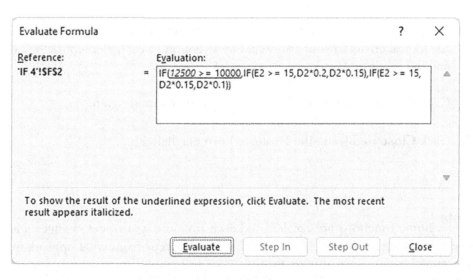

4. Click **Evaluate** again to evaluate the underlined statement. Excel shows the result in italics and underlines the next item to be evaluated.

=IF(*TRUE*,IF(E2 >= 15,D2*0.2,D2*0.15),IF(E2 >= 15,D2*0.15,D2*0.1))

In this case, the result of the test is TRUE. Hence, Excel will process elements of the first nested IF statement.

5. Click **Evaluate** to step through the formula and view the results until the final value is displayed in the **Evaluation** box.

   The process of stepping through the formula like this should help you to identify any logical errors in your formula. Pay attention to each element being evaluated, and the result returned.

6. Click **Restart** if you want to step through the formula again.

7. Click **Close** to dismiss the Evaluate Formula dialog box.

Note Some functions are recalculated each time the worksheet changes. Hence the Evaluate Formula tool could give results that are different from what appears in the cell if those functions are part of your formula. The following functions may not work well with Evaluate Formula: RAND, OFFSET, CELL, INDIRECT, NOW, TODAY, RANDBETWEEN, RANDARRAY, INFO, SUMIF (in some scenarios).

Using the Watch Window

Another way to troubleshoot logical errors in formulas is to use the **Watch Window** in Excel. You can use the Watch Window to inspect formula calculations and results in large worksheets. With the Watch Window, you don't need to scroll continually or go to different parts of your worksheet to see different results.

The Watch Window toolbar can be moved or docked like other toolbars in Excel. For example, you can move it and dock it at the bottom of the window. To undock the Watch Window toolbar, click its title bar and drag it from the docking position.

The Watch Window keeps track of the following properties of a cell: workbook, worksheet, name, cell reference, cell value, and the formula in a cell. You can only have one watch entry per cell. You can change data on the worksheet and view the Watch Window for how the change affects other cells with formulas.

The following example uses the Watch Window to monitor the value in cell B11 in our worksheet.

B11			fx	=IF(AVERAGE(A2:A9)>50,SUM(B2:B9),0)

▲	A	B	C	D	E	F	G	H
1	AVG	SUM						
2	45	47						
3	74	30						
4	26	40						
5	39	30						
6	90	77						
7	72	79						
8	28	48						
9	68	29						
10								
11	Result	380	*Result if the average of A1:A8 is greater than 50*					
12								

Follow the steps below to add a Watch item to the Watch Window:

1. Select the cells that you want to watch.

    To select all cells with formulas on your worksheet, select **Home** > **Editing** group > **Find & Replace** > **Go To Special** > **Formulas** > **OK**.

2. On the **Formulas** tab, in the **Formula Auditing** group, click the **Watch Window** button to display the Watch Window toolbar.

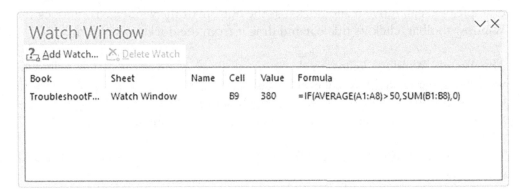

3. Click **Add Watch**.

4. Click **Add** in the **Add Watch** dialog. Here you can select a cell to watch (if it differs from the one selected in step 1).

5. Move the Watch Window toolbar and dock it to the bottom, left, or right side of the Excel window. To change the width of a column, for example, the **Book** column, drag the boundary on the right side of the column heading.

6. To display the cell for an entry in the Watch Window, double-click the entry to select the cell on the worksheet. Note that cells with references to other workbooks are only displayed in the Watch Window when the referenced workbook is open.

7. To close the Watch Window toolbar, on the **Formulas** tab, in the **Formula Auditing** group, click the **Watch Window** button to toggle it off.

Removing cells from the Watch Window

1. If the Watch Window toolbar is not open, click the **Watch Window** command button on the **Formulas** tab to display it.

2. Select the entry you want to remove. To select multiple entries, hold down the Ctrl key while clicking the entries.

3. Click **Delete Watch**.

4. To close the Watch Window toolbar, on the **Formulas** tab, in the **Formula Auditing** group, click the **Watch Window** button to toggle it off.

Chapter 5

Use Macros to Automate Excel Tasks

This chapter will cover the following:

- How to record and run macros in Excel.
- Adding macro command buttons on the ribbon.
- Assigning a macro to a graphic object in your worksheet.
- Macro security, including the Trust Center and Trusted Locations.
- How to view and edit your macros in the Visual Basic Editor.

Macros enable you to automate pretty much any task you can manually carry out in Excel. You can use Excel's macro recorder to record tasks you perform routinely. Macros enable you to do the work faster, as Excel can play back keystrokes and mouse actions much faster than when you perform them manually. Also, a macro ensures a particular task is performed in a consistent way, which reduces the likelihood of errors.

Excel uses the Visual Basic for Applications (VBA) programming language to record all the commands and keystrokes you make while recording the macro. VBA is a programming language developed and used primarily for Microsoft 365 applications like Access, Word, Excel, PowerPoint, etc. You don't need to have any knowledge of VBA to record and use macros in Excel, but you can use the Visual Basic Editor to view and edit your macros after recording them if needed.

Overview

There are two ways you can create a macro in Excel:

1. You can use Excel's macro recorder to record your actions as you perform a task in the worksheet.

2. Use the VBA editor to write the code that performs the task from scratch. VBA programming is outside the scope of this book, but we will briefly look at the code editor.

Whichever method you use, Excel will create a special code module that holds the actions and instructions recorded in the macro. These are stored as Visual Basic code. In fact, one way to create VBA code for Excel is to start the macro recorder and manually perform the task for which you want to write code. Then you open the macro in the Visual Basic Editor and put the finishing touches to the code. This method is how developers can quickly create code to automate Excel.

Displaying the Developer Tab

A default installation of Excel does not add the **Developer** tab to the ribbon. When working with macros and the Visual Basic Editor, it is much easier to access commands on the Developer tab.

Follow the steps below to display the **Developer** tab on the ribbon (if it is not already added):

1. Right-click anywhere on the ribbon (below the buttons) and select **Customize the Ribbon**. You can also open the Excel Options dialog box by selecting **File > Options > Customize Ribbon**.

   Excel opens the **Customize the Ribbon** pane in the Excel Options dialog box.

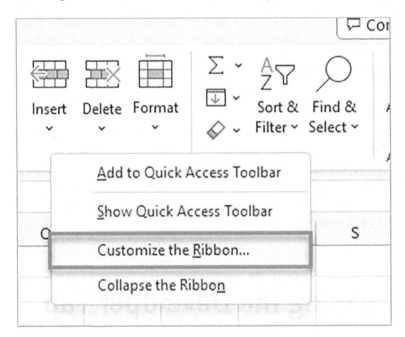

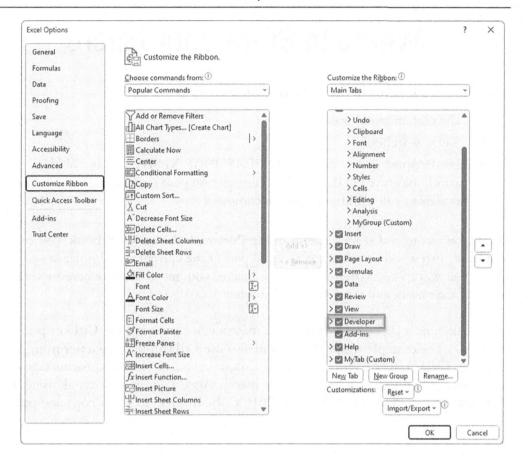

2. On the right side of the dialog box, select **Main Tabs** in the dropdown list. Select the **Developer** check box in the list below.

3. Click **OK**.

Where to Store Your Macro

You can store macros in the following locations:

- The current workbook.

- A new workbook.

- The Personal Macro Workbook (PERSONAL.XLSB). This is a hidden workbook stored in the XLSTART folder on your computer. This workbook is available to all workbooks on the computer.

When you record and store a macro in the **Personal Macro Workbook**, you can run it from any open workbook. Macros saved as part of the current workbook can only be run inside that workbook. When recording a macro, you get to select where to save it, the name of the macro, and what keyboard shortcut to assign to it.

When assigning a keyboard shortcut to a macro, you can assign the **Ctrl** key plus a letter from A-Z. For example, Ctrl+M. You can also use Ctrl+Shift and a letter from A-Z, for example, Ctrl+Shift+M. You can't assign some keyboard shortcut, for instance, Ctrl+ (any number) or Ctrl+ (a punctuation mark). Also, you should avoid using known Windows shortcut keys like Ctrl+C or Ctrl+V (the shortcut keys for copy and paste).

How to Start the Macro Recorder

There are three ways you can start the macro recorder in Excel:

- **From the Status bar**

  On the Excel Status bar, click the **Record Macro** button (bottom left of the window, next to the Ready indicator). Having the Record Macro button on the status bar is convenient as it means you don't have to switch from your current tab on the ribbon to start and stop the recording.

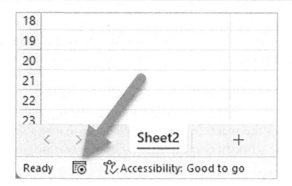

- **From the View tab**

  On the **View** tab, click the dropdown arrow on the **Macros** button, and then select **Record Macro** from the dropdown menu.

- **From the Developer tab**

  On the **Developer** tab, click the **Record Macro** command button.

View Tab Macro Options

On the **View** tab of the ribbon, the **Macros** button has three options on its dropdown list (you can also find these options as command buttons in the Code group in the Developer tab):

- **View Macros**: This opens the **Macro** dialog box, which enables you to select and run a macro that has already been recorded. You can also choose to edit macros from here.

261

- **Record Macro**: This opens the **Record Macro** dialog box, which allows you to define settings for the macro you want to record and start the macro recorder.

- **Use Relative References**: This setting, which you can turn on before recording a macro, uses relative cell references when recording macros. Using relative cell references makes the macro more flexible because it enables you to run it anywhere on the worksheet rather than where it was originally recorded.

Absolute Reference vs Relative Reference

The macro recorder uses absolute references by default, which means that Excel will store specific cell references as part of the code instructions. For example, if the macro was recorded in range A2:A5 in one worksheet, Excel will only perform the tasks in that range when you run the macro in any worksheet.

If you want a macro to perform the tasks in any range in a worksheet, enable the **Use Relative Reference** setting on the **View** or **Developer** tabs of the ribbon before recording the macro.

With the reference type set to relative, the macro will perform the actions relative to the active cell when the macro is run.

Recording a Macro

In the following example, we'll create reusable column and row headers. Once the process is recorded as a macro, we can run the macro whenever we want to insert those headers in a new worksheet.

The worksheet looks like this:

◢	A	B	C	D	E
1	**Sales**				
2					
3		**New York**	**Los Angeles**	**London**	**Paris**
4	Jan				
5	Feb				
6	Mar				
7	Apr				
8	May				
9	Jun				
10	Jul				
11	Aug				
12	Sep				
13	Oct				
14	Nov				
15	Dec				
16					

The process of creating the above template involves the following actions:

- Enter the text "Sales" in the first row. Set the font to bold and the font size to 14 points.

- Enter New York, Los Angeles, London, and Paris in cells B3 to E3.

- Select B3:E3, then Center and Bold the text.

- Increase the column width for B3:E3 to display all the text.

- Select B3:E3 and change the **Fill Color** to *Green, Accent 6, Lighter 40%*.

- Enter Jan to Dec in cells A4 to A15.

- Select A4:A15 and set the font to bold.

Follow the steps below to record the macro:

1. Open an Excel workbook and a blank worksheet. On the **View** tab, click the dropdown button of the **Macros** button (not the command button itself), then select **Use Relative References** from the menu.

2. On the **View** tab, click the dropdown button of the **Macros** button and click **Record Macro**. Excel opens the **Records Macro** dialog box.

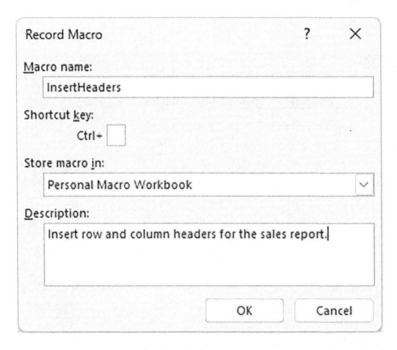

3. In the **Macro Name** field, enter the macro name. For example, *InsertHeaders*.

4. For the **Shortcut key**, hold down the **Shift** key and press **M**. This will enter Ctrl+Shift+M for the shortcut key. This keystroke can be used to run the macro. You can use other key combinations but avoid using popular Windows shortcut keys.

Note The shortcut key is optional, and you don't necessarily need to assign one to every macro you create.

---

5. In the **Store macro in** dropdown list, select **Personal Macro Workbook**. This ensures that the macro is saved in the global PERSONAL.XLSB workbook and not the current workbook.

6. In the **Description** box, enter a brief description of what the macro does. A description is optional but useful if you have a lot of macros. A brief description of each macro helps to differentiate between the macros and make maintenance easier.

7. Click **OK** to start recording.

    The Record Macro box is closed. On the status bar, next to Ready, you'll see a small square button indicating that the macro recorder is currently running.

    Next, we'll perform the Excel actions we'll be recording.

8. In cell A1, enter the text "Sales", then set the font to Bold and font size to 14 points.

9. Enter "New York", "Los Angeles", "London", and "Paris" in cells B3 to E3.

10. Select cells B3 to E3 and perform the following actions:

    - Set the column width to 12 (**Home** > **Cells** > **Format** > **Column Width**)
    - Set the text alignment to **Center**.
    - Set the font to **Bold**.
    - Change the **Fill Color** to *Green, Accent 6, Lighter 40%*.

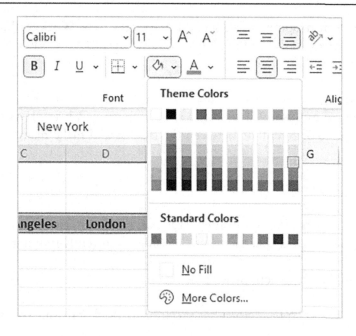

11. Enter "Jan" to "Dec" in cells A4 to A15.

12. Select cells A4 to A15 and set the font to Bold.

13. **Stop recording**: On the status bar, to the immediate right of **Ready**, you'll see a square button (the Record Macro/Stop Recording button). Click that button to stop recording the macro.

With that, your macro recording has been completed. Next, we'll run the macro.

Running a Macro

It is best to test a macro in a new worksheet (or a different range in the current worksheet) to see if the macro replicates actions you performed when recording it.

⚠️ **Important** If you run a new macro in a worksheet with existing data, there is a risk that the macro will overwrite your existing data or formatting. Always test the macro in a new worksheet to ensure you don't mistakenly overwrite data. Only run the macro against production data when you're satisfied it is working as intended. For example, you may create a macro that adds formatting to existing data. In such cases, ensure you test the macro first against test copies of the data before running it against your production data.

To run a recorded macro, do the following:

1. Open the Macro dialog box.

    There are three ways you can open the **Macro** dialog box:

    - On the **View** tab, in the **Macros** group, click the dropdown button on the **Macros** button and select **View Macros**.

    - On the **Developer** tab, in the **Code** group, click the **Macros** button.

    - Select **Alt+F8** on your keyboard to open the **Macro** dialog box.

    Excel opens the **Macro** dialog box, which lists all the macros you have created in the **Macro name** box.

2. To run a macro, select the macro name on the list and click the **Run** button.

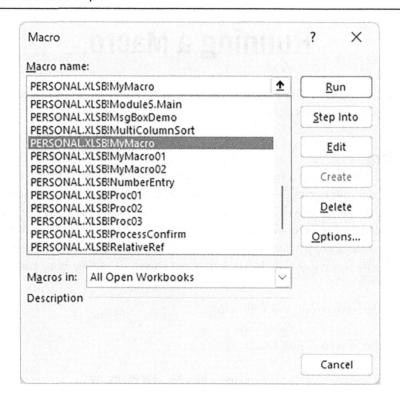

-ॆ-Tip If you assigned a keyboard shortcut to the macro, for example, Ctrl+Shift+M, you could use the keystroke to automatically run the macro without needing to open the Macro dialog box.

Adding a Macro Button to the Ribbon

If you need to run your macro often, assigning it to a command button on the ribbon would be a good idea instead of running it from the Macros dialog box each time.

You must create a new custom group for your macro button, as you can't add the button to one of the default groups in Excel. You can create a new custom group in one of the default tabs and add your macro button. Alternatively, you can create a new custom tab to add your new custom group and a macro command button.

Creating a New Custom Tab and Group

Follow the steps below to create a new tab and then add a command button to it:

1. To create a **new tab**, click the **New Tab** button at the bottom of the Main Tabs list box. Inside the tab, you must create at least one group before adding a command button from the left side of the dialog box.

2. To give the tab a display name, select the **New Tab (Custom)** item and click the **Rename** button at the bottom of the Main Tabs list box. Enter your preferred name for the tab in the **Rename** dialog box and click **OK**.

3. You can use the arrow buttons to the right of the Main Tabs list box to move your new tab item up or down the list, depending on where you want to place it.

4. To create a new **custom group**, select the tab where you want to create the group. This could be one of the default tabs or the new one you've created. Click **New Group** (at the bottom of the dialog box). Excel creates a new group in the currently selected tab.

5. To create a name for the group, select the **New Group (Custom)** item and click the **Rename** button. Enter your preferred name in the **Rename** dialog box, for example, *MyMacros*.

6. Click **OK**.

You now have a custom group in which you can add your macro command buttons.

Assigning A Macro Command to The New Group

Follow the steps below to add a macro command button to the new custom group:

1. Select your custom group in the **Main Tabs** list box.

2. Click the dropdown list box named **Choose commands from** (on the left of the dialog box) and select **Macros** from the dropdown list. In the list box on the left, you'll see a list of macros created in the current workbook and saved in the PERSONAL.XLSB workbook.

3. Select the macro name that you want to add to your custom group in the list box on the left, then click the **Add** button to add the macro command to the new custom group in the list box on the right.

Note If you mistakenly added the wrong command, select it in the list box on the right and click the **Remove** button to remove it.

---

4. Click **OK** on the Excel Options dialog box to confirm the change.

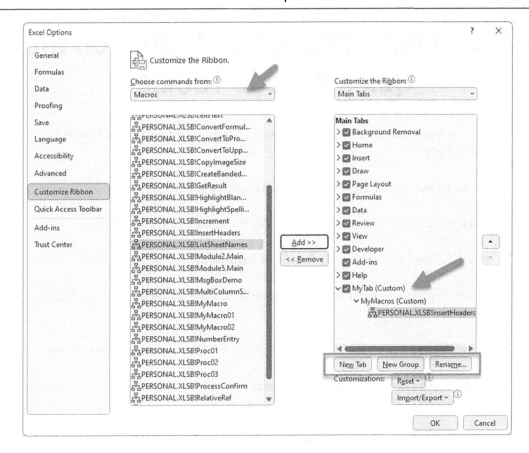

After adding the macro, the macro's name appears on a button with a generic icon (a program diagram chart). When you click the button, Excel runs the macro.

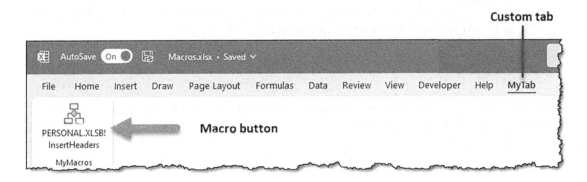

Assigning a Macro to a Button on the Quick Access Toolbar

You can also add a macro button to the Quick Access Toolbar if you have it displayed and use it regularly.

Follow the steps below to add a custom macro button to the Quick Access Toolbar:

1. Click the dropdown arrow at the end of the Quick Access toolbar.

2. On the dropdown menu, click **More Commands**.

   Excel displays the **Customize the Quick Access Toolbar** pane in Excel Options.

3. Select **Macros** from the dropdown list named **Choose commands from**.

   The list box below will display all macros created in the current workbook and those saved in the PERSONAL.XLSB workbook.

4. In the list box on the left, select the macro you want to add to the Quick Access Toolbar and click the **Add** button to add it to the list on the right.

Note If you add the wrong command by mistake, select it in the list on the right and click the **Remove** button to remove it.

---

5. Click **OK**.

Excel displays your macro button as a generic macro icon on the Quick Access Toolbar. To run the macro, click the button.

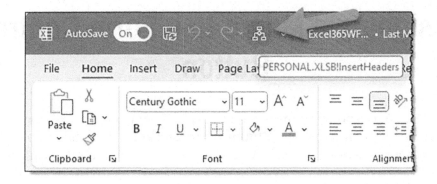

Assigning a Macro to an Image

You can assign macros to images you've inserted in your worksheet, including Pictures, Shapes, and Icons that you can insert from the **Illustrations** group on the **Insert** tab. You can also assign macros to images you have drawn using tools on the **Draw** tab.

To assign a macro to an image, do the following:

1. Insert the image in the worksheet area. For example, an icon from **Insert > Illustrations > Icons**.

2. Right-click the icon, and then click **Assign Macro** on its shortcut menu.

3. In the **Assign Macro** dialog box, select the macro name from the **Macro name** list box and click **OK.**

Now when you hover over the icon, the mouse pointer changes to a hand with a pointing index finger, indicating that you can click it to run the macro.

Assigning a Macro to a Form Control Button

You can add an Excel **Form Control** from the Developer tab in your worksheet, which you can use to execute macros. The **Button Form Control** is like a button on a form to which you can assign a macro. When you click the button, the macro runs in the current worksheet.

To add a Button Form Control to your worksheet, do the following:

1. On the **Developer** tab, in the **Controls** group, click the **Insert** button. Then select the **Button** under **Form Controls**.

2. In the body of the worksheet, draw the button with your mouse.

3. As soon as you release the left mouse button, the **Assign Macro** dialog box will open. Select the macro you want to assign to the button from the Macro name box and click **OK**.

4. To edit the button's caption, right-click the button and select **Edit Text** on the shortcut menu, then type the caption you want for the button.

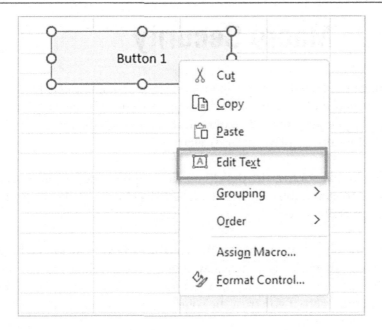

5. Click anywhere in the worksheet to exit the design mode. Excel deselects the button.

Your button is now set and ready for use. When you click the button, the macro assigned to it will run in the current worksheet.

Note When you right-click the button, the worksheet goes into design mode, and the button becomes inactive. To reactivate the button, click anywhere else in the worksheet. Excel deselects the button, and it responds to clicks again.

Formatting Controls

To format the button and change other properties, for example, the font or caption, right-click the button and select **Format Control** from the shortcut menu. Excel opens the **Format Control** dialog box, where you can change several control properties. When you're done, click **OK** on the Format Control dialog box. Then, click any cell in your worksheet to exit design mode.

Macro Security

Excel uses an authentication system called Microsoft Authenticode to digitally sign macro projects or add-ins created with Visual Basic for Applications. The macros you create locally on your computer are automatically authenticated. Hence, when you run them on your computer, Excel does not display a security alert.

For macros from an external source, the developer can acquire a certificate issued by a reputable authority or a trusted publisher. In such cases, Excel will run the macro if it can verify that it is from a trusted source.

If Excel cannot verify the digital signature of a macro from an external source because it perhaps doesn't have one, a security alert is displayed in the message bar (below the Excel ribbon). This alert allows you to enable the macro or ignore it. You can click the **Enable Content** button to run the macro if you trust the source and are sure that the macro poses no security threat to your computer.

If you try to create a macro in an Excel workbook that was saved as an XLSX file, Excel will display a message on the message bar prompting you to save the workbook as a macro-enabled file first. When you get this message, click the **Save As** button on the message bar, and select the **Excel Macro-Enabled Workbook (*.xlsm)** file type from the filter list.

File type	File extension
Excel Workbook	xlsx
Excel Macro-Enabled Workbook	xlsm

If you save the macro to the **Personal Macro Workbook**, it will be saved in the PERSONAL.XLSB file, which is an Excel Binary Workbook in the XLSTART folder. In this case, you'll not need to save your workbook as a macro-enabled workbook.

As much as possible, store macros in the **Personal Macro Workbook**. This means the macro is global to the computer and can be run from any workbook on the computer. It also means you don't need to convert your workbooks to macro-enabled files. Only create a macro-enabled workbook if it is necessary. For example, if you want to distribute the file to other people.

Trust Center Macro Settings

Microsoft Office security and privacy settings are located in the **Trust Center**. The Macro Settings tab of the Trust Center contains the macro security settings for your computer. Macro security is important to protect your computer against the threat of malicious code that can be inserted in Microsoft Office macros.

You can access the **Macro Settings** in the Trust Center in the following ways:

- On the **Developer** tab, in the **Code** group, click the **Macro Security** button. Excel opens the **Macro Settings** pane of the Trust Center dialog box.

- To go to macro settings, select **File** > **Options** > **Trust Center** > **Trust Centre Settings** > **Macro Settings**.

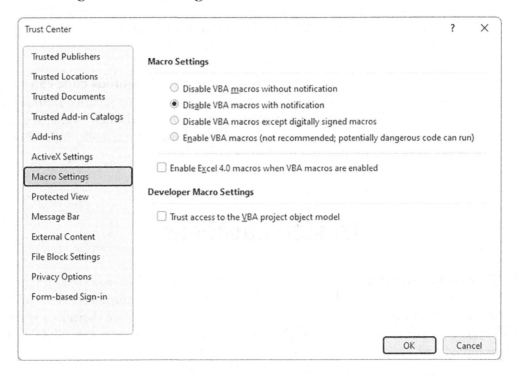

By default, Excel disables all macros from external sources with a security alert on the message bar, allowing you to enable the macro or ignore it. This setting is the default when you install Excel. However, there are other security options you can select.

You can also select one of these options in Macro Settings:

- **Disable all macros without notification**: This automatically disables macros in your computer. This setting means no macros will run on your computer, and you'll not get a security alert giving you the option to run the macro. This option is useful for shared computers, for instance, where you don't want anyone using the computer to run macros.

- **Disable all macros with notification**: This option is the default. All macros from external sources are disabled, with a security alert on the message bar. With this option, you have to specifically choose to enable the macro before it can run.

- **Disable all macros except digitally signed macros**: This option disables all macros apart from the digitally signed macros from publishers you have added to your **Trusted Publishers** in the Trust Center. With this option, a macro from a publisher not in your Trusted Publishers list will generate an alert with a message asking if you want to **Trust All Documents from this Publisher**. You can then choose to add them to your trusted publishers.

- **Enable all macros (not recommended; potentially dangerous code can run)**: This option enables all macros without any notifications or security alerts, even macros that are not digitally signed or authenticated. As indicated by the title, this option is not recommended because you can inadvertently run malicious code that corrupts your data or damages your computer.

Trusted Locations

The **Trusted Locations** tab of the Trust Center dialog box enables you to add, remove or modify trusted locations. If you are receiving macros from an external source that you need to run on your computer without alerts, then you need to place them in a trusted location on your computer. In doing so, Excel knows that these files are safe, and you are not prompted with security alerts when you open them.

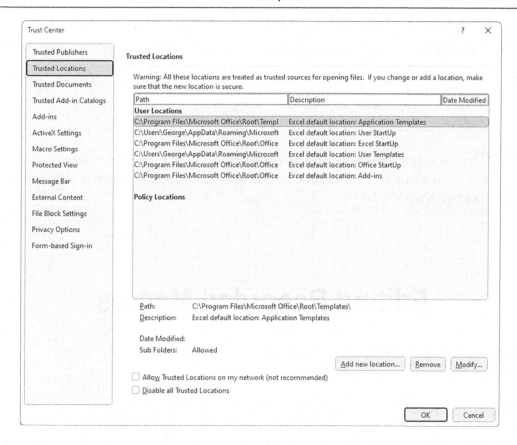

You can use the following options to change Trusted Locations settings:

- **Add new location**: To add a new trusted location, click the **Add new location** button at the bottom of the dialog box. On the **Microsoft Office Trusted Location** dialog box, click **Browse** and navigate to the folder you want to add to the list of trusted locations. After selecting the folder, click **OK** twice.

  Excel adds a new trusted location on your computer, and you can store any externally created macro-enabled files in that folder.

- **Allow trusted locations on my network (not recommended):** Select this option if you want to add folders on your network to your trusted locations. As indicated by the title, this is not recommended by Microsoft, as you can't entirely trust the safety of external locations. However, if you're working on a shared network drive that you trust and is the only way you can collaborate with others, this may be an option for sharing macro-enabled files. Only use it as a last option.

- **Disable all trusted locations**: Select this option if you want to immediately disable all trusted locations. With this option enabled, macros in your trusted locations will not run. Only the macros digitally signed and recognized as trustworthy by Excel will run on the computer.

Note The macro-enabled worksheets you create locally on your computer do not need to be stored in a trusted location to run on your computer. They're automatically digitally authenticated by Excel.

Editing Recorded Macros

As mentioned earlier in this chapter, the macros recorded in Excel are stored as Visual Basic for Applications (VBA) code instructions.

VBA programming is outside the scope of this book. However, knowing how to view the source code for your macro is useful, as you can identify and fix simple errors or make small changes to values. Sometimes, editing the macro in the Visual Basic Editor to change how it behaves is more expedient than recording it again.

Even if you have no programming skills, you may still be able to identify errors and make small changes. For example, you can fix spelling errors in the text, change number values, and correct formula errors. You don't need programming skills to make simple changes like these. You may also see something out of place in the code that helps you to avoid the error if you decide to re-record the macro.

Unhiding the Personal Macro Workbook

If the macro you want to edit is stored in your Personal Macro Workbook, you must unhide this workbook before you edit it in the Visual Basic Editor.

Follow the steps below to unhide the Personal Macro Workbook:

1. On the **View** tab, click the **Unhide** command button.

    Excel displays the **Unhide** dialog box showing the PERSONAL.XLSB workbook in the Unhide Workbook list.

2. Select PERSONAL.XLSB in the list box and click **OK** to unhide the workbook.

With the Personal Macro Workbook unhidden, you can edit macros saved in the Visual Basic Editor.

Editing the Macro in the Visual Basic Editor

Follow the steps below to open a macro for editing in the Visual Basic Editor:

1. Switch back to your main workbook.

2. On the **View** tab, click the **Macros** command button, then select **View Macros**.

    Excel opens the **Macro** dialog box listing the names of the macros created in the current workbook and the Personal Macro Workbook.

3. Select the macro you want to edit in the **Macro Name** box, and click the **Edit** button.

    Excel will display the macro in the Visual Basic Editor.

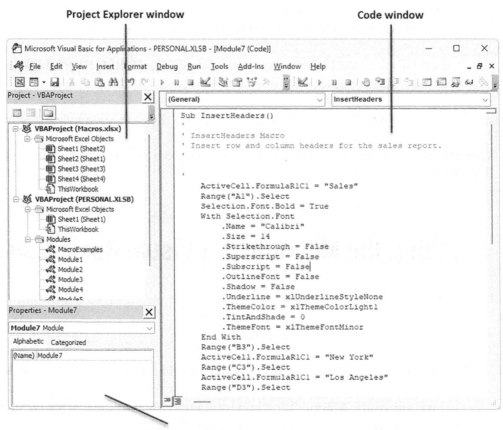

Project Explorer window   Code window

Properties window

The **Code window** shows the code instructions for the macro, and this is where you would edit the macro. The Project Explorer enables you to navigate to macros saved in different modules or workbooks currently open.

In the Code window, the macro code is between a starting keyword and an ending keyword. The beginning of the macro has the keyword **Sub InsertHeaders()** because **InsertHeaders** is the name given to the macro when it was created. The keyword **End Sub** indicates the end of the macro. To make changes to the macro, ensure you keep your edits within this area.

4. After making your changes, click the **Save** button on the Visual Basic Editor toolbar to save your changes (the blue disk icon).

5. Click the **Close** button to close the Visual Basic Editor. The close button is the x icon on the top right of the window. You can also close the window by selecting **File** > **Close and Return to Microsoft Excel**.

6. In the PERSONAL.XLSB workbook, select **View** tab > **Window** group > **Hide**.

   Hiding the file again prevents Excel from displaying the file when you next open Excel.

The code below was generated from the macro created earlier in this chapter.

```
Sub InsertHeaders()
'
' InsertHeaders Macro
' Insert row and column headers for the sales report.
'
    ActiveCell.FormulaR1C1 = "Sales"
    Range("A1").Select
    Selection.Font.Bold = True
    With Selection.Font
        .Name = "Calibri"
        .Size = 14
        .Strikethrough = False
        .Superscript = False
        .Subscript = False
        .OutlineFont = False
        .Shadow = False
        .Underline = xlUnderlineStyleNone
        .ThemeColor = xlThemeColorLight1
        .TintAndShade = 0
        .ThemeFont = xlThemeFontMinor
    End With
    Range("B3").Select
    ActiveCell.FormulaR1C1 = "New York"
    Range("C3").Select
    ActiveCell.FormulaR1C1 = "Los Angeles"
    Range("D3").Select
    ActiveCell.FormulaR1C1 = "London"
    Range("E3").Select
    ActiveCell.FormulaR1C1 = "Paris"
```

```
    Range("B3:E3").Select
    Selection.ColumnWidth = 12
    With Selection
        .HorizontalAlignment = xlCenter
        .VerticalAlignment = xlBottom
        .WrapText = False
        .Orientation = 0
        .AddIndent = False
        .IndentLevel = 0
        .ShrinkToFit = False
        .ReadingOrder = xlContext
        .MergeCells = False
    End With
    Selection.Font.Bold = True
    With Selection.Interior
        .Pattern = xlSolid
        .PatternColorIndex = xlAutomatic
        .ThemeColor = xlThemeColorAccent6
        .TintAndShade = 0.399975585192419
        .PatternTintAndShade = 0
    End With
    Range("A4").Select
    ActiveCell.FormulaR1C1 = "Jan"
    Range("A4").Select
    Selection.AutoFill Destination:=Range("A4:A15"),
Type:=xlFillDefault
    Range("A4:A15").Select
    Selection.Font.Bold = True
    Range("B4").Select
End Sub
```

Chapter 6

Analyze Alternative Data Sets with What-If Analysis

This chapter covers the following:

- What-If Analysis for one-variable and two-variable data tables.

- Using the Scenario Manager to create and compare different scenarios for your data.

- Using the Goal Seek tool to adjust variables in a data set to meet a goal.

- Using the Solver add-in tool to generate alternate scenarios for more complex data.

Spreadsheet formulas are excellent at automatically updating results based on your input. For that reason, spreadsheets are one of the best tools for carrying out financial projections based on assumptions. Excel provides a whole raft of tools for just this purpose.

In Excel, there are different types of What-If Analysis you can perform. In this chapter, we will cover four commonly used types in Excel.

- **Data tables**: This feature enables you to generate a series of projections based on one or two changing variables.

- **Goal seeking**: This feature enables you to set a predetermined goal and then choose the variables that will change to meet this goal.

- **Scenarios**: In this type of What-If Analysis, you create different scenarios using alternative figures, which you can compare side-by-side in a generated report.

- **Solver**: The Solver is an Excel add-in that you can use to create more complex What-If Analysis, enabling you to use multiple variables and constraints.

Data Tables

A data table gives you a projection of how your bottom line would look if one or two variables in your data were changed. For example, what would be our profit if we achieved a growth rate in sales of 1.5% rather than 1%? What would be our net profit next year if we reduced our expenses by 3%? These are the kinds of questions that a data table can answer.

Creating a One-Variable Data Table

The one-variable data table is a projection based on a series of values you want to substitute for a single input value. To demonstrate this data table, we will use an example where we create a series of projected sales for the next quarter.

In this example, we have the following figures:

- Sales for quarter one: $45,000.
- Projected growth in sales for quarter two: 2.0%.
- Projected sales for quarter two: 45,000 + (45,000 x 0.02).

For this projection, we want to substitute different growth rates into the projected growth for Qtr 2 to see a series of projected sales based on different growth rates.

For the column values, we enter rates ranging from 1% to 5% in range B8:B16, with an increment of 0.5%. You can use different increments based on your requirements.

For the row value, cell **C8**, we enter =*B5*, which is a reference to the master formula which calculates **Projected Sales Qtr 2**. The data table will use this master formula as the base figure to make the projections.

B5		⌄ : ✕ ✓ ƒx	=B3+(B3*B4)		
◢	A	B	C	D
1	**Projected sales for Quarter 2 - one-variable data table**			
2				
3	Sales Qtr 1	$45,000.00		
4	Growth Qtr 2	2.00%		
5	Projected Sales Qtr 2	$45,900.00		
6				
7			$45,900.00	
8		1.00%		
9		1.50%		
10		2.00%		
11		2.50%		
12		3.00%		
13		3.50%		
14		4.00%		
15		4.50%		
16		5.00%		
17				
18	*B8:B16 = Growth rates*			
19	*C7 = Master formula*			
20				

Once your data has been prepared, as shown above, follow the steps below to generate the data table:

1. Select the table. For this example, it is B7:C16.

2. On the **Data** tab, in the **Forecast** group, select **What-If Analysis > Data Table**.

Excel displays the **Data Table** dialog box.

3. Click in the **Column input cell** box, and on the worksheet, select the growth percentage, cell **B4**. This example is a one-variable data table, so we only need the column input.

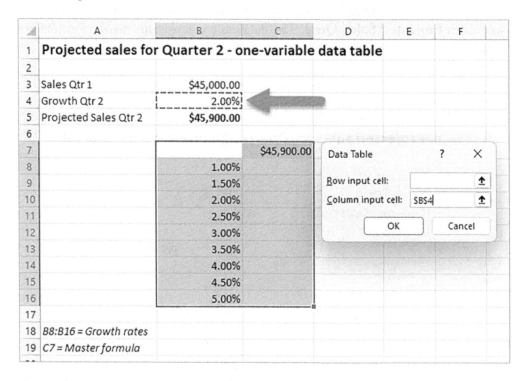

4. Click **OK** to generate the projected sale values in cells C8:C16.

	A	B	C	D	E	F	G
	C8		fx {=TABLE(,B4)}				

	A	B	C	D	E	F	G
1	Projected sales for Quarter 2 - one-variable data table						
2							
3	Sales Qtr 1	$45,000.00					
4	Growth Qtr 2	2.00%					
5	Projected Sales Qtr 2	$45,900.00					
6							
7			$45,900.00		B8:B16 = Growth rates		
8			1.00%	$45,450.00	C7 = Master formula		
9			1.50%	$45,675.00	C8:C16 = Projected sales		
10			2.00%	$45,900.00			
11			2.50%	$46,125.00			
12			3.00%	$46,350.00			
13			3.50%	$46,575.00			
14			4.00%	$46,800.00			
15			4.50%	$47,025.00			
16			5.00%	$47,250.00			

The data table is created as an array formula using the TABLE function. The TABLE function takes two arguments *row_ref* and/or *column_ref*, but only needs one for a one-variable data table.

{=TABLE(,B4)}

The formula shows that the value in cell B4 represents its *column_ref* argument for which alternate values are provided in cells B8:B16. The process simply substitutes the original rate in B4 with the series of rates in B8:B16 to generate the projected values.

As the data table uses an array formula, Excel will not allow you to delete only some of the values in the array. To delete values in the data table, you must select all the generated values, cells C8:C16, and select the **Delete** key.

Creating a Two-Variable Data Table

A two-variable data table enables you to create projections based on the changing values of two variables.

Creating a two-variable table is similar to the one-variable data table described above. But, in this case, we have two variables that can change instead of one. A two-variable data table requires input for the column and row fields, so we need a series of values for the table's first column and first row. At the intersection of the row and column, we enter the master formula, which would have the figure we want to use as the basis of the projection.

To demonstrate this type of data table, we will use an example where we create a series of projected sales for the next quarter based on two variables.

In this example, we have the following figures:
- Sales for quarter one: $45,000.
- Projected growth in sales for quarter two: 2.0%.
- Expenses for quarter two: 15%.
- Projected sales for quarter two: 45,000 + (45,000*0.02).

We want to see a projection of our sales with different growth rates (between 1% and 5%) and expense rates (between 15% and 30%).

B6			f_x	=B3+(B3*B4)-(B3*B5)		

▲	A	B	C	D	E	F
1	**Projection on sales - two-variable data table**					
2						
3	Sales Qtr 1	$45,000.00				
4	Growth Qtr 2	1.80%				
5	Expenses Qtr 2	15%				
6	Projected Sales Qtr 2	£39,060.00				
7						
8		£39,060.00	15%	20%	25%	30%
9		1.00%				
10		1.50%				
11		2.00%				
12		2.50%				
13		3.00%				
14		3.50%				
15		4.00%				
16		4.50%				
17		5.00%				
18						
19	B9:B17 = Growth rates, B8 = Master formula, C8:F8 = Expenses					

For the row entries we want to substitute in **Expenses Qtr 2**, we enter values ranging from 15% to 30% in cells C8:F8.

For the column entries we want to substitute in **Growth Qtr 2**, we enter values ranging from 1% to 5% (increasing by 0.5%) in cells B9:B17.

In cell B8, we enter =*B6,* a reference to the master formula that calculates **Projected Sales Qtr 2**.

As shown in the image above, with the worksheet model prepared, follow the steps below to generate the data table:

1. Select the table. For this example, the range is B8:F17.

2. On the **Data** tab, in the **Forecast** group, select **What-If Analysis > Data Table**.

   Excel displays the **Data Table** dialog box.

We must enter both input values in the Data Table dialog because this is a two-variable data table.

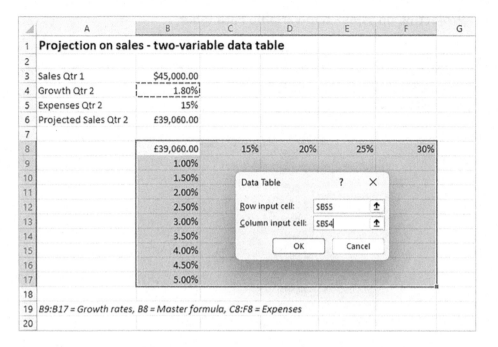

3. Click in the **Row input cell** box, and on the worksheet, select the expenses for quarter two, cell **B5**.

4. Next, click in the **Column input cell** box, and then on the worksheet, select the growth percentage, cell **B4**.

5. Click **OK** to generate the projected values in the data table.

| C9 | | ⌄ | : | ✕ ✓ | *fx* | {=TABLE(B5,B4)} | |

◢	A	B	C	D	E	F	G
1	**Projection on sales - two-variable data table**						
2							
3	Sales Qtr 1	$45,000.00					
4	Growth Qtr 2	1.80%					
5	Expenses Qtr 2	15%					
6	Projected Sales Qtr 2	£39,060.00					
7							
8		£39,060.00	15%	20%	25%	30%	
9		1.00%	£38,700.00	£36,450.00	£34,200.00	£31,950.00	
10		1.50%	£38,925.00	£36,675.00	£34,425.00	£32,175.00	
11		2.00%	£39,150.00	£36,900.00	£34,650.00	£32,400.00	
12		2.50%	£39,375.00	£37,125.00	£34,875.00	£32,625.00	
13		3.00%	£39,600.00	£37,350.00	£35,100.00	£32,850.00	
14		3.50%	£39,825.00	£37,575.00	£35,325.00	£33,075.00	
15		4.00%	£40,050.00	£37,800.00	£35,550.00	£33,300.00	
16		4.50%	£40,275.00	£38,025.00	£35,775.00	£33,525.00	
17		5.00%	£40,500.00	£38,250.00	£36,000.00	£33,750.00	
18							
19	*B9:B17 = Growth rates, B8 = Master formula, C8:F8 = Expenses, C9:F17 = Projected sales*						
20							

The two-variable data table uses the TABLE function to create an array formula in the output range of C9:F17. The TABLE function takes two arguments *row_ref* and/or *column_ref*.

{=TABLE(B5,B4)}

The formula shows that cell B5 is the *row_ref* argument for which alternate values have been provided in cells C8:F8. The *column_ref* argument has cell B4, for which there are alternate values in cells B9:B17.

The process substitutes the original values with those in B9:B17 and C8:F8 to generate the projection.

As the data table uses an array formula, you can't delete only some of the values in the array. To delete the generated data in the table, select all values in cells C9:F17 and select the **Delete** key.

Scenario Manager

Another tool provided by Excel that you can use to create a What-If Analysis is the Scenario Manager. The Scenario Manager enables you to create different scenarios where certain input values are changed to produce different results.

You can assign names to the different scenarios in the scenario manager. For example, *Most Likely*, *Best Case*, and *Worst Case*. Once you've created the scenarios in the Scenario Manager, you can view the different scenarios in your worksheet. You can also generate a summary report with all the scenarios to compare them side-by-side.

Adding Scenarios

In the following example, we will create projections for the next year based on figures from the current year. The scenarios will apply different growth rates to the current figures so that we can compare the scenarios together in a summary report.

Figures – Current Year
- Sales: $627,198.00
- Cost of production: $200,000
- Office supplies: $5,000
- Vehicle: $10,500.00
- Building: $50,000.00

C4		⌄	⋮	✕ ✓ f_x	=B4+(B4*D4)	

◢	A	B	C	D
1	**Projection Scenarios**			
2				
3		Current	Projected	Growth assumptions
4	Sales	$627,198.00	$639,741.96	2.00%
5	Cost of production	($200,000.00)	($203,000.00)	1.50%
6	Office supplies	($5,000.00)	($5,075.00)	1.50%
7	Vehicle	($10,500.00)	($10,657.50)	1.50%
8	Building	($50,000.00)	($50,750.00)	1.50%
9	Profit	$361,698.00	$370,259.46	
10				

The projected value in C4 is calculated with the following formula:

=B4+(B4*D4)

The formula under **Projected** increments the current value by the growth assumption (percentage rate). The same formula is used to derive the values in cells C5:C8.

We want to create more scenarios using different growth assumptions without overwriting the original data, as we want to compare multiple scenarios. The Scenario Manager comes in handy for scenarios like this.

🔅Tip
When using the Scenario Manager, it is a good idea to name each cell you intend to change. It makes it easier to know what each cell represents when you enter the new values in a subsequent dialog box. It also makes your subsequent reports of the scenarios easier to understand.

Follow the steps below to create different scenarios with the Scenario Manager:

1. Select the changing cells in the worksheet. In this case, the changing cells are D4:D8.

2. On the **Data** tab, in the **Forecast** group, select **What-If Analysis > Scenario Manager**.

295

Excel opens the **Scenario Manager** dialog box.

3. Click the **Add** button to add a new scenario.

4. Enter a name for the scenario in the **Scenario name** field. These can be names like *Most likely*, *Best case*, *Worst case,* etc.

5. The **Changing cells** box should already have the reference to the cells you selected before opening the Scenario Manager dialog box. However, if the right cells have not been selected, click the Expand Dialog button on the field (up arrow) and select the cells in the worksheet.

6. The **Comment** box is optional. You can enter a short description for the scenario or leave the default text, a log of when it was last updated.

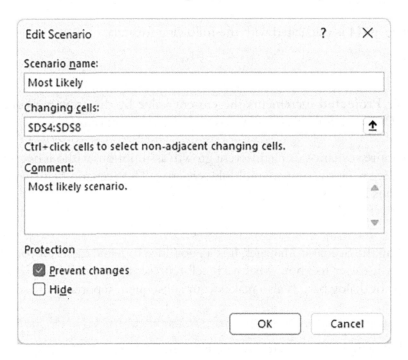

7. In the **Protection** portion of the screen, accept the default selection for the **Prevent changes** checkbox. This setting means Excel protects the scenario from changes when worksheet protection is turned on. If you don't want to protect the scenario when the worksheet is protected, uncheck Prevent changes.

8. Leave the **Hide** checkbox unselected if you don't want the scenario hidden when worksheet protection is on. Alternatively, select the Hide checkbox if you want Excel to hide the scenario when the worksheet is protected.

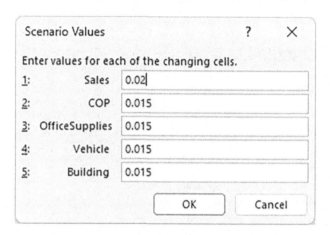 **Note** Worksheet protection is a separate topic not related to What-If Analysis and is covered elsewhere in this book.

---

9. Click **OK** to open the **Scenario Values** dialog box.

Scenario Values		? ☒
Enter values for each of the changing cells.		
1:	Sales	0.02
2:	COP	0.015
3:	OfficeSupplies	0.015
4:	Vehicle	0.015
5:	Building	0.015
	OK	Cancel

10. The Scenario Values dialog box contains several boxes for the changing cells. As shown in the image above, naming the changing cells becomes useful here as each box is labeled with a cell name rather than a cell reference.

   For the first scenario, you may want to accept the values already in the text box (if you had values in the cells before starting the Scenario Manager). If you want a different set of values for your first scenario, you can change them here.

11. When done, click the **Add** button to save the scenario and return to the **Add Scenario** dialog box.

12. Repeat steps **4** to **11** above to add the other scenarios you want to create.

13. When you're done, close the Scenario Values dialog box and return to the Scenario Manager.

Viewing and Editing Scenarios

1. Open the Scenario Manager dialog box if it's not already open (**Data** > **Forecast** >**What-If Analysis** > **Scenario Manager)**.

    In the Scenario Manager dialog box, you'll see the names of all the scenarios you've added under **Scenarios**.

2. To view a scenario, select its name under **Scenarios** and click the **Show** button.

    You can also double-click a scenario name to view it in the worksheet. For example, double-click *Best Case* in the **Scenarios** box to display the *Best Case* scenario.

    Excel closes the Scenario Manager dialog box and inserts the rates entered for the *Best Case* scenario in our table.

3. To delete a scenario, select it and click **Delete**. Excel removes that scenario from the Scenario Manager.

4. To edit a scenario, select the scenario under **Scenarios** and click **Edit**. Excel takes you through the editing process, where you can change the name of the scenario, the changing cells, and the values for the cells. If you only want to change the values, click through to the **Scenario Values** dialog box and change the values there.

Merging Scenarios

The Scenario Manager dialog box also enables you to merge scenarios from other Excel workbooks that are open. Note that the workbooks must share the same data layout and changing cells for you to merge their scenarios.

To merge scenarios from another workbook, do the following:

1. Click the **Merge** button in the Scenario Manager dialog box. Excel displays the **Merge Scenarios** dialog box.

2. Select the workbook name from the **Book** dropdown list box.

3. In the **Sheet** box, select the worksheet and then click **OK**.

All the scenarios in that worksheet are then copied and merged with the current worksheet.

Summary Reports

After creating the different scenarios, you can compare them in a summary report.

To generate a summary report for the scenarios you have entered:

1. In the **Scenario Manager** dialog box, click the **Summary** button.

    Excel opens the **Scenario Summary** dialog box.

2. Select **Report type** if it is not already selected.

3. Click the **Results cells** text box and select the result cells in your worksheet. These would be the cells with the totals for your projection. For our example, our **Profit** cell is C9.

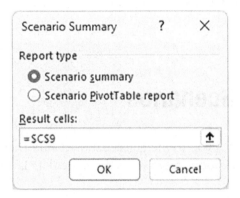

4. Click **OK** to generate the report.

Excel will generate a report in a separate worksheet showing all the scenarios you have created.

Scenario Summary				
	Current Values:	Most Likely	Best Case	Worst Case
Changing Cells:				
Sales	2.00%	2.00%	5.00%	1.00%
COP	1.50%	1.50%	1.00%	8.00%
OfficeSupplies	1.50%	1.50%	1.00%	2.50%
Vehicle	1.50%	1.50%	1.00%	5.00%
Building	1.50%	1.50%	1.20%	5.00%
Result Cells:				
Profit	$370,259.46	$370,259.46	$390,302.90	$348,819.98

Notes: Current Values column represents values of changing cells at time Scenario Summary Report was created. Changing cells for each scenario are highlighted in gray.

As you can see from the image above, assigning names to the changing cells and result cells in your worksheet comes in handy when generating a scenario summary.

You may wonder why we need to use the scenario manager when we could have just entered the different scenarios directly in the Excel worksheet area. The example used here with the scenario manager is simple for demonstration purposes only. However, the scenario manager comes in handy when the complexity of the data model makes it difficult to enter the different scenarios side-by-side in Excel in a meaningful way.

Goal Seeking

On some occasions, when working with data in Excel, you already have the outcome you want to achieve in mind, and you would like to know the various input values that will achieve that outcome or goal. For example, you may have a goal of $600,000 in revenue, and to achieve that goal, you need a certain amount for your sales against the cost of expenses. This kind of scenario is where the Goal Seek feature in Excel comes in handy.

The **Goal Seek** command in Excel enables you to set a goal in one cell and then choose the cell whose value you would like Excel to adjust in other to meet your goal. So, this is like working backward, stating the results first and allowing Goal Seek to determine the inputs needed to meet that goal. The goal cell will have a formula based on the input from other cells, including the cell that Excel will change.

For example, let's say we want to find how much sales we need to generate to reach a certain income level. Instead of making several adjustments to the sales figure to produce the desired result, we can simply set the desired result and let Goal Seek work out the sales figure required to achieve the result.

Example

To demonstrate the Goal Seek feature in Excel, we'll use an example to forecast the income based on a range of input values.

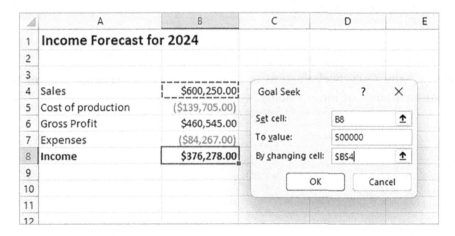

	A	B	C
1	**Income Forecast for 2024**		
2			
3			
4	Sales	$600,250.00	
5	Cost of production	($139,705.00)	
6	Gross Profit	$460,545.00	
7	Expenses	($84,267.00)	
8	Income	$376,278.00	
9			

In the table above, cell **B8** has a formula that calculates the *Income*, which is the sum of the *Gross Profit* and the *Expenses* (this is a negative value as indicated by brackets).

=B6+B7

Our goal-seeking question is:

What amount should our sales be if we want to generate an income of $500,000?

Once the figures have been entered in the worksheet, follow the steps below to perform the goal-seeking:

1. On the **Data** tab, in the **Forecast** group, select **What-If Analysis** > **Goal Seek**.

   Excel displays the **Goal Seek** dialog box.

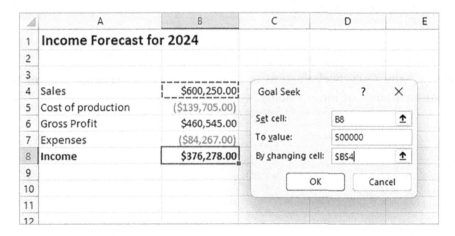

2. Click in the **Set cell** box and select the cell in the worksheet that contains the formula that will return the value you're seeking. For our example, this is cell **B8**.

3. In the **To value** box, enter the goal value. For our example, the value will be 500,000.

4. Click in the **By changing cell** box and select the cell that contains the value you want Excel to adjust to achieve the goal. For this example, this will be cell **B4**.

5. Click **OK**.

Excel displays the **Goal Seek Status** dialog box, which informs you that a solution has been found and that the result value is now the same as the target value.

◢	A	B	C	D	E
1	**Income Forecast for 2024**				
2					
3					
4	Sales	$723,972.00	Goal Seek Status	?	X
5	Cost of production	($139,705.00)			
6	Gross Profit	$584,267.00	Goal Seeking with Cell B8	Step	
7	Expenses	($84,267.00)	found a solution.		
8	Income	$500,000.00	Target value: 500000	Pause	
9			Current value: $500,000.00		
10				OK	Cancel
11					
12					

If the Goal Seek does not find a solution, it will enable the **Step** and **Pause** buttons to enable you to step through different options to find a solution.

6. Click **OK** to accept this result, or click **Cancel** if you don't want to keep the result.

Excel will overwrite your existing values if you click OK to accept the value.

If you want to return to the previous values, you can undo the change by clicking the **Undo** button on the **Home** tab or selecting Ctrl+Z on your keyboard.

To switch back and forth between the previous value and the new value returned by Goal Seek, use the **Undo** and **Redo** buttons on the Home tab. Alternatively, you can select Ctrl+Z to display the original values and Ctrl+Y to display the Goal Seek values.

Using The Solver for Complex Problems

The Data Table and Goal Seek commands are great for creating What-If Analysis solutions for simpler problems requiring a direct relationship between the inputs and the outputs. However, for more complex problems, Excel provides another tool, which is the **Solver** add-in utility.

The Solver can be used when you create a solution that requires changing multiple input values in your model. The Solver also enables you to impose constraints on the input and output values.

The Solver uses an iterative method to find the optimum solution based on the inputs, the desired result, and the constraints you have set.

Complex problems can have different ways they're solved, and the Solver tries to present the best solution for you. Sometimes, the solution returned may not be the best for your situation. For example, suppose several variables need to be changed. In that case, the Solver may produce a combination of figures that may not suit your specific needs (even if the result meets the objective). Hence, you may want to run the Solver multiple times to get the best solution.

To set up the problem in the Solver, you will need to define the following items:

- **Objective cell**: The target cell that you can set to maximum, minimum, or a specific value. The objective cell needs to be a formula.

- **Variable cells**: These are the changing cells in your worksheet. The Goal Seek method, for example, enables you to only specify one cell that can be changed. The difference with the Solver is that you can have multiple cells that can be changed to achieve the objective.

- **Constraints**: The cells containing the values you want to use to set a limit or restriction to the range of changes that can be made. For instance, you could set a constraint that says the *Sales* figure cannot be increased by more than 10% to achieve the solution (perhaps because a sales figure of more than 10% would be unrealistic for this particular problem).

After setting the parameters in the Solver, Excel returns the optimum solution by changing the values in your worksheet. At this point, you can retain the changes in your worksheet or restore your original values. The Solver also enables you to save the solution as a scenario you can view later.

The Solver can be used with the Scenario Manager to set up a problem to solve. The variable cells you define when you use the Scenario Manager to set up a scenario are available and picked up by the Solver. The Solver also allows you to save solutions as scenarios which will then be available to the Scenario Manager.

Enabling the Solver Add-in

The Solver is an add-in and may not be available on your ribbon if it hasn't been manually added, as it is not added by the default Excel installation.

Follow the steps below to add the Solver command button to your Excel ribbon:

1. Select **File** > **Options** > **Add-ins**.
2. At the bottom of the Add-ins tab, ensure that the **Manage** dropdown list has **Excel Add-ins** selected.
3. Click **Go**.
4. Select the **Solver Add-in** option in the **Add-ins** dialog and click **OK**.

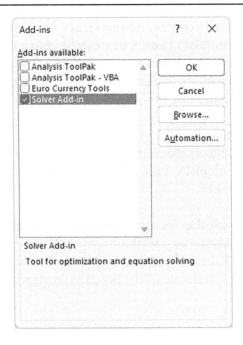

The **Solver** command button can be found on the **Data** tab in the **Analyze** group.

Solver Example

In the following example, we will use the Solver to find a solution to what combination of figures can generate an income of $680,500.00. The worksheet model created for the problem is shown below.

C4			f_x	=$B$4+($B$4*SalesGrowth)	

	A	B	C	D
1	Sales Forecast			
2				
3		Qtr 1	Qtr 2	Assumptions
4	Sales	$800,250.40	$840,262.92	5%
5	Cost of production	($139,705.00)	($148,087.30)	6%
6	Gross Profit	$660,545.40	$692,175.62	
7	Expenses	($84,267.00)	($90,165.69)	7%
8	Income	$576,278.40	$602,009.93	
9				

The value in C4 is calculated with the following formula:

=$B$4+($B$4*SalesGrowth)

SalesGrowth is the name given to cell **D4,** which is currently 5%. The formulas in the **Qtr 2** column simply increment the **Qtr 1** values by the growth rates under **Assumptions**.

For this example, the changing/variable cells will be those in the Assumptions column, while the result/objective cell will be **C8** (which is named **Income_Qtr2**).

Once you have loaded the Solver add-in and created your worksheet model, follow the steps below to define a problem with the Solver:

1. On the **Data** tab, in the **Analyze** group, click the **Solver** command button.

    Excel opens the **Solver Parameters** dialog box.

2. In the **Solver Parameters** dialog box, the **Set Objective** box is the result you want to achieve. Enter a reference to a cell on the worksheet with a formula. Click in the **Set Objective** box and select the cell on your worksheet.

    For our example, this is cell **C8** on the worksheet. The name of the cell is **Income_Qtr2**, so the name is inserted in the text box.

3. You can set the Objective to the following options:

    ▪   **Max**: As large as possible based on the input values available.

- **Min**: As small as possible.
- **Value Of**: A specific value.

For this example, we are using a specific value for our objective. Select **Value Of** and enter 680500.

4. Click the **By Changing Variable Cells** text box and select the cells you want to change in the worksheet.

   To select non-adjacent cells, hold down the **Ctrl** key while clicking the cells. Excel will enter cell names in place of cell references if they have been named.

5. In the **Subject to the Constraints** box, you can add constraints to limit the changes the Solver can make. To add a constraint, click the **Add** button.

   Excel displays the **Add Constraint** dialog box.

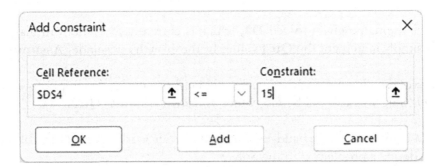

6. In the **Add Constraints** dialog box, click in the **Cell Reference** box, then select the cell on the worksheet for which you want to create a constraint.

   Select the relationship from the dropdown list box in the middle. The options are =, <=, >=, int (for integer), and bin (for binary). For our example, we select <= from the dropdown list.

   In the **Constraint** box, enter the constraint. For this example, we don't want the *SalesGrowth* to be more than 15%, so we enter 15%.

   Click **Add** to insert the constraint and continue adding more constraints (or click **OK** to return to the Solver Parameters dialog box if you're done).

The constraint you added will now be listed in the **Subject to the Constraints** box.

7. For our example, we'll leave the **Make Unconstrained Variables Non-Negative** checkbox selected, which is the default. Clear this checkbox if you want to allow negative values in variable cells for which you've set no constraints.

8. The default value for the **Select a Solving Method** dropdown list will have the default value is **GRG Nonlinear**.

   There are three solving methods:

   - **GRG Nonlinear** is for solving smooth nonlinear problems.

   - **Simplex LP** method is for linear problems.

   - **Evolutionary** method is for non-smooth problems.

   Accept the GRG Nonlinear default, unless you're sure one of the other methods is more optimal for your problem. Excel displays a brief description of the solving methods in the label below the dropdown list box.

9. After entering all the parameters in the Solver Parameters dialog box, click the **Solve** button.

Solver Results

When you click **Solve** on the Solver Parameters dialog box, the box will disappear. Depending on your problem's complexity, you may see an indicator on Excel's status bar informing you of the progress of the Solver. On most occasions, however, the solution would be generated quickly, and Excel will display the **Solver Results** dialog box.

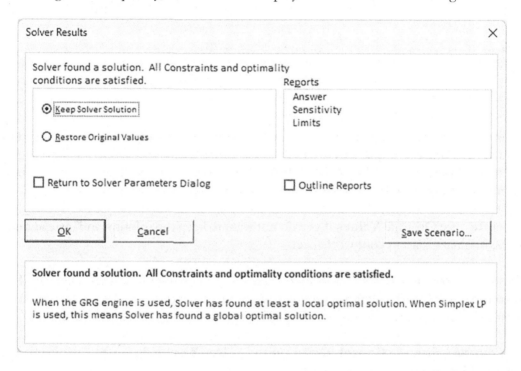

The **Solver Results** dialog box informs you whether a solution was found for your problem. If a solution is not found, the dialog box will inform you that a solution cannot be found, and you will have the opportunity to go back and adjust the parameters.

The Solver will display the new values in your worksheet if a solution is found. However, the Solver Results dialog box will allow you to keep the values provided by the solution or restore your original values.

To keep the solution, select **Keep Solver Solution** (if it is not already selected), and click **OK**.

	A	B	C	D	E
1	**Sales Forecast**				
2					
3		Qtr 1	Qtr 2	Assumptions	
4	Sales	$800,250.40	$915,620.72	14%	
5	Cost of production	($139,705.00)	($145,790.62)	4%	
6	Gross Profit	$660,545.40	$769,830.10		
7	Expenses	($84,267.00)	($89,330.10)	6%	
8	Income	$576,278.40	$680,500.00		
9					
10					
11					
12					

From the worksheet model in the image above, you can see that the Solver changed the growth percentages for *Sales* (14%), *Cost of Production* (4%), and *Expenses* (6%) to achieve the target *Income* for *Qtr 2* of $680,500.00. You may also notice that the Solver stayed within the 15% constraint set for the *SalesGrowth* cell.

Select **Restore Original Values** if you do not want to keep the solution and instead return to the original values in your worksheet.

To save the solution as a scenario before restoring your original values, click the **Save Scenario** button and assign a name to it. Once you have saved it, you can select the Restore Original Values option and click **OK** to close the Solver Results dialog box.

You can also click the **Cancel** button on the Solver Results dialog box to dismiss the Solver and return your original values.

Note If you keep the solution provided by the Solver, unlike the Goal Seek command, you can't undo the changes by clicking the Undo command on the Quick Access Toolbar. If you want to retain your original values, select **Restore Original Values,** and then click **Save Scenario** to save the scenario for later viewing. That way, you can keep your original values in the worksheet and use the Scenario Manager (covered previously in this chapter) to display the solution generated by the Solver.

Solver Options

The default options used by the Solver are adequate for most problems. However, for some scenarios, you may want to change the options before generating a solution with the Solver.

To change the Solver options, click the **Options** button in the Solver Parameters dialog box.

Excel opens the **Options** dialog box with three tabs: All Methods, GRG Nonlinear, and Evolutionary.

Options	?	×

All Methods | GRG Nonlinear | Evolutionary

Constraint Precision: 0.000001

☐ Use Automatic Scaling

☐ Show Iteration Results

Solving with Integer Constraints

☐ Ignore Integer Constraints

Integer Optimality (%):   1

Solving Limits

Max Time (Seconds):

Iterations:

Evolutionary and Integer Constraints:

Max Subproblems:

Max Feasible Solutions:

OK   Cancel

The following settings apply to the Solver options:

- **Constraint Precision**: This specifies the precision of the constraints added. To satisfy a constraint, the relationship between the cell reference and the value of the constraint cannot be more than this amount. The smaller this number is, the higher the precision.

- **Use Automatic Scaling**: Select this option if you want the Solver to automatically scale the results.

- **Show Iteration Results**: Select this option if you want the Solver to show the results for the iterations it followed in solving the problem.

- **Ignore Integer Constraints**: Select this checkbox if you want the Solver to ignore any specified constraints that use integers.

- **Integer Optimality (%)**: This option specifies the percentage of Integer Optimality the Solver applies when solving the problem.

- **Max Time (Seconds)**: Specifies the maximum number of seconds that you want the Solver to spend in finding a solution before it times out.

- **Iterations**: This value specifies the maximum number of iterations you want the Solver to make in recalculating the worksheet when finding the solution.

- **Max Subproblems**: Specifies the maximum number of subproblems you want the Solver to take when using the Evolutionary method to solve the problem.

- **Max Feasible Solutions**: This value specifies the maximum number of feasible solutions you want the Solver to pursue when using the Evolutionary method to solve the problem.

Note that the Options dialog box also has the **GRG Nonlinear** and **Evolutionary** tabs where you can make additional changes to the settings.

After making changes to the Solver options, click **OK** to return to the Solver Parameters dialog box.

Tip Only change to an option in the Solver if you understand what that setting represents and how the change will affect your worksheet model. Otherwise, the default values will suffice for most Solver problems.

Saving Solver Problem Models

When you save your workbook, the objective cell, variable cells, constraint, and Solver options that were last entered in the Solver Parameters dialog box are saved as part of the worksheet. These parameters will be loaded in the Solver Parameters dialog box the next time it is opened.

When you create other problem models for the worksheet you want to save, you must use the **Load/Save** button in the **Solver Parameters** dialog box to save them.

To save an additional Solver model, do the following:

1. In the **Solver Parameters** dialog box, click the **Load/Save** button.

   Excel displays the **Load/Save Model** dialog box.

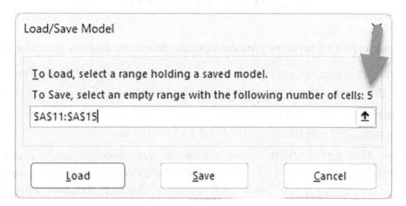

2. On the **Load/Save** dialog, click in the text box and select an empty vertical range in your worksheet with enough cells to hold all the parameters you entered for the problem model. The text above in the text box will tell you how many cells you need to select.

315

3. Click **Save** after entering the range in the text box.

    Excel saves the values to that range in your worksheet.

Loading a Saved Solver Model

To load a saved Solver model, do the following:

1. In the **Solver Parameters** dialog box, click the **Load/Save** button.

    Excel displays the **Load/Save Model** dialog box.

2. In the **Load/Save** dialog box, click inside the text box, and then select the range in your worksheet with the saved model. For example, A11:A15.

3. Click **Load**. Excel loads the parameters saved in the selected range in the Solver Parameters dialog box.

Solver Reports

There are three types of reports you can create from the Solver Results dialog box:

- **Answer**: This report lists the result and the variable cells with their original values, final values, and any constraints used as parameters.
- **Sensitivity**: This report shows how sensitive an optimal solution is to changes in the formulas behind the objective cell and constraints.
- **Limits**: This report displays the values for the objective and variable cells, the lower and upper limits, and the results. The lower limit is the lowest value the variable cells can have while still meeting the constraints. The upper limit represents the highest value that will do this.

To generate a report, in the Solver Results dialog box, select one or more of the reports in the **Reports** list box before clicking **OK**.

You can generate one or all of the reports, as the Reports list box allows you to select more than one item on the list. When you click **OK**, Excel will generate the selected reports in separate worksheets, adding them to the beginning of the workbook.

Chapter 7

Analyze Data Dynamically with PivotTables and PivotCharts

This chapter will cover the following:

- Creating PivotTables with the Quick Analysis tool.

- Creating a Recommended PivotTable.

- Manually creating a PivotTable.

- Filtering, sorting, and formatting PivotTables.

- Creating a PivotChart.

There are different ways you can create pivot tables in Excel. We will focus here on the different methods you can use to create PivotTables, including how to generate pivot charts from the pivoted data. An Excel PivotTable is a powerful tool that lets you dynamically summarize, calculate, and analyze large data sets from different perspectives.

There are several methods for creating a new PivotTable in Excel:

- **Quick Analysis tool**: This option auto-generates a PivotTable for you. When you select all the cells in your data list and click the Quick Analysis tool on the Tables tab, you get a list of pre-designed PivotTables for your data from which you can select. When you select one, Excel inserts the PivotTable in a new worksheet.

- **Recommended PivotTables button**: This option auto-generates a PivotTable for you. When you select one cell in your data list and click the Recommended PivotTables button on the Insert tab, you get a list of recommended PivotTables from which you can select. When you select one, Excel inserts the PivotTable in a new worksheet.

- **PivotTable button**: This option enables you to create a PivotTable manually. When you select one cell in your data list and click the PivotTable button on the Insert tab, Excel opens the Create PivotTable dialog box where you specify your data source and location of the PivotTable before manually selecting the fields to use from the data.

Preparing Your Data

Some preparation is required to get a data list ready for a PivotTable. The source data used for a PivotTable needs to be organized as a list or converted to an Excel table (this is recommended, although not essential).

A few steps to prepare the source data for a PivotTable:

1. The data should have column headings in a single row on top.

2. Remove any temporary totals or summaries not part of the core data.

3. The data cannot have empty rows. So, delete any empty rows.

4. Ensure you do not have any extraneous data surrounding the list.

5. You may also want to convert the range to an Excel table (but this is optional).

Once the data has been prepared, you can now create a PivotTable.

Creating a PivotTable with the Quick Analysis Tool

Using the Quick Analysis tool, you can quickly create a pivot table for your data list in Excel. If you're not that familiar with creating PivotTables, but you have an idea of want you want to summarize, the Quick Analysis tool will recommend a series of pre-designed options from which you can choose.

Follow the steps below to create a PivotTable from the Quick Analysis tool:

1. Select all the data in your data list (including the headings).

    If you have assigned a range name to your data list, you can select the whole list by selecting the name from the Name box dropdown menu.

2. The Quick Analysis tool appears on the lower right of the selection. Click the **Quick Analysis** tool to open the Quick Analysis palette.

3. Click the **Tables** tab to display various PivotTable options for your data.

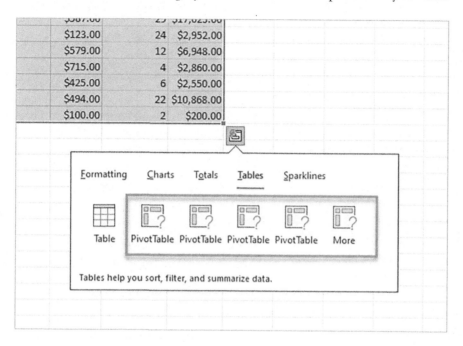

4. To see a preview of each PivotTable option, hover over each button. Excel displays a live preview of the type of PivotTable that option will generate (with your data).

5. View previews to identify the option you want, then click its button to generate. For this example, we've selected the second PivotTable option to generate a PivotTable where **Total Cost** is summed for each **Employee**.

Excel generates the PivotTable in a new worksheet (inserted in front of the worksheet with the source data). You can rename and move this worksheet to a different part of your workbook.

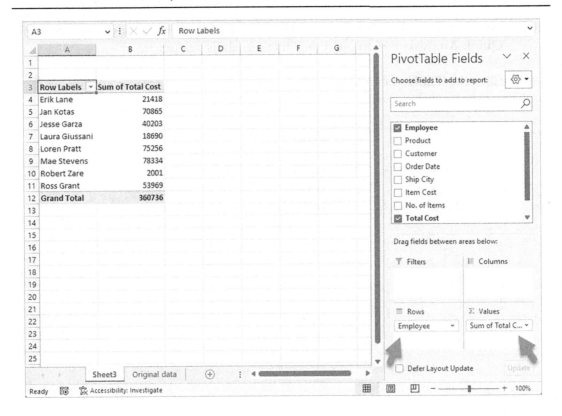

Remarks:

- When you select any area in the new PivotTable, Excel displays the **PivotTable Fields** pane on the right side of the worksheet window. The **PivotTable Analyze** and **Design** contextual tabs are also displayed on the ribbon. These contextual tabs provide several tools and commands for modifying and formatting the PivotTable, just as you would if you had created it manually.

- On some occasions, Excel may not be able to suggest PivotTable options with the Data Analysis tool, particularly if it can't analyze the data due to how it is structured. When this happens, on the Tables tab of the Quick Analysis palette, a single blank PivotTable button will be displayed after the Table button. You can click that button to manually create your PivotTable. We will cover how to manually create a PivotTable later in this chapter.

Creating a Recommended PivotTable

Another way to create a pivot table is by using the **Recommended PivotTables** command on the ribbon. This method is even faster than using the Quick Analysis tool (as long as you have prepared the data list with column headings as described earlier in this chapter).

Follow the steps below to use this method to create a PivotTable:

1. Click anywhere within the data list for which you want to create a new PivotTable.

2. On the **Insert** tab, in the **Tables** group, click the **Recommended PivotTables** button.

Excel displays the **Recommended PivotTables** pane on the right side of the window with several PivotTable options for your data. Scroll down the list to view all recommended PivotTable options.

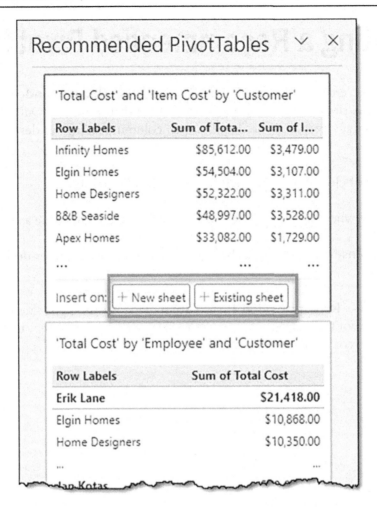

3. After identifying a PivotTable you want from the recommended list, do one of the following:

    - Select the **New sheet** button to create the PivotTable in a new worksheet in the current workbook.

    Or

    - Select the **Existing sheet** button to add the PivotTable to the current worksheet. Excel will prompt you to select where the PivotTable should be placed in the current sheet.

4. Clear the fields in the **PivotTable Fields** pane that you don't want to include in the summary. In the example below, the **Item Cost** field was cleared so that the PivotTable only showed the sum of Total Cost per Customer.

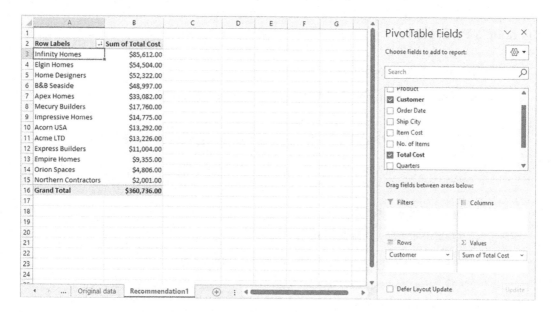

When you select the PivotTable on the worksheet, Excel displays the **PivotTable Fields** pane on the right side of the window and the **PivotTable Analyze** and **Design** contextual tabs on the ribbon.

If none of the Recommended PivotTables are suitable for your requirements, create the PivotTable manually.

Creating a PivotTable Manually

To create a PivotTable:

1. Select any cell in your range or table.

2. On the **Insert** tab, in the **Tables** group, click the **PivotTable** button.

   Excel displays the **PivotTable from table or range** dialog box.

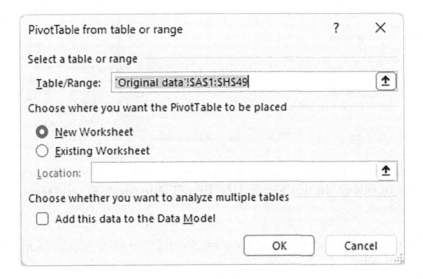

3. **Select the table/range**: Excel will attempt to figure out the table or range you want to use for your PivotTable and insert the reference in the **Table/Range** box. If this is inaccurate, you can manually select the range by clicking the Expand Dialog button (up arrow) on the box.

4. Select where you want to place the PivotTable. The default location is in a new worksheet. Having your PivotTable on a separate worksheet from your source data is best. Thus, select the **New Worksheet** option if it's not already selected.

5. Click **OK**.

Excel creates a new worksheet with a PivotTable placeholder in the worksheet area and the PivotTable Fields pane on the right side of the window.

Selecting PivotTable Fields

The PivotTable Fields pane has four areas where you can place fields:

- **Filters**: The fields added here act as filters at the top of the report that enable you to display values in the PivotTable based on different criteria.

- **Columns**: The fields placed in this area are displayed as column labels in the PivotTable.

- **Rows**: The fields placed in this area become row labels (or row headings) of the PivotTable.

- **Values**: These fields are aggregated as numeric values in the PivotTable.

To add a field to your PivotTable, select the checkbox next to the field name in the PivotTable Fields pane. When you select fields, they are added to their default areas. Non-numeric fields are added to the **Rows** area. Date and time fields are added to the **Columns** area. Numeric fields are added to the **Values** area.

You can also drag fields from the list to one of the four areas. To move a field from one area to another, you can drag it there.

To remove a field from an area, click the dropdown arrow on the field and select **Remove Field** on the shortcut menu. You can also clear the checkbox for the field in the fields list or drag it out of the box and drop it back on the fields list.

Example

In this example, let's say we want a summary of our data that shows the total spent by each Customer.

Do the following to add fields to the PivotTable placeholder generated previously:

1. Select the **Customer** field on the list to add it to the **Rows** box. The PivotTable will also be updated with the list of customers as row headings.

2. Select the **Total Cost** field to add it to the **Values** box.

The PivotTable will now be updated with the **Sum of Total Cost** for each Customer.

Row Labels	Sum of Total Cost
Acme LTD	13226
Acorn USA	13292
Apex Homes	33082
B&B Seaside	48997
Elgin Homes	54504
Empire Homes	9355
Express Builders	11004
Home Designers	52322
Impressive Homes	14775
Infinity Homes	85612
Mecury Builders	17760
Northern Contractors	2001
Orion Spaces	4806
Grand Total	360736

So, as you can see in the image above, we have been able to get a quick summary of our data with just a few clicks. If we had hundreds of thousands of records, this task could have taken many hours to accomplish manually.

We can add more values to the table by dragging them to the **Values** area from the fields list.

For example, to add the total number of items bought per customer, select **No. of Items** on the list or drag it to the **Values** box.

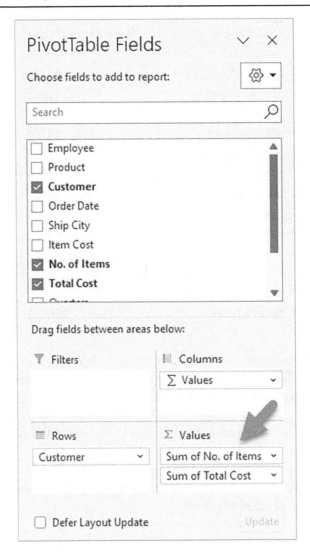

Excel adds the **Sum of No. of Items** for each customer to the PivotTable, as shown in the image below.

The order in which you enter the fields in the Values area affects how Excel organizes the columns in the PivotTable. You can move fields up or down in the Values area by dragging or using the **Move Up/Move Down** commands on the shortcut menu displayed when you select a field in the area.

Row Labels	Sum of No. of Items	Sum of Total Cost
Acme LTD	43	13226
Acorn USA	53	13292
Apex Homes	73	33082
B&B Seaside	88	48997
Elgin Homes	123	54504
Empire Homes	40	9355
Express Builders	14	11004
Home Designers	94	52322
Impressive Homes	31	14775
Infinity Homes	143	85612
Mecury Builders	52	17760
Northern Contractors	7	2001
Orion Spaces	33	4806
Grand Total	**794**	**360736**

To view the summary from the perspective of **Products**, i.e., the total number of items sold and the total cost for each product, drag the **Product** field to the Rows area and then drag both **Total Cost** and **No. of Items** in the **Values** area.

To view the summary from the perspective of **Employees**, place **Employee** in the Rows box, and **No. of Items** and **Total Cost** in the Values box.

Here we see the data summarized by Employee, i.e., how many items each employee sold and the revenue generated.

Row Labels	Sum of No. of Items	Sum of Total Cost
Erik Lane	40	21418
Jan Kotas	110	70865
Jesse Garza	105	40203
Laura Giussani	26	18690
Loren Pratt	181	75256
Mae Stevens	176	78334
Robert Zare	7	2001
Ross Grant	149	53969
Grand Total	794	360736

To see the number of items sold per city, place **Ship City** in the Rows area and **No. of Items** in the Values area.

	Row Labels	Sum of No. of Items
3		
4	Boise	40
5	Chicago	106
6	Denver	45
7	Las Vegas	95
8	Los Angeles	43
9	Memphis	53
10	Miami	44
11	Milwaukee	94
12	New York	93
13	Portland	143
14	Salt Lake City	7
15	Seattle	31
16	Grand Total	794
17		

Summarizing Data by Date

To display the columns split into years, drag a date field into the Columns area, for example, Order Date. The PivotTable tool will automatically generate PivotTable fields for Quarters and Years. Once these fields have been generated, remove the Order Date field from the Columns area. Then drag the Quarter or Year field into the Columns area (depending on which one you want to use for your summary).

To display the row headings by date, place **Order Date** (or your date field) in the Rows area.

Excel displays the following results.

Sum of Total Cost	Column Labels		
Row Labels	**2022**	**2023**	**Grand Total**
Jan	39569	7772	47341
Feb		22819	22819
Mar	5502	1854	7356
Apr	22724	57618	80342
May	3105	14510	17615
Jun	24021	596	24617
Jul	16060		16060
Aug	316	12141	12457
Sep	42763	9615	52378
Oct	16752		16752
Nov	34347	9756	44103
Dec	18896		18896
Grand Total	**224055**	**136681**	**360736**

As you can see, we can dynamically change how we want to view our data with just a few clicks.

Applying Formatting

You can apply formatting to the appropriate columns when you're happy with your summary. For example, to change values in the report to the Currency format, select the cells in the report and apply the **Currency** format (**Home > Numbers > Currency**).

The good thing about PivotTables is that you can explore different types of summaries with the PivotTable without changing the source data. If you make a mistake that you can't figure out how to undo, you can simply delete the PivotTable worksheet and recreate it in a new worksheet.

Filtering and Sorting PivotTables

Sometimes, you may want to limit what is displayed in a PivotTable. You can sort and filter a PivotTable similar to a range or table.

Filtering a PivotTable with Slicers

An Excel Slicer is a graphical tool for filtering the data in your PivotTable. A Slicer gives you a visual indication of which items are displayed or hidden in your PivotTable.

Instead of filtering the data using the AutoFilter buttons attached to row and column labels, you can use slicers, which offer a better visual representation. Slicers are floating objects on the worksheet which can be moved around. You can insert multiple slicers to filter a PivotTable using multiple fields.

To filter your PivotTable with a slicer, select any field in the PivotTable to display the PivotTable Analyze contextual tab. On the ribbon, click the **PivotTable Analyze** tab, and in the Filter group, select **Insert Slicer**.

Excel displays the **Insert Slicers** dialog box listing all the fields you can use to filter the PivotTable.

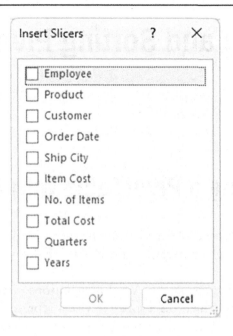

In the Insert Slicers dialog box, select the fields for which you want to display a slicer and click **OK**. Excel adds a slicer for each selected field in the worksheet.

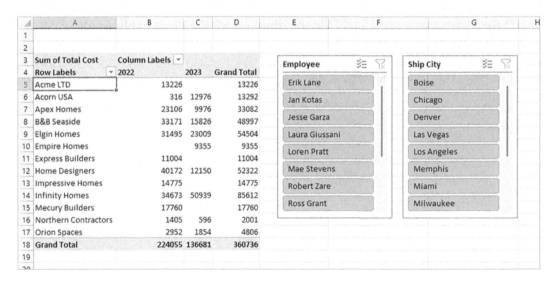

A slicer displays the values from the PivotTable field it represents. When you select a value in a slicer, the other values are deselected, indicating which value is used to filter the PivotTable. You can toggle selected values on or off by clicking them again. The values deselected or greyed out do not appear in the PivotTable.

To select multiple items, hold down the Ctrl key as you click the values in the slicer. To select multiple values in sequence, select the first value, hold down the Shift key, and select the last value. Excel selects the two values and all values between them.

You can also select multiple items by enabling the **Multi-Select** button on the slicer's title bar. With Multi-Select enabled, Excel adds additional selections to the filter instead of replacing the original selection. To clear the filter, click the **Clear Filter** button on the slicer's title bar.

As you select values in the slicer, Excel displays the filtered PivotTable in real time, only showing list entries associated with the selected value(s) in the slicer. In the example below, the PivotTable was filtered to only show customer orders processed by employee Erik Lane.

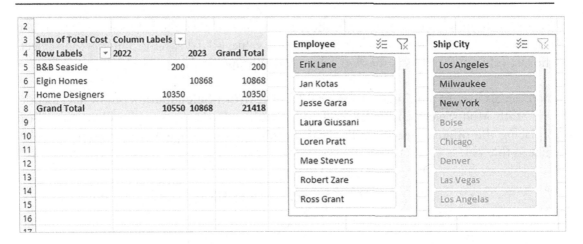

When you've finished filtering the values, you can clear the slicer filter and delete the slicer from the worksheet.

💡-Tip To change the formatting of a slicer, select the slicer to display the **Slicer** context tab on the Excel ribbon. You can select different styles in the **Slicer Styles** group. In the **Arrange** group, you have commands that enable you to move and arrange groups of slicers.

Applying a Quick Filter with AutoFilter

To apply a quick filter to a PivotTable, do the following:

1. Select the AutoFilter button on the Row Labels header.

   The shortcut menu provides a list of the row headings in your PivotTable. You can select/deselect items on this list to limit the data displayed in the PivotTable.

2. Clear the **Select All** checkbox.

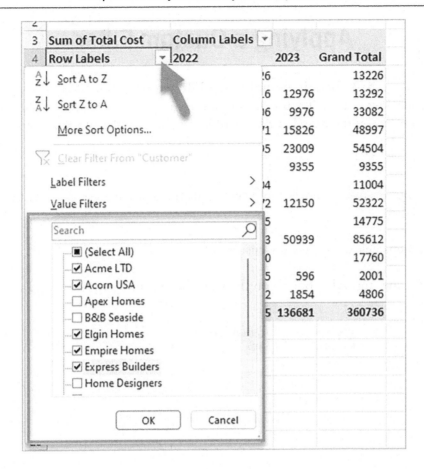

3. Scroll through the list and manually select the items you want to display in the PivotTable.

4. Click **OK**.

The PivotTable will now show only the selected columns.

Excel indicates that a PivotTable is filtered by placing a filter indicator on the AutoFilter of the Row Labels or Column Labels header. There will also be a filter indicator next to the filtered field's name in the PivotTable Fields pane.

Applying a Custom Filter

You can also use the **Label Filters** and **Value Filters** menu commands to apply a custom filter to your PivotTable. To use a conditional expression for your filter, click the AutoFilter button on the Row Labels or Column Labels header of the PivotTable.

Example

Let's say in our example, we want to display only the rows that contain "Homes" as part of the row label.

Follow the steps below to apply the custom filter:

1. Click the AutoFilter button on the Row Labels header of the PivotTable.

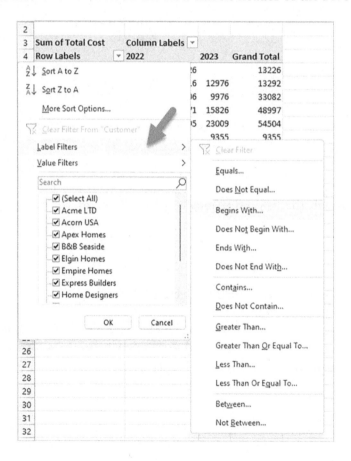

2. On the dropdown menu, select **Label Filter** > **Begins With**.

   Excel displays the Label Filter dialog box.

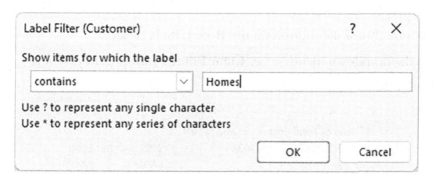

3. Ensure "contains" is selected in the dropdown list box.

4. Enter "Homes in the criteria box.

5. Click **OK**.

Excel applies the filter to the report using the condition you have set.

Sum of Total Cost	Column Labels		
Row Labels	2022	2023	Grand Total
Apex Homes	23106	9976	33082
Elgin Homes	31495	23009	54504
Empire Homes		9355	9355
Impressive Homes	14775		14775
Infinity Homes	34673	50939	85612
Grand Total	104049	93279	197328

Clearing a Filter

To clear a filter, do the following:

1. Click the AutoFilter button on the **Row Labels** header.

2. On the dropdown menu, select **Clear Filter From [*Field Name*]**.

3. Click **OK**.

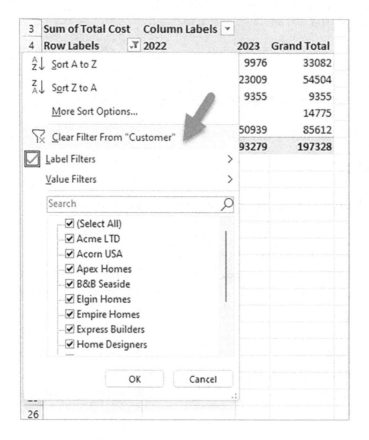

Sorting PivotTable Data

To arrange the order of the data in a PivotTable, use the same sorting methods you would use for a range or table.

1. Click the AutoFilter button on the column named **Row Labels**.

2. On the dropdown menu, select **Sort A to Z** (to sort in ascending order) or **Sort Z to A** (to sort in descending order). If your column headings are dates, you'll get **Sort Oldest to Newest** (for ascending) and **Sort Newest to Oldest** (for descending).

Creating PivotCharts

Another way to present your PivotTable data is by using charts. Book 1 covered creating, editing, and formatting regular Excel charts. Here we will focus on generating charts from PivotTables. A PivotChart in Excel is a chart based on a PivotTable. Hence, instead of manually summarizing your data before creating a regular Excel chart, generate a PivotTable on which your base the chart. This process enables you to create a dynamic chart just like the source PivotTable.

To create a PivotChart from a PivotTable, do the following:

1. Select any cell in the PivotTable. On the **Insert** tab, in the **Charts** group, select **PivotChart**.

   Excel opens the **Insert Chart** dialog box, which allows you to select the type and subtype of the pivot chart you want to create.

2. On the Insert Chart dialog box, select the type and subtype of the chart you want to create and click **OK**.

   Excel inserts an embedded PivotChart in the worksheet with the PivotTable used as the data source.

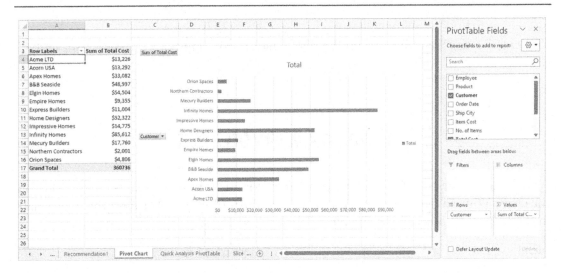

Tip To move the chart around the window, hover over the chart until the mouse pointer changes to a crosshair, then click and drag the chart to any part of the screen you want.

Sorting and Filtering PivotCharts

There are several ways you can sort and filter a PivotChart. You can filter or sort the chart using the source PivotTable or elements on the chart itself.

Sorting Axis Labels

To sort axis labels on the chart, sort the Row Labels header in the source PivotTable:

1. On the PivotTable, click the AutoFilter button on the **Row Labels** header.

2. On the dropdown menu, select **Sort A to Z** (to sort in ascending order) or **Sort Z to A** (to sort in descending order). If axis values are dates, you'll get **Sort Oldest to Newest** (for ascending) and **Sort Newest to Oldest** (for descending).

You can also use Field Buttons on the PivotChart to sort and filter the chart as described below.

Filtering a PivotChart

After generating a new PivotChart, you'll see Axis Field Buttons representing fields on the chart. You can use these dropdown buttons to AutoFilter or AutoSort the PivotChart in the same way you can with the PivotTable.

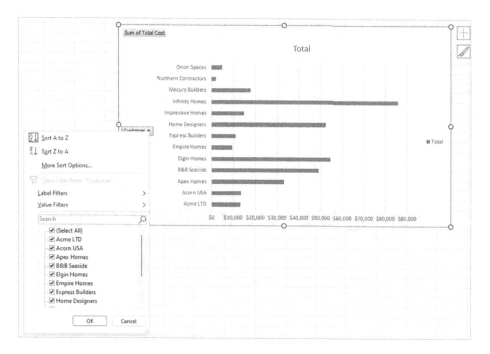

The example above has the **Customer** field button on the chart representing the y-axis labels.

For instance, to exclude some customers from the chart, do the following:

1. Click the **Customer** field button, and on the shortcut menu, clear **Select All**.

2. On the shortcut menu, select the values you want to display in the PivotChart individually.

3. Click **OK**.

Excel filters the PivotChart to only display the selected names.

Note You can also sort the PivotChart using the shortcut menu on an Axis Field Button.

To hide the Field Buttons on the chart, for example, if you want to print the chart without the buttons, do the following:

1. On the ribbon, click the **PivotChart Analyze** tab.

2. In the **Show/Hide** group, click **Field Buttons** (click the button's image rather than its dropdown arrow). You can toggle this button to show or hide the field buttons on the chart.

Customizing a PivotChart

When you select the PivotChart, three additional tabs appear on the ribbon, **PivotChart Analyze**, **Design**, and **Format**. You can use commands on these tabs to modify the format and design of the PivotChart. For example, the **Add Chart Elements** button on the **Design** tab enables you to add or remove elements from the PivotChart. Among many elements, you can add or remove Data Labels, Axis Titles, Gridlines, and a Legend.

Adding Data Labels

To add Data Labels to your PivotChart, do the following:

1. Select the PivotChart to display its related contextual tabs.

2. On the **Design** tab, in the **Chart Layouts** group, select **Add Chart Elements > Data Labels > Outside End**.

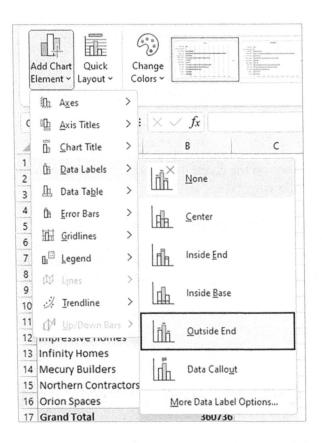

Excel adds data labels to the bars on the chart.

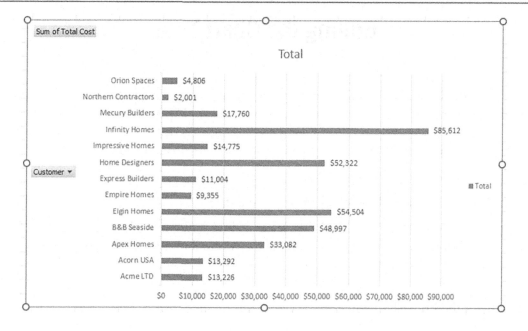

Adding Axis Titles

You can add axis titles to the left and bottom of the chart. The left side is the y-axis, and the bottom is the x-axis.

1. Select the PivotChart to display its related contextual tabs.

2. On the **Design** tab, in the **Chart Layouts** group, select **Axis Titles** > **Primary Vertical**.

Excel adds a title to the y-axis of the chart. You can double-click the label and edit the title.

Editing the Chart Title

To change the Chart Title, you can simply select it and type in the title. Alternatively, you can set the name to a cell reference in your worksheet to display the text in that cell.

To change the chart title to a value in cell A1 of the worksheet, do the following:

1. Enter the text value in cell A1.

2. Select the **Chart Title** element on the chart.

3. In the formula bar, type "=" and select cell A1 in the worksheet area. Excel enters **= 'Pivot Chart'!$A$1** in the formula bar where 'Pivot Chart' represents the name of your worksheet.

The title of the PivotChart will now show the text entered in cell A1.

Quick Chart Layouts

Quick layouts provide several layout options for your chart that add or remove certain chart elements. You can use layout options to reposition the Legend, add Axis Titles, and add Data Labels.

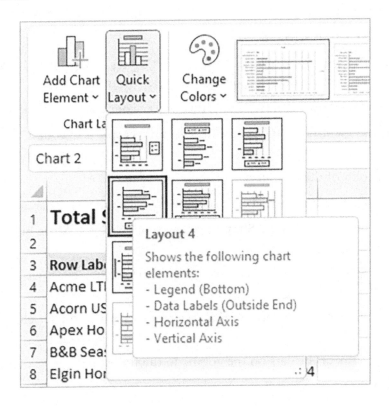

To change the layout of your chart, do the following:

1. Select the chart.

2. On the **Design** tab, in the **Chart Layouts** group, click **Quick Layout**.

3. Select one of the layout options from the gallery. To preview a layout option without selecting it, hover over it, and Excel displays a preview of how your chart will look with that layout option.

Chart Styles

The **Design** tab shows up on the ribbon when you select a PivotChart. On this tab, you have various **Chart Styles** you can choose from to change your chart's overall look and color.

To change your chart style to one of the predefined styles, do the following:

5. Click the chart to select it.

6. On the **Design** contextual tab, in the **Chart Styles** group, click the **More** button (dropdown arrow) and select one of the styles from the gallery.

7. You can hover over each style to preview how your chart will look with that style.

8. When you identify a suitable option, select it to apply it to your chart.

To change the color of the plot area:

5. Click a blank space in the chart's plot area to select the whole area.

6. On the **Format** tab, in the **Shape Styles** group, click the **More** button to expand the styles gallery.

7. Hover over each style to see a preview of what your chart would look like if selected.

8. When you identify a suitable option, select it to apply it to your chart.

To change the colors of the bars on the graph, do the following:

4. Click the chart to select it.

5. On the **Design** tab, in the **Chart Styles** group, click **Change Colors**.

6. You can hover over each color combination on the palette to preview the result on your chart.

7. When you identify an option you want, select it to apply it to your chart.

Moving a PivotChart

To move the chart to another worksheet, do the following:

1. Select the PivotChart.

2. On the ribbon, select **PivotChart Analyze** > **Actions** > **Move Chart**.

   Excel displays the **Move Chart** dialog box.

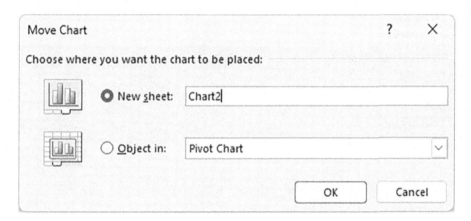

3. Select **New sheet,** and in the corresponding text box, you can accept the default name provided for the new worksheet or type in another name of your choosing.

4. Click **OK** when you're done.

Excel moves the chart to a new worksheet.

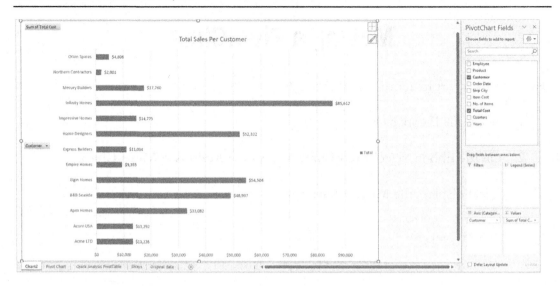

Generate a PivotTable and a PivotChart Simultaneously

You can generate a PivotTable and a PivotChart simultaneously from your table or data list instead of creating them separately.

To generate a PivotTable and PivotChart together, do the following:

1. Click anywhere in the data list.
2. On the **Insert** tab, click the dropdown arrow on the **PivotChart** button.
3. Select **PivotChart & PivotTable** from the dropdown menu on the command button.
4. In the Create PivotTable dialog box, click the **OK** button.

Excel will create a new worksheet with the placeholders for a PivotTable and a PivotChart.

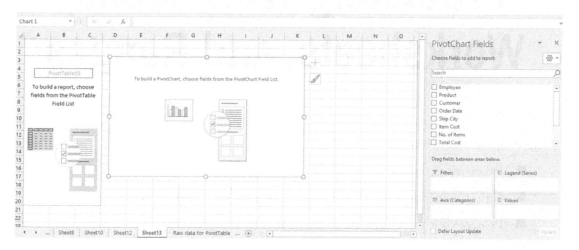

In the **PivotChart Fields** pane, select the fields to display in your PivotTable and PivotChart. As you select the fields you want for the chart in the PivotChart Fields pane, the PivotTable and PivotChart are updated simultaneously.

Follow the steps described in the sections titled **Creating PivotTables Manually** and **Creating PivotCharts** in this chapter to finalize the PivotTable and PivotChart.

Chapter 8

Protecting Workbooks, Worksheets, and Ranges

This chapter covers how to:

- Password-protect your Excel file.

- Set different access levels for your workbook with passwords.

- Protect your workbook structure from unauthorized changes.

- Protect individual worksheets within a workbook.

- Protect specific ranges within a worksheet.

Excel provides security at different levels of granularity. You can protect workbooks, worksheets, ranges, and individual cells from unauthorized access and changes. This chapter will cover the various methods you can use to protect your workbook.

⚠ Important

Before you protect your workbook with a password, ensure that you've got the password written down and stored in a safe place where it can be retrieved if necessary. Microsoft does not provide any methods to access a password-protected Excel file where the password has been lost. Without an advanced password-cracking tool, it is impossible to gain access to an Excel file that has been password-protected if the password has been forgotten.

How to set a password for your Excel workbook:

To set a password on your Excel workbook, do the following:

1. From the Excel ribbon, select **File** > **Info** > **Protect Document** > **Encrypt with Password**.

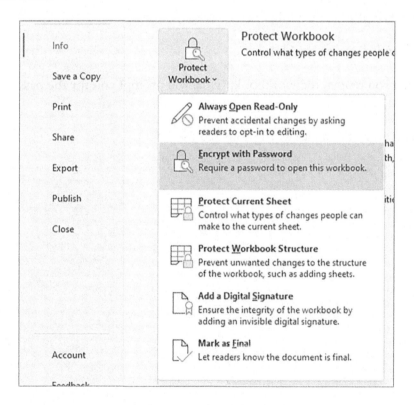

2. At the prompt, enter your password, then confirm it.

3. Click **OK** after confirming the password.

4. Save and close the workbook.

5. When you reopen the workbook, Excel will prompt you for the password.

That's it! You now have a password protected file.

Removing a Password from an Excel Workbook

Sometimes, you may want to remove a password from an Excel workbook. Setting a password encrypts the workbook, so you'll need to remove the encryption. Carry out the following steps to remove the password.

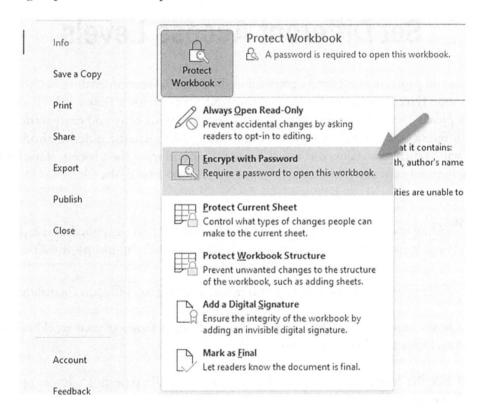

1. Open the workbook and enter the password in the **Password** box.

2. Select **File** > **Info** > **Protect Workbook** > **Encrypt with Password**.

   Excel displays the Encrypt Document dialog box.

3. Delete the contents of the **Password** box.

4. Click **OK**.

5. Save the workbook and close it.

When you reopen the workbook, Excel will not challenge you for a password.

Set Different Access Levels

The password protection method described in the previous section enables you to quickly protect your Excel workbook from unauthorized access with a password. However, it does not provide a way to set different access levels, like **read-only** and **read-write** access. To set different access levels with passwords, you need to use the older method to save the file with a different name and insert the passwords during the process. This method allows you to set separate passwords for opening and modifying the file.

Note Only use this method (over the encryption method described in the previous section) if you want to create different access levels for different groups of users.

To set different passwords for opening and modifying an Excel file, do the following:

1. On the ribbon, select **File** > **Save As** (or **Save a Copy** if your workbook is on OneDrive and AutoSave is set to **On**).

2. Click the **More options** link (directly under the file type box). Excel opens the **Save As** dialog box.

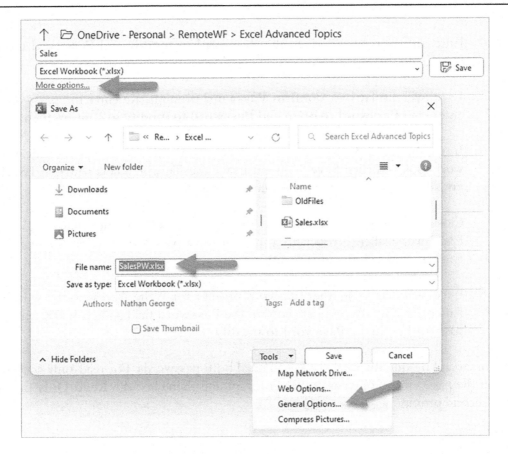

3. In the **Save As** dialog box, click the **Tools** button and select **General Options** from the menu.

Excel displays the **General Options** dialog box, which enables you to set one password for opening the workbook and another for modifying the workbook.

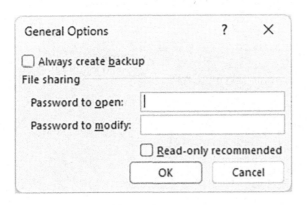

4. Enter different passwords in the **Password to modify** and **Password to open** boxes, and then click **OK**.

5. Excel will display two **Confirm Password** prompts. Re-enter the password you entered in **Password to open** and **Password to modify** to confirm them.

6. In the **Save As** dialog box, in the **File name** field, enter a new name for the workbook and click **Save**. You must save the file with a new name, as Excel will not allow you to save it with the current name.

7. Close and reopen the workbook (the file saved with the new name). This time Excel will challenge you with a prompt for a password to open the workbook. Enter the password and click **OK**.

8. Excel will display another password prompt for Write Access to the workbook. Enter the Write Access password in the **Password** field and click **OK** (this is the password set in the **Password to modify** box).

To open and modify the workbook, you need both passwords. For read-only access, you enter the password to open at the first prompt and then click the **Read Only** button at the second prompt.

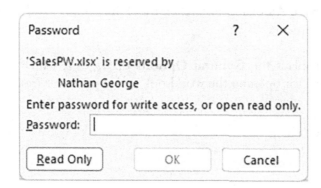

Removing the Passwords Set in General Options

There may be situations when you want to remove file protection and make the file accessible to all users. To remove the passwords set in General Options, you can delete them from General Options and save the file again.

Do the following to remove the passwords:

1. Open the Excel file with the current passwords.

2. Select **File** > **Save As** (or **Save a Copy** if your file is saved on OneDrive).

3. Click the **More options** link (directly under the file type box).

    Excel opens the **Save As** dialog box.

4. In the **Save As** dialog box, select **Tools** > **General Options**. Excel displays the **General Options** dialog box where you entered the passwords.

5. Clear the passwords from the **Password to modify** and **Password to open** boxes, and click **OK** to dismiss the dialog box.

6. In the **Save As** dialog box, click **Save** to save the file.

    If you use the same file name, Excel will display a message asking if you want to replace the current file.

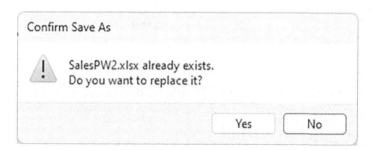

7. Select **Yes** to replace the file or **No** to go back to the Save As dialog and change the name.

8. Close the workbook and reopen it. It will no longer prompt you for a password.

Protecting the Workbook Structure

You can protect your workbook structure with a password to prevent other users from adding, moving, deleting, renaming, hiding, or viewing hidden worksheets. Protecting the workbook structure differs from protecting an Excel file or worksheet with a password. When you protect your workbook structure, the file is still accessible to everyone with access, but they can't change the workbook's structure. This type of protection does not protect the data from being modified, only the workbook's structure.

To protect your workbook, carry out the following steps:

1. On the **Review** tab, in the **Protect** group, select **Protect Workbook**.

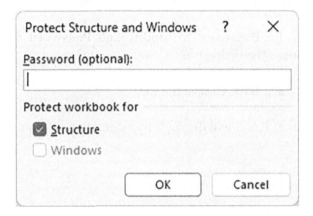

2. In the **Protect Structure and Windows** dialog, enter a password in the **Password** box.

3. Click **OK**.

4. In the **Confirm Password** dialog box, re-enter the password and click **OK**.

The **Protect Workbook** button on the Review tab will be enabled, indicating that the workbook is protected.

With the workbook protected, all the commands that involve changing the workbook's structure, like add, delete, move, or rename worksheets are disabled. To re-enable these commands, you'll need to remove the password protection.

Unprotecting the Workbook Structure

To unprotect your workbook's structure, do the following:

1. On the **Review** tab of the ribbon, in the **Protect** group, click **Protect Workbook**.

2. In the **Unprotect Workbook** dialog box, enter the password used to protect the workbook and click **OK**.

Protecting Worksheets

Instead of protecting the whole workbook with a password, you could protect individual worksheets and even narrow it down to restricting certain actions within the sheet. For example, you can lock certain cells in the worksheet with formulas from being editable so that other users do not accidentally delete formulas.

In a shared workbook, users could inadvertently delete formulas as they may not be aware that some cells contain formulas rather than values. Hence, cells with formulas are often protected in shared workbooks. Another reason to protect parts of your worksheet is that you may have core data that you don't want users to change. You can protect those ranges only on the worksheet.

Worksheet protection involves two steps:

1. First, unlock the cells that you want to keep editable. If you don't take this step, all cells in the worksheet will be locked when you protect it.

2. Protect the worksheet with or without a password.

Step 1 - Unlock any cells/ranges that need to be editable:

1. Click the tab of the worksheet you want to protect. In the worksheet area, select the range(s) to be left unprotected.

> -💡-**Tip** You can select multiple ranges by holding down the **Ctrl** key while selecting additional ranges.

2. On the **Home** tab, in the **Cells** group, select **Format > Format Cells**.

3. In the **Format Cells** dialog box, select the **Protection** tab and clear the **Locked** checkbox.

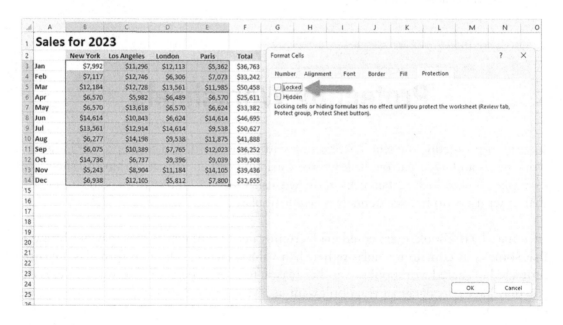

Step 2 - Protect the worksheet:

Next, you can choose specific actions that users can carry out in the worksheet.

1. On the **Review** tab, in the **Protect** group, click **Protect Sheet**.

   Excel displays the **Protect Sheet** dialog box.

2. Ensure the **Protect worksheet and contents of locked cells** setting is selected. This setting should be enabled by default.

3. In the list box, select the actions users can perform on the worksheet. For example, you could allow users to insert rows and columns, sort data, format cells, use AutoFilter, etc., among the many options on the list.

4. You can specify a password that a user will require to unprotect the sheet, but this is optional.

   You can protect the sheet without a password, but users can click the **Unprotect Sheet** button to unprotect the sheet. If you want to prevent users from doing this, enter a password in the **Password to unprotect sheet** box and click **OK**. Re-enter the password at the **Confirm Password** prompt and click **OK** to complete the action.

⚠ **Important**
If you set a password to protect your worksheet, you'll need the password whenever you want to unprotect it. Hence, it is critical that you remember your password. Ideally, you want to have it written down somewhere under lock and key for easy retrieval if needed. If the password is lost, Microsoft provides no tools to retrieve it.

Unprotect a Worksheet

In a protected worksheet, in place of the **Protect Sheet** command button on the **Review** tab, you'll see an **Unprotect Sheet** command button.

To unprotect the sheet, click the **Unprotect Sheet** button. You'll be challenged with a password prompt if it is protected with a password. Enter the password and click **OK** to unprotect the worksheet.

Protecting Specific Ranges

Excel locks all cells by default when you protect a worksheet unless you specifically unlock some cells before you enable protection (as described above). Hence, you must remove the sheet protection to access the locked parts of the sheet.

What if we have situations where we want some users to access locked ranges without removing the sheet protection?

Excel provides a solution with the **Allow Edit Ranges** command. You can password-protect specific ranges in the worksheet rather than the whole sheet. Also, if you're using a Microsoft Windows machine on a network domain, you can give specific users in your domain permission to edit ranges in a protected worksheet.

The process involves two steps:

1. Specify the ranges to be password protected.

2. Protect the worksheet.

Step 1 - Follow these steps to specify the ranges to be password protected:

1. If the worksheet is already protected, you need to unprotect the sheet first.

2. Select the worksheet you want to protect by clicking its tab at the bottom of the Excel window.

3. On the **Review** tab, in the **Protect** group, click the **Allow Edit Ranges** button. This button is only available when the worksheet is unprotected.

   Excel displays the **Allow Users to Edit Ranges** dialog box.

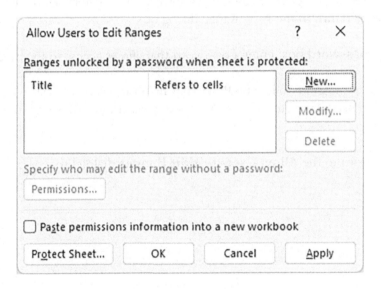

4. Click **New** to add a new range that you want editable using a password.

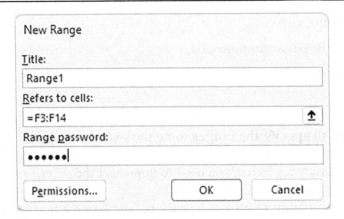

5. In the **New Range** dialog box, in the **Title** box, name the range you want to password-protect.

6. In the **Refers to cells** box, enter the cell reference of the range, starting with an equal sign (=). Alternatively, select the Collapse Dialog button (the up arrow on the right of the box) and select the range on the worksheet. Then click the Expand Dialog button to return to the New Range dialog box.

7. In the **Range password** box, enter a password that allows access to the range.

   To use domain permissions, click the **Permissions** button and follow the process to add a domain user. This button only applies to network domains with multiple user accounts.

8. Click **OK** to return to the **Allow Users to Edit Ranges** dialog box.

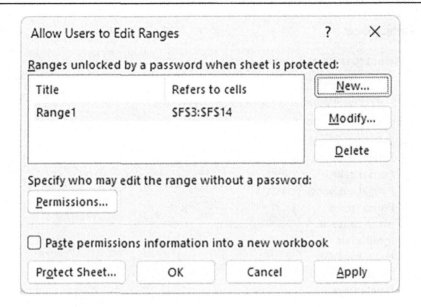

Step 2 - Protect the worksheet:

If you have closed the **Allow Users to Edit Ranges** dialog box, open it again by selecting **Review > Protect > Protect Sheet**.

1. In the **Allow Users to Edit Ranges** dialog box, select the **Protect Sheet** button.

   Excel displays the **Protect Sheet** dialog box.

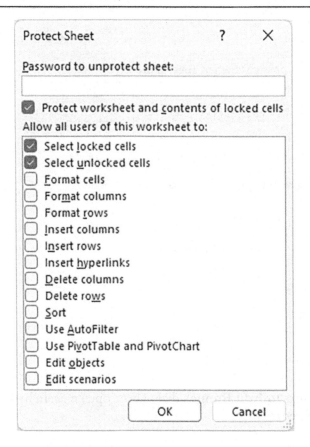

2. Accept the default selection of the **Protect worksheet and contents of locked cells** checkbox. If it is not enabled, then select it.

3. In the **Allow all users of this worksheet to** list, select the actions users can perform in the worksheet. For example, you could allow users to insert rows and columns, sort data, format cells, or use AutoFilter, among the many options on the list.

4. In the **Password to unprotect sheet** box, enter a password and click **OK**. Re-enter the password to confirm it and click **OK** again.

As mentioned previously, the password is optional. If you don't set a password, the sheet will be protected, but any user can click the **Unprotect Sheet** button on the ribbon to unprotect the sheet.

Once a range has been protected, users will be prompted to enter the password set in Step 1 when they try to edit the range. A user will only need to enter the password once per session.

⚠ Important

Although mentioned earlier in this chapter, this is worth repeating. If you protect any part of your worksheet with a password, you'll need the password to unprotect it. Hence, it is critical that you remember your password. Ideally, you want to have it written down somewhere under lock and key for easy retrieval if needed. If you forget the password, Microsoft provides no tools to retrieve it.

Book 3

Excel Functions

Chapter 1

Function Basics

This chapter covers the following:

- How to enter a formula in Excel.

- Operators in Excel and how operator precedence affects your formula results.

- How to step through a formula and fix errors using Evaluate Formula.

How to Enter a Function

To insert a function in a cell, do the following:

1. Click the cell where you want to display the result.

2. Click in the formula bar.

3. Enter your formula, starting your entry with the equal sign (=). The equal sign tells Excel that your entry is a formula, not a static value.

4. Press **Enter** on your keyboard to confirm the entry. Alternatively, click the **Enter** button (check mark).

For example:

=SUM(A2:A10)

A11			✕ ✓ *fx*	=SUM(A2:A10)|

◢	A	B	C	D	E	
1						
2	12					
3	40					
4	68					
5	409					
6	217					
7	327					
8	85					
9	312					
10	369					
11	A10)					
12						

Tip As much as possible, avoid typing cell references directly into the formula bar, as it could introduce errors. Instead, enter the name of the formula and then an open bracket. For example, enter =SUM(. Then select the cells you want for your argument in the worksheet itself before entering the closing bracket.

The Insert Function Dialog Box

A second way to enter a function is by using the **Insert Function** dialog box.

Click in the formula bar to place the cursor there. And then, click the **Insert Function** command on the **Formulas** tab or the Insert Function button next to the formula bar.

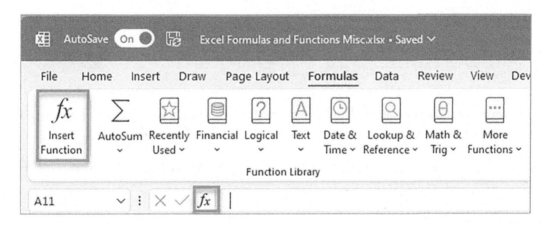

Excel displays the **Insert Function** dialog box. This dialog box provides the option to search for the function or select it from a category.

To search for the function, enter the function's name in the **Search for a function** box. For example, if you were searching for the IF function, you would enter IF in the search box and click **Go**. The **Select a function** list will display all the functions related to your search term.

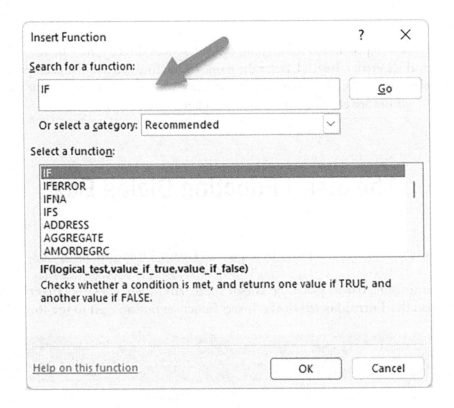

You can also use the **category** drop-down list to select a function if you know its category in Excel. For example, you can find the IF function in the **Logical** category.

If you have used a function recently, it'll be listed in the **Most Recently Used** category.

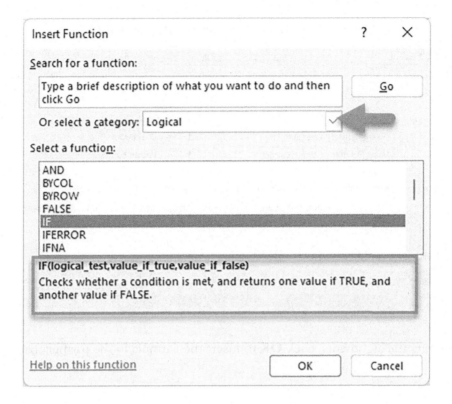

When you select a function on the list, you'll see the syntax and a description of what the function does below the list.

Once you've selected the function you want, click **OK** to open the Function Arguments dialog box.

The **Function Arguments** dialog box enables you to enter the arguments for the function. A function argument is a value the function needs to run.

The Function Arguments dialog box is particularly useful if you are unfamiliar with a function. It describes each argument, a preview of your entries, and the result returned by the function.

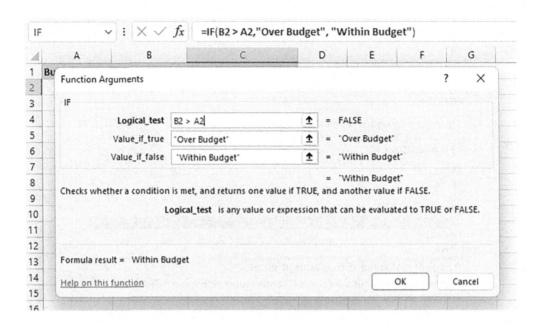

After entering the arguments, click **OK** to insert the formula in the formula bar.

Chapter 2

Lookup and Reference Functions

In this chapter, we'll cover functions that enable you to:

- Lookup data in a list, table, or range based on one or more lookup values.

- Perform complex vertical and horizontal lookups.

- Transpose a column or row of data using.

- Choose a value from a list, table, or range based on a search index.

- Return the address of a cell in your worksheet.

- Display the formula of a cell (rather than the return value).

- Return the number of rows or columns in a range.

- Select and return a subset of rows or columns.

The Lookup and Reference functions can be found by clicking the **Lookup & Reference** command button on the **Formulas** tab on the Ribbon. Excel provides many functions to enable you to look up one piece of data using another. Reference functions allow you to find and return specific information about your data.

Looking Up Values in a Range

The functions in this section enable you to look up one value based on another. You can perform complex lookups using more than one value to search for and return a value or an array.

Find Data with XLOOKUP

XLOOKUP was introduced as an improvement on the VLOOKUP function. Like its predecessor, XLOOKUP searches a range or an array and returns a value corresponding to the first match it finds on the same row in another range.

For instance, you can look up the **price** of a product in a data list using the **Product ID** or **name**. Similarly, you can return an employee's name using their employee ID. If XLOOKUP does not find a match, you can tell it to return the closest (approximate) match.

Unlike VLOOKUP, which only allows you to return values from a column to the right of the lookup range, XLOOKUP can return values from columns to the left or the right of the lookup range. XLOOKUP also returns exact matches by default, making it easier and more convenient than its predecessor.

Syntax:

Note The XLOOKUP function is available in Excel for Microsoft 365 and Excel 2021. If you're using an older 'standalone' version of Excel, XLOOKUP will not be available, so you should use VLOOKUP.

=XLOOKUP(lookup_value, lookup_array, return_array, [if_not_found], [match_mode], [search_mode])

Arguments and Descriptions

Argument	Description
lookup_value	Required. What value are you searching for? Excel will look for a match for this value in the lookup_array. You can provide a value here or a cell reference containing the value you want to find.
lookup_array	Required. Where do you want to search? This value is the lookup range containing the columns you want to include in your search, for example, A2:D10.
return_array	Required. Which range contains the values you want to return? This value is the return range. The return range can have one or more columns, as XLOOKUP is about to return more than one value.
[if_not_found]	Optional. This optional argument enables you to enter a piece of text to return if a valid match is not found. If this argument is omitted and a valid match is not found, XLOOKUP will return the #N/A error.
[match_mode]	Optional. This optional argument enables you to specify a match mode from four options: 0 (or omitted) = Exact match. If no match is found, Excel returns an error (#N/A), the default if you omit this argument. -1 = Exact match or the next smallest item if an exact match is not found.

	1 = Exact match or the next largest item if an exact match is not found. 2 = Performs a wildcard match where you can use the characters *, ?, and ~ for wildcard searches.
[search_mode]	Optional. This optional argument enables you to specify the order in which you want to perform the search: 1 (or omitted) = Search first to last. This setting is the default if this argument is omitted. -1 = Perform the search in reverse order - last to first. 2 = Perform a binary search for data sorted in ascending order. If lookup_array is not sorted in ascending order, invalid results will be returned. -2 = Perform a binary search for data sorted in descending order. If lookup_array is not sorted in descending order, invalid results will be returned.

-̇☋-**Tip**   Regarding the *search_mode* argument, in earlier versions of Excel, performing binary searches on sorted lists produced quicker results, but in Microsoft 365, non-binary searches are equally fast. Hence, using binary search options for sorted lists is no longer beneficial. Using 1 or -1 for the search_mode argument is easier because you don't require a sorted table.

Vertical Lookup

In this example, we use XLOOKUP to return the Reorder Level of the product entered in cell F1. The formula is in cell F2.

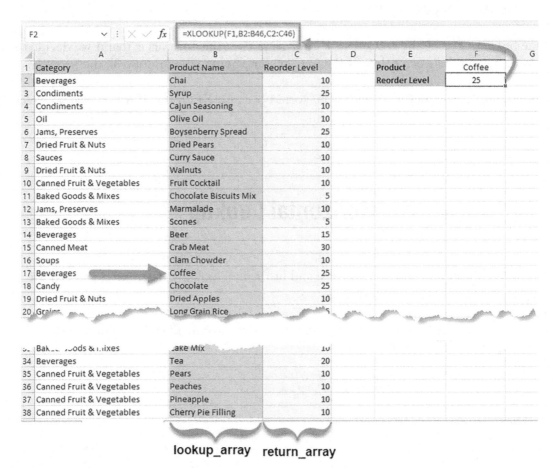

lookup_array   return_array

Formula explanation:

=XLOOKUP(F1,B2:B46,C2:C46)

The formula says, in range B2:B46, find the value in cell F1 (which in this case is "Coffee") and return the value on the same row in range C2:C46.

The *if_not_found* argument has not been provided here, so if a match is not found, it will return an error which is the default behavior.

The VLOOKUP equivalent of this formula would look like this:

=VLOOKUP(F1,B2:C46,2,0)

One benefit of using the XLOOKUP equivalent over this formula is that if we decide to insert a column between columns B and C at some point, it will not break the formula.

The lookup_array does not need to be sorted because XLOOKUP will return an exact match by default.

Horizontal Lookup

XLOOKUP can perform both vertical and horizontal lookups. Therefore, you can use it in place of the HLOOKUP function.

In the example below, we can retrieve the value associated with a month using the abbreviation of the month.

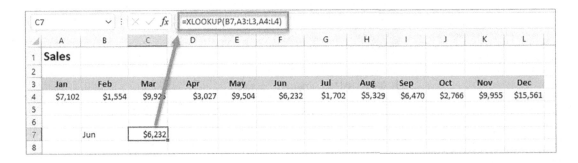

=XLOOKUP(B7,A3:L3,A4:L4)

The formula uses only the first three arguments of the XLOOKUP function. B7 is the lookup_value, A3:L3 is the lookup_array, and A4:L4 is the return_array.

Note that a horizontal lookup_array must contain the same number of columns as the return_array.

Simultaneous Vertical and Horizontal Lookup

This example will use two XLOOKUP functions to perform both a vertical and horizontal match. Here, the formula will first look for a "Mark" in the cell range A4:A15, then look for "Q3" in the top row of the table (range B3:E3) and return the value at the intersection of the two. Previously, you would need to use the INDEX/MATCH/MATCH combination to achieve the same result.

	A	B	C	D	E	F	G	H	I	J
				fx	=XLOOKUP(G4,A4:A15,XLOOKUP(H4,B3:E3,B4:E15))					
1	**Sales data**									
2										
3	**Salesperson**	**Q1**	**Q2**	**Q3**	**Q4**					
4	Penny	17,526	23,972	61,066	22,596		Mark	Q3	19,062	
5	Leslie	49,405	36,646	21,899	62,629					
6	Sally	78,658	16,529	14,976	68,184					
7	Shaun	80,176	84,918	66,561	65,326					
8	Julie	86,988	29,692	30,197	80,960					
9	Velma	94,514	13,333	78,000	59,718					
10	Ian	23,183	21,547	40,408	57,767					
11	Cassandra	70,597	19,615	54,664	68,175					
12	Mark	16,832	91,907	19,062	23,467					
13	Kathy	45,446	14,638	52,312	92,069					
14	Renee	34,583	78,213	21,295	26,964					
15	Judith	18,689	91,081	66,795	96,860					

Formula explanation:

=XLOOKUP(G4,A4:A15,XLOOKUP(H4,B3:E3,B4:E15))

The first XLOOKUP function has the following arguments:
- lookup_value = G4
- lookup_array = A4:A15
- return_array = XLOOKUP(H4,B3:E3,B4:E15)

The second XLOOKUP, executed first, performs a horizontal search on B3:E3, using the value in cell H4 ("Q3") as the lookup_value, then returns the range **D4:D15**. Notice that the second XLOOKUP returns a range rather than a value. This range is used as the return_array argument for the first XLOOKUP.

So, after the second XLOOKUP has been executed, the first XLOOKUP will look like this:

=XLOOKUP(G4,A4:A15,D4:D15)

Examining the Formula with Evaluate Formula

To examine how the formula performs the task, you can use the **Evaluate Formula** dialog box in Excel to see how each formula part is evaluated.

Follow the steps below to open the Evaluate Formula dialog box:

1. Select the cell with the formula you want to evaluate. In this case, it is cell **I4**.

2. On the Formulas tab, in the **Formula Auditing** group, click the **Evaluate Formula** command button.

3. In the Evaluate Formula dialog box, click the **Evaluate** button until the nested XLOOKUP function has been evaluated and its result is displayed in the formula.

   For this example, we need to click the Evaluate button three times.

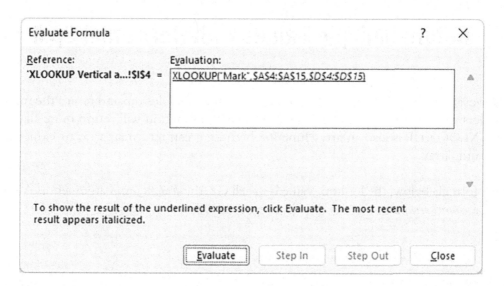

You will notice that the second XLOOKUP performs a search using the lookup_value, "Q3", and then returns the range **D4:D15** (displayed as an absolute reference **$D$4:$D$15**). We can use XLOOKUP here as the *return_array* argument of the first XLOOKUP function because XLOOKUP can return a range and value.

Next, the main XLOOKUP performs a lookup using the value in cell G4, "Mark" as the lookup_value, cells A4:A15 as the lookup_array, and cells D4:D15 as the return_array to return the final result.

Return Multiple Values with Horizontal Spill

In this example, we want to be able to enter the name of a sales rep and return the number of orders and sales associated with them. Hence, the function will return more than one value. XLOOKUP is also an array function because it can return an array of values from the return_array.

In the formula below, the lookup_value is in cell G2, the *lookup_array* argument is A2:A12, and the *return_array* argument is the cell range C2:D12.

H2			fx	=XLOOKUP(G2,A2:A12,C2:D12)						
	A	B	C	D	E	F	G	H	I
1	Name	State	# Orders	Sales			Name	# Orders	Sales
2	Bruce	New York	51	$74,298			Bruce	51	$74,298
3	Louis	New York	39	$46,039					
4	Earl	Washington	60	$65,252					
5	Sean	Washington	100	$61,847					
6	Benjamin	Texas	28	$33,340					
7	Joe	California	31	$95,778					
8	Shawn	Texas	35	$58,808					
9	Kenneth	California	39	$52,593					
10	Cynthia	California	51	$42,484					
11	Susan	Texas	80	$44,390					
12	David	New York	70	$66,109					
13									

Horizontal spill

Formula explanation:

=XLOOKUP(G2,A2:A12,C2:D12)

As you can see from the formula, the return_array contains columns C and D. When we enter the name "Bruce" in cell G2, XLOOKUP returns the values in columns C and D from the same row. As the function returns more than one value, the result spills into cell I2.

The range containing the spilled result has a blue border, which is how you can tell the result has spilled into other cells.

Return Multiple Values with Vertical Spill

To get the formula to spill vertically, we can use another example where we need to return the sales for more than one person on our list.

In this example, we first use the FILTER function to generate a filtered list of names based in **New York**. The function returns an array of names that spill vertically in the range G2:G4.

G2			fx	=FILTER(A2:A12,B2:B12="New York")			
	A	B	C	D	E	F	G	H
1	**Name**	**State**	**# Orders**	**Sales**			**Name**	**Sales**
2	Bruce	New York	51	$74,298			Bruce	
3	Louis	New York	39	$46,039			Louis	
4	Earl	Washington	60	$65,252			David	
5	Sean	Washington	100	$61,847				
6	Benjamin	Texas	28	$33,340				
7	Joe	California	31	$95,778				
8	Shawn	Texas	35	$58,808				
9	Kenneth	California	39	$52,593				
10	Cynthia	California	51	$42,484				
11	Susan	Texas	80	$44,390				
12	David	New York	70	$66,109				
13								

Next, we want to get the **Sales** associated with the names on our filtered list and insert them in column H. To do this, we use XLOOKUP in cell H2 and select cells G2:G4 for our lookup_value argument.

When you select the *lookup_value* (G2:G4), Excel recognizes the range as a spilled range and references the range with the spilled range operator, i.e., G2#.

	A	B	C	D	E	F	G	H
							H2 ✓ : ✕ ✓ fx =XLOOKUP(G2#,A2:A12,D2:D12)	
1	**Name**	**State**	**# Orders**	**Sales**			**Name**	**Sales**
2	Bruce	New York	51	$74,298			Bruce	$74,298
3	Louis	New York	39	$46,039			Louis	$46,039
4	Earl	Washington	60	$65,252			David	$66,109
5	Sean	Washington	100	$61,847				
6	Benjamin	Texas	28	$33,340				
7	Joe	California	31	$95,778				
8	Shawn	Texas	35	$58,808				
9	Kenneth	California	39	$52,593				
10	Cynthia	California	51	$42,484				
11	Susan	Texas	80	$44,390				
12	David	New York	70	$66,109				
13								
14								
15								

Formula explanation:

=XLOOKUP(G2#,A2:A12,D2:D12)

The lookup_value argument in the formula is G2#.

G2# (note the hash) designates the entire range of the spilled data. It tells us that G2 is the starting point of the array of values returned from a dynamic array formula.

The lookup_array is the Name column (A2:A12), and the return_array is the Sales column (D2:D12).

When you type in the formula in cell H2 and press Enter, XLOOKUP will return all the sales related to the names in the dynamic array in column G. As we have more than one value, it will spill down vertically in column H2.

One benefit of using XLOOKUP is that the formula will adjust to the dynamic array in column G. If we change the filter and add more names to column G, the formula in cell H2 would still work in finding the values corresponding to the new names. We don't have to worry about copying the formula to additional cells.

Common XLOOKUP Errors and Solutions

#N/A error

If an exact match is not found, and the **if_not_found** and **match_mode** arguments are omitted, XLOOKUP will return a #N/A error.

There may be scenarios where you will not know if your formula will generate this error, for example, when a formula is copied to multiple cells in a column. If you want to catch and replace this error with a meaningful message, specify the message in the **if_not_found** argument.

For example:
=XLOOKUP(F2,B2:B12,D2:D12,"Item not found")

#VALUE! error

This error is often generated because the lookup and return arrays are not the same length. When you get this error, check that these ranges are the same length. The lookup_array and return_array should have the same number of rows for vertical lookups. If the lookup is horizontal, they should have the same number of columns.

#NAME? in cell

This error usually means that there is an issue with a cell reference. A typo in the cell reference or omitting the colon can generate this error. When you get this error, check your cell references. To help avoid errors and typos in your formula, select cell references on the worksheet with your mouse rather than typing them in the formula.

#REF! error

If XLOOKUP is referencing another workbook that is closed, you will get a #REF! error. Ensure all workbooks referenced in your formula are open to avoid this error.

#SPILL! error

When returning multiple values, if there is already data in the spill range, Excel returns the #SPILL! error. To avoid this error, ensure there is no existing data in the cells that will contain the returned results.

Find Data with VLOOKUP

VLOOKUP is still one of the most popular lookup functions in Excel despite the introduction of XLOOKUP. If you intend to share your workbook with people using older versions of Excel without XLOOKUP, you might want to use VLOOKUP for looking up data. VLOOKUP enables you to find one piece of information in a workbook based on another piece of information. For example, if you have a product list, you can find and return a **Product Code** by providing the corresponding **Product Name** to the VLOOKUP function.

Syntax

=VLOOKUP (lookup_value, table_array, col_index_num, [range_lookup])

Arguments

Argument	Description
lookup_value	Required. What value are you searching for? This argument is the lookup value. Excel will look for a match for this value in the leftmost column of your chosen range. You can provide a value here or a cell reference.
table_array	Required. What columns do you want to search? This argument is the range you want to include in your search, e.g., A2:D10.
col_index_num	Required. Which column contains the search result? Count from the first column to determine what this number should be, starting from 1.
range_lookup	Optional.
	For an exact match, enter FALSE/0.
	For an approximate match, enter TRUE/1.
	For TRUE, ensure the leftmost column is sorted in ascending order for correct results.
	This argument defaults to TRUE if omitted.

Example 1 – Standard lookup

In the example below, we use VLOOKUP to find the **Price** and **Reorder Level** of a product by entering the **Product Name** in cell G2. The formula is in cell G3, and as you can see from the image below, it searches the table for **Pears** and returns the price from the next column.

| G3 | : | × ✓ fx | =VLOOKUP(G2,B2:D46,2,FALSE) | | | | | |

	A	B	C	D	E	F	G
1	Product Code	Product Name	Price	Reorder Level	Category		
2	NWTB-1	Chai	$18.00	10	Beverages	Protuct name:	Pears
3	NWTB-34	Beer	$14.00	15	Beverages	Price:	$1.30
4	NWTB-43	Coffee	$46.00	25	Beverages	Reorder Level:	10
5	NWTB-81	Green Tea	$2.99	100	Beverages		
6	NWTB-87	Tea	$4.00	20	Beverages		
7	NWTBGM-19	Chocolate Biscuits Mix	$9.20	5	Baked Goods & Mixes		
8	NWTBGM-21	Scones	$10.00	5	Baked Goods & Mixes		
9	NWTBGM-85	Brownie Mix	$12.49	10	Baked Goods & Mixes		
10	NWTBGM-86	Cake Mix	$15.99	10	Baked Goods & Mixes		
11	NWTC-82	Granola	$4.00	20	Cereal		
12	NWTC-82	Hot Cereal	$5.00	50	Cereal		
13	NWTCA-48	Chocolate	$12.75	25	Candy		
14	NWTCFV-17	Fruit Cocktail	$39.00	10	Canned Fruit & Vegetables		
15		Pears	$1.30	10	Canned Fruit & Vegetables		
16	NWTCFV-89	Peaches	$1.50	10	Canned Fruit & Vegetables		
17	NWTCFV-90	Pineapple	$1.80	10	Canned Fruit & Vegetables		

Formula Explanation

The following formula looks up the **Price** for **Pears**:

=VLOOKUP(G2, B2:D46, 2, FALSE)

The function uses a lookup_value from cell **G2** to search a table_array which is **B2:D46**.

The col_index_num is **2,** so it returns a value from the second column in the search range (table_array), the **Price** column.

The range_lookup is **FALSE**, meaning we want an exact match.

To look up the **Reorder Level** for Pears, we use the same formula and just change the column containing the search result (col_index_num) to 3 to return a value from the third row of the table array.

=VLOOKUP(G2, B2:D46, **3**, FALSE)

In this case, the VLOOKUP search for Pears returns a Reorder Level of **10**.

Example 2 - Approximate match

In the following example, we want to find an approximate match if an exact match is not found. The worksheet calculates the commission for each Sales Rep based on their sales. We have a Commission table to the right of the Sales report with a graduated scale of rates against sales.

We want to ensure that if an exact match is not found on the commission table, an approximate match is applied for the sales rep. $5,000 or more in sales is 2% commission, $10,000 or more is 5%, $20,000 or more is 10%, and so on.

C3		fx	=VLOOKUP(B3,table_array,2,TRUE)		
	A	B	C	D	E	F

	A	B	C	D	E	F
1	**Sales**				**Commission table**	
2	Sales Rep	Sales	Commisson		Sales	Rate
3	Berna Alger	$7,372	2%		$0	0%
4	Rich Donaldson	$23,895	10%		$5,000	2%
5	Erwin Wofford	$31,323	15%		$10,000	5%
6	Arvilla Leon	$3,024	0%		$20,000	10%
7	Simone Sharkey	$73,033	25%		$30,000	15%
8	Guillermina Canales	$7,735	2%		$40,000	20%
9	Stacey Lovett	$22,417	10%		$50,000	25%
10	Jaunita Headrick	$1,483	0%			
11	Romaine Ashford	$9,028	2%			
12	Juliann Keane	$26,980	10%			
13						
14						

Formula Explanation:

=VLOOKUP(B3,table_array,2,TRUE)

The *lookup_value* is cell B3, the value for which we want an approximate match in the lookup range (cells E3:F9).

Note that the lookup range (E3:F9) is a named range, **table_array**. Named ranges are absolute references, ensuring cell references do not change when the formula is filled down to other cells.

The *col_index_num* is set to 2, meaning we want to return values from the second column in table_array.

The optional *range_lookup* argument is set to TRUE, which tells Excel to return an approximate match if an exact match is not found. The default for the *range_lookup* argument is TRUE if omitted, so you do not need to set this argument explicitly to TRUE. This example specifies it for demonstration purposes only.

Best Practices for VLOOKUP

- **Use absolute references for the table array.**

  Using absolute references allows you to fill down a formula without changing the cell references. An absolute reference ensures that VLOOKUP always looks at the same table array when the formula is copied to other cells.

- **Do not store a number or date as a text value.**

  When searching for numbers or dates, ensure the data in the first column of the table array is not stored as text. Otherwise, the formula might return an incorrect or unexpected value. Number and date values are right-aligned, while text values are left-aligned by default. Therefore, if your numbers or dates are left-aligned in the cell, you must check that they are using the right cell format.

- **Sort the first column.**

  If you want VLOOKUP to find the next best match when the **range_lookup** argument is TRUE, make sure the first column in **table_array** is sorted.

- **Use wildcard characters.**

  You can use a wildcard in **lookup_value** if **range_lookup** is FALSE and lookup_value is text. A question mark (?) matches any single character, and an asterisk (*) matches any sequence of characters. If you want to find an actual question mark or asterisk as part of the search criteria, type a tilde (~) in front of the character.

For example, =VLOOKUP("Dried*",B2:D46,2,FALSE) will find the first item starting with "Dried" in the first column of table_array.

- **Make sure your data does not contain erroneous characters.**

  If you are searching for text values in the first column of the table array, ensure the data in the first column does not have leading or trailing spaces, non-printable characters, and inconsistent use of straight and curly quotation marks. In cases like these, the formula might return an unexpected value.

  To clean up your data, you can use the TRIM function to remove any extra spaces or the CLEAN function to remove all nonprintable characters.

Common VLOOKUP Errors and Solutions

- **Wrong value returned**

  If you omit the **range_lookup** argument or set it to TRUE (for an approximate match), you need to sort the first column of **table_array** in alphanumeric order. Excel may return an unexpected value if the first column is not sorted. Use FALSE for an exact match or sort the first column of the table array for an approximate match.

- **#N/A error in cell**

  If the range_lookup argument is FALSE, and an exact match is not found, you will get a #N/A error. You will also get a #N/A error if **range_lookup** is TRUE and the **lookup_value** is smaller than the smallest value in the first column of **table_array**.

- **#REF! error in cell**

  You will get the #REF error if the col_index_num argument exceeds the number of columns in the table array.

- **#VALUE! error in cell**

  You will encounter a #VALUE! error if the **lookup_value** argument is over 255 characters. Use wildcards for partial matches if the values in the lookup range are over 255 characters.

  Excel will also generate the #VALUE! error if the **col_index_num** argument contains text or is less than 1. Ensure **col_index_num** is not less than 1.

- **#NAME? error in cell**

  This error usually means that the formula is missing quotes. If you enter a text value directly in your formula (instead of a cell reference), ensure you enclose the value in quotes. For example, =VLOOKUP("Dried Pears", B2:D46, 2, FALSE). You will also get this error if you make a mistake when typing in the cell reference. Select cell references on the worksheet with your mouse rather than typing them in the formula to avoid cell reference typos.

Find Data with HLOOKUP

HLOOKUP is now a legacy function in Excel, as you can perform horizontal lookups with XLOOKUP (see the section on XLOOKUP). However, if you have an older version of Excel without XLOOKUP, then you may need to use this function for horizontal lookups.

-`Ò`-**Tip** You can now use the new XLOOKUP function for horizontal lookups. It is an improvement on HLOOKUP. XLOOKUP does everything HLOOKUP can do and more. It is also easier and more convenient to use.

HLOOKUP searches for a value in the top row of a range or table and returns a value in the same column from a row you specify in the range or table. The function performs a horizontal search on the first column of the specified range for the lookup value (criteria). Then it uses the criteria to return another value from the same column but on a row below.

Use HLOOKUP when your lookup values are in a row at the top of a range or table, and you want to look down a specified number of rows. Conversely, VLOOKUP is suitable when your lookup values are in a column to the left of the data you want to search for.

Syntax

=HLOOKUP(lookup_value, table_array, row_index_num, [range_lookup])

Arguments

Argument	Description
lookup_value	Required. The search criteria. The value should be in the first row of table_array. Lookup_value can be text, a value, or a reference.
table_array	Required. A range or table which contains the data being looked up. You can use cell references or a named range.
row_index_num	Required. The row number from which you want the value returned, counting from 1 from the first row of the range.
range_lookup	Optional. This argument is to specify whether HLOOKUP should find an exact match or an approximate match. TRUE is for an approximate match, while FALSE is for an exact match. If this argument is omitted, it'll default to TRUE.

Example

E2			⌄ ⁝ ✕ ✓ *fx*	=HLOOKUP("Bolts",myList,6,FALSE)	

◢	A	B	C	D	E	F
1	Spanners	Bolts	Wrenches		Result	Formula text
2	7	4	11		5	=HLOOKUP("Bolts",myList,6,FALSE)
3	6	7	10		6	=HLOOKUP("Spanners",myList,3,FALSE)
4	1	5	8		10	=HLOOKUP("Wrenches",myList,3,TRUE)
5	2	3	12		6	=HLOOKUP("Spanners",myList,3,FALSE)
6	9	5	8			
7						

Note that the range **A1:C6** has been named as **myList**. This type of name is known as a *named range* in Excel.

Formula explanations:

=HLOOKUP("Bolts",myList,6,FALSE)

This formula uses "Bolts" as the lookup value to return a value on row 6 from the same column.

=HLOOKUP("Spanners",myList,3,FALSE)

This formula uses "Spanners" as the lookup value to return a value on row 3 from the same column.

=HLOOKUP("Wrenches",myList,3,TRUE)

This formula uses "Wrenches" as the lookup value to return a value on row 3 from the same column.

MATCH Function

The MATCH function searches for a given item in a list and then returns the relative position of the item in the list. MATCH tells you where in your list you can locate your value after you provide search parameters. For example, if the range A1:A5 has the values 10, 30, 26, 44, and 100, the formula =MATCH(44,A1:A5,0) will return 4 because 44 is the fourth item in the range. If MATCH cannot find an exact match, it will find the closest item to the lookup criteria, which can be useful when you want to identify the cut-off point in a list of values.

MATCH is most useful when used as an argument inside another function where you need to return the position of a specific item on your list as one of the arguments for that function. MATCH is often used with the INDEX function to find and return items in a table.

-ৄৣৄ-**Tip** If you're using Microsoft 365, try using the new XMATCH function. XMATCH is an improved version of MATCH that is easier and more convenient to use than its predecessor.

Syntax

=MATCH(lookup_value, lookup_array, [match_type])

Arguments

Argument	Description
lookup_value	Required. The value you want to match in your list. This argument can be a number, cell reference, text, or logical value.
lookup_array	Required. The list or range to be searched.
match_type	Optional. This argument specifies how the function will behave.

You have three options for this argument -1, 0, or 1. The default is 1 if the argument is omitted.

1 (or omitted) = MATCH finds the largest value that is less than or equal to the lookup value. The values in the list must be in ascending order.

0 = MATCH finds the first value that's exactly equal to lookup_value. The values in the range can be in any order.

-1 = MATCH finds the smallest value greater than or equal to lookup_value. The values in the list must be in descending order.

Remarks

- MATCH is not case-sensitive.

- If MATCH cannot find a matching, it returns a #N/A error.

- If the lookup_value is a text string and match_type is 0, you can use the wildcard characters, question mark (?), and asterisk (*) in the lookup_value argument. A question mark (?) matches any single character, while an asterisk (*) is used to match a sequence of characters. To find a question mark or asterisk as part of the criteria in lookup_value, type a tilde (~) before the character.

Example

In this example, MATCH is used to query the range A2:A10, named Products, to find the position of the lookup values entered in column C.

D2			f_x	=MATCH(C2,Products,0)	
⊿	A	B	C	D	E	F
1	**Product Name**		**Lookup value**	**Matched row**	**Formula text**	
2	Curry Sauce		Curry Sauce	1	=MATCH(C2,Products,0)	
3	Dried Pears		*Oil	4	=MATCH(C3,Products,0)	
4	Boysenberry Spread		Syrup	6	=MATCH(C4,Products,0)	
5	Olive Oil		Cajun*	5	=MATCH(C5,Products,0)	
6	Cajun Seasoning		Cha?	8	=MATCH(C6,Products,0)	
7	Syrup					
8	Walnuts					
9	Chai				*Products = A2:A10*	
10	Tomato Sauce					
11						
12						

Formula explanation

=MATCH(C2,Products,0)

In the above formula, the lookup_value is in cell C2, the lookup_array is the range Products, and the match_type is 0, indicating that we want an exact match.

Notice that some of the lookup values in column C have wildcard characters. When the match_type is 0, you can provide only part of the lookup_value with a question mark (?) or asterisk (*) to perform a wildcard search.

XMATCH Function

The XMATCH function is an improved version of the MATCH function. The MATCH function searches for a given item in a list and then returns the relative position of the item in the list. MATCH tells you where you can locate the value you've provided as the criteria in your list.

For example, if the range A1:A5 has the values 10, 30, 26, 44, and 100, the formula =MATCH(44,A1:A5,0) will return 4 because 44 is the fourth item in the range.

XMATCH is multidirectional and returns exact matches by default, which makes it easier to use than its predecessor.

XMATCH is often used in combination with another function. For example, you may want to find the position of a value in a list to use as an argument in another function. XMATCH is often used with the INDEX function for performing lookups.

Syntax

=XMATCH(lookup_value, lookup_array, [match_mode], [search_mode])

Argument	Description
lookup_value	Required. The value you want to match in your list. This argument can be a number, cell reference, text, or logical value.
lookup_array	Required. The list or range to be searched.
[match_mode]	Optional. This argument enables you to specify a match mode from four options: **0 (or omitted)** = Exact match. An error will be returned if no match is found (#N/A). This option is the default if you omit this argument. **-1** = Exact match or the next smallest item if an exact match is not found. **1** = Exact match or the next largest item if an exact match is not found. **2** = Performs a wildcard match where you use *, ?, and ~.
[search_mode]	Optional. This argument enables you to specify the search mode to use: **1 (or omitted)** = Search first to last. This option is the default if this argument is omitted. **-1** = Perform the search in reverse order - last to first. **2** = Perform a binary search (for data sorted in ascending order). If lookup_array is not sorted in ascending order, invalid results will be returned. **-2** = Perform a binary search (for data sorted in descending order). If lookup_array is not sorted in descending order, invalid results will be returned.

Examples

In the example below, we use XMATCH to find the relative position of products on the list based on different search criteria. The formulas also use different optional arguments to determine the function's behavior.

	D2			f_x	=XMATCH(C2,$A$2:$A$12)	
	A	B	C	D	E	
1	Product		Product	Position	Formula Text	
2	Chai		Walnuts	7	=XMATCH(C2,$A$2:$A$12)	
3	Syrup		Wal?	7	=XMATCH(C3,$A$2:$A$12,1)	
4	Cajun Seasoning		*Oil	4	=XMATCH(C4,$A$2:$A$12,2)	
5	Olive Oil		*Sauce	6	=XMATCH(C5,$A$2:$A$12,2)	
6	Dried Pears		*Sauce	11	=XMATCH(C6,$A$2:$A$12,2,-1)	
7	Curry Sauce					
8	Walnuts					
9	Fruit Cocktail					
10	Chocolate Biscuits Mix					
11	Marmalade					
12	Tomato Sauce					

Formula explanation:

=XMATCH(C2,$A$2:$A$12)

This example is a straightforward search for "Walnuts" (cell C2), and the formula returns its relative position of 7 on the list. The optional arguments have been omitted here, so the function uses its default search behavior.

=XMATCH(C3,$A$2:$A$12,1)

In this example, the *match_mode* argument has been set to 1, which tells XMATCH to find the position of the first item that is an exact match or the next largest value that starts with "Wal."

=XMATCH(C4,$A$2:$A$12,2)

In this example, the *match_mode* argument has been set to 2, which specifies that we are performing a wildcard search. Thus, the wildcard characters (*, ?, and ~) are treated as special characters.

=XMATCH(C6,$A$2:$A$12,2,-1)

In this example, the *match_mode* argument has been set to **2** for a wildcard search. The *search_mode* argument is set to **-1**, telling XMATCH to start from the last item.

You can see that the same search term, "*Sauce" in cells C5 and C6 returned different relative positions (6 and 11) because the formula in D5 is searching from the top. As a result, it finds "Curry Sauce" first. Conversely, the formula in D6 starts searching from the bottom, so it finds "Tomato Sauce" first.

INDEX Function

The INDEX function enables you to return a value or a series of values from a given location in range. The INDEX function is often combined with XMATCH (or its predecessor, MATCH) to perform horizontal and vertical lookups.

There are two forms of the INDEX function:
- Array form
- Reference form

Both INDEX forms are similar in behavior, but the Reference form enables you to specify multiple arrays, including an optional argument to select which array to use.

INDEX Function - Array Form

The array form of this function can return a single value or multiple values. If your formula returns more than one value, the results are spilled into adjacent cells to the right of the cell with the formula.

Syntax

=INDEX(array, row_num, [column_num])

Arguments

Argument	Description
array	Required. The array argument is a range of cells or an array constant. If the range contains only one row or column, the corresponding row_num or column_num is optional.
row_num	Required if column_num is omitted. This value specifies the row in the array argument from which to return a value.
column_num	Optional. Specifies the column in the array argument from which to return a value. If omitted, row_num is required.

Remarks

- If the *array* has more than one row and more than one column, and only row_num or column_num is used, INDEX returns an array of the entire row or column in the *array* argument.

- INDEX returns an array of values, i.e., the entire row or column if you set row_num or column_num to 0 (zero).

- INDEX returns a single value (at the intersection of row_num and column_num) if both arguments are used.

- To return several values, enter the formula in the first cell and press **Enter**. Excel will spill the return values to other cells.

Example 1

In the following example, we can return the sum of the entire row for Q1. We can return this result by combining the INDEX and SUM functions.

The example uses a drop-down list in cell H3 to select the row. The formula in cell I3 references H3 for the row_num argument.

When we select **1** in H3, we're setting the row_num to 1. The column_num argument is 0 (zero) in the formula, specifying that we want to return all the values in the range B4:E4.

=SUM(INDEX(B4:E7,H3,0))

I3		fx	=SUM(INDEX(B4:E7,H3,0))						
	A	B	C	D	E	F	G	H	I
1	**Quaterly Data**								
2									
3		London	Paris	New York	Toronto		Sum for quarter:	1	$19,082.00
4	Q1	$2,635.00	$2,194.00	$7,217.00	$7,036.00				
5	Q2	$7,227.00	$2,459.00	$9,269.00	$8,442.00		Sum for city:	London	$23,062.00
6	Q3	$4,426.00	$3,920.00	$6,803.00	$6,306.00				
7	Q4	$8,774.00	$2,566.00	$5,775.00	$2,390.00				
8									
9									
10									
11									

Example 2

In the following example, we want to return the sum of an entire column, for instance, B4:B7. We can achieve this result by combining the INDEX, SUM, and XMATCH functions.

=SUM(INDEX(B4:E7,0,XMATCH(H5,B3:E3)))

411

I5				f_x	=SUM(INDEX(B4:E7,0,XMATCH(H5,B3:E3)))				

▲	A	B	C	D	E	F	G	H	I
1	**Quaterly Data**								
2									
3		London	Paris	New York	Toronto		Sum for quarter:	1	$19,082.00
4	Q1	$2,635.00	$2,194.00	$7,217.00	$7,036.00				
5	Q2	$7,227.00	$2,459.00	$9,269.00	$8,442.00		Sum for city:	London	$23,062.00
6	Q3	$4,426.00	$3,920.00	$6,803.00	$6,306.00				
7	Q4	$8,774.00	$2,566.00	$5,775.00	$2,390.00				
8									
9									
10									

Formula explanation

=SUM(INDEX(B4:E7,0,XMATCH(H5,B3:E3)))

The INDEX function in the formula uses a nested XMATCH to return its column_num argument:

XMATCH(H5,B3:E3)

The XMATCH function uses the value in cell H5 as its lookup_value. Its lookup_array is B3:E3 (the column headers with the city names). The match_mode is omitted as we want an exact match. XMATCH returns a number corresponding to the column that matches the lookup value. In this example, the lookup value is **London**, so XMATCH returns **1**.

Thus, for the INDEX function, the array is B4:E7; the row_num is 0, meaning we want to return all rows; and the column_num is 1, which returns every value in the first column of the range B4:E7.

The SUM function then sums all values returned from the first column.

INDEX Function - Reference Form

The reference form of the INDEX function returns the value of the cell at the intersection of a row and column. The reference argument can be made up of non-contiguous ranges, and you can pick which range to search using the area_num argument.

Syntax

=INDEX(reference, row_num,[col_num],[area_num])

Arguments

Argument	Description
reference	Required. A reference to one or more ranges. If you are entering more than one range, enclose this argument in parentheses. For example, INDEX((A1:B10,D1:D10),3,4).
row_num	Required. The row number in *reference* from which to return a value. If row_num is omitted, column_num is required.
column_num	Optional. Selects the column in the *array* argument from which to return a value. If column_num is omitted, row_num is required.
area_num	Optional. Selects a range in *reference* from which the intersection of *row_num* and *column_num* will be returned. The areas are numbered 1, 2, 3, etc. If area_num is omitted, the default, 1, is used. The areas need to be on the same worksheet.

Remarks

- If you specify areas in *reference* that are not on the same worksheet as each other, the function will return an error (#VALUE!). If you need to use ranges on different worksheets, it is recommended that you use the array form of INDEX and use another function to generate the range that makes up the array. For example, you could use the CHOOSE function to specify the ranges.

- If each area in *reference* contains only one row or column, the row_num or column_num argument is optional. For example, use INDEX(reference, column_num) for a single-row reference.

- *row_num* and *column_num* must point to a cell within *reference,* or the function will return a #REF! error.

Example

In this example, we have four named ranges making up the *reference* argument:

Reference	Range name	Area_num
B6:E9	Year1	1
H6:K9	Year2	2
B13:E16	Year3	3
H13:K16	Year4	4

To return a value from one of these ranges, we specify the range with a *rea_num*. The ranges are numbered by order of entry, starting from 1.

Year1 = 1; Year2 = 2; Year3 = 3; Year4 = 4

In the following formula, we want to return the value in Year 4, Q3, for Toronto.

=INDEX((Year1,Year2,Year3,Year4),3,4,J2)

A cell reference, J2, is used for the *area_num* so that the value can be easily changed on the worksheet to point to a different range when needed.

K2			fx	=INDEX((Year1,Year2,Year3,Year4),3,4,J2)						

	A	B	C	D	E	F	G	H	I		K
1	Quaterly Data										
2									Year:	4	$9,851.00
3											
4		Year 1						Year 2			
5		London	Paris	New York	Toronto			London	Paris	New York	Toronto
6	Q1	$2,635.00	$2,194.00	$7,217.00	$7,036.00		Q1	$7,062.00	$9,851.00	$6,499.00	$6,824.00
7	Q2	$7,227.00	$2,459.00	$9,269.00	$8,442.00		Q2	$6,945.00	$5,746.00	$7,611.00	$5,690.00
8	Q3	$4,426.00	$3,920.00	$6,803.00	$6,306.00		Q3	$9,400.00	$6,173.00	$8,901.00	$6,528.00
9	Q4	$8,774.00	$2,566.00	$5,775.00	$2,390.00		Q4	$5,848.00	$6,937.00	$6,945.00	$5,746.00
10											
11		Year 3						Year 4			
12		London	Paris	New York	Toronto			London	Paris	New York	Toronto
13	Q1	$8,442.00	$4,227.00	$6,067.00	$2,036.00		Q1	$4,408.00	$9,095.00	$9,879.00	$6,692.00
14	Q2	$6,306.00	$8,998.00	$4,213.00	$7,062.00		Q2	$4,227.00	$6,067.00	$2,036.00	$3,063.00
15	Q3	$2,390.00	$5,848.00	$6,937.00	$6,945.00		Q3	$8,998.00	$4,213.00	$7,062.00	$9,851.00
16	Q4	$7,734.00	$3,375.00	$9,024.00	$9,400.00		Q4	$6,306.00	$8,998.00	$4,213.00	$7,062.00
17											

The formula returns **$9,851.00** from the fourth range in the third row and fourth column.

The INDEX function is most useful when combined with other functions like XMATCH.

Finding Matches with INDEX and XMATCH

In the example below, we want to identify the sales amount for a Sales Rep for a given quarter. The combination of INDEX/XMATCH/XMATCH enables us to perform a simultaneous vertical and horizontal lookup.

D3			fx	=INDEX(C6:F17,XMATCH(B3,B6:B17),XMATCH(C3,C5:F5))				

	A	B	C	D	E	F	G	H	I
1									
2		Sales Rep	Quarter	Sales					
3		Shaun	Q3	$66,561					
4									
5		Sales Rep	Q1	Q2	Q3	Q4			
6		Penny	$17,526	$23,972	$61,066	$22,596			
7		Leslie	$49,405	$36,646	$21,899	$62,629			
8		Sally	$78,658	$16,529	$14,976	$68,184			
9		Shaun	$80,176	$84,918	$66,561	$65,326			
10		Julie	$86,988	$29,692	$30,197	$80,960			
11		Velma	$94,514	$13,333	$78,000	$59,718			
12		Ian	$23,183	$21,547	$40,408	$57,767			
13		Cassandra	$70,597	$19,615	$54,664	$68,175			
14		Mark	$16,832	$91,907	$19,062	$23,167			
15		Kathy	$45,446	$14,638	$52,312	$92,069			
16		Renee	$34,583	$78,213	$21,295	$26,964			
17		Judith	$18,689	$91,081	$66,795	$96,860			
18									

Second XMATCH

First XMATCH

Formula explanation:

=INDEX(C6:F17,XMATCH(B3,B6:B17),XMATCH(C3,C5:F5))

The INDEX function has three arguments. The first argument is the range C6:F17. The first XMATCH function represents *row_num,* while the second XMATCH function represents the *column_num* argument.

The first XMATCH function returns **4**, which is the relative position of "Shaun" in range B6:B17, while the second XMATCH function returns **3**, which is the relative position of "Q3" in range C5:F5.

You can use the **Evaluate Formula** command (on the **Formulas** tab) to step through the formula and see the results at each evaluation stage until it gets to the final arguments used to execute the INDEX function. The image below shows that the *row_num* and *column_num* arguments evaluate to 4 and 3.

=INDEX(C6:F17,4,3)

Manipulating Columns and Rows

The functions in this category enable you to select and return several columns or rows in your specified order. You can also transpose columns or rows.

CHOOSECOLS Function

The CHOOSECOLS function returns the specified columns from a range in the order specified in the arguments. This function enables you to select a subset of columns or rearrange their order. You can use CHOOSECOLS to return an array as an argument in another formula.

Syntax

=CHOOSECOLS(array,col_num1,[col_num2],…)

Arguments

Arguments	Description
array	Required. The range or array that has the columns you want to return.
col_num1	Required. A number representing the first column to return from the range specified in *array*.
[col_num2], …	Optional. A number representing an additional column to return. You can have several optional columns, for example, col_num3, col_num4, col_num5, etc.

Remarks

- Excel returns a #VALUE error if any of the col_num arguments exceeds the number of columns in the array.

- Excel returns a #VALUE error if any of the col_num arguments is 0.

Example 1

The formula below selects columns 2 and 4 from the range B2:E17.

=CHOOSECOLS(B2:E17,1,4)

	A	B	C	D	E	F	G	H
	G2				fx	=CHOOSECOLS(B2:E17,1,4)		
1	**Sales by Quarter**							
2		QTR1	QTR2	QTR3	QTR4		QTR1	QTR4
3	Chai	$672.00	$921.00	$344.00	$131.00		$672.00	$131.00
4	Beer	$966.00	$595.00	$136.00	$416.00		$966.00	$416.00
5	Coffee	$442.00	$564.00	$570.00	$427.00		$442.00	$427.00
6	Green Tea	$163.00	$284.00	$801.00	$713.00		$163.00	$713.00
7	Tea	$744.00	$282.00	$169.00	$142.00		$744.00	$142.00
8	Chocolate Biscuits Mix	$592.00	$104.00	$449.00	$652.00		$592.00	$652.00
9	Scones	$917.00	$814.00	$796.00	$593.00		$917.00	$593.00
10	Brownie Mix	$502.00	$270.00	$614.00	$313.00		$502.00	$313.00
11	Cake Mix	$555.00	$384.00	$250.00	$612.00		$555.00	$612.00
12	Granola	$555.00	$807.00	$244.00	$856.00		$555.00	$856.00
13	Hot Cereal	$770.00	$916.00	$858.00	$288.00		$770.00	$288.00
14	Chocolate	$258.00	$765.00	$578.00	$900.00		$258.00	$900.00
15	Fruit Cocktail	$552.00	$118.00	$335.00	$366.00		$552.00	$366.00
16	Pears	$763.00	$509.00	$374.00	$368.00		$763.00	$368.00
17	Peaches	$199.00	$998.00	$200.00	$264.00		$199.00	$264.00
18								
19								

419

Example 2 – Rearrange columns with **CHOOSECOLS**

The following example combines VLOOKUP and CHOOSECOLS to perform left lookups. By default, VLOOKUP is limited to only being able to perform right lookups, but we can use CHOOSECOLS to rearrange the columns so that our formula performs left lookups.

=VLOOKUP(B3,CHOOSECOLS(E3:F47,2,1),2,FALSE)

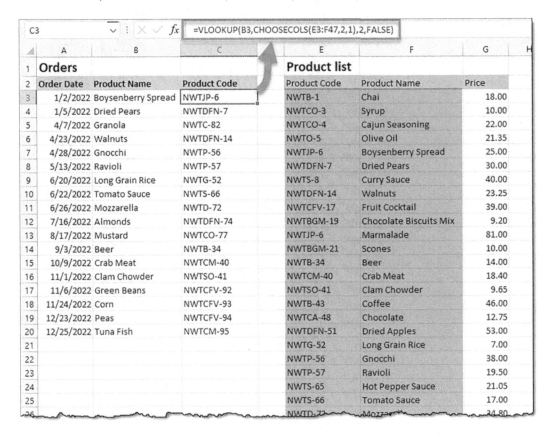

Formula explanation:

=VLOOKUP(B3,CHOOSECOLS(E3:F47,2,1),2,FALSE)

The formula reverses the order of the columns, placing column E to the right of column F with the following:

CHOOSECOLS(E3:F47,2,1).

The nested function has the following arguments:
- array = E3:F47
- col_num1 = 2
- col_num2 = 1

The formula returns an array with the first column as F3:F47 and the second column as E3:E47. Hence, VLOOKUP can now look up values in the first column (F3:F47) and return values from the second column, E3:E47.

See the section on VLOOKUP for a more detailed explanation of the function.

CHOOSEROWS Function

The CHOOSEROWS function returns several rows in the specified order from a range. This function is useful for returning an array as an argument in another formula.

Syntax

=CHOOSEROWS(array,row_num1,[row_num2],...)

Arguments

Argument	Description
array	Required. The range or array with the rows you want to return.
row_num1	Required. An integer representing the first row to return from the range specified in array.
[row_num2], ...	Optional. An integer representing an additional row to return. You can return several additional rows, for example, row_num3, row_num4, row_num5, etc.

Remarks

- Excel returns a #VALUE error if any of the row_num arguments exceeds the number of columns in the array.

- Excel returns a #VALUE error if any of the row_num arguments is 0.

Example 1

The following formula selects the first, fourth, and tenth rows from the array A2:C14.

=CHOOSEROWS(A2:C14,1,4,10)

	A	B	C	D	E	F	G
					E2 ✓ : × ✓ fx =CHOOSEROWS(A2:C14,1,4,10)		
1	Array				Returned rows		
2	NWTB-1	Chai	$18.00		NWTB-1	Chai	$18.00
3	NWTB-2	Syrup	$10.00		NWTB-4	Olive Oil	$21.35
4	NWTB-3	Cajun Seasoning	$22.00		NWTB-10	Chocolate Biscuits Mix	$9.20
5	NWTB-4	Olive Oil	$21.35				
6	NWTB-5	Boysenberry Spread	$25.00				
7	NWTB-6	Dried Pears	$30.00				
8	NWTB-7	Curry Sauce	$40.00				
9	NWTB-8	Walnuts	$23.25				
10	NWTB-9	Fruit Cocktail	$39.00				
11	NWTB-10	Chocolate Biscuits Mix	$9.20				
12	NWTB-11	Marmalade	$81.00				
13	NWTB-12	Scones	$10.00				
14	NWTB-13	Beer	$14.00				
15							
16							

Example 2

The following formula selects the last three rows in reverse order from the array A2:C14 by using negative numbers for the row_num arguments. -1 returns the last row in the array, -2 returns the second to the last, and so on.

=CHOOSEROWS(A2:C14,-1,-2,-3)

	A	B	C	D	E	F	G
					=CHOOSEROWS(A2:C14,-1,-2,-3)		

	A	B	C	D	E	F	G
1	Array				Returned rows		
2	NWTB-1	Chai	$18.00		NWTB-13	Beer	$14.00
3	NWTB-2	Syrup	$10.00		NWTB-12	Scones	$10.00
4	NWTB-3	Cajun Seasoning	$22.00		NWTB-11	Marmalade	$81.00
5	NWTB-4	Olive Oil	$21.35				
6	NWTB-5	Boysenberry Spread	$25.00				
7	NWTB-6	Dried Pears	$30.00				
8	NWTB-7	Curry Sauce	$40.00				
9	NWTB-8	Walnuts	$23.25				
10	NWTB-9	Fruit Cocktail	$39.00				
11	NWTB-10	Chocolate Biscuits Mix	$9.20				
12	NWTB-11	Marmalade	$81.00				
13	NWTB-12	Scones	$10.00				
14	NWTB-13	Beer	$14.00				
15							

Using an Array Constant

You can use an array constant in place of an argument to return multiple rows and simplify the formula. An array constant is a set of values enclosed in curly brackets {} often used in formulas to create or manipulate several values simultaneously rather than a single value.

For example, {"apple","orange","pear"}.

Example 3

The following formula uses an array constant to specify the rows returned by CHOOSEROWS.

=CHOOSEROWS(A3:C12,{1,2,3})

Notice the array constant {1,2,3} takes up only one argument in the formula but returns three rows.

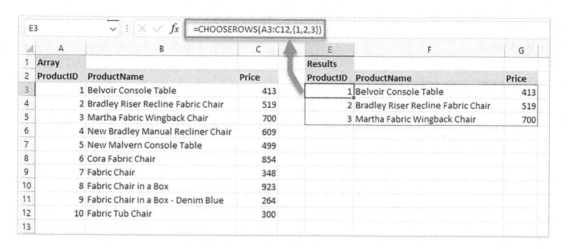

CHOOSE Function

The CHOOSE function allows you to use an index number to return a value from a list of arguments. The arguments can be values or cell references. You can use CHOOSE to select one out of a maximum of 254 values based on the index number.

CHOOSE is more useful when used in with another function in a formula. For example, you can use CHOOSE to rearrange columns in a list to perform left lookups with VLOOKUP.

Syntax

=CHOOSE(index_num, value1, [value2], ...)

Arguments

Argument	Description
index_num	Required. This argument specifies the value to be selected from the list. The value must be a number between 1 and 254. It can be a formula or a cell reference that returns a number between 1 and 254.
value1	Required. The first value is required. Values can be numbers, cell references, ranges, formulas, functions, or text.
[value2], ...	Optional. You can have up to 253 additional optional values.

Remarks

If the index_num argument is less than 1 or greater than the number of the last value in the list, CHOOSE returns a #VALUE! error. If index_num is a fraction, it will be truncated to the lowest integer.

Example 1

The CHOOSE function is most useful when used in combination with another function. For example, we can nest the CHOOSE function within the SUM function.

The example below has one SUM formula that can calculate the total of individual quarters. We just need to specify the quarter number to determine which quarter to calculate.

| C20 | ⌄ | : | × ✓ | *fx* | =SUM(CHOOSE(B20,B3:B17,C3:C17,D3:D17,E3:E17)) |

◢	A	B	C	D	E	F	G
1	**Sales by Quarter**						
2		QTR1	QTR2	QTR3	QTR4		
3	Chai	$672.00	$921.00	$344.00	$131.00		
4	Beer	$966.00	$595.00	$136.00	$416.00		
5	Coffee	$442.00	$564.00	$570.00	$427.00		
6	Green Tea	$163.00	$284.00	$801.00	$713.00		
7	Tea	$744.00	$282.00	$169.00	$142.00		
8	Chocolate Biscuits Mix	$592.00	$104.00	$449.00	$652.00		
9	Scones	$917.00	$814.00	$796.00	$593.00		
10	Brownie Mix	$502.00	$270.00	$614.00	$313.00		
11	Cake Mix	$555.00	$384.00	$250.00	$612.00		
12	Granola	$555.00	$807.00	$244.00	$856.00		
13	Hot Cereal	$770.00	$916.00	$858.00	$288.00		
14	Chocolate	$258.00	$765.00	$578.00	$900.00		
15	Fruit Cocktail	$552.00	$118.00	$335.00	$366.00		
16	Pears	$763.00	$509.00	$374.00	$368.00		
17	Peaches	$199.00	$998.00	$200.00	$264.00		
18							
19							
20	CHOOSE QTR	4	$7,041.00				
21							

Formula explanation

The following formula is entered in cell C20:

=SUM(CHOOSE(B20,B3:B17,C3:C17,D3:D17,E3:E17))

The value in **B20** is **4**, which represents **QTR4**. So, the result returned by the formula is for the range E3:E17.

The CHOOSE function is first evaluated, and it returns the range E3:E17. The SUM function then sums up E3:E17 to provide the total for that quarter.

Of course, looking at the example above, it may appear that it would be easier to just sum up each quarter separately. However, there may be scenarios when we want to produce dynamic summaries by changing the target range.

Example 2 – Rearrange columns with CHOOSE

One limitation of VLOOKUP is that we can only return values in a column to the right of the lookup range. In the example below, the lookup range is F3:F47, and the return range is E3:E47. The return values are in a column to the left of the lookup column.

For example, imagine that we're not allowed to rearrange the columns of the original data. We can use the CHOOSE function to rearrange the columns for the table_array argument of VLOOKUP.

Applying the CHOOSE function to our formula produces the following:

=VLOOKUP(B3,CHOOSE({1,2},ProductNames,ProductCodes),2,FALSE)

Note that this formula uses two range names:

- ProductCodes = E3:E47

- ProductNames = F3:F47

-Tip Use range names instead of absolute references, as they're easier to read in formulas.

| C3 | ⌄ : X ✓ fx | =VLOOKUP(B3,CHOOSE({1,2},ProductNames,ProductCodes),2,FALSE) |

⏴	A	B	C	D	E	F	G
1	**Orders**				**Product list**		
2	Order Date	Product Name	Product Code		Product Code	Product Name	Price
3	01/02/2016	Boysenberry Spread	NWTJP-6		NWTB-1	Chai	18.00
4	01/05/2016	Dried Pears	NWTDFN-7		NWTCO-3	Syrup	10.00
5	04/07/2016	Granola	NWTC-82		NWTCO-4	Cajun Seasoning	22.00
6	04/23/2016	Walnuts	NWTDFN-14		NWTO-5	Olive Oil	21.35
7	04/28/2016	Gnocchi	NWTP-56		NWTJP-6	Boysenberry Spread	25.00
8	05/13/2016	Ravioli	NWTP-57		NWTDFN-7	Dried Pears	30.00
9	06/20/2016	Long Grain Rice	NWTG-52		NWTS-8	Curry Sauce	40.00
10	06/22/2016	Tomato Sauce	NWTS-66		NWTDFN-14	Walnuts	23.25
11	06/26/2016	Mozzarella	NWTD-72		NWTCFV-17	Fruit Cocktail	39.00
12	07/16/2016	Almonds	NWTDFN-74		NWTBGM-19	Chocolate Biscuits Mix	9.20
13	08/17/2016	Mustard	NWTCO-77		NWTJP-6	Marmalade	81.00
14	09/03/2016	Beer	NWTB-34		NWTBGM-21	Scones	10.00
15	10/09/2016	Crab Meat	NWTCM-40		NWTB-34	Beer	14.00
16	11/01/2016	Clam Chowder	NWTSO-41		NWTCM-40	Crab Meat	18.40
17	11/06/2016	Green Beans	NWTCFV-92		NWTSO-41	Clam Chowder	9.65
18	11/24/2016	Corn	NWTCFV-93		NWTB-43	Coffee	46.00
19	12/23/2016	Peas	NWTCFV-94		NWTCA-48	Chocolate	12.75
20	12/25/2016	Tuna Fish	NWTCM-95		NWTDFN-51	Dried Apples	53.00
21					NWTG-52	Long Grain Rice	7.00
22					NWTP-56	Gnocchi	38.00
23					NWTP-57	Ravioli	19.50
24					NWTS-65	Hot Pepper Sauce	21.05

CHOOSE column 2   CHOOSE column 1

Formula explanation:

=VLOOKUP(B3,CHOOSE({1,2},ProductNames,ProductCodes),2,FALSE)

Our table_array is E3:F47, and we want to return values in column E. We want a method in our formula that reverses the order of the columns, that is, put column E to the right of column F. The CHOOSE formula can do this:

CHOOSE({1,2},ProductNames,ProductCodes)

This formula has F3:F47 (ProductName) as the *value1* argument and E3:E47 (ProductCodes) as the *value2* argument. Both ranges are absolute references in the formula, as range names are absolute references by default.

The *index_num* argument of our CHOOSE function is an array constant {1,2}, which tells the function to return the data in the order *value1* and *value2*, that is, ProductNames before ProductCodes.

With the columns of *table_array* now rearranged by CHOOSE, VLOOKUP can now look up a value in ProductNames, and return a corresponding value in ProductCodes.

We can fill down the formula to populate the other cells in column C.

TRANSPOSE Function

The TRANSPOSE function enables you to transpose data in your worksheet.
If you want to rotate data on your worksheet, you can use the Transpose option on the paste command. The TRANSPOSE function provides a way to perform the same task automatically with a formula. TRANSPOSE can be useful when you want to copy and transpose data from several ranges across different worksheets.

Tip To manually copy and transpose a range as a one-off task, use the **Transpose** option on the **Paste** command (or the **Paste Special** dialog box).

Syntax

=TRANSPOSE(array)

Argument

Argument	Description
array	Required. The range of cells that you want to transpose.

Example:

In this example, we want to transpose the data in cells A1:B4 in the table below.

Follow the steps below to copy and transpose a range:

1. Click the top-left cell of the destination range.

2. In the formula bar, type **=TRANSPOSE(**

3. Select the source range on the worksheet with your mouse.

4. Enter the closing bracket.

5. Press **Enter**.

Excel transposes the data from the top-left of the destination cell and spills it to adjacent cells.

A7			fx	=TRANSPOSE(A1:B4)		
	A	**B**	**C**	**D**	**E**	
1	QTR1	$2,000.00				
2	QTR2	$3,000.00				
3	QTR3	$1,400.00				
4	QTR4	$5,000.00				
5						
6						
7	QTR1	QTR2	QTR3	QTR4		
8	2000	3000	1400	5000		
9						

Note If you're using a standalone version of Excel before Excel 2021, you need to select all cells needed for the result and then press **CTRL+SHIFT+ENTER** to paste the result of the formula.

COLUMNS and ROWS Functions

The COLUMNS function returns the number of columns in an array or range. The ROWS function returns the number of rows in an array or range. These two functions are often used in formulas where you need to return the number of columns or rows in a specified range as an argument of another function.

As these two functions are very similar, this section covers them simultaneously.

Syntax

=COLUMNS(array)

=ROWS(array)

Argument	Description
array	Required. An array or a reference to a range you want to count.

Example

The following example counts the number of rows and columns in a range.

The formulas used to get the count are:

=COLUMNS(A1:E23)

=ROWS(A1:E23)

	A	B	C	D	E	F	G	H	I
								Count	Formula Text
1	$2,635	$7,227	$4,426	$8,774	$9,829				
2	$2,194	$2,459	$3,920	$2,566	$4,894		Rows:	23	=ROWS(A1:E23)
3	$7,217	$9,269	$6,803	$5,775	$4,857		Columns:	5	=COLUMNS(A1:E23)
4	$7,036	$8,442	$6,306	$2,390	$7,734				
5	$4,408	$4,227	$8,998	$5,848	$3,375				
6	$9,095	$6,067	$4,213	$6,937	$9,024				
7	$9,879	$2,036	$7,062	$6,945	$9,400				
8	$6,692	$3,063	$9,851	$5,746	$6,173				
9	$3,513	$4,434	$6,499	$7,611	$8,901				
10	$4,032	$4,280	$6,824	$5,690	$6,528				
11	$7,217	$9,269	$6,803	$5,775	$4,857				
12	$7,036	$8,442	$6,306	$2,390	$7,734				

Returning Cell Information

The functions under this category enable you to create formulas that return information about a cell. For example, the formula in the cell or its reference.

FORMULATEXT Function

The FORMULATEXT function enables you to display the formula from one cell in another cell in your worksheet. This function is useful for identifying errors in your syntax or comparing different formulas side by side. Instead of only checking your formulas one at a time by clicking on each cell, you can use FORMULATEXT to reveal the formulas in several cells simultaneously.

Syntax

FORMULATEXT(reference)

Argument

Argument	Description
reference	Required. A reference to a cell in the current workbook or another open workbook.

Remarks

FORMULATEXT will return the #N/A error if:

- The cell used as the reference argument does not contain a formula.

- The reference argument is in an external workbook that is not open.

- The formula can't be displayed due to worksheet protection.

If the reference argument points to more than one cell, for example, a range, FORMULATEXT will return the value in the upper leftmost cell in the range.

Example

In this example, we have some values in range A2:A9. In range C2:C7, different aggregate formulas calculate the values in A2:A9. The worksheet uses FORMULATEXT to display the formulas in column D.

D2		fx	=FORMULATEXT(C2)
	A	B	C	D
1	Values		Aggregate	Formula text
2	$18.00	Sum	$181.35	=SUM(A2:A9)
3	$10.00	Avg	$22.67	=AVERAGE(A2:A9)
4	$22.00	Count	8	=COUNT(A2:A9)
5	$21.35	Max	$40.00	=MAX(A2:A9)
6	$25.00	Min	$10.00	=MIN(A2:A9)
7	$30.00	Median	$21.68	=MEDIAN(A2:A9)
8	$15.00			
9	$40.00			
10				

ADDRESS Function

You can use the ADDRESS function to return the address of a cell in a worksheet when you provide the row and column numbers as arguments. For example, =ADDRESS(4,6) returns $F$4. This function is useful when you need to return the address of a cell in your formula.

Syntax

=ADDRESS(row_num, column_num, [abs_num], [a1], [sheet_text])

Arguments

Argument	Description
row_num	Required. A number that specifies the row number to use in the cell reference.
column_num	Required. A number that specifies the column number to use in the cell reference.
abs_num	Optional. Specifies the reference type to return, e.g., absolute, relative, or mixed reference. The default is Absolute reference, which will be used if abs_num is omitted. Argument values 1 (or omitted) = Absolute reference 2 = Mixed reference. Absolute row, relative column 3 = Mixed reference. Relative row, absolute column 4 = Relative reference
a1	Optional. A logical value that specifies whether to use the A1 or R1C1 style of reference. TRUE is A1, and FALSE is R1C1. If this argument is omitted, A1 is used.
sheet_text	Optional. A string specifying the name of the worksheet from which to get the cell reference. To be used when connecting to an external sheet. If this argument is omitted, the current sheet is used.

Note In Excel, A1 referencing means columns are labeled alphabetically and rows numerically. R1C1 referencing means both columns and rows are labeled numerically.

The A1 reference style is the default and the recommendation for most occasions. However, if you need to change the reference style, click **File** > **Options** > **Formulas**. Under **Working with formulas**, check or uncheck the **R1C1 reference style** checkbox. The default reference style is A1, so R1C1 should be unchecked by default.

Examples

Example 1	
Formula:	=ADDRESS(2,4)
Description:	Absolute reference in the current sheet.
Result:	$D$2

Example 2	
Formula:	=ADDRESS(2,4,2)
Description:	Mixed reference. Absolute row; relative column.
Result:	D$2

Example 3	
Formula:	=ADDRESS(2,4,2,FALSE)
Description:	Mixed reference. Absolute row; relative column using the R1C1 reference style.
Result:	R2C[4]

Example 4	
Formula:	=ADDRESS(2,4,1,FALSE,"[Book2]Sheet1")
Description:	An absolute reference to another workbook (Book2) and worksheet.
Result:	[Book2]Sheet1!R2C4

Example 5	
Formula:	=ADDRESS(2,4,1,FALSE,"Accounts sheet")
Description:	An absolute reference to another worksheet.
Result:	'Accounts sheet'!R2C4

Filtering and Sorting Ranges

The dynamic array functions in this section allow you to select data from lists and return arrays that are filtered or sorted without changing the source data.

UNIQUE Function

Excel's UNIQUE function is a dynamic array function that returns a list of unique values in an array or range. UNIQUE returns an array, which spills across the required range if it's the final output of a formula. When you press ENTER, Excel will dynamically create the required sized range for the output.

Note that you can use the **Remove Duplicates** command button in Excel to create unique rows in a list manually. However, UNIQUE comes in handy when you need to return an array of unique values in a formula or to create a dynamic list of unique values without changing the original data source.

Syntax

=UNIQUE(array,[by_col],[exactly_once])

Arguments

Argument	Description
array	Required. The range or array from which to return unique values.
by_col	Optional. A logical value specifying how to perform the comparison. TRUE = compare columns against each other. FALSE (or omitted) = compare rows against each other.
exactly_once	Optional. This argument is a logical value to indicate whether to return rows/columns that only occur once in array. TRUE = return values that occur only once in the range/array. FALSE (or omitted) = return all distinct values (i.e., eliminate duplicates).

Example

The following example uses Excel's UNIQUE to generate a list of unique states from the range B2:B19. A lookup list like this can be used as the data source for a dropdown list somewhere else in the worksheet. Dynamically generating the list saves you from manually creating the lookup list.

Formula explanation

=SORT(UNIQUE(B2:B19,FALSE,FALSE))

The range B2:B19 is the array argument. The by_col and exactly_once arguments are FALSE, meaning the formula returns all unique values, i.e., removes duplicates. The result is displayed in the range E2:E12. Note that the formula uses the SORT function to sort the returned array in alphabetical order.

| E2 | | fx | =SORT(UNIQUE(B2:B19,FALSE,FALSE)) | |

	A	B	C	D	E	F
1	Salesperson	State	Sales		States - Unique	
2	Hill, Virginia	Minnesota(MN)	$4,061		Arizona(AZ)	
3	Johnson, Cheryl	Texas(TX)	$2,746		Georgia(GA)	
4	Griffin, Ruth	Kentucky(KY)	$5,183		Illinois(IL)	
5	Morris, Andrea	Minnesota(MN)	$5,048		Kentucky(KY)	
6	Walker, Steven	Georgia(GA)	$3,851		Louisiana(LA)	
7	Hall, Ruby	Louisiana(LA)	$4,562		Massachusetts(MA)	
8	Rogers, Marilyn	Kentucky(KY)	$6,942		Minnesota(MN)	
9	Scott, Amanda	Georgia(GA)	$5,141		Mississippi(MS)	
10	Taylor, Christina	Mississippi(MS)	$2,634		Pennsylvania(PA)	
11	Diaz, Jerry	Texas(TX)	$1,149		Texas(TX)	
12	Russell, Jack	Texas(TX)	$6,586		Washington(WA)	
13	Mitchell, Linda	Washington(WA)	$5,473			
14	Sanchez, Shawn	Texas(TX)	$1,971			
15	Campbell, Dorothy	Pennsylvania(PA)	$6,027			
16	Ross, Kimberly	Illinois(IL)	$4,670			
17	Thompson, Raymond	Massachusetts(MA)	$2,018			
18	Simmons, Shirley	Texas(TX)	$1,270			
19	Morgan, Gary	Arizona(AZ)	$5,224			
20						
21						

FILTER Function

The FILTER function is a dynamic array function that filters and returns an array based on the specified criteria. You can filter a range using the **Filter** command on the Excel ribbon. However, the FILTER function is useful when supplying the range as an argument inside a formula to display the result as an array in a different range. FILTER will return several values, which will spill across the cells required to hold the result when you enter the formula and press ENTER.

Syntax

=FILTER(array,include,[if_empty])

441

Arguments

Argument	Description
array	Required. The range you want to filter. This can be a row of values, a column of values, or several rows and columns of values.
include	Required. A Boolean array or an expression specifying the criteria that returns a Boolean array. For example, A2:A10="Apples".
[if_empty]	Optional. You can specify a string value to return if the filter returns nothing. For example, "No data".

Remarks

- FILTER will return a #CALC! error if the return value is empty, as Excel does not currently support empty arrays. To avoid this error, if there is a possibility that your formula will return no records, use the if_empty argument to specify a value to return in place of the error.

- FILTER will return an error (#N/A, #VALUE, etc.) if any value in the criteria range is an error or cannot be converted to a Boolean value with the expression in the *include* argument.

- The *include* argument should be a Boolean array or an expression that returns a Boolean array whose height or width is the same as the array argument.

Example

The example below has a list of sales data in the range A3:D50. On the right of the worksheet, we want to view a subset of sales data filtered by product category.

We can combine FILTER and CHOOSECOLS to achieve the desired result as in the formula below.

=FILTER(CHOOSECOLS(A3:D50,1,2,4),C3:C50=G3,"No data")

| F6 | ⌄ : | × ✓ ƒx | =FILTER(CHOOSECOLS(A3:D50,1,2,4),C3:C50=G3,"No data") | | | | | |

◢	A	B	C	D	E	F	G	H
1	Sales					Filtered by product category		
2	Salesperson	Product	Category	Price				
3	Ross Grant	Cora Fabric Chair	Chair	$706		Enter Category:	Sofa	
4	Jan Kotas	Lukah Leather Chair	Chair	$1,049				
5	Mae Stevens	Habitat Oken Console Table	Table	$1,706		Product	Product	Price
6	Jesse Garza	Tessa Fabric Sofa	Sofa	$1,213		Jesse Garza	Tessa Fabric Sofa	$1,213
7	Ross Grant	Harley Fabric Cuddle Chair	Chair	$1,317		Mae Stevens	Tessa Fabric Sofa	$1,213
8	Jan Kotas	Windsor 2 Seater Cuddle Chair	Chair	$1,687		Ross Grant	Trieste Leather Sofa	$628
9	Mae Stevens	Fabric Tub Chair	Chair	$1,060		Jesse Garza	Tessa Fabric Sofa	$1,213
10	Laura Giussani	Verona 1 Shelf Table	Table	$1,265		Ross Grant	Tessa Fabric Sofa	$1,213
11	Ross Grant	Floral Fabric Tub Chair	Chair	$915				
12	Jan Kotas	Fabric Chair in a Box	Box	$856				
13	Mae Stevens	Slimline Console Table	Table	$762				
14	Loren Pratt	Martha Fabric Wingback Chair	Chair	$883				
15	Loren Pratt	Slimline Console Table	Table	$626				
16	Loren Pratt	Fabric Wingback Chair	Chair	$1,786				
17	Loren Pratt	Fabric Chair in a Box	Box	$888				
18	Loren Pratt	Verona Chair in a Box	Box	$765				
19	Robert Zare	Cora Fabric Chair	Chair	$1,772				
20	Jesse Garza	Fabric Wingback Chair	Chair	$773				
21	Mae Stevens	Tessa Fabric Sofa	Sofa	$1,213				

Formula explanation

=FILTER(CHOOSECOLS(A3:D50,1,2,4),C3:C50=G3,"No data")

This formula is in two parts. The first part uses CHOOSECOLS to return all values in columns 1, 2, and 4 from the range A3:D50.

The second part of the formula uses the FILTER function to filter the result using the expression **C3:C50=G3**. This expression is the *include* argument for the FILTER function. It uses the criteria in cell G3 to filter the values in the range C3:C50 to return rows where the product category matches the criteria.

The value in the *if_empty* argument ensures the formula returns "No data" instead of an error for instances where no results match the entered criteria.

SORT Function

The SORT function is a dynamic array function that takes in an array and returns a sorted list based on the sort_index and sort_order you have specified. SORT will spill the result across the required range. The SORT function is more useful for sorting an array as an argument. To sort data directly on the worksheet, use the SORTBY function, which supports multi-level sorting.

Syntax:

=SORT(array,[sort_index],[sort_order],[by_col])

Arguments

Argument	Description
array	Required. The range or array to sort.
sort_index	Optional. A number that specifies the row or column within the array to sort by. The default is 1 if omitted.
sort_order	Optional. The sort order to use. 1 = ascending (default). -1 =descending. If omitted, the default is ascending.
by_col	Optional. A logical value to indicate whether to sort by column or by row. FALSE = sort by row (default) TRUE = sort by column If omitted, the default is FALSE, i.e., sort by row.

Example

In the following example, we want to return records filtered by State to show the best-performing salespeople first. The following formula combines the SORT and FILTER functions to achieve the desired result.

=SORT(FILTER(A3:C20,B3:B20=F1),3,-1)

E5				f_x	=SORT(FILTER(A3:C20,B3:B20=F1),3,-1)		
	A	B	C	D	E	F	G
1	Array				Enter State:	TX	
2	Salesperson	State	Sales				
3	Hill, Virginia	MN	$4,061		Filtered list		
4	Johnson, Cheryl	TX	$2,746		Salesperson	State	Sales
5	Griffin, Ruth	KY	$5,183		Russell, Jack	TX	$6,586
6	Morris, Andrea	MN	$5,048		Johnson, Cheryl	TX	$2,746
7	Walker, Steven	GA	$3,851		Sanchez, Shawn	TX	$1,971
8	Hall, Ruby	LA	$4,562		Simmons, Shirley	TX	$1,270
9	Rogers, Marilyn	KY	$6,942		Diaz, Jerry	TX	$1,149
10	Scott, Amanda	GA	$5,141				
11	Taylor, Christina	MS	$2,634				
12	Diaz, Jerry	TX	$1,149				
13	Russell, Jack	TX	$6,586				
14	Mitchell, Linda	WA	$5,473				
15	Sanchez, Shawn	TX	$1,971				
16	Campbell, Dorothy	PA	$6,027				
17	Ross, Kimberly	IL	$4,670				
18	Thompson, Raymond	MA	$2,018				
19	Simmons, Shirley	TX	$1,270				
20	Morgan, Gary	AZ	$5,224				
21							

Formula explanation:

=SORT(FILTER(A3:C20,B3:B20=F1),3,-1)

The above formula has A3:C20 as the array from which we want to extract a filtered and sorted list.

The FILTER function has **B3:B20=F1** as its *include* argument. This expression filters the data in cells A3:C20 and returns only rows where the State matches the value entered in cell F1.

The SORT function's sort_index argument is **3**, indicating the formula uses the third column (Sales) for the sort. The sort_order is **-1**, which sorts the data in descending order.

The result is a list filtered by state and sorted in descending order by sales.

SORTBY Function

The SORTBY function sorts the values of a range or array based on specified 'sort by' ranges and sort orders. SORTBY is an array function and spills the result across the required range. The 'sort by' range does not necessarily need to be part of the source range but must have the same number of rows as the source range. You can perform a multi-level sort by providing additional pairs of by_array and sort_order arguments.

Syntax

=SORTBY(array, by_array1, [sort_order1], [by_array2, sort_order2],…)

Arguments

Argument	Description
array	Required. The range or array to sort.
by_array1	Required. The range or array to sort by.
[sort_order1]	Optional. The sort order to use.
	1 = ascending
	-1 =descending
	If omitted, the default is ascending.
[by_array2, sort_order2],…	Optional. Additional pairs of by_array/sort_order arguments to sort the array by more than one field.

Remarks

- All range/array arguments must be the same size.

- SORTBY will return a #VALUE! error if you enter a sort order argument that's not 1 or -1. If you omit the sort order argument, Excel will use ascending order.

Example 1

In the following example, we use SORTBY to sort and return the range B3:C20 by the **State** and **Sales** amount (B3:B20 and C3:C20). So, the formula has a two-level sort. The sorted data is displayed in cell E20:F20.

=SORTBY(B3:C20,B3:B20,1,C3:C20,-1)

	A	B	C	D	E	F
					fx =SORTBY(B3:C20,B3:B20,1,C3:C20,-1)	
	A	B	C	D	E	F
1	Array				Sorted Result	
2	Salesperson	State	Sales		State	Sales
3	Hill, Virginia	Minnesota(MN)	$4,061		Arizona(AZ)	$5,224
4	Johnson, Cheryl	Texas(TX)	$2,746		Georgia(GA)	$5,141
5	Griffin, Ruth	Kentucky(KY)	$5,183		Georgia(GA)	$3,851
6	Morris, Andrea	Minnesota(MN)	$5,048		Illinois(IL)	$4,670
7	Walker, Steven	Georgia(GA)	$3,851		Kentucky(KY)	$6,942
8	Hall, Ruby	Louisiana(LA)	$4,562		Kentucky(KY)	$5,183
9	Rogers, Marilyn	Kentucky(KY)	$6,942		Louisiana(LA)	$4,562
10	Scott, Amanda	Georgia(GA)	$5,141		Massachusetts(MA)	$2,018
11	Taylor, Christina	Mississippi(MS)	$2,634		Minnesota(MN)	$5,048
12	Diaz, Jerry	Texas(TX)	$1,149		Minnesota(MN)	$4,061
13	Russell, Jack	Texas(TX)	$6,586		Mississippi(MS)	$2,634
14	Mitchell, Linda	Washington(WA)	$5,473		Pennsylvania(PA)	$6,027
15	Sanchez, Shawn	Texas(TX)	$1,971		Texas(TX)	$6,586
16	Campbell, Dorothy	Pennsylvania(PA)	$6,027		Texas(TX)	$2,746
17	Ross, Kimberly	Illinois(IL)	$4,670		Texas(TX)	$1,971
18	Thompson, Raymond	Massachusetts(MA)	$2,018		Texas(TX)	$1,270
19	Simmons, Shirley	Texas(TX)	$1,270		Texas(TX)	$1,149
20	Morgan, Gary	Arizona(AZ)	$5,224		Washington(WA)	$5,473
21						

Formula explanation

=SORTBY(B3:C20,B3:B20,1,C3:C20,-1)

This formula has B3:C20 as the source array. B3:B20 is the first by_array (i.e., sort by) argument, and its sort order is 1 (ascending). The second by_array argument is C3:C20, and its sort order is -1 (descending).

The result is a list sorted by state alphabetically, then sales, in descending order. Thus, for each state, you'll see the highest sales first.

Chapter 3

Logical Functions

This chapter covers functions that enable you to:

- ■ Select which statement to execute based on the result of a logical test.

- ■ Check that multiple conditions are met with nested functions before executing a statement.

- ■ Check that at least one of several conditions is met before executing a statement.

- ■ Identify values in a list and provide replacement values.

- ■ Trap errors in formulas and return a user-friendly message or a meaningful value.

The logical functions in Excel can be found by clicking the Logical command button on the Formulas tab of the Ribbon. A logical function requires a logical test before carrying out one evaluation from several options. If the test evaluates to TRUE, it executes one statement, and if the test is FALSE, it executes a different statement. A statement can be a calculation, a value, a string, or even another function. Logical functions can be nested, enabling you to perform multiple logical tests before executing the statement.

Creating Conditional Formulas

Logical functions allow you to create conditional formulas that can perform logical tests before returning a value based on the test result.

IF Function

The IF function is one of the popular functions in Excel used to create conditional formulas. The IF function allows you to perform a logical test (using comparison operators) that evaluates to TRUE or FALSE. The function executes one statement if the test is TRUE and another statement if the test is FALSE.

Syntax:

=IF(logical_test, value_if_true, [value_if_false])

Arguments

Argument	Description
logical_test	Required. A value or expression that can evaluate to TRUE or FALSE.
value_if_true	Required. The value returned if the logical test is true.
value_if_false	Optional. The value returned if the logical test is false. If the logical test is FALSE and this argument is omitted, nothing happens.

In its simplest form, this is what the function says:

IF (something is TRUE, then do A, otherwise do B)

Thus, the IF function will return a different result for TRUE and FALSE.

Example 1

A common way the IF function is used is to determine whether or not a referenced cell has any value. If the result is 0, then it returns a blank cell.

In the example below, the formula calculating the total for **Jan** was entered in cell **F2** and filled down to populate the totals for **Feb** to **Dec.** Without the IF function, the worksheet would display $0 for the unpopulated months. We want the totals for the unpopulated months to be blank instead of $0, even with the formula in place.

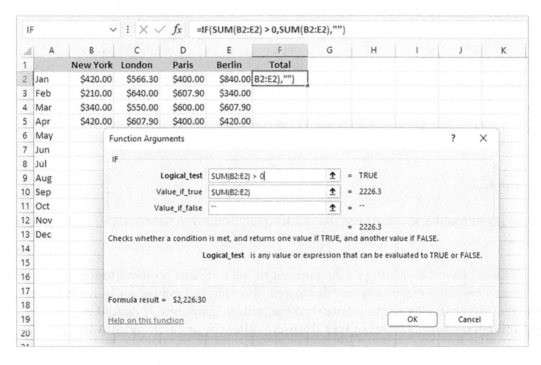

Thus, the formula for Jan in cell **F2** is:

=IF(SUM(B2:E2) > 0,SUM(B2:E2),"")

The IF function checks to see if the sum of Jan is greater than 0. If the test is TRUE, the formula returns the sum. Otherwise, it returns a blank string.

When we populate the other fields with the formula, we get the following:

F2				fx	=IF(SUM(B2:E2) > 0,SUM(B2:E2),"")	
	A	B	C	D	E	F	G
1		New York	London	Paris	Berlin	Total	
2	Jan	$420.00	$566.30	$400.00	$840.00	$2,226.30	
3	Feb	$210.00	$640.00	$607.90	$340.00	$1,797.90	
4	Mar	$340.00	$550.00	$600.00	$607.90	$2,097.90	
5	Apr	$420.00	$607.90	$400.00	$420.00	$1,847.90	
6	May						
7	Jun						
8	Jul						
9	Aug						
10	Sep						
11	Oct						
12	Nov						
13	Dec						
14							

Example 2

In another example, we could use the results of an evaluation to return different values in our worksheet.

Let's say we have a budgeting sheet and want to use a "Status" column to report how the "Actual" amount compares to the "Budgeted" amount. We can use an IF formula to test whether the actual amount is greater than the budgeted amount. If **Actual** is greater than **Budgeted**, the formula enters **Over Budget**. Otherwise, it enters **Within Budget**.

D2			f_x	=IF(C2 > B2,"Over Budget", "Within Budget")			

	A	B	C	D	E	F	G
1	**Project**	**Budgeted**	**Actual**	**Status**			
2	Project1	$1,000.00	$900.00	Within Budget			
3	Project2	$2,000.00	$2,100.00	Over Budget			
4	Project3	$2,500.00	$1,500.00	Within Budget			
5	Project4	$2,300.00	$2,100.00	Within Budget			
6	Project5	$2,500.00	$2,300.00	Within Budget			
7	Project6	$1,200.00	$2,100.00	Over Budget			
8	Project7	$2,050.00	$2,030.00	Within Budget			
9	Project8	$5,000.00	$4,100.00	Within Budget			
10	Project9	$3,000.00	$2,100.00	Within Budget			
11							

=IF(C2 > B2,"Over Budget", "Within Budget")

The IF function checks to see if the value in C2 is greater than the value in B2. If it is, Excel returns **Over Budget**. Otherwise, it returns **Within Budget**.

Note that the example uses conditional formatting to automatically highlight the rows where the **Status** is **Over Budget**. You can apply conditional formatting to a range by selecting **Home** > **Conditional Formatting** > **New Rule**.

You can learn how to apply conditional formatting to your ranges in Book 1, chapter 5.

Example 3

In another example, we want to apply a **10%** promotional discount when **10 or more** items are purchased. We can use an IF formula to perform this conditional calculation.

| E4 | | ⌄ | : | X ✓ | fx | =IF(C4>=10,D4 - (D4 * 0.1),D4) | |

▲	A	B	C	D	E	F
1	**Sales**					
2						
3	Product	Cost	Qty	Sub total	Total (with discount)	Formulatext
4	Beer	$1.50	15	$22.50	$20.25	=IF(C4>=10,D4 - (D4 * 0.1),D4)
5	Brownie Mix	$4.20	10	$42.00	$37.80	=IF(C5>=10,D5 - (D5 * 0.1),D5)
6	Cake Mix	$4.80	10	$48.00	$43.20	=IF(C6>=10,D6 - (D6 * 0.1),D6)
7	Chai	$1.80	10	$18.00	$16.20	=IF(C7>=10,D7 - (D7 * 0.1),D7)
8	Chocolate Biscuits Mix	$5.20	5	$26.00	$26.00	=IF(C8>=10,D8 - (D8 * 0.1),D8)
9	Coffee	$2.00	25	$50.00	$45.00	=IF(C9>=10,D9 - (D9 * 0.1),D9)
10	Green Tea	$2.00	50	$100.00	$90.00	=IF(C10>=10,D10 - (D10 * 0.1),D10)
11	Scones	$4.90	5	$24.50	$24.50	=IF(C11>=10,D11 - (D11 * 0.1),D11)
12	Tea	$1.30	20	$26.00	$23.40	=IF(C12>=10,D12 - (D12 * 0.1),D12)
13						
14						
15	*Apply a 10% discount if the quantity sold per item is 10 or more.					
16						

Formula explanation

=IF(C4>=10,D4 - (D4 * 0.1),D4)

The logical test checks if C4 (**Qty**) is greater than or equal to 10.

If the test is TRUE, the formula returns the sub-total minus 10%.

If the test is FALSE, the formula returns the sub-total.

We can use the fill handle of the cell to copy the formula to the other cells in the range E4:E12.

💡**Tip** The fill handle appears as a plus sign (+) when you hover your mouse pointer over the lower-right corner of the active cell.

Nested IF Functions

You can nest an IF function by inserting one IF function as an argument in another one. This formula is called a nested IF statement. You can nest up to seven IF statements. A nested IF statement might be required if you need to carry out more than one logical test in your formula.

Example 4

In the example below, we use a nested IF statement to test for three possible values and return a different result for each one.

We have a spreadsheet to record the score of exams, and we want to mark everything under 40 as FAIL, between 40 and 69 as CREDIT, and 70 or more as MERIT.

The formula would look like this:

=IF(B2 < 40, "FAIL",IF(B2 < 70,"CREDIT","MERIT"))

| C2 | | fx | =IF(B2 < 40, "FAIL",IF(B2 < 70,"CREDIT","MERIT")) |

	A	B	C	D	E	F	G
1	**Student**	**Mark**	**Grade**				
2	Judith	67	CREDIT				
3	Paul	57	CREDIT				
4	David	51	CREDIT				
5	Randy	74	MERIT				
6	Mary	50	CREDIT				
7	Dorothy	30	FAIL				
8	Kimberly	95	MERIT				
9	Raymond	8	FAIL				
10	Shirley	30	FAIL				
11	Gary	57	CREDIT				
12	Lori	67	CREDIT				
13	Fred	81	MERIT				
14	Virginia	50	CREDIT				
15	Cheryl	30	FAIL				
16	Ruth	79	MERIT				

Formula explanation

=IF(B2 < 40, "FAIL",IF(B2 < 70,"CREDIT","MERIT"))

The first IF statement checks if B2 is less than 40. If TRUE, it returns "FAIL" and ends the evaluation there. If B2 < 40 is FALSE, the second IF test is executed.

The second IF function checks if B2 is less than 70. If true, it returns "CREDIT," and if false, it returns "MERIT."

Tip The IFS function provides a better way of addressing multiple logical tests in one formula. As much as possible, use IFS instead of multiple nested IF statements. It is much cleaner and easier to read for multiple tests.

Example 5

In the following example, we want to calculate the commission paid to sales reps based on performance.

The formula calculates the following:

- If a sales rep generates $10,000 in sales AND 15 signups, they earn a 20% commission on their sales amount.

- If a sales rep generates $10,000 in sales OR 15 signups, they earn a 15% commission on their sales amount.

- If a sales rep generates less than $10,000 in sales and less than 15 signups, they earn a 10% commission on their sales amount.

The following formula returns the result we want:

=IF(D2 >= 10000,IF(E2 >= 15,D2*0.2,D2*0.15),IF(E2 >= 15,D2*0.15,D2*0.1))

fx | =IF(D2 >= 10000,IF(E2 >= 15,D2*0.2,D2*0.15),IF(E2 >= 15,D2*0.15,D2*0.1))

	C	D	E	F	G	H
	Sales rep	Sales	Signups	Commission		
	Gilbert Higgins	$12,500	20	$2,500		
	Clinton Bradley	$14,300	25	$2,860		
	Bob Nash	$9,000	10	$900		
	Lee Powers	$8,050	5	$805		
	Mae Stevens	$5,000	7	$500		
	Inez Griffith	$8,900	10	$890		
	Theresa Hawkins	$7,900	10	$790		
	Felix Jacobs	$6,000	17	$900		
	Erik Lane	$11,000	18	$2,200		
	Jesse Garza	$12,676	12	$1,901		
	Alberta Fletcher	$13,163	14	$1,975		
	Melody Mendoza	$8,795	20	$1,319		
	Abraham Graves	$12,875	26	$2,575		
	Van Sims	$6,646	16	$997		

Formula explanation

=IF(D2 >= 10000,IF(E2 >= 15,D2*0.2,D2*0.15),IF(E2 >= 15,D2*0.15,D2*0.1))

The outer IF function runs the test **D2 >= 10000** to check if D2 (Sales) is $10,000 or greater. If the result is TRUE, it runs the first nested IF function. If the result is FALSE, it runs the second nested IF function.

The first nested IF function checks whether signups are 15 or greater. If the result is TRUE, the formula returns 20% commission (D2*0.2) as its final result. If the test is FALSE, the formula returns a 15% commission (D2*0.15).

The second nested IF function is only executed if D2 is less than $10,000. It checks whether signups are 15 or greater. If the result is TRUE, the formula returns a 15% commission (D2*0.15) as its final result. If the test is false, the formula returns a 10% commission (D2*0.1).

457

Advanced IF Functions

An advanced IF function combines a logical function and a statistics or mathematics function. Advanced IF functions are covered in more detail in this book in the chapters for **Math Functions** and **Statistical Functions**. This section briefly examines some advanced IF functions you can use as one solution instead of combining two.

AVERAGEIF

Syntax:

=AVERAGEIF(range, criteria, [average_range])

This function returns the average (arithmetic mean) of numbers that meets the value you've entered as the criteria. The optional *average_range* argument allows you to specify another range for the values if it is separate from the one with the criteria.

Example:

=AVERAGEIF(A2:A20,"<2000")

The above formula calculates the average of all the values in the range A2:A20 that are greater than 2000.

AVERAGEIFS

Syntax:

=AVERAGEIFS(average_range, criteria_range1, criteria1, [criteria_range2, criteria2], ...)

This function is similar to AVERAGEIF, but it allows you to specify multiple ranges and criteria in the arguments. You can specify up to 127 ranges and criteria.

COUNTIF

This function returns the count of the values in a range that meets the specified criteria.

Syntax:

=COUNTIF(range, criteria)

In its simplest form, this function says:

=COUNTIF(Where do you want to look?, What do you want to look for?)

Example:

=COUNTIF(A2:A10," New York")

This formula will return the count of the number of cells in A2:A10 with the value "New York."

COUNTIFS

=COUNTIFS(criteria_range1, criteria1, [criteria_range2, criteria2]...)

This function is like the COUNTIF function in that it returns a count based on a condition you specify. However, you can specify multiple ranges and criteria. You can specify up to 127 range/criteria pairs.

SUMIF

=SUMIF(range, criteria, [sum_range])

This function returns the sum of values in a range based on the criteria.

Example:

=SUMIF(A2:A10, ">10")

This formula returns the sum of all the values in cells A2:A10 that are greater than 10.

SUMIFS

Syntax:

SUMIFS(sum_range, criteria_range1, criteria1, [criteria_range2, criteria2], ...)

This function returns the sum of values that meet several criteria. You can specify up to 127 range/criteria pairs.

Note All advanced IF functions mentioned above are covered in more detail elsewhere in this book. Check the table of contents for which chapter a function has been covered.

IFS Function

The IFS function enables you to carry out multiple logical tests and execute a statement corresponding to the first test that evaluates to TRUE. The tests need to be entered in the order you want the statements executed so that the right result is returned as soon as a test is passed. IFS was created as a better approach to nested IF statements, which can quickly become too complex.

Syntax

=IFS(logical_test1, value_if_true1, [logical_test2, value_if_true2], [logical_test3, value_if_true3],…)

Arguments

Argument	Description
logical_test1	Required. The condition that is being tested. It can evaluate to TRUE or FALSE.
value_if_true1	Required. The value returned if logical_test1 evaluates to TRUE.
logical_test2... logical_test127	Optional. An expression that evaluates to TRUE or FALSE. You can have up to 127 tests.
value_if_true2... value_if_true127	Optional. The value returned if a corresponding logical test evaluates to TRUE. You can have up to 127 values.

Remarks

The IFS function allows you to test up to 127 different tests. However, it is generally advised not to use too many tests with IF or IFS statements. Multiple tests need to be entered in the right order, and it can become too complex to update or maintain.

Tip As much as possible, use IFS instead of multiple nested IF statements. It is much easier to read when you have multiple conditions.

Example 1

In the example below, we use the IFS function to solve a problem we addressed earlier with nested IF statements. Notice how we don't need a nested function to achieve the same result.

In this problem, we want to assign grades to different ranges of exam scores.

Score and Grades
- 70 or above = MERIT
- 50 to 69 = CREDIT

- 40 to 49 = PASS
- less than 40 = FAIL

The following formula provides an ideal solution:

=IFS(B2>=70,"MERIT",B2>=50,"CREDIT", B2>=40,"PASS", B2<40,"FAIL")

C2		fx	=IFS(B2>=70,"MERIT",B2>=50,"CREDIT", B2>=40,"PASS", B2<40,"FAIL")

	A	B	C	D	E	F	G	H	I	J
1	Student	Mark	Grade							
2	Bruce	67	CREDIT							
3	Louis	57	CREDIT							
4	Earl	51	CREDIT							
5	Sean	74	MERIT							
6	Benjamin	50	CREDIT							
7	Joe	30	FAIL							
8	Shawn	95	MERIT							
9	Kenneth	8	FAIL							
10	Cynthia	30	FAIL							
11	Susan	57	CREDIT							
12	John	67	CREDIT							
13	Bruce	81	MERIT							
14	Louis	50	CREDIT							
15	Earl	30	FAIL							
16	Kenneth	79	MERIT							
17										

Formula explanation

=IFS(B2>=70,"MERIT",B2>=50,"CREDIT", B2>=40,"PASS", B2<40,"FAIL")

The IFS formula above has four logical tests in sequential order:

1. B2>=70,"MERIT"
2. B2>=50,"CREDIT"
3. B2>=40,"PASS"
4. B2<40,"FAIL"

B2 is a reference to the score. Each score is tested against each condition in sequential order. When a test returns TRUE, the corresponding grade is returned, and no further tests are carried out.

Example 2

In this example, we want to set different priority levels for re-ordering items depending on the number of items in stock.

Priority Level:
1. 5 or less = 1
2. 10 or less = 2
3. Less than 20 = 3

The formula we use to accomplish this task is:

=IFS(B2>20,"N/A",B2<=5,1, B2<=10,2, B2<20,3)

C2			fx	=IFS(B2>20,"N/A",B2<=5,1, B2<=10,2, B2<20,3)		
	A	B	C	D	E	
1	Product	# In stock	Reorder Priority			
2	Cora Fabric Chair	10	2			
3	Tessa Fabric Chair	25	N/A			
4	Fabric Chair in a Box	9	2			
5	Lukah Leather Chair	10	2			
6	Fabric Tub Chair	4	1			
7	Fabric Wingback Chair	10	2			
8	Floral Fabric Tub Chair	15	3			
9	Habitat Oken Console Table	10	2			
10	Harley Fabric Cuddle Chair	10	2			
11	Leather Effect Tub Chair	5	1			
12	Habitat Fabric Chair	10	2			
13	Hygena Fabric Chair in a Box	5	1			
14	Hygena Lumina Console Table	15	3			

Formula explanation

=IFS(B2>20,"N/A",B2<=5,1, B2<=10,2, B2<20,3)

First, the formula has a test to mark the Reorder Priority of products greater than 20 as "N/A" (not applicable) as those have no re-order priority yet. Then several tests are defined in sequential order from the smallest value to the largest to ensure that the right corresponding value is returned as soon as a test is passed.

-💡-**Tip** You can also apply **conditional formatting** to highlight the records with the highest priority. In this case, 1 is the highest priority. See Chapter 5 in Book 1 for how to conditionally format a range.

SWITCH Function

The SWITCH function evaluates an expression against a list of values and returns the value corresponding to the first match. If no match is found, an optional default value may be returned. SWITCH allows you to identify values in your list and replace them with something more meaningful to your audience.

Syntax

=SWITCH(expression, value1, result1, [default or value2, result2],…[default or value3, result3])

Arguments

Argument	Description
expression	Required. The value that's compared against the list of values in value1 to value126. This argument can be a number, date, or text.
value1 to value126	Value1 is required. A value that will be compared with the expression argument. You can have up to 126 values.
result1 to result126	Result1 is required. The value that is returned when the corresponding argument matches the expression argument. A result must be supplied for each corresponding value argument. You can have up to 126 results to match each value argument.
default	Optional. The default value to return if no match is found. The argument must be the last one in the function. It is identified by not having a corresponding result value.

Remarks:

Excel functions are limited to 254 arguments, so you can only use up to 126 pairs of *value/result* arguments.

Example

The following example shows a column in our data representing the quarter. To make the data more understandable, we want to switch the numbers to text descriptions that describe the numbers more meaningfully.

List of values to switch:
- 1 = QTR1
- 2 = QTR2
- 3 = QTR3
- 4 = QTR4

Formula:

=SWITCH(C2,1,"QTR1",2,"QTR2",3,"QTR3",4,"QTR4","No match")

D2			fx	=SWITCH(C2,1,"QTR1",2,"QTR2",3,"QTR3",4,"QTR4","No match")					
	A	B	C	D	E	F	G	H	I
1	Amount	Year	QTR	Switched					
2	$1,242.00	2022	3	QTR3					
3	$3,221.00	2022	2	QTR2					
4	$2,349.00	2022	4	QTR4					
5	$2,951.00	2022	1	QTR1					
6	$1,903.00	2023	3	QTR3					
7	$2,648.80	2023	2	QTR2					
8	$2,754.00	2023	3	QTR3					
9	$2,859.20	2023	4	QTR4					
10	$2,964.40	2023	1	QTR1					
11									

A "No match" result would reveal an error in the data.

Tip The *result* arguments have been entered directly in the formula here for demonstration purposes only. In a production worksheet, it would be better to enter the values in a lookup range in your worksheet and then use cell references in your formula. That way, it is easier to maintain.

AND Function

The AND function is used to determine if all conditions in a test are TRUE. This function is useful for scenarios where you want to perform more than one logical test and check that they all evaluate to TRUE before a condition is applied or calculated.

Syntax

=AND(logical1, [logical2], ...)

Arguments

Argument	Description
Logical1	Required. The first condition that you want to test that can either evaluate to TRUE or FALSE.
Logical2, ...	Optional. You can have up to 254 additional conditions you want to test that can evaluate to either TRUE or FALSE.

Remarks

- The arguments must evaluate to logical values (i.e., TRUE or FALSE) or must be references to cells that contain logical values.

- If an argument contains a reference that points to text values or empty cells, those values will be ignored.

- Excel returns the #VALUE! error if any referenced ranges contain no logical values.

Example

In this example, we want to apply a discount for order items that meet a certain criterion.

We want a formula that:

1. Checks that a product is on promotion.

2. Checks that the number of units ordered is three or more.

3. Applies a discount if the item is on promotion **and** three or more have been ordered.

◢	A	B	C
1	**Product Name**	**On Promotion**	**Units Ordered**
2	Chai	Yes	3
3	Syrup	Yes	1
4	Cajun Seasoning	Yes	6
5	Olive Oil	No	7
6	Boysenberry Spread	Yes	1
7	Dried Pears	No	1
8	Curry Sauce	Yes	2
9	Walnuts	Yes	3
10	Fruit Cocktail	No	4
11	Chocolate Biscuits Mix	Yes	2
12	Marmalade	Yes	3
13	Scones	Yes	5
14	Beer	Yes	10
15	Crab Meat	No	7

The AND formula we use to carry out both tests is:

AND(B2="yes",C2>=3)

Next, we use the AND function as an argument inside an IF function. The IF statement returns "Yes" if the AND statement returns TRUE and "No" if the AND statement returns FALSE.

The final formula looks like this:

=IF(AND(B2="yes",C2>=3)=TRUE,"Yes","No")

D2		⌄ ⋮ ✕ ✓	*fx*	=IF(AND(B2="yes",C2>=3)=TRUE,"Yes","No")	

◢	A	B	C	D	E
1	**Product Name**	**On Promotion**	**Units Ordered**	**Discount applied**	
2	Chai	Yes	3	Yes	
3	Syrup	Yes	1	No	
4	Cajun Seasoning	Yes	6	Yes	
5	Olive Oil	No	7	No	
6	Boysenberry Spread	Yes	1	No	
7	Dried Pears	No	1	No	
8	Curry Sauce	Yes	2	No	
9	Walnuts	Yes	3	Yes	
10	Fruit Cocktail	No	4	No	
11	Chocolate Biscuits Mix	Yes	2	No	
12	Marmalade	Yes	3	Yes	
13	Scones	Yes	5	Yes	
14	Beer	Yes	10	Yes	
15	Crab Meat	No	7	No	
16					

Our formula uses the AND function to extend the power of the IF function. Using AND as an argument in IF enabled us to perform two logical tests within its *logical_test* argument and return one logical value.

469

OR Function

The OR function is used to determine if any conditions in a test are TRUE. This function is useful for formulas where you want to perform more than one logical test and return a value if at least one of them evaluates to TRUE.

This function is best used in conjunction with other logical functions for more complex test scenarios involving multiple logical tests. For example, the IF function requires you to test a condition to determine which return statement to execute. If you combine IF and OR, it enables you to test multiple conditions instead of just one.

Syntax

=OR(logical1, [logical2], ...)

Arguments

Argument	Description
Logical1	Required. The first condition that you want to test that can either evaluate to TRUE or FALSE.
Logical2, ...	Optional. You can have up to 254 additional conditions you want to test that can evaluate to either TRUE or FALSE.

Remarks

- The maximum number of arguments you can have for the OR functions is 255.

- The arguments must evaluate to logical values (i.e., TRUE or FALSE) or must be references to cells that contain logical values.

- If an argument contains references that point to text or empty cells, those values will be ignored.

- If the specified range contains no logical values, Excel returns the #VALUE! error.

Example

In this example, we need to determine which sales staff qualify for a sales commission based on their generated sales.

The sales figures are in the table below. Under the main table, we have a lookup table for the Amount per **Criteria**. These are the goals referenced in our formula to calculate the **Commission** for each salesperson.

The IF function can be combined with OR to achieve our aim.

The following formula is entered in cell D2 and copied to the other cells in column D using the Fill Handle.

=IF(OR(B2>=$B$15,C2>=$B$16),B2*$B$17,0)

D2		fx	=IF(OR(B2>=$B$15,C2>=$B$16),B2*$B$17,0)	
	A	B	C	D	E
1	**Name**	**Sales**	**Signups**	**Commission**	**Bonus**
2	Nancy Freehafer	$12,500	20	$250	$188
3	Andrew Cencini	$14,300	25	$286	$215
4	Jan Kotas	$9,000	10	$180	$0
5	Mariya Sergienko	$8,050	5	$161	$0
6	Steven Thorpe	$5,000	7	$0	$0
7	Michael Neipper	$8,900	10	$178	$0
8	Robert Zare	$7,900	10	$0	$0
9	Laura Giussani	$6,000	17	$120	$0
10	Anne Hellung-Larsen	$11,000	18	$220	$0
11					
12				- Sales people need to exceed **Sales Goal**
13				OR **Signup Goal** to earn a **Commission**.
14	**Criteria**	**Amount**		
15	Sales Goal	$8,000		- Sales people need to exceed **Bonus Goal**
16	Signup Goal	15		AND **Signup Goal** to earn a **Bonus**.
17	Commission	2.0%		
18	Bonus Goal	$12,000		
19	Bonus %	1.5%		

Formula explanation

=IF(OR(B2>=$B$15,C2>=$B$16),B2*$B$17,0)

The formula says:

If the sales value is greater than or equal to the **Sales Goal**, OR signups are greater than or equal to the **Signup Goal**, then multiply Sales by the Commission (2.0%). Otherwise, return 0.

Trapping and Replacing Error Values

Excel provides formulas that enable you to catch error return values and replace them with a more user-friendly message. These functions are used with formulas where you anticipate error values in certain scenarios. Instead of displaying the error value on the worksheet, you can swap in a more meaningful message.

IFERROR Function

You can use IFERROR to trap errors in Excel formulas and return a custom message. This function provides a more user-friendly experience, especially if you're developing a worksheet for end-users and anticipate errors in certain data cells. Otherwise, you often do need to see the errors Excel generates so you can fix them.

This method is similar to how errors are trapped and handled in computer code. IFERROR can trap the following error types: #VALUE!, #N/A, #DIV/0!, #REF!, #NAME?, #NUM!, or #NULL!.

Syntax

=IFERROR(value, value_if_error)

Arguments

Argument	Description
value	Required. A cell reference or formula that's checked for an error.
value_if_error	Required. The value to be returned if the formula identifies an error.

Remarks

- If either *value* or *value_if_error* points to an empty cell, IFERROR treats it as an empty string value (""").

- If *value* is an array formula, IFERROR returns an array, one for each cell in the results range.

Example

In the following example, we use the IFERROR formula to trap any errors in our formula in column C and return a text message **Entry error**.

The FORMULATEXT function used in D2:D9 reveals the formulas in C2:C9.

C2		✓ : ✕ ✓ *fx*	=IFERROR(B2/A2,"Entry error")

◢	A	B	C	D
1	**Target**	**Actual sold**	**Percentage**	**Formula text**
2	200	35	18%	=IFERROR(B2/A2,"Entry error")
3	10	0	0%	=IFERROR(B3/A3,"Entry error")
4	120	50	42%	=IFERROR(B4/A4,"Entry error")
5	300	5	2%	=IFERROR(B5/A5,"Entry error")
6	0	60	Entry error	=IFERROR(B6/A6,"Entry error")
7	50	0	0%	=IFERROR(B7/A7,"Entry error")
8		10	Entry error	=IFERROR(B8/A8,"Entry error")
9	250	120	48%	=IFERROR(B9/A9,"Entry error")
10				

IFNA Function

The IFNA function is for handling #N/A errors. Excel displays the #NA error when a value is unavailable to a formula or function. Use IFNA when you want to trap and handle only #N/A errors.

You're more likely to encounter #N/A errors with lookup and reference functions when a value referenced in the formula is not in the source. You usually want to display other errors as they may reveal bugs in your formula that need fixing.

IFNA returns the value you specify if your formula encounters the #N/A error. Otherwise, it returns the result of the formula.

Syntax:

= IFNA(value, value_if_na)

Arguments

Argument	Description
value	Required. The expression that is checked for an error. It can be a value, cell reference, or formula. When using IFNA with VLOOKUP, the VLOOKUP formula will be this argument.
value_if_na	Required. The value the formula returns when it encounters a #N/A error.

Example

The following example uses the IFNA function to handle a #N/A error generated when the VLOOKUP function cannot find the provided lookup_value in the table_array.

The formula in E2, without IFNA, returns #N/A. Conversely, the formula in E3 traps the error with IFNA and provides a more user-friendly message.

=IFNA(VLOOKUP(D3,A3:B11,2,FALSE),"Not found")

E3			f_x	=IFNA(VLOOKUP(D3,A3:B11,2,FALSE),"Not found")		
	A	B	C	D	E	F
1	**Product**	**Cost**		**Product**	**Cost**	**Formula text**
2	Beer	$1.50		Walnuts	#N/A	=VLOOKUP(D2,A2:B10,2,FALSE)
3	Brownie Mix	$4.20		Walnuts	Not found	=IFNA(VLOOKUP(D3,A3:B11,2,FALSE),"Not found")
4	Cake Mix	$4.80				
5	Chai	$1.80				
6	Chocolate Biscuits Mix	$5.20				
7	Coffee	$2.00				
8	Green Tea	$2.00				
9	Scones	$4.90				
10	Tea	$1.30				
11						

Chapter 4

Math Functions

This chapter covers functions that enable you to:

- Sum up data in contiguous or non-contiguous ranges.
- Sum up data based on certain criteria using a single function.
- Use multiple criteria to determine which data to add up.
- Generate random numbers between two given numbers.
- Generate a sequence of numbers based on given parameters.
- Automatically round up or round down numbers with a function.
- Calculate the square root of a number.

The mathematics functions in Excel can be found by clicking the Math & Trig command button on the Formulas tab of the ribbon. The dropdown menu lists all the Math & Trig functions. This category of functions in Excel ranges from common arithmetic functions to complex functions used by mathematicians and engineers.

Our focus here will be on the arithmetic functions, as many Excel trigonometric functions apply to math problems requiring specialist knowledge outside the scope of this book.

Summing and Aggregating Values

Excel offers an array of functions to sum values for different scenarios. You can create formulas that sum single ranges, multiple ranges, or values that meet certain criteria.

SUM Function

The SUM function enables you to sum up values on your spreadsheet. You can add individual values, cell references, ranges, or a mix of all three. You can sum up contiguous cells or non-contiguous cells.

Syntax

=SUM(number1,[number2],...)

Arguments

Argument	Description
Number1	Required. The first cell reference, range, or number for which you want to calculate the sum. The argument can be a number like 4, a cell reference like A10, or a range like A2:A10.
Number2, ...	Optional. Additional cell references, ranges, or numbers for which you want to calculate the sum - up to a maximum of 255.

Example 1

The following example sums up the values in cells B2 to B13. The SUM function was entered in the formula bar, but you can also use the AutoSum command on the ribbon to sum up the range.

=SUM(B2:B13)

| IF | | ⌄ | ⋮ | ✕ ✓ *fx* | =SUM(B2:B13) |

◢	A	B	C	D	E
1	**Month**	**Expenses**			
2	Jan	$547.00			
3	Feb	$880.00			
4	Mar	$717.00			
5	Apr	$540.00			
6	May	$620.00			
7	Jun	$423.00			
8	Jul	$937.00			
9	Aug	$683.00			
10	Sep	$633.00			
11	Oct	$551.00			
12	Nov	$680.00			
13	Dec	$766.00			
14	**Total**	=SUM(B2:B13)			
15		SUM(**number1**, [number2], ...)			
16					

Example 2

To sum up data in different ranges, i.e., non-contiguous data, you can enter the ranges as different arguments in the SUM function.

=SUM(B2:B13,D2:D13,F2:F13,H2:H13)

IF				✗ ✓ *fx*	=SUM(B2:B13,D2:D13,F2:F13,H2:H13)			

▲	A	B	C	D	E	F	G	H	I
1	Month	Year1		Year2		Year3		Year4	
2	Jan	$547.00		$934.00		$412.00		$447.00	
3	Feb	$880.00		$590.00		$961.00		$605.00	
4	Mar	$717.00		$961.00		$460.00		$652.00	
5	Apr	$540.00		$542.00		$574.00		$754.00	
6	May	$620.00		$497.00		$531.00		$462.00	
7	Jun	$423.00		$874.00		$799.00		$699.00	
8	Jul	$937.00		$755.00		$877.00		$446.00	
9	Aug	$683.00		$715.00		$792.00		$742.00	
10	Sep	$633.00		$421.00		$877.00		$576.00	
11	Oct	$551.00		$941.00		$675.00		$598.00	
12	Nov	$680.00		$520.00		$867.00		$916.00	
13	Dec	$766.00		$524.00		$401.00		$707.00	
14									
15	Total								H13)
16									

SUMIF Function

The SUMIF function combines a math function and a logical function. It allows you to sum up data in a range based on the specified criteria.

Syntax

=SUMIF(range, criteria, [sum_range])

Arguments

Argument	Description
range	Required. The range you want to evaluate based on the condition in *criteria*.
criteria	Required. The condition (or logical test) that is used to determine which cells are summed up in range. This value can be an expression, cell reference, text, or function. If this argument is text or includes logical or math symbols like greater than (>), it must be enclosed in double quotes (""). If criteria is numeric, quotation marks are not required.
sum_range	Optional. Used to specify the sum range if it is different from the range specified in the range. If omitted, the range argument is used.

Remarks

- Cells in the range argument must be numbers, names (for example, named ranges or tables), arrays, or references that contain numbers. Text values and blanks are ignored.

- You can use wildcard characters (like a question mark "?" or an asterisk "*") as the criteria argument. A question mark matches any single character, while an asterisk matches any sequence of characters. Type a tilde (~) before the character if you want to find an actual question mark or asterisk.

Example

The following example uses SUMIF to calculate the following:

- Total of all sales over $5,000.

- Total commissions paid out to salespeople who generated over $5,000 in sales.

We can achieve the desired results with two formulas:

=SUMIF(B2:B11,">5000")

=SUMIF(B2:B11,">5000", C2:C11)

	A	B	C	D	E	F	G
					fx	=SUMIF(B2:B11,">5000")	
	Salesperson	Sales	Commission		Sales over $5K		Formula text
1							
2	Geraldine Simpson	$2,635	$132		Total	$59,250	=SUMIF(B2:B11,">5000")
3	Earnest Lambert	$7,227	$361		Total comm.	$2,963	=SUMIF(B2:B11,">5000", C2:C11)
4	Pauline Turner	$4,426	$221				
5	Miriam Abbott	$4,774	$239				
6	Willis Goodwin	$9,829	$491				
7	Claire Wilkerson	$20,000	$1,000				
8	Jamie Newman	$2,459	$123				
9	Andres Craig	$11,300	$565				
10	Dominic Gilbert	$2,566	$128				
11	Luz Fitzgerald	$10,894	$545				

Formula explanation

=SUMIF(B2:B11,">5000")

This formula uses the criteria argument of ">5000" to filter which values will be added to the sum from the range B2:B11.

=SUMIF(B2:B11,">5000", C2:C11)

Our second formula uses the criteria argument ">5000" to select the values in range B2:B11 (Sales) for which the corresponding values in range C2:C11 (Commission) will be added to the sum. So, even though we applied the criteria to B2:B11, the calculated values returned by the formula come from C2:C11.

SUMIFS Function

The SUMIFS function is like the SUMIF function, but you can use multiple criteria to determine which cells in a range are included in the sum. SUMIFS enables you to have up to 127 range/criteria pairs.

Syntax

=SUMIFS(sum_range, criteria_range1, criteria1, [criteria_range2, criteria2], ...)

Arguments

Argument	Description
sum_range	Required. The range of cells to sum up.
criteria_range1	Required. The range that is tested using Criteria1.
	Criteria_range1 and criteria1 are a pair where criteria1 is used to search criteria_range1 for matching values. Once items in the range are found, Excel sums up their corresponding values in sum_range.
criteria1	Required. The criteria used to filter criteria_range1 to select a subset of data. For example, criteria can be entered as 40, ">40", C6, "bolts", or "125".
criteria_range2, criteria2, ...	Optional. You can have additional range/criteria pairs up to 127.

Remarks

- If you are testing for text values, ensure the criteria are in quotation marks.

- You can use wildcard characters like the question mark (?) and asterisk (*) in your criteria to enable you to find matches that are not exact but similar. The question mark matches one character, and the asterisk matches a sequence of characters. To find a character like a question mark or asterisk, type a tilde sign (~) in front of the character.

- The criteria_range argument must reference a range with the same number of rows and columns as the sum_range argument.

Example

The following example sums up sales data using two criteria:

1. State name.

2. Items with 40 or more Orders (>=40).

The following formula achieves the result:

=SUMIFS($D$2:$D$12,$B$2:$B$12,F2,$C$2:$C$12,G2)

H2			fx	=SUMIFS($D$2:$D$12,$B$2:$B$12,F2,$C$2:$C$12,G2)			
	A	B	C	D	E	F	G	H

	A	B	C	D	F	G	H
1	Name	States	No. Orders	Sales	States	Orders	Total Sales for matching orders
2	Bruce	New York	51	$74,298	New York	>=40	$140,407
3	Louis	New York	39	$46,039	Texas	>=40	$44,390
4	Earl	Washington	60	$65,252	California	>=40	$42,484
5	Sean	Washington	100	$61,847	Washington	>=40	$127,099
6	Benjamin	Texas	28	$33,340			
7	Joe	California	31	$95,778			
8	Shawn	Texas	35	$58,808			
9	Kenneth	California	39	$52,593			
10	Cynthia	California	51	$42,484			
11	Susan	Texas	80	$44,390			
12	Dav	New York	70	$66,109			
13							

Formula explanation

=SUMIFS($D$2:$D$12,$B$2:$B$12,F2,$C$2:$C$12,G2)

- The sum_range argument references the Sales column **D2:D12** (an absolute reference has been used - **$D$2:$D$12**).

- The criteria_range1 is **B2:B12** (an absolute reference has also been used here - **$B$2:$B$12**).

- Press F4, with the argument selected, to make this an absolute reference.

- The criteria1 argument is **F2**, which is a reference to the states we want to use as our criteria. Using a cell reference makes it easier to change this value. This argument has a relative reference because we want the cell reference to change as we copy the formula to other cells.

- The criteria_range2 is **$C$2:$C$12** (in absolute reference form).

- The criteria2 argument is **G2** (>=40). A cell reference has been used for this argument to make it easier to change.

We enter the formula in cell **H2** and then copy it down the column to calculate the **Total Sales** for orders that match the criteria for each state.

-🔅-**Tip** To convert a relative reference to an absolute reference, manually add the dollar signs in the formula bar or select the reference in the formula (i.e., D2:D12) and press the **F4** key. Making the references absolute ensures they don't change when the formula is copied to other cells.

Using Named Ranges

One way to make a formula with absolute references easier to read is to use named ranges. Name ranges are absolute references by default and provide a cleaner look to your formula.

For example:
- Sales = D2:D12
- States = B2:B12
- Orders = C2:C12

With the named ranges in place, the formula looks like this:

=SUMIFS(Sales,States,F2,Orders,G2)

Instead of this:

=SUMIFS($D$2:$D$12,$B$2:$B$12,F2,$C$2:$C$12,G2)

IF			∨ : × ✓ fx	=SUMIFS(Sales,States,F2,Orders,G2)			

	A	B	C		SUMIFS(sum_range, criteria_range1, criteria1, [criteria_range2, cr

	A	B	C			States	Orders	Total Sales for matching orders
1	Name	States	No. Orders	Sales		States	Orders	matching orders
2	Bruce	New York	51	$74,298		New York	>=40	Orders,G2)
3	Louis	New York	39	$46,039		Texas	>=40	$44,390
4	Earl	Washington	60	$65,252		California	>=40	$42,484
5	Sean	Washington	100	$61,847		Washington	>=40	$127,099
6	Benjamin	Texas	28	$33,340				
7	Joe	California	31	$95,778				
8	Shawn	Texas	35	$58,808				
9	Kenneth	California	39	$52,593				
10	Cynthia	California	51	$42,484				
11	Susan	Texas	80	$44,390				
12	Dav	New York	70	$66,109				
13								

AGGREGATE Function

The AGGREGATE function returns an aggregate in a list or database. This function brings together all the aggregate functions into one. Instead of using individual aggregate functions, like SUM, AVG, MAX, etc., you simply enter a number in one of its arguments to specify the type of aggregate you want to perform. You can also set the option to ignore hidden rows and error values. You can perform 19 aggregate operations with this function.

There are two forms of the AGGREGATE function:

- Reference form
- Array form

Syntax

Reference form

=AGGREGATE(function_num, options, ref1, [ref2], …)
Array form

=AGGREGATE(function_num, options, array, [k])

Arguments

- **Function_num:** Required. The function_num argument is a number between 1 and 19. This argument is the number that specifies which aggregate function to use. See the list below.

Function_num	Function
1	AVERAGE
2	COUNT
3	COUNTA
4	MAX
5	MIN
6	PRODUCT
7	STDEV.S
8	STDEV.P
9	SUM
10	VAR.S
11	VAR.P
12	MEDIAN
13	MODE.SNGL
14	LARGE
15	SMALL
16	PERCENTILE.INC
17	QUARTILE.INC
18	PERCENTILE.EXC
19	QUARTILE.EXC

- **Options:** Required. This argument is a numerical value from 1 to 7 that determines which values to ignore in the range evaluated.

Option	Behavior
0 or omitted	Ignore nested AGGREGATE and SUBTOTAL functions
1	Ignore hidden rows, nested AGGREGATE and SUBTOTAL functions
2	Ignore error values, nested AGGREGATE and SUBTOTAL functions
3	Ignore hidden rows, error values, nested AGGREGATE and SUBTOTAL functions
4	Ignore nothing
5	Ignore hidden rows
6	Ignore error values
7	Ignore hidden rows and error values

- **Ref1:** Required. The first argument for functions that take multiple numeric arguments. Ref1 can be a range, an array (for functions that take an array), or a formula.

- **Ref2:** Optional. For additional numeric arguments. You can have up to 253 arguments in total for which you want the aggregate value.

For the functions that take an array argument, ref1 will be an array, an array formula, or a reference to a range for which you want the aggregate. Ref2 is a second argument that is required for some functions. The functions listed below require a ref2 argument:

Function
LARGE(array,k)
SMALL(array,k)
PERCENTILE.INC(array,k)
QUARTILE.INC(array,quart)
PERCENTILE.EXC(array,k)
QUARTILE.EXC(array,quart)

Remarks

- As soon as you type **=AGGREGATE(** in the formula bar, you'll see a dropdown list of all functions that you can use as arguments for function_num. You'll also get a dropdown list of the values you can enter for the options argument.

- AGGREGATE will return a #VALUE! error if a second ref argument is required but not provided.

- The AGGREGATE function is designed for columns of data, i.e., vertical ranges. It is not designed for rows of data, i.e., horizontal ranges.

Examples

In the following example, we'll use different instances of the AGGREGATE function to evaluate the data in range A2:B12. The calculations use different function_num arguments for the AGGREGATE function.

	A	B	C	D	E	F
1	Table of numbers			Calculation	Result	Formula text
2	#DIV/0!	56		MAX (4)	150	=AGGREGATE(4, 6, A2:A12)
3	90	81		LARGE (14)	95	=AGGREGATE(14, 6, A2:B12, 3)
4	31	95		SMALL (15)	#VALUE!	=AGGREGATE(15, 6, A2:A12)
5	#NUM!	49		MEDIAN (12)	77.5	=AGGREGATE(12, 6, A2:A12, B2:B12)
6	41	34		MAX function	#DIV/0!	=MAX(A2:B12)
7	150	92				
8	34	58				
9	87	93				
10	33	120				
11	53	89				
12	74	92				
13						

Formulas and descriptions

Example 1 - MAX	
Formula	=AGGREGATE(4, 6, A2:B12)
Result	150
Description	Returns the maximum value in range A2:B12 while ignoring error values.

Example 2 - LARGE	
Formula	=AGGREGATE(14, 6, A2:B12, 3)
Result	95
Description	Returns the third largest value in range A2:B12 while ignoring error values.

Example 3 - SMALL

Formula	=AGGREGATE(15, 6, A2:B12)
Result	#VALUE!
Description	Returns a #VALUE! error because AGGREGATE is expecting a second ref argument here. The function referenced (SMALL) requires one.

Example 4 - MEDIAN

Formula	=AGGREGATE(12, 6, A2:A12, B2:B12)
Result	77.5
Description	Returns the median from both columns while ignoring error values in the range.

Example 5

Formula	=MAX(A2:B12)
Result	#DIV/0!
Description	The regular MAX function is used here for comparisons. It returns an error value since error values are in the referenced range.

-💡-**Tip**   The AGGREGATE function would be overkill for common aggregate calculations in Excel, like sum, average, and count. Hence, use standard functions like SUM, AVG, MIN, and MAX for common aggregate calculations. Only use AGGREGATE if you're calculating one of the more complex aggregate types like STDEV.S, QUARTILE.INC, PERCENTILE.INC etc.

Generating Random and Sequential Numbers

The functions in this category enable you to generate a series of random or sequential numbers between a given start and end number, including an interval if required.

RANDBETWEEN Function

The RANDBETWEEN function returns a random integer between two numbers you specify. This function comes in handy whenever you need to generate sample data between two numbers. For example, if you want to generate sample data between 1 and 100 in several cells, you could use RANDBETWEEN to generate a random number in one cell and copy the formula over the required range.

Syntax

=RANDBETWEEN(bottom, top)

Arguments

Argument	Description
Bottom	Required. The smallest integer to be returned.
Top	Required. The largest integer to be returned.

Random values from RANDBETWEEN are regenerated each time the worksheet is recalculated. If you don't want the values to change each time the worksheet is recalculated, copy them to the clipboard, then use **Paste Special** > **Values** to convert them to static values.

To generate a random number that doesn't change, enter the formula in the formula bar, press F9 to convert the formula to a static value, then press **Enter** to insert the value in the cell.

Example

The following example uses RANDBETWEEN to generate sample data for student scores between 0 and 100.

= RANDBETWEEN(0,100)

B4				fx	=RANDBETWEEN(0,100)

	A	B	C	D	E	F
1	**Test Score Sample Data**					
2						
3	**Student**	Score				
4	Bruce	70				
5	Louis	82				
6	Earl	28				
7	Sean	44				
8	Benjamin	3				
9	Joe	19				
10	Shawn	38				
11	Kenneth	34				
12	Cynthia	5				
13	Susan	7				

💡**Tip** To keep only the generated values without the formula, generate the sample data in a different part of your worksheet and copy and paste only the values into your target range. For example, if you wanted random values in cells B2:B10, generate the values using RANDBETWEEN in cells C2:C10 and then copy and paste only the values in B2:B10, then delete the values in C2:C10.

RANDARRAY Function

RANDARRAY is a dynamic array function that returns random numbers. An array can be seen as a row of values, a column of values, or a combination of both. This function is an improvement on RANDBETWEEN, which returns only one value and must be copied to the entire range for multiple random numbers. RANDARRAY can return multiple values with one formula for your specified range. You can also specify whether you want whole numbers or decimal values.

Note This function is currently only available to Microsoft 365 subscribers.

Syntax

=RANDARRAY([rows],[columns],[min],[max],[whole_number])

Argument	Description
rows	Optional. The number of rows returned. If omitted, RANDARRAY will return a single row.
columns	Optional. The number of columns returned. If omitted, RANDARRAY will return a single column.
min	Optional. The minimum number to return.
max	Optional. The maximum number to return.
whole_number	Optional. Set this option to TRUE for whole numbers and FALSE for decimal values. If omitted, the default is FALSE, i.e., decimal values.

Remarks:

- If you omit both the rows and columns arguments, RANDARRAY returns a single value.

- If you omit the min and max arguments, RANDARRY returns numbers between 0 and 1.

- The max argument must be greater than the min argument. Otherwise, RANDARRAY returns a #VALUE! error.

Example

The following example generates sample numbers to be used as test data. The RANDARRAY formula is in cell B2, spilling the result over the range B2:E13. Note that we do not need to copy the formula to the other cells.

=RANDARRAY(12,4,500,1000,TRUE)

B2			f_x	=RANDARRAY(12,4,500,1000,TRUE)		
	A	B	C	D	E	F	G
1		**2022**	**2023**	**2024**	**2025**		
2	Jan	$501.00	$817.00	$530.00	$711.00		
3	Feb	$959.00	$887.00	$710.00	$739.00		
4	Mar	$532.00	$794.00	$727.00	$894.00		
5	Apr	$668.00	$972.00	$759.00	$839.00		
6	May	$945.00	$683.00	$751.00	$698.00		
7	Jun	$978.00	$509.00	$561.00	$911.00		
8	Jul	$626.00	$669.00	$911.00	$915.00		
9	Aug	$662.00	$573.00	$849.00	$971.00		
10	Sep	$829.00	$699.00	$966.00	$962.00		
11	Oct	$822.00	$813.00	$719.00	$720.00		
12	Nov	$751.00	$823.00	$889.00	$998.00		
13	Dec	$692.00	$983.00	$878.00	$884.00		
14							

Formula explanation

=RANDARRAY(12,4,500,1000,TRUE)

The row and column numbers are 12 and 4. The min and max numbers are 500 and 1000. The whole_number argument is set to TRUE to return whole numbers. The range is formatted as Currency.

Note Random values from RANDARRAY are regenerated each time the worksheet is recalculated. If you don't want the values to change each time the worksheet is recalculated, copy them to the clipboard, then use **Paste Special** > **Values** to convert them to static values.

Paste Special	? ✕
Paste	
○ All	○ All using Source theme
○ Formulas	○ All except borders
◉ Values	○ Column widths
○ Formats	○ Formulas and number formats
○ Comments and Notes	○ Values and number formats
○ Validation	○ All merging conditional formats
Operation	
◉ None	○ Multiply
○ Add	○ Divide
○ Subtract	
☐ Skip blanks	☐ Transpose
Paste Link	OK Cancel

SEQUENCE Function

SEQUENCE is a dynamic array function that allows you to generate a list of sequential numbers in an array. You can also specify an interval. An array can be a row of values, a column of values, or a combination of both. You can manually generate a series of numbers in Excel using the AutoFill feature. SEQUENCE offers the function equivalent of creating a series.

Note This function is currently only available to Microsoft 365 subscribers.

Syntax

=SEQUENCE(rows,[columns],[start],[step])

Arguments

Argument	Description
rows	Required. The number of rows to create.
columns	Optional. The number of columns to create. The default is 1 if this argument is omitted.
start	Optional. The starting number. The default is 1 if this argument is omitted.
step	Optional. The increment applied to each subsequent value in the array. The default is 1 if this argument is omitted.

Remarks

The result from SEQUENCE will spill on the worksheet if it's the final result of a formula. Excel will create the right-sized range to display the result. You can also use SEQUENCE as an argument within another formula to generate an array of values.

Example 1

The following example uses SEQUENCE to generate even numbers in five columns and five rows.

=SEQUENCE(5,5,0,2)

The formula has 5 for both the rows and columns arguments. The start argument is 0, and the step is 2.

A1			fx	=SEQUENCE(5,5,0,2)	
	A	B	C	D	E	F
1	0	2	4	6	8	
2	10	12	14	16	18	
3	20	22	24	26	28	
4	30	32	34	36	38	
5	40	42	44	46	48	
6						
7						

Example 2

Excel stores date values internally as serial numbers, so you can use SEQUENCE to generate dates with a specified interval. To display the result as a date, ensure the spill range is formatted as an Excel **Date**.

The following example generates the Monday date for 10 weeks from our specified starting date, 10/10/2022.

B2		✓ : ✕ ✓	fx	=SEQUENCE(10,,DATEVALUE("10/10/2022"),7)					
⎮	A	B	C	D	E	F	G	H
1	**Week starting Monday**							
2	Week 1	10/10/2022						
3	Week 2	17/10/2022						
4	Week 3	24/10/2022						
5	Week 4	31/10/2022						
6	Week 5	07/11/2022						
7	Week 6	14/11/2022						
8	Week 7	21/11/2022						
9	Week 8	28/11/2022						
10	Week 9	05/12/2022						
11	Week 10	12/12/2022						
12								

Formula explanation:

=SEQUENCE(10,,DATEVALUE("10/10/2022"),7)

The rows argument is 10 to specify the ten rows of dates we want to return. The columns argument has been omitted as we only want one column. For the starting date, the formula uses the DATEVALUE function to return the serial number for the provided date string. The step argument is 7, which increments each subsequent number by 7. Excel displays the serial numbers returned by DATEVALUE as dates because the spill range has the Date number format.

📝**Note** You might be thinking that it would just be easier to generate the list of dates on the worksheet by adding 7 to the second week and using autofill to populate the other cells. That's correct. The SEQUENCE function is more useful when you need to generate sequential values as an array argument within another formula.

Rounding Numbers

The functions in this category enable you to create formulas that round numbers up or down in different ways, based on the settings you provide.

ROUND Function

The ROUND function rounds a number to a specified number of digits. For example, if you have 25.4568 in cell A1 and you want to round the figure to two decimal places, you can use the following formula:

=ROUND(A1, 2)

The function will return: 25.46

Syntax

=ROUND(number, num_digits)

Arguments

Argument	Description
number	Required. This argument is the number that you want to round.
num_digits	Required. The number of decimal places to which you want to round the number.

Remarks
- The number is rounded to the specified number of decimal places if num_digits is greater than 0 (zero).
- The number is rounded to the nearest integer if num_digits is 0.
- The number is rounded to the left of the decimal point if num_digits is less than 0.

- Use the ROUNDUP function to always round up (away from zero).

- Use the ROUNDDOWN function to always round down (toward zero).

Examples

In the following examples, the ROUND function is applied to several values. The table displays the formula, the result, and a description of the outcome.

Formula	Result	Description
=ROUND(3.15, 1)	3.2	Rounds 3.15 to one decimal place.
=ROUND(4.149, 1)	4.1	Rounds 4.149 to one decimal place.
=ROUND(-2.475, 2)	-2.48	Rounds -2.475 to two decimal places.
=ROUND(57.5, -1)	60	Rounds 57.5 to one decimal place to the left of the decimal point.
=ROUND(671.3,-3)	1000	Rounds 671.3 to the nearest multiple of 1000.
=ROUND(1.78,-1)	0	Rounds 1.78 to the nearest multiple of 10.
=ROUND(-70.45,-2)	-100	Rounds -70.45 to the nearest multiple of 100.

ROUNDUP Function

The ROUNDUP function rounds a number up, away from 0 (zero).

Syntax

=ROUNDUP(number, num_digits)

Arguments

Argument	Description
number	Required. This argument is for the number that you want to round up.
num_digits	Required. The number of decimal places to which you want to round up the number.

Remarks

- ROUNDUP is like ROUND but always rounds a number up.
- Number is rounded up to the specified number of decimal places if num_digits is greater than 0 (zero).
- Number is rounded up to the nearest integer if num_digits is 0.
- Number is rounded up to the left of the decimal point if num_digits is less than 0.

Examples

In the following examples, ROUNDUP is applied to several values. The table displays the value, result, formula, and description.

	A	B	C	D
1	Value	Rounded up	Formula text	Description
2	3.15	3.2	=ROUNDUP(A2, 1)	Rounds 3.15 up to one decimal place.
3	4.149	5	=ROUNDUP(A3, 0)	Rounds 4.149 up to zero decimal places.
4	-2.475	-2.48	=ROUNDUP(A4, 2)	Rounds -2.475 to two decimal places.
5	57.5	60	=ROUNDUP(A5, -1)	Rounds 57.5 to one decimal place to the left of the decimal point.
6	671.3	700	=ROUNDUP(A6,-2)	Rounds 671.3 to two decimal places to the left of the decimal point.
7	1.78	2	=ROUNDUP(A7,0)	Rounds 1.78 up to zero decimal places.
8	-70.45	-100	=ROUNDUP(A8,-2)	Rounds -70.45 to the nearest multiple of 100.
9				
10				
11				
12				
13				

Formula explanations

=ROUNDUP(A2, 1)

In the formula above, A2 is the cell reference to the value to be rounded up. The num_digits argument is 1, specifying that we want to round up to 1 decimal place.

=ROUNDUP(A3, 0)

In the formula above, A3 is the cell reference to the value to round up. The num_digits argument is 0, specifying that we want to round up to a whole number, i.e., zero decimal places.

=ROUNDUP(A5, -1)

In the formula above, the num_digits argument is -1, specifying that we want to round up to one decimal place to the left of the decimal point. So, 57.5 is rounded up to 60.

ROUNDDOWN Function

The ROUNDDOWN function rounds a number down towards zero.

Syntax

=ROUNDDOWN(number, num_digits)

Arguments

Argument	Description
number	Required. The number you want to round down.
num_digits	Required. The number of decimal places you want to round the number down to.

Remarks

- ROUNDDOWN works like ROUND but always rounds a number down.

- Number is rounded down to the specified number of decimal places if num_digits is greater than 0 (zero).

- Number is rounded down to the nearest integer if num_digits is 0.

- Number is rounded down to the left of the decimal point if num_digits is less than 0.

Examples

In the following examples, ROUNDDOWN is applied to several values. The table displays the value, result, formula, and description.

	A	B	C	D
	Value	Result	Formula text	Description
1				
2	3.15	3.1	=ROUNDDOWN(A2, 1)	Rounds 3.15 down to one decimal place.
3	4.149	4	=ROUNDDOWN(A3, 0)	Rounds 4.149 down to zero decimal places.
4	-2.475	-2.47	=ROUNDDOWN(A4, 2)	Rounds -2.475 down to two decimal places.
5	57.5	50	=ROUNDDOWN(A5, -1)	Rounds 57.5 down to one decimal place to the left of the decimal point.
6	671.3	600	=ROUNDDOWN(A6,-2)	Rounds 671.3 down to the nearest multiple of 100.
7	1.78	1	=ROUNDDOWN(A7,0)	Rounds 1.78 down to zero decimal places.
8	-71.45	-70	=ROUNDDOWN(A8,-1)	Rounds -71.45 down to the nearest multiple of 10.
9				

Formula explanations

= ROUNDDOWN(A2, 1)

In the formula above, A2 is the cell reference holding the value to be rounded down. The num_digits argument is 1, specifying that we want to round down to 1 decimal place. So, 3.15 is rounded down to 3.1.

= ROUNDDOWN(A3, 0)

In the formula above, A3 is the cell reference to the value to round down. The num_digits argument is 0, specifying that we want to round down to a whole number, i.e., zero decimal places. So, 4.149 is rounded down to 4.

=ROUNDDOWN(A5, -1)

In the formula above, A5 is the cell reference to the value to round down. The num_digits argument is -1, specifying that we want to round down to one decimal place to the left of the decimal point. So, 57.5 is rounded down to 50.

Other Math Functions

The functions in this section are useful for performing calculations that return values as arguments within other functions.

Returning the Reminder with MOD

The MOD function is useful for calculations where you want to return the remainder of a division between two numbers. The result has the same sign as the divisor.

Syntax

=MOD(number, divisor)

Arguments

Argument	Description
Number	Required. The number being divided for which you want to find the remainder.
Divisor	Required. The number being used for the division. MOD will return the #DIV/0! error value if the divisor is 0.

Examples

The following examples use MOD in column C to calculate the remainder by dividing the values in column A by the values in column B.

| C2 | | | f_x | =MOD(A2,B2) | |

◢	A	B	C	D
1	Number	Divisor	Result	Description
2	100	40	20	Reminder of 100/40
3	7	5	2	Reminder of 7/5
4	30	45	30	
5	-4	3	2	The result is always the same sign as the divisor.
6	-3	2	1	
7	4	-3	-2	Result is always the same sign as the divisor.
8	-4	-3	-1	
9				

Returning The Square Root with SQRT

This function returns a positive square root of any number.

Syntax

=SQRT(number)

Argument	Description
number	Required. The number for which you want to calculate the square root.
	The function returns an error value (#NUM!) if this value is negative.

Example

The SQRT function has been applied to the following numbers.

	A	B	C
	B2		=SQRT(A2)
1	Number	Square root	
2	16	4	
3	6602	81.25269226	
4	4414	66.43794097	
5	5788	76.07890641	
6	1216	34.87119155	
7	0	0	
8	1	1	
9	820	28.63564213	
10	852	29.18903904	
11	6358	79.73706792	
12	924	30.39736831	
13	8689	93.21480569	
14	6614	81.32650245	
15	-10	#NUM!	Negative numner
16	4163	64.52131431	
17	8942	94.56214888	
18	2628	51.26402247	
19	4010	63.3245608	
20	9465	97.28823156	
21			

Chapter 5

Statistical Functions

This chapter covers functions that enable you to:

- Calculate the average, min, max, and median values in a range.
- Use criteria to determine which values to aggregate.
- Count the number of values in a range of cells that meet a certain condition.
- Count the number of values in a range that meet multiple criteria.
- Count the number of cells that contain numbers in a range or table.
- Count the number of empty cells in a range or table.

You can access the statistical functions in Excel by clicking on the More Functions button on the Formulas tab. On the drop-down menu, highlight the Statistical option to display a list of all the statistical functions in alphabetical order. The statistical functions in Excel range from everyday statistical functions like AVERAGE, MIN, MAX, etc., to more specialized functions used by statisticians.

Counting Values

Excel provides an array of functions that enable you to count values in your worksheet. You can count all populated cells, only numeric values, blank values, or values that meet certain criteria.

COUNT Function

The COUNT function will count the number of cells that contain numbers in a range or a list of numbers provided as arguments. The COUNT function only counts populated cells. For example, if you have a range with 20 cells, and only 5 cells have numbers, the count function will return 5.

Syntax

=COUNT(value1, [value2], ...)

Arguments

Argument	Description
Value1	Required. The first range in which you want to count numbers.
Value2	Optional. Additional cell references or ranges in which you want to count numbers. You can have a maximum of 255 arguments for this function.

Remarks

- You can have a maximum of 255 arguments for this function. Each argument could be a number, a cell reference, or a range.

- The COUNT function counts numbers, dates, or text representations of numbers (i.e., a number enclosed in quotation marks, like "1").

- Error values or text that cannot be translated into numbers are not counted.

- Use the COUNTA function if you want to count text, logical values, or error values.

- Use the COUNTIF function or the COUNTIFS function to count only numbers that meet a specific condition.

Example

The following formula counts the values in two ranges:

=COUNT(A3:D20,F3:I20)

This formula has two arguments to represent the ranges in which we want to count values: A3:D20 and F3:I20. Note that the blank cells are not counted.

| L2 | | | ⌄ | : | ✕ ✓ | fx | =COUNT(A3:D20,F3:I20) | | | | |

◢	A	B	C	D	E	F	G	H	I	J	K	L
1		Year1					Year2					
2	QTR1	QTR2	QTR3	QTR4		QTR1	QTR2	QTR3	QTR4		Count:	131
3	70	83	16	37		26	56	47	17			
4	73	71	88	52		87	57	36	87			
5	38	65		19		38	50	51	68			
6	87	56	91	55		62	40	26	77			
7	18	97	39	82			98	98	25			
8	86	15		85		47	59	60	61			
9	28		98	86		41	19	10	11			
10	45	80	43	73			92	95	59			
11	60	92	98	34		51	38	13	91			
12	51	64	25	50		81	84		60			
13	79	29	69	27		62	69	17	65			
14	65	54	95	22		73	53	40	67			
15	91		10	91		66		83	74			
16	88	97	91	89		48	58	78	25			
17	40	88		15		66	12	55	85			
18	12	54	22	87		59	10	66	20			
19	42	17	51	33			67		26			
20	78			32		52	32	62	61			
21												

COUNTIF Function

The COUNTIF function is a combination of a statistical function and a logical function. It allows you to count the number of cells that meet a criterion. For example, you can count only the values in a list of orders that exceed $1,000.

Syntax

=COUNTIF(range, criteria)

Arguments

Argument	Description
range	Required. The group of cells that you want to count. This argument can contain numbers, a named range, or references that contain numbers.
criteria	Required. The condition used to determine which cells will be counted. This argument can be a cell reference, text, expression, or function. For example, you can use a number like 40, a logical comparison like ">=40", a cell reference like D10, or a word like "bolts."

Remarks

- If the criteria argument is a text value or includes logical or math symbols, like greater than (>), it must be enclosed in double quotes ("").
- If criteria is a numeric value, quotation marks are not required.

Example

In this example, we're using COUNTIF to count all Sales over $5,000.

The formula we use is:

=COUNTIF(B2:B11,">5000")

	A	B	C	D
			fx	=COUNTIF(B2:B11,">5000")
1	Salesperson	Sales	Commission	Formula text
2	Bruce	$2,635	$132	
3	Louis	$7,227	$361	
4	Earl	$4,426	$221	
5	Sean	$4,774	$239	
6	Benjamin	$9,829	$491	
7	Joe	$20,000	$1,000	
8	Shawn	$2,459	$123	
9	Kenneth	$11,300	$565	
10	Cynthia	$2,566	$128	
11	Susan	$10,894	$545	
12				
13	Report			
14	Count of sales over $5,000		5	=COUNTIF(B2:B11,">5000")
15	Count of commissions over $200		7	=COUNTIF(C2:C11,">200")
16				

The first argument is the range we want to count - **B2:B11**.

The second argument is the criteria - greater than $5,000 ("> 5000").

Note that the criteria argument is enclosed in quotes because it includes a comparison operator.

Other examples

In the following examples, we have a list of orders that we query with different COUNTIF formulas in a report. The results and formulas are shown in the image below.

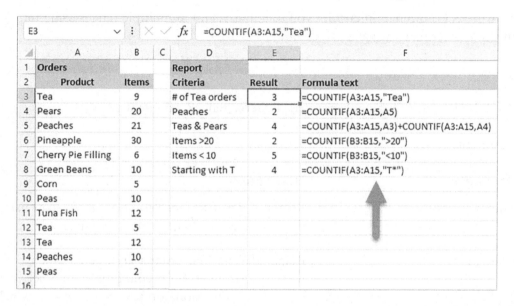

COUNTIFS Function

The COUNTIFS function enables you to count values in multiple ranges using multiple criteria to determine the values to count.

Syntax

=COUNTIFS(criteria_range1, criteria1, [criteria_range2, criteria2]…)

Arguments

Argument	Description
criteria_range1	Required. The first range you want to evaluate using the associated criteria, which is criteria1.
criteria1	Required. The first criteria argument, which pairs with criteria_range1. It could be a number, cell reference, expression, or text that defines which cells will be counted. For example, criteria can be expressed as 40, ">=40", D10, "bolts", or "40".
criteria_range2, criteria2, ...	Optional. Additional ranges and criteria pairs. You can have a total of 127 range/criteria pairs.

Remarks

- Each additional range must have the same number of rows and columns as criteria_range1. The ranges do not have to be adjacent to each other.

- If the criteria argument points to an empty cell, the COUNTIFS function treats the empty cell as a 0 value.

- If you are testing for text values, for example, "apples," make sure the criterion is in quotation marks.

- You can use wildcard characters like the question mark (?) and asterisk (*) in your criteria to enable you to find matches that are similar but not the same. The question mark matches any character, and the asterisk matches a sequence of characters. To find a character like a question mark or asterisk, type a tilde sign (~) in front of the character.

Example

The following example counts the number of people for each State with 40 or more Orders. This problem requires using two criteria to evaluate two columns. We will use the state name and ">=40" to filter the rows to be counted.

We apply the following formula to solve the problem:

=COUNTIFS(State,F2,Orders,G2)

Range names:
- State = B2:B12
- Orders = C2:C12

	A	B	C	D	E	F	G	H	I
1	Name	State	Orders	Sales		States	Orders	# People	Formula text
2	Bruce	New York	51	$74,298		New York	>=40	2	=COUNTIFS(State,F2,Orders,G2)
3	Louis	New York	39	$46,039		Texas	>=40	1	=COUNTIFS(State,F3,Orders,G3)
4	Earl	Washington	60	$65,252		California	>=40	1	=COUNTIFS(State,F4,Orders,G4)
5	Sean	Washington	100	$61,847		Washington	>=40	2	=COUNTIFS(State,F5,Orders,G5)
6	Benjamin	Texas	28	$33,340					
7	Joe	California	31	$95,778					
8	Shawn	Texas	35	$58,808					
9	Kenneth	California	39	$52,593					
10	Cynthia	California	51	$42,484		State = B2:B12			
11	Susan	Texas	80	$44,390		Orders = C2:12			
12	Dav	New York	70	$66,109					
13									

Formula explanation:

=COUNTIFS(State,F2,Orders,G2)

- The criteria_range1 argument references the range B2:B12 for which the range name **State** has been used.

- The criteria1 argument is cell **F2**, which has the State we want to use as our criteria. Using a cell reference here makes it easier to change the value.

This argument is a relative cell reference because we want it to change (relatively) as we copy the formula to other cells.

- The criteria_range2 is the range C2:C12, which has the range name **Orders** in the worksheet. We will be using criteria2 to evaluate this range.

- The criteria2 argument is **G2**, which is the expression **>=40**. A cell reference is used for this argument to make it easier to change the criteria.

We enter the formula in cell **H2** and copy it down the column to count the number of people with orders that match the criteria for each state.

COUNTA Function

The COUNTA function counts the number of cells that are not empty in a group of cells or range. The difference between the COUNTA and COUNT is that COUNTA counts all cells containing an entry, including empty text ("") and even error values. COUNT, on the other hand, only counts cells that contain numeric values.

Syntax

=COUNTA(value1, [value2], ...)

Arguments

Argument	Description
value1	Required. The first argument represents the range in which you want to count cells with an entry.
value2, ...	Optional. You can have additional value arguments up to a maximum of 255 arguments in total.

Remarks

- If you want to count only cells that contain numeric values, use the COUNT function.

- Use the COUNTIF function or the COUNTIFS function if you only want to count cells that meet certain criteria.

Example

In the following example, we use the COUNTA function to count cells with entries in our range of cells. The group of cells containing our data, A1:D14, is a named range called *Orders_Range*.

The COUNTA function is demonstrated next to other functions like COUNT and COUNTBLANK to show the difference in the results.

Formula: =COUNTA(Orders_Range)

Result: 37

Orders_Range	⌄	:	✕ ✓ fx	Orders		

◢	A	B	C	D	E
1	**Orders**				
2		**Customer**	**Order Date**	**Order Total**	
3	**Sector 1**	Bruce Henderson	1/15/2022	$2,635	
4		Louis Anderson	2/2/2022	$7,227	
5		Earl Foster	3/3/2022	$4,426	
6		Sean Hill	4/4/2022	$8,774	
7					
8	**Sector 2**	Benjamin Martinez	4/12/2022	$9,829	
9		Joe Perez	4/15/2022	$2,194	
10		Shawn Johnson	4/17/2022	$2,459	
11		Kenneth Roberts	5/8/2022	$3,920	
12		Cynthia Martin	5/19/2022	$2,566	
13		Susan Mitchell	6/10/2022	$7,034	
14				$51,064	
15					
16	Total # cells	56	=ROWS(Orders_Range)*COLUMNS(Orders_Range)		
17	Occupied cells	37	=COUNTA(Orders_Range)		
18	Numeric values	21	=COUNT(Orders_Range)		
19	Blank cells	19	=COUNTBLANK(Orders_Range)		
20					

COUNTBLANK Function

The COUNTBLANK function counts the number of empty cells in a range.

Syntax

=COUNTBLANK(range)

Argument	Description
range	Required. The first argument represents the range in which you want to count the blank cells.

Cells with formulas that return an empty string ("") are also counted. Cells with 0 (zero) are not counted.

Example

In the following example, we use the COUNTBLANK function to count the blank cells in the range A1:D14 named *Orders_Range*.

Formula: =COUNTBLANK(Orders_Range)

Result: 19

	A	B	C	D	E
1	**Orders**				
2		**Customer**	**Order Date**	**Order Total**	
3	**Sector 1**	Bruce Henderson	1/15/2022	$2,635	
4		Louis Anderson	2/2/2022	$7,227	
5		Earl Foster	3/3/2022	$4,426	
6		Sean Hill	4/4/2022	$8,774	
7					
8	**Sector 2**	Benjamin Martinez	4/12/2022	$9,829	
9		Joe Perez	4/15/2022	$2,194	
10		Shawn Johnson	4/17/2022	$2,459	
11		Kenneth Roberts	5/8/2022	$3,920	
12		Cynthia Martin	5/19/2022	$2,566	
13		Susan Mitchell	6/10/2022	$7,034	
14				$51,064	
15					
16	**Total # cells**	56	=ROWS(Orders_Range)*COLUMNS(Orders_Range)		
17	**Occupied cells**	37	=COUNTA(Orders_Range)		
18	**Numeric values**	21	=COUNT(Orders_Range)		
19	**Blank cells**	19	=COUNTBLANK(Orders_Range)		
20					

Calculating Averages and Extreme Values

The functions in this section enable you to create formulas that return the average, median, and extreme values like maximum and minimum values. You can also use corresponding advanced functions to create formulas that evaluate only a subset of values based on the criteria you provide.

AVERAGE Function

The AVERAGE function is one of the widely used aggregate functions in Excel. It returns the average of the arguments. The average is the arithmetic mean of a series of numbers and is calculated by adding up the numbers and then dividing by the count of those numbers.

Syntax

=AVERAGE(number1, [number2], ...)

Arguments

Argument	Description
number1	Required. The first cell reference, range, or number for which you want to calculate an average.
number2, ...	Optional. Additional cell references, ranges, or numbers for which you want to calculate an average up to a maximum of 255.

Remarks

- Arguments can include numbers, named ranges, or cell references containing numbers.

- If any of the cells referenced in the arguments contain an error value, AVERAGE returns an error.

- Text, logical values, and empty cells are ignored, but cells with the value zero (0) are included.

- Use the AVERAGEA function to include logical values and text representations of numbers as part of the calculation.

- Use AVERAGEIF and AVERAGEIFS to calculate the average of a subset of values that meet a set of criteria.

Example

In the example below, we use the AVERAGE function to calculate the average of the scores in C2:C16.

Formula

=AVERAGE(C2:C16)

| F2 | | ⌄ | ⋮ | ✕ | ✓ | fx | =AVERAGE(C2:C16) | |

◢	A	B	C	D	E	F
1	**Student**	**Subject**	**Score**		**Average score**	
2	Bruce	Math	75		All subjects	64.7
3	Louis	Chemistry	61			
4	Earl	Biology	67			
5	Sean	English	74			
6	Benjamin	Math	86			
7	Joe	Chemistry	58			
8	Shawn	Biology	74			
9	Kenneth	English	70			
10	Cynthia	Math	55			
11	Susan	Chemistry	49			
12	John	Math	76			
13	Bruce	English	60			
14	Louis	Biology	68			
15	Earl	Chemistry	47			
16	Kenneth	Math	50			
17						

AVERAGEIF Function

The AVERAGEIF function is a combination of a statistical function and a logical function. AVERAGEIF returns the average (or arithmetic mean) of all the cells in a range that meet a specified condition.

Syntax

=AVERAGEIF(range, criteria, [average_range])

Arguments

Argument	Description
range	Required. A reference to one or more cells to average. This argument can include numbers, cell references, or named ranges.
criteria	Required. An expression that determines which cells are included in the average.
average_range	Optional. The actual set of cells to average, if not the cells in the *range* argument. If this argument is omitted, *range* is used.

Remarks

- AVERAGEIF will return the error #DIV/0! if no cells in *range* meet the criteria.

- AVERAGEIF will return the error #DIV/0! if *range* is a blank or text string.

- If a cell in *criteria* is empty, it is treated as zero (0).

- Cells in the range argument that contain logical values like TRUE or FALSE are ignored.

- You can use wildcard characters like the question mark (?) and asterisk (*) in your criteria to find matches that are similar but not the same. A question mark matches any single character, while an asterisk matches a sequence of characters. To find a character like a question mark or asterisk, type a tilde sign (~) in front of the character.

- *Average_range* does not necessarily need to be the same number of rows and columns as *range*. The average is performed by using the top-left cell in average_range plus cells that match the same number of rows and columns in the range argument. See examples in the table below:

range	average_range	Cells evaluated and averaged
A1:A10	B1:B10	B1:B10
A1:A10	B1:B5	B1:B10
A1:B5	C1:C3	C1:D5

Example

In the following example, we use the AVERAGEIF function to calculate the average test scores for students per subject. We want to group the data by **Subject** (for example, Biology, Chemistry, Math, etc.) and average each group by **Score**.

The range used to filter the averaged data is B2:B16, and the range that averaged is C2:C16. The formula uses range names for the referenced ranges to make them absolute references.

F2				fx	=AVERAGEIF(Subjects,E2,Scores)	
	A	B	C	D	E	F	G
1	Student	Subject	Score		Subject	Average	Formula text
2	Bruce	Math	75		Math	68.4	=AVERAGEIF(Subjects,E2,Scores)
3	Louis	Chemistry	61		Chemistry	53.8	=AVERAGEIF(Subjects,E3,Scores)
4	Earl	Biology	67		English	68.0	=AVERAGEIF(Subjects,E4,Scores)
5	Sean	English	74		Biology	69.7	=AVERAGEIF(Subjects,E5,Scores)
6	Benjamin	Math	86				
7	Joe	Chemistry	58				
8	Shawn	Biology	74				
9	Kenneth	English	70				
10	Cynthia	Math	55				
11	Susan	Chemistry	49				
12	John	Math	76		Subjects = B2:B16		
13	Bruce	English	60		Scores = C2:C16		
14	Louis	Biology	68				
15	Earl	Chemistry	47				
16	Kenneth	Math	50				
17							

Formula explanation:

=AVERAGEIF(Subjects,E2,Scores)

Subjects = B2:B16
Scores = C2:C16

- The range argument references cells B2:B16 (named Subjects), which is used to filter the values to be averaged.

- The criteria argument is **E2**, which is a reference to our criteria. Using a cell reference makes it easier to change the criteria on the worksheet. This argument is a relative reference because we want the criteria to change (relatively) as we copy the formula to other cells.

- The average_range argument references cells C2:C16 (named Scores), which is the range we want to average based on the criteria.

We enter the formula in cell F2 to return the average for Math, then copy the formula to cells F3:F5 to display the average for the other subjects.

AVERAGEIFS Function

The AVERAGEIFS function returns the average (arithmetic mean) of all cells that meet a set of criteria. This function allows you to specify several criteria pairs to select the data to be included in the average. An IFS function enables you to create several range/criteria pairs to select the data that meet the criteria.

The function identifies items that meet the criteria in one column and averages corresponding items in another. You can have up to a maximum of 127 range/criteria pairs, as you can only have 255 arguments in an Excel function.

Syntax

=AVERAGEIFS(average_range, criteria_range1, criteria1, [criteria_range2, criteria2], ...)

Arguments

Argument	Description
average_range	Required. The range of cells for which you want the average calculated.
criteria_range1	Required. The range to evaluate using criteria1.

criteria1	Required. The criteria used to evaluate criteria1_range to select matching data. For example, criteria can be entered as 40, ">40", C6, "bolts", or "125".
Criteria_range2, criteria2, …	Optional. You can have additional range/criteria pairs, up to 127 total pairs.

Example

This example shows a list of orders from different sales reps for several states. We want to find the average sales per state for entries with 10 or more orders (>=10).

We can use the following formula to achieve the result:

=AVERAGEIFS(Sales,States,F2,Orders,G2)

Sales = D2:D12
States = B2:B12
Orders = C2:C12

H2			fx	=AVERAGEIFS(Sales,States,F2,Orders,G2)				
	A	B	C	D	E	F	G	H	I
1	**Name**	**State**	**Orders**	**Sales**		**States**	**Orders**	**Avg Sales 10+ orders**	**Formula text**
2	Bruce	New York	12	$74,298		New York	>=10	$70,204	=AVERAGEIFS(Sales,States,F2,Orders,G2)
3	Louis	New York	5	$46,039		Texas	>=10	$58,808	=AVERAGEIFS(Sales,States,F3,Orders,G3)
4	Earl	Washington	15	$65,252		California	>=10	$52,593	=AVERAGEIFS(Sales,States,F4,Orders,G4)
5	Sean	Washington	11	$61,847		Washington	>=10	$63,550	=AVERAGEIFS(Sales,States,F5,Orders,G5)
6	Benjamin	Texas	9	$33,340					
7	Joe	California	3	$30,000					
8	Shawn	Texas	20	$58,808		Sales = D2:D12			
9	Kenneth	California	12	$52,593		States = B2:B12			
10	Cynthia	California	8	$42,484		Orders = C2:C12			
11	Susan	Texas	2	$20,000					
12	Dav	New York	10	$66,109					
13									
14									
15	The average sales per state for entries with 10 or more orders.								
16									
17									

Formula explanation:

=AVERAGEIFS(Sales,States,F2,Orders,G2)

- The average_range argument references D2:D12 (named Sales), the range for which we calculate the average.

- The criteria_range1 is B2:B12 for which a range name States has been used.

- The criteria1 argument is F2, a cell reference to the value used as the criteria. A cell reference makes it easier to change the criteria on the worksheet.

  This argument is a relative reference as we want it to change as we copy the formula to other cells.

- The criteria_range2 argument is C2:C12 (named Orders) has been used.

- The criteria2 argument is cell G2, which references our criteria (>=10). This argument is a matching pair for criteria_range2. A cell reference has been used to make it easier to change the criteria if needed.

The first criteria_range/criteria pair filters the data by State, and the second criteria_range/criteria pair filters the data by Orders. The formula then returns the average of the filtered data.

The formula is entered in cell H2 and copied to H3:H5 to calculate the average for the other states.

MAX, MIN, and MEDIAN Functions

The MAX, MIN, and MEDIAN functions are some of the most commonly used functions in Excel and are very similar in their arguments and usage. In a set of values, MAX returns the largest number, MIN returns the smallest number, and MEDIAN returns the number in the middle. We can cover these functions simultaneously as they're similar in arguments.

Syntax

=MAX(number1, [number2], ...)

=MIN(number1, [number2], ...)

=MEDIAN(number1, [number2], ...)

Arguments – similar for all three functions

Argument	Description
Number1	Required. A number, range, array, or cell reference that contains numbers.
number2, ...	Optional. You can have additional numbers, cell references, or ranges up to a maximum of 255 arguments that you want to evaluate.

Remarks

- MEDIAN calculates the average of the two middle numbers if there is an even number of values.

- The functions will return 0 (zero) if the arguments contain no numbers.

- Excel uses only the numbers in a reference or array argument. Logical values, text values, and empty cells in the reference or array are ignored.

- The functions will return an error if arguments contain error values or text that cannot be translated into numbers.

- Text representations of numbers and logical values that you directly type into the arguments list are counted.

- Use the MAXA and MINA functions if you want to include logical values and text representations of numbers as part of the result for MAX and MIN. You can search for the MAXA or MINA with the **Insert Function** command on Excel's Formulas tab.

Example

The example below shows the maximum, minimum, and median values for the **Sales** column (D2:D12).

The following formulas return the desired results:

- MAX(D2:D12)

- MIN(D2:D12)

- MEDIAN(D2:D12)

	A	B	C	D	E	F	G	H
1	Name	State	Orders	Sales		Summary Report		Formula text
2	Bruce	New York	51	$74,298		Highest sales	$95,778	=MAX(D2:D12)
3	Louis	New York	39	$46,039		Lowest sales	$33,340	=MIN(D2:D12)
4	Earl	Washington	60	$65,252		Median	$58,808	=MEDIAN(D2:D12)
5	Sean	Washington	100	$61,847				
6	Benjamin	Texas	28	$33,340				
7	Joe	California	31	$95,778				
8	Shawn	Texas	35	$58,808				
9	Kenneth	California	39	$52,593				
10	Cynthia	California	51	$42,484				
11	Susan	Texas	80	$44,390				
12	Dav	New York	70	$66,109				
13								

To add more cell references or ranges to the arguments, separate them with a comma. For example, MAX(C1:C5, G1:G5).

MAXIFS and MINIFS Functions

The MAXIFS and MINIFS functions are an extension of the MAX and MIN functions to include a conditional component in their functionality. MAXIFS returns the maximum value of all cells that meet the specified criteria. MINIFS returns the minimum value of all cells that meet the specified criteria. You can specify more than one set of criteria to determine which data is selected to be part of the evaluation.

An IFS function enables you to create several range/criteria pairs to narrow down the data to only those that meet the criteria. The functions identify items that meet the criteria in one column and calculate corresponding items in another.

You can have up to a maximum of 127 range/criteria pairs, as you can only have 255 arguments in an Excel function.

Syntax

=MAXIFS(max_range, criteria_range1, criteria1, [criteria_range2, criteria2], ...)

=MINIFS(min_range, criteria_range1, criteria1, [criteria_range2, criteria2], ...)

Arguments – similar for both functions

Argument	Description
max_range (MAX function) min_range(MIN function)	Required. The actual range of cells for which we want the maximum or minimum value determined.
criteria_range1	Required. The range evaluated using criteria1.
criteria1	Required. The criteria used to determine which cells in criteria_range1 will be part of the calculation. This argument can be a number, expression, or text. For example, criteria can be entered as 40, ">40", C6, "bolts", or "125".
criteria_range2, criteria2, ...	Optional. You can have additional range/criteria pairs, up to 127 total pairs.

Remarks

- The max_range (or min_range) and criteria_range arguments must have the same number of rows and columns. Otherwise, these functions return the #VALUE! error.

- The range we use to filter the data does not necessarily have to be the same range from which we want to generate the max or min value.

Example

In this example, we want to produce reports that show the minimum and maximums sales per state. However, we only want to evaluate entries with 10 or more orders (>=10). So, we have different criteria that we want to use to determine the data to be evaluated.

Formulas

The following formulas return the desired results.

Maximum:
=MAXIFS(Sales,States,F3,Orders,G3)

Minimum:
=MINIFS(Sales,States,F10,Orders,G10)

	A	B	C	D	E	F	G	H	I
1	Name	State	Orders	Sales		Max Sales			
2	Bruce	New York	12	$74,298		States	Orders	Max Sales	Formula Text
3	Louis	New York	5	$46,039		New York	>=10	$74,298	=MAXIFS(Sales,States,F3,Orders,G3)
4	Earl	Washington	15	$65,252		Texas	>=10	$58,808	=MAXIFS(Sales,States,F4,Orders,G4)
5	Sean	Washington	11	$61,847		California	>=10	$52,593	=MAXIFS(Sales,States,F5,Orders,G5)
6	Benjamin	Texas	10	$33,340		Washington	>=10	$65,252	=MAXIFS(Sales,States,F6,Orders,G6)
7	Joe	California	3	$30,000					
8	Shawn	Texas	20	$58,808		Min Sales			
9	Kenneth	California	12	$52,593		States	Orders	Min sales	Formula Text
10	Cynthia	California	8	$42,484		New York	>=10	$66,109	=MINIFS(Sales,States,F10,Orders,G10)
11	Susan	Texas	2	$20,000		Texas	>=10	$33,340	=MINIFS(Sales,States,F11,Orders,G11)
12	Dav	New York	10	$66,109		California	>=10	$52,593	=MINIFS(Sales,States,F12,Orders,G12)
13						Washington	>=10	$61,847	=MINIFS(Sales,States,F13,Orders,G13)
14									

Formula explanation

Both functions use identical cell references and criteria arguments. So, they can be described together.

=MAXIFS(Sales,States,F3,Orders,G3)

=MINIFS(Sales,States,F10,Orders,G10)

- The first argument references D2:D12, which has the range name **Sales**. We want to evaluate this range for the maximum and minimum values.

- The criteria_range1 argument is referencing B2:B12 (named **States**). This argument makes up the first range/criteria pair we're using to filter the data to be evaluated.

- The criteria1 argument is **F2**, a cell reference to the criteria - **New York**. Using a cell reference makes it easier to change the criteria.

- The criteria_range2 argument is C2:C12 (named **Orders**). Criteria_range2 is part of the second range/criteria pair.

- The criteria2 argument is cell **G2** which holds the criteria for the number of orders, ">=10". Criteria2 is part of the second range/criteria pair used to filter the data to be evaluated. A cell reference has been used to make it easier to change the criteria.

To display the results, we enter the MAXIFS formula in cell H3 and copy it to the other cells for which we want to display maximum sales. For the minimum values, the MINIFS formula is entered in cell H10 and copied to the other cells displaying the minimum sales.

Chapter 6

Date and Time Functions

This chapter covers functions that enable you to:

- Return the day, month, or year from a given date.

- Add or subtract days, months, and years from dates.

- Combine different values into a single date.

- Return the number of days, months, or years between two dates.

- Convert date values entered as text into recognized Excel dates, for example, in the case of imported data.

- Return the number of whole working days between two dates.

- Return the current date or the date and time.

- Return the decimal number for a given time.

The date and time functions can be found in Excel by clicking the Date & Time command on the Formulas tab on the Ribbon. The dropdown menu lists all the date and time functions in Excel.

Excel stores dates and times as serial numbers internally, for example, 45280.83583. The numbers to the left of the decimal point represent the date, and the numbers to the right of the decimal point represent the time. Excel calculates dates and times using serial numbers like this. Any entry formatted as a date/time in Excel is automatically converted internally into a serial number. For example, by default, 1/1/1900 is serial number 1, and 1/1/2023 is serial number 44927 because 1/1/2023 is 44927 days after 1/1/1900.

Date Formats

Before delving into the date functions, we need to look at date formats in Excel and how to set cells to different date formats. The default date and time formats used by Excel will be the ones you have set in your regional settings in Windows (or macOS for Macs).

The short date format used in Europe is Day/Month/Year (i.e., dd/mm/yy), while in the United States, the short date format is Month/Day/Year (i.e., m/dd/yy).

You can change how dates are displayed in your Excel worksheet regardless of your regional date settings in Windows or macOS.

To change the date format in Excel, do the following:

1. Select the cell(s) for which you want to change the date format.

2. Right-click and select **Format Cells** on the shortcut menu.

3. Under **Category**, select **Date**.

4. Under **Locale (location)**, select the region. For example, English (United States).

5. Under **Type**, select the date format you want.

6. To select a different time format, select **Time** under Category and follow the same steps above to choose a time format.

7. Click OK.

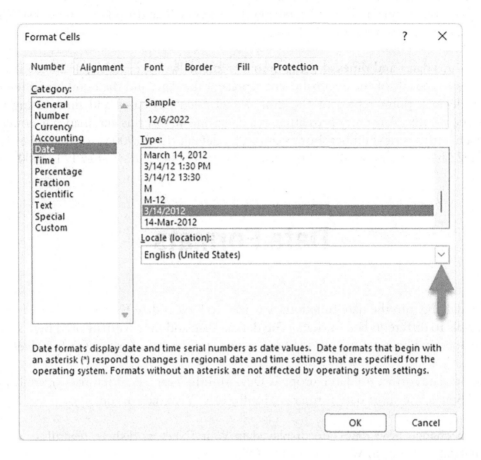

For the examples in this chapter, we will use the United States short date convention **m/d/yyyy**. If you're in a region using the dd/mm/yyyy convention, simply swap the month and day of the dates used in the examples.

Add Days, Months, and Years to a Date

This section covers functions that enable you to add and subtract dates. You can combine date functions to create formulas that add or subtract dates, including days, months, and years.

DAY, MONTH, and YEAR Functions

The DAY, MONTH, and YEAR functions are very similar and are often used together, so this section covers them simultaneously. They all take a single argument, a serial number representing a date.

DAY returns the day (an integer between 1 to 31) corresponding to a date entered as its argument.

MONTH returns the month (an integer between 1 to 12, representing January to December) corresponding to a date entered as its argument.

YEAR returns the year (as an integer in the range 1900-9999) corresponding to a date entered as its argument.

Syntax

=DAY(serial_number)

=MONTH(serial_number)

=YEAR(serial_number)

Arguments

Argument	Description
Serial_number	Required. All three functions have the same kind of argument. This argument must be a recognized date. It is the date for the day, month, or year you want to return.
	You can use the DATE function in this argument to ensure a proper date is entered, for example, DATE(2019,4,28). Problems may occur if dates are entered as text.

Remarks

The values returned by the YEAR, MONTH, and DAY functions are always Gregorian values regardless of the date format of the argument. For example, if the entered date is Hijri (Islamic Calendar), the values returned by DAY, MONTH, and YEAR will be the equivalent in the Gregorian calendar.

Example 1

In the example below, we use the DAY, MONTH, and YEAR functions to extract the day, month, and year from a given date in cell A1.

Formulas:
    =DAY(A1)
    =MONTH(A1)
    =YEAR(A1)

| D4 | | | f_x | =DAY(A4) |

▲	A	B	C	D	E
1	**Extract the day, month, and year from a date**				
2					
3	**Date**			**Date portion**	**Formula text**
4	1/18/2024		Day	18	=DAY(A4)
5			Month	1	=MONTH(A4)
6			Year	2024	=YEAR(A4)
7					
8					

📝**Note** In the next section, see examples of how to add or subtract days, months, or years from a date by combining DAY, MONTH, and YEAR with the DATE function.

DATE Function

The DATE function enables you to combine different values into a single date.

Syntax

=DATE (year, month, day)

Arguments

Argument	Description
year	Required. This argument can have one to four digits. Excel uses the date system on your computer to interpret the year argument.
month	Required. The month argument should be a positive or negative integer between 1 to 12, representing January to December. If the month argument is a negative number (*-n*), the function returns a date *n* months from the last month of the previous year. For example, DATE(2019,-4,2) will return the serial number representing August 2, 2018.
day	Required. This argument can be a positive or negative integer from 1 to 31, representing the day of the month.

Remarks

- If the month argument is greater than 12, the function adds that number of months to the last month of the specified year. For example, DATE(2022,14,4) will return the serial number representing February 4, 2023.

- If day is greater than the number of days in the specified month, the function adds that number of days to the first day of the next month of the specified date. For example, DATE(2022,2,30) returns the serial number representing March 2, 2022.

- If day is less than 1, Excel subtracts that number of days from the last day of the previous month. For example, DATE(2022,12,-10) will return the serial number that represents November 20, 2022. Excel subtracted 10 from the 30 days in November, which is the previous month.

- Excel sometimes automatically detects a date entry and formats the cell accordingly. However, if you copied and pasted a date from another source, you may need to manually format the cell to a date to display the date properly.

-ͷ́-**Tip** Always use four digits for the year argument to prevent unwanted results. For example, 04 could mean 1904 or 2004. Using four-digit years prevents any confusion.

Example 1

In this example, we want to combine values from different cells for the month, day, and year into a date value recognized in Excel.

When we use the DATE function to combine values into a single date, we get the following formula:

=DATE(C4,A4,B4)

	A	B	C	D	E
	D4		fx	=DATE(C4,A4,B4)	
1	**Combining numbers into dates**				
2					
3	**Month**	**Day**	**Year**	**Date**	
4	4	14	1985	04/14/1985	
5	8	28	1995	08/28/1995	
6	6	5	2023	06/05/2023	
7	12	30	2025	12/30/2025	
8					

Example 2

When we combine the DATE function with the DAY, MONTH, and YEAR functions, we can perform the following date calculations:

- Add 5 years to 12/15/2022

- Add 15 months to 12/15/2022

- Add 60 days to 10/15/2022

The image below shows the formulas used to perform these calculations.

	A	B	C	D
1	**Contract duration**			
2				
3	**Start date**	**Years**	**End date**	**Formula Text**
4	12/15/2022	5	12/15/2027	=DATE(YEAR(A4)+B4,MONTH(A4),DAY(A4))
5				
6	**Start date**	**Months**	**End date**	
7	12/15/2022	15	3/15/2024	=DATE(YEAR(A7),MONTH(A7)+B7,DAY(A7))
8				
9	**Start date**	**Days**	**End date**	
10	12/15/2022	60	2/13/2023	=DATE(YEAR(A10),MONTH(A10),DAY(A10)+B10)
11				
12				
13	*Adds the duration of the contract to the start date to calculate the end date.*			
14				
15				

Formula Explanation

Add 5 years to 12/15/2022

=DATE(YEAR(A4)+B4,MONTH(A4),DAY(A4))

The **year** argument of the DATE function has **YEAR(A4)+B4** (i.e., 2022 + 5, which returns 2027). The other nested functions return the month and day in the **month** and **day** arguments. To subtract years, use the minus sign (**−**) in place of the plus sign (**+**) in the formula.

Add 15 Months to 12/15/2022

=DATE(YEAR(A7),MONTH(A7)+B7,DAY(A7))

In this formula, **MONTH(A7)+B7** adds 15 months to the start date. The other nested functions return the year and day, respectively, in the year and day arguments of the DATE function. To subtract months, use the − sign in place of the + sign in the formula.

Add 60 days to 12/15/2022

=DATE(YEAR(A10),MONTH(A10),DAY(A10)+B10)

In this formula, **DAY(A10)+B10** adds 60 days to the start date. The other nested functions return the year and month, respectively, in the year and month arguments of the DATE function. To subtract days, use the − sign in place of the + sign in the formula.

EDATE Function

The EDATE function allows you to add or subtract months from a given date. EDATE is useful for calculating end dates on the same day of the month as the start date.

Syntax

=EDATE(start_date, months)

Arguments

Argument	Description
start_date	Required. This argument should be a date representing the start date. It can be a cell reference or a value. Cell references should have the Date format. Use the DATE function for values directly entered. For example, use DATE(2023,1,25) for January 25, 2023. You may get inconsistent results if dates are entered as text.
months	Required. An integer representing the number of months before or after start_date. A positive value returns a future date, and a negative value returns a date in the past.

Remarks

- If start_date is not a valid date, EDATE will return a #VALUE! error.
- If the months argument is not an integer, it is truncated.

Example

In the following example, we use the EDATE function to calculate the expiry dates for a series of property lease contracts with start dates (A3:A15) and lease lengths in months (B3:B15).

Formula:

=EDATE(A3,B3)

The formula was entered in cell A3 and copied to the other cells in the column with the fill handle.

	A	B	C
	C3		=EDATE(A3,B3)
1	**Property Lease**		
2	**Start Date**	**Length (Months)**	**Expiry Date**
3	1/28/2023	24	1/28/2025
4	4/4/2023	12	4/4/2024
5	4/16/2023	12	4/16/2024
6	5/21/2023	24	5/21/2025
7	5/28/2023	36	5/28/2026
8	10/27/2023	6	4/27/2024
9	11/9/2023	24	11/9/2025
10	12/7/2023	12	12/7/2024
11	12/14/2023	24	12/14/2025
12	2/21/2024	36	2/21/2027
13	5/6/2024	6	11/6/2024
14	7/25/2024	24	7/25/2026
15	11/29/2024	12	11/29/2025
16			
17			

Note that the cells in A3:A15 and C3:C15 were set to the **Date** format so that Excel displays the dates properly.

NOW Function

The NOW function returns the current date and time. It's a straightforward function with no arguments. The function displays the date using the date and time format of your regional settings. Check the **Date Formats** section of this book for how to change the date format of a cell.

You can use the NOW function to display the current date and time in a cell and have it updated every time you open the worksheet. You can also use the NOW function as arguments in other functions to calculate dates based on the current date and time.

Syntax

=NOW()

Remarks

- The results of the NOW function are not continuously updated. It only updates when the worksheet is recalculated, i.e., when new values or formulas are entered or a macro that contains the function is run.

- If the cell containing the NOW function was changed to a General format, it would display the current date as a serial number, for instance, 43454.83583. Numbers to the left of the decimal point represent the date, and numbers to the right represent the time. For example, serial number 0.5 represents the time 12:00 noon.

Example

In the example below, the NOW function is used in different formulas to display date calculations based on the current date and time.

Formulas:
    =NOW()
    =NOW()-10.5
    =NOW()+10
    =NOW()+2.25
    =EDATE(NOW(),3)

	A	B	C
1	Result	Formula text	Description
2	09/07/2022 13:19	=NOW()	Returns the current date and time
3	44811.55532	=NOW()	Returns the current date and time (General Number cell format)
4	08/28/2022 01:19	=NOW()-10.5	Returns the date and time 10 days and 12 hours ago (-10.5 days ago)
5	09/17/2022 13:19	=NOW()+10	Returns the date and time 10 days in the future
6	09/09/2022 19:19	=NOW()+2.25	Returns the date and time 2 days and 6 hours in the future
7	12/07/2022 00:00	=EDATE(NOW(),3)	3 months in the future, time removed
8			

TODAY Function

The TODAY function returns the serial number of the current date. When you use this function, Excel automatically changes the cell's number format to a **Date**, which displays the value as a date instead of a serial number. To see the date value as a serial number, you must change the cell format to **General** or Number.

The TODAY function is useful for displaying the current date on a worksheet. The function is also useful for calculating the difference between dates. For instance, you can calculate the number of years between two dates by combining the TODAY and YEAR functions.

= YEAR(TODAY())-1979

The formula above uses the TODAY function as an argument in the YEAR function to return the current year. The formula then subtracts 1979 from the current year to return the number of years between 1979 and today.

Syntax

=TODAY()

Example

In the example below, the TODAY function is used in different formulas to display the current date and to calculate other dates based on today's date.

Formulas:
    =TODAY()
    =TODAY()+10
    =DAY(TODAY())
    =MONTH(TODAY())
    =YEAR(TODAY())-2000

	A	B	C
1	Result	Formula text	Description
2	9/7/2022	=TODAY()	Returns the current date.
3	9/17/2022	=TODAY()+10	Returns the current date plus 10 days.
4	7	=DAY(TODAY())	Returns the current day of the month (1 - 31).
5	9	=MONTH(TODAY())	Returns the current month of the year (1 - 12).
6	22	= YEAR(TODAY())-2000	TODAY is used in YEAR to calculate the number of years between the current date and the subtracted date.
7			
8			
9			

Note If the TODAY function does not update when you open the worksheet, you might need to change the settings in Excel Options that determine when the workbook recalculates.

If your worksheet is not recalculating, you can enable the automatic calculation option in Excel Options:

1. Click **File** > **Options** > **Formulas** to display the Formulas tab of the Excel Options dialog.

2. Under **Calculation options**, select **Automatic** (if it is not already selected).

Calculate the Difference between Two Dates

The functions in this category enable you to create formulas that calculate the difference between two dates. For example, the number of days, months, or years between a start and an end date.

DATEDIF Function

The DATEDIF function calculates the difference between two dates. This function provides one of the easiest ways in Excel to calculate the difference between two dates. It can return the number of days, months, or years between two dates.

DATEDIF is a "hidden" function in Excel because you'll not find it on the list of date functions or when you search for it using the Insert Function dialog box. You must enter it manually any time you want to use it. It is a legacy function from Lotus 1-2-3, but it has been operational on all versions of Excel.

Syntax

=DATEDIF(start_date, end_date, unit)

Arguments

Argument	Description
start_date	Required. This argument represents the start date of the period.
end_date	Required. This argument represents the end date of the period.
unit	Required. This argument represents the unit of measurement you want to return - days, months, or years. It should be entered as a string. It can be one of Y, M, D, YM, or YD: "Y" = Calculates the number of years in the period. "M" = Calculates the number of months in the period. "D" = Calculates the number of days in the period. "YM" = Calculates the difference between the months in start_date and end_date. The days and years of the dates are ignored. "YD"= Calculates the difference between the days of start_date and end_date. The years of the dates are ignored.

Remarks

This function also has an "MD" argument that calculates the number of days while ignoring the month and years. However, Microsoft no longer recommends using the MD argument because, under some conditions, it could return a negative number, which would be an incorrect value.

Example 1

The example below calculates the age from the date of birth of different people.

Formula:

=DATEDIF(A2,TODAY(),"Y")

B2		✓ : ✕ ✓ fx	=DATEDIF(A2,TODAY(),"Y")			

	A	B	C	D	E	F
1	Date of Birth	Years				
2	1/8/1957	65				
3	1/12/1965	57				
4	12/1/1980	41				
5	11/6/1992	29				
6	7/26/2001	21				
7						

The formula combines the DATEDIF function with the TODAY function to get the desired result. The TODAY function returns today's date, so this formula will always use today's date to calculate the age. The "Y" argument returns the difference in years.

Example 2

To calculate the number of months between two dates, we use the "M" argument of the DATEDIF function.

=DATEDIF(A2,B2,"M")

C11		✓ : ✕ ✓ fx	=DATEDIF(A11,B11,"M")	

	A	B	C	D	E
10	Start Date	End Date	Months		
11	12/1/2022	12/1/2023	12		
12	12/1/2022	12/1/2024	24		
13	12/1/2022	6/1/2025	30		
14	12/6/2024	12/1/2027	35		
15	12/6/2023	12/1/2028	59		
16					

DAYS Function

The DAYS function returns the number of days between two dates.

Syntax

=DAYS (end_date, start_date)

Arguments

Argument	Description
end_date	Required. A date that represents the end date of the period.
start_date	Required. A date that represents the start date of the period.

Example

The table below calculates the difference between two dates in several examples.

Formula:

=DAYS(B2, A2)

	A	B	C	D
				=DAYS(B2, A2)
	A	**B**	**C**	**D**
1	**Start Date**	**End Date**	**Days**	
2	1-Dec-2018	1-Dec-2019	365	
3	1-Dec-2022	1-Jun-2023	182	
4	1-Apr-2024	1-Jul-2025	456	
5	1-Oct-2013	1-Dec-2015	791	
6	29-Nov-2022	30-Dec-2023	396	
7	1-Dec-2015	1-Dec-2014	-365	Reversed dates
8	1-Jan-2020	1-Jan-2021	366	2000 is a leap year
9				
10				

If you're entering the dates directly into the function, you need to enclose them in quotation marks.

For example:

=DAYS("12/01/2023","12/01/2022") will return 365 days.

NETWORKDAYS Function

The NETWORKDAYS function returns the number of whole working days between two dates. Working days exclude weekends and any dates specified in the holidays argument. You can use NETWORKDAYS to calculate employee pay and other benefits based on the number of days worked in a specific period.

Syntax

=NETWORKDAYS(start_date, end_date, [holidays])

Arguments

Argument	Description
start_date	Required. A date that represents the start date.
end_date	Required. A date that represents the end date.
holidays	Optional. A range, list, or table with one or more dates to be excluded from the working calendar, for example, state holidays, federal holidays, and floating holidays.

Remarks

If you're entering a date directly as an argument, you should use the DATE function to ensure the argument is converted to a date. For example, use DATE(2023,5,23) instead of "May 23, 2023". Problems can occur if dates are entered as text. If you are referencing a date in a cell, ensure the date format is applied to the cell.

Example

The example below uses the NETWORKDAYS function to calculate the workdays between the project start and end dates. The worksheet also has a range named **Holiday_range** used for the holidays argument. Holiday_range contains the holiday dates to exclude from the count of workdays.

Formula:

=NETWORKDAYS(A4,B4,Holidays_range)

C4			f_x	=NETWORKDAYS(A4,B4,Holidays_range)

	A	B	C	D
1	**Projects - Workdays**			
2				
3	**Start date**	**End date**	**Workdays**	**Formula text**
4	2/1/2023	2/1/2024	259	=NETWORKDAYS(A4,B4,Holidays_range)
5	4/1/2023	4/1/2024	258	=NETWORKDAYS(A5,B5,Holidays_range)
6	6/1/2023	6/1/2024	259	=NETWORKDAYS(A6,B6,Holidays_range)
7				
8	**Holidays**			
9	1/2/2023			*Holidays_range = A9:A13*
10	7/4/2023			
11	12/25/2023			
12	1/2/2024			
13	7/4/2024			
14				

The answers are displayed under **Workdays** in the table.

Column D displays the formulas in range C4:C6 (Workdays).

Tip If you want to be able to specify weekend days that are different from the default Saturday and Sunday used in the Gregorian calendar, use the NETWORKDAYS.INTL function instead of NETWORKDAYS.

To access the NETWORKDAYS.INTL function, on the Ribbon, click **Formulas > Date & Time > NETWORKDAYS.INTL**.

Convert Values to Date and Time

The functions discussed in this section enable you to create formulas that convert values in other formats to Excel date and time formats. These formulas are useful for combining values from different cells into one date or time value.

DATEVALUE Function

The DATEVALUE function converts a date entered as text to a serial number in Excel that is recognized as a date. The DATEVALUE function is useful when a worksheet contains dates imported from another application, and Excel reads that data as text. In those instances, you must convert the values to recognized dates in Excel to perform date calculations. Once the values have been converted to dates, you can sort, filter, add, or subtract dates.

DATEVALUE returns a serial number internally recognized as a date. To format this number as a date, you must apply a **Date** format to the cell. For example, the formula =DATEVALUE("1/1/2023") returns 44927, its internal serial number. A cell formatted as a date will display the value as 1/1/2023.

Syntax

=DATEVALUE(date_text)

Arguments

Argument	Description
date_text	Required. Text that represents a date in an Excel date format or a cell reference containing text that represents a date in an Excel date format. For example, "1/30/2008" or "30-Jan-2008" are text strings in quotation marks representing dates.

Remarks

- The date_text argument must represent a date between January 1, 1900, and December 31, 9999. DATEVALUE will return an error if the date_text argument falls outside this range.

- If you omit the year part of the date in the date_text argument, the DATEVALUE function will use the current year from your computer's internal clock.

Example

The following example converts several date textual values to serial numbers using the DATEVALUE function.

C2		⌄ ⋮ ✕ ✓ *fx*	=DATEVALUE(A2)	

◢	A	B	C	D
1	Date as Text	General number format	Date format (US)	Formula text
2	22 May 2011	40685	5/22/2011	=DATEVALUE(A2)
3	5 Jul	44747	7/5/2022	=DATEVALUE(A3)
4	01/01/2023	44927	1/1/2023	=DATEVALUE(A4)
5	April 1990	32964	4/1/1990	=DATEVALUE(A5)
6				

Formula Explanation

=DATEVALUE(A2)

- In the image above, the cells in column A have the text format, the cells in column B have the general number format, and the cells in column C have the date format.

- The DATEVALUE function has been used to convert the text values in A2:A5 to date values in B2:B5. The results are displayed as date serial numbers because the cells have the General number format.

- The DATEVALUE function has been used to convert the text values from A2:A5 to date values in C2:C5. However, Excel displays the same results as dates because the **Date** format was applied to the range.

TIME Function

The TIME function returns the decimal number representing a specified time. Excel stores dates and times as serial numbers internally.

Example: 43454.83583

The numbers to the left of the decimal point represent the date, and the numbers to the right of the decimal point represent the time. The TIME function will return a decimal number ranging from 0 to 0.99988426, representing the times from 0:00:00 (12:00:00 AM) to 23:59:59 (11:59:59 PM). If a cell had the General format before the function was entered, Excel formats the result as a date to properly display the time instead of a decimal number.

Syntax

TIME(hour, minute, second)

Arguments

Arguments	Descriptions
Hour	Required. This argument can be a number from 0 (zero) to 32767, representing the hour. Any value larger than 23 will be divided by 24, and the remainder will be treated as the hour value. For example, TIME(29,0,0) = TIME(5,0,0) = .20833 or 5:00 AM.
Minute	Required. This argument can be a number from 0 to 32767, representing the minute. Any value larger than 59 will be divided by 60 and converted to hours and minutes. For example, TIME(0,810,0) = TIME(13,30,0) = .5625 or 1:30 PM.
Second	Required. This argument can be a number from 0 to 32767, representing the second. Any value larger than 59 will be divided by 60 and converted to hours, minutes, and seconds. For example, TIME(0,0,2120) = TIME(0,35,22) = .02456 or 0:35:22 AM

Example

In this example, the range B3:C4 has values for Hour, Minute, and Second that we want to use for our calculation. E3:E4 and F3:F4 show the results of using the TIME function to combine the values into a single date value.

Formulas:
=TIME(A3,B3,C3)
=TIME(A4,B4,C4)

	A	B	C	D	E	F	G	H
1					Result	Result		
2	Hr	Min	Sec		(Time format)	(Decimal)	Formula text	Description
3	12	0	0		12:00 PM	0.5	=TIME(A3,B3,C3)	Decimal part of a day (12 hours, 0 minutes, 0 seconds)
4	18	58	5		6:58 PM	0.790335648	=TIME(A4,B4,C4)	Decimal part for the time specified in row 3
5								
6								
7								
8								

Column E shows the results as times because Excel automatically applies the **Time** format to a cell as it knows the TIME function returns a time.

Column F shows the results as decimal values because the cell Number format was set to General.

Chapter 7

Text Functions

This chapter covers functions that enable you to:

- Find one text string within another one.

- Extract a portion of text from the right, middle, or left of another string.

- Extract a portion of a string based on a character or space within the string.

- Combine values from multiple ranges or strings into one string.

- Trim text by removing all extra spaces except single spaces between words.

- Convert text to uppercase, lowercase, or proper case.

The text functions in Excel can be found by going to **Formulas > Function Library > Text** on the Ribbon. The drop-down menu lists all the text functions in Excel. Text functions are useful for manipulating and rearranging text values.

For example, when you import data into Excel from other applications, you may encounter irregular text spacing or data with the wrong case. You may want to remove extra spaces from the data or change the case to uppercase or lowercase.

-💡-Tip The **Flash Fill** command on the Home tab enables you to automatically perform many text manipulation tasks for which you previously needed functions. Flash Fill is covered in the Excel Basics portion of this book.

Find and Extract Substrings

The functions in this category enable you to create formulas that can extract a substring from the left, right, or middle of a string. Support functions like FIND, TRIM, and LEN are often combined with other text functions to manipulate text. Recently introduced text functions allow you to perform tasks for which you previously needed to combine several functions.

TEXTBEFORE Function

The TEXTBEFORE function returns text that occurs before a given delimiter or string. If multiple instances of a delimiter exist in the text, you can specify which instance to use for the text portion extraction. TEXTBEFORE offers the same functionality (and more) to handle tasks previously needing a combination of the LEFT and FIND functions.

Note This function is currently only available in Excel for Microsoft 365.

Syntax

=TEXTBEFORE(text,delimiter,[instance_num],   [match_mode],   [match_end],
[if_not_found])

Arguments

Argument	Description
text	Required. A value or cell reference representing the text from which you want to extract a substring.
delimiter	Required. The character or text marking the point you want to extract text before.
instance_num	Optional. The instance of the delimiter marking the end point from which you want to extract the text. Use when *text* has more than one instance of *delimiter,* and you want an instance other than the first. The first delimiter instance is 1 (default), the second is 2, and so on. A negative number starts the search from the end.
match_mode	Optional. Determines if the delimiter match is case-sensitive. 0 = case-sensitive; 1= case-insensitive. The default is case-sensitive if omitted.
match_end	Optional. You can enable this option to treat the end of the text as the delimiter for instances where the delimiter is not found. 0 = disabled; 1 = Enabled The default is disabled if omitted.
if_not_found	Optional. Specifies the value to return if no match is found. If this argument is omitted and no match is found, the default returned is #N/A.

Remarks

- TEXTBEFORE returns a #VALUE! error if instance_num is 0 or greater than the length of text.

- TEXTBEFORE returns a #N/A error if the specified delimiter is not in text.

- TEXTBEFORE returns a #N/A error if the value entered for the instance_num argument exceeds the number of occurrences of delimiter in text.

Examples

The examples in the image below use TEXTBEFORE (in column B) to extract part of the string in column A. The formulas are shown in column C.

B2		fx	=TEXTBEFORE(A2," ")	
	A	B	C	D
1	Text	Extracted text	Formula text	Description
2	Linda Mitchell	Linda	=TEXTBEFORE(A2," ")	Finds space as delimiter
3	Christina Taylor, Analyst	Christina Taylor	=TEXTBEFORE(A3,",")	Finds comma as delimiter
4	Sanchez, Shawn, Manager	Sanchez, Shawn	=TEXTBEFORE(A4,",",2)	Find 2nd comma as delimiter
5	Andrew Steven James	Andrew Steven	=TEXTBEFORE(A5," ",2)	Finds 2nd space as delimiter
6	NWTCFV-91	NWTCFV	=TEXTBEFORE(A6,"-")	Finds dash as delimiter
7	Connecticut - CT	Connecticut	=TEXTBEFORE(A7," - ")	Finds dash and space
8	GTECH-365-4001	GTECH-365	=TEXTBEFORE(A8,"-",2)	Finds 2nd instance of dash
9	GTECH-365-4002-402	GTECH-365-4002	=TEXTBEFORE(A9,"-",-1)	Starts search from the end
10	15 x 45 x 30	15 x 45	=TEXTBEFORE(A10," x ",2)	Finds 2nd instance of x
11				
12				
13				

Formula explanations

=TEXTBEFORE(A2," ")

This formula has A2 as the text from which to extract a substring. The delimiter is a space specified by the double quotes.

=TEXTBEFORE(A3,",")

The delimiter here is a comma.

=TEXTBEFORE(A4,",",2)

The text is in A4, and the delimiter is a comma. The instance_num is 2, which matches the second instance of a comma.

=TEXTBEFORE(A7," - ")

The delimiter is a hyphen with a space on both sides.

=TEXTBEFORE(A8,"-",2)

The delimiter here is a hyphen, and we want to extract all text before the second instance of a hyphen.

=TEXTBEFORE(A9,"-",-1)

The delimiter here is a hyphen. The instance_num is -1, which searches for the first hyphen starting from the end of the text. The formula then returns all text before the hyphen.

=TEXTBEFORE(A10," x ",2)

The delimiter here is a lowercase x bordered by two spaces. The instance_num is 2, which means the formula finds the second instance of x and returns all text before it.

TEXTAFTER Function

The TEXTAFTER function returns text that occurs after a specified delimiter or substring. If multiple instances of a delimiter exist in the text, you can specify which instance to use for the text extraction. You can use TEXTAFTER in instances where you would have previously needed to combine the RIGHT, FIND, and LEN functions to achieve the same result.

 Note This function is currently only available in Excel for Microsoft 365.

Syntax

=TEXTAFTER(text,delimiter,[instance_num], [match_mode], [match_end], [if_not_found])

Arguments

Argument	Description
text	Required. A value or cell reference representing the text from which you want to extract a substring.
delimiter	Required. This argument is a character or text marking the point after which you want to extract text.
instance_num	Optional. The instance of the delimiter marking the point after which you want to extract the text. Use when *text* has more than one instance of *delimiter,* and you want an instance other than the first. The first delimiter instance is 1 (default), the second is 2, and so on. A negative number starts the search from the end of the list.
match_mode	Optional. Determines if the delimiter match is case-sensitive. 0 = case-sensitive; 1= case-insensitive.

	The default is case-sensitive if omitted.
match_end	Optional. Treats the end of the text as the delimiter, for example, where the delimiter is not found. 0 = disabled; 1 = Enabled.
if_not_found	Optional. Specifies the value to return if no match is found. If this argument is omitted and no match is found, the default returned is #N/A.

Remarks

- TEXTAFTER returns a #VALUE! error if instance_num is 0 or greater than the length of *text*.

- TEXTAFTER returns a #N/A error if the specified delimiter is not in *text*.

- TEXTAFTER will return a #N/A error if instance_num is greater than the number of instances of delimiter in *text*.

Examples

The examples in the image below use TEXTAFTER (in column B) to extract part of the string in column A. The formulas are displayed in column C.

	A	B	C	D
1	Text	Extracted	Formula text	Description
2	Linda Mitchell	Mitchell	=TEXTAFTER(A2," ")	Finds space as delimiter
3	Sanchez, Shawn	Shawn	=TEXTAFTER(A3,", ")	Find comma and space as delimiter
4	Delaware - DE	DE	=TEXTAFTER(A4," - ")	Finds dash and space
5	NWTCFV-91	91	=TEXTAFTER(A5,"-")	Finds dash as delimiter
6	GTX-365-PH	PH	=TEXTAFTER(A6,"-",2)	Finds 2nd instance of dash
7	15 ft x 10 ft	10 ft	=TEXTAFTER(A7," x ")	Finds x as delimiter
8	Andrew Steven James	Steven	=TEXTBEFORE(TEXTAFTER(A8," ")," ")	Returns text from the middle of the string
9	Minnesota (MN)	MN	=TEXTBEFORE(TEXTAFTER(A9,"("),")")	Returns the abbreviation without the brackets
10	Cora Fabric Chair	Chair	=TEXTAFTER(A10," ",-1)	Returns the first item from the right of the string
11	Habitat Oken Console Table	Table	=TEXTAFTER(A11," ",-1)	Returns the first item from the right of the string
12	Windsor 2 Seater Cuddle Chair	Chair	=TEXTAFTER(A12," ",-1)	Returns the first item from the right of the string
13	Fabric Chair in a Box	Box	=TEXTAFTER(A13," ",-1)	Returns the first item from the right of the string
14				
15				
16				

Formula explanations

=TEXTAFTER(A2," ")

In this formula, A2 is the cell reference to the text from which to extract a substring after the delimiter. The delimiter argument is a space character denoted by a space in quotes.

=TEXTAFTER(A3,", ")

A3 is the cell reference to the text from which to extract a substring after the delimiter. The delimiter argument is a comma and a space character.

=TEXTAFTER(A4," - ")

The delimiter here is a hyphen with a space on each side.

=TEXTAFTER(A5,"-")

The delimiter argument here is a hyphen with no spaces.

=TEXTAFTER(A6,"-",2)

The delimiter argument here is a hyphen. The instance_num is 2, which finds the second instance of a hyphen and returns all text after.

=TEXTAFTER(A7," x ")

The delimiter argument here is a lowercase x with a space character on each side.

=TEXTBEFORE(TEXTAFTER(A8," ")," ")

A8 = Andrew Steven James
Result = Steven

This formula combines TEXTBEFORE and TEXTAFTER to extract the middle name from a full name in cell A8. TEXTAFTER first selects the text after the first space, which is **Steven James**. TEXTBEFORE selects the name before the space in the returned result, **Steven**. This formula provides an easier solution than using the MID and FIND functions to achieve the same result.

=TEXTBEFORE(TEXTAFTER(A9,"("),")")

A9 = Minnesota (MN)
Result = MN

This formula combines TEXTBEFORE and TEXTAFTER to extract the abbreviation from the value in cell A9. TEXTAFTER first returns the text after the opening bracket **MN)**. TEXTBEFORE then returns the characters before the closing bracket, which is **MN**.

=TEXTAFTER(A10," ",-1)

The delimiter argument in the above formula is a space. The instance_num is -1, which tells Excel to find the last space in the text string and return the text after it.

TRIM Function

The TRIM function removes all spaces from a text string causing irregular spacing except for single spaces between words. The TRIM function is useful when you've imported data into Excel from another application, and the text has irregular spacing.

Note The TRIM function does not remove the non-breaking space commonly used in HTML code or web pages - ** **. To remove this type of space, you need to use the Find and Replace function in an HTML editor.

Syntax

=TRIM(text)

Argument	Description
Text	Required. The text you want to trim. This argument can be a text string value or cell reference.

Example

In the following example, we use the TRIM function to remove all extra spaces from the text values in column A.

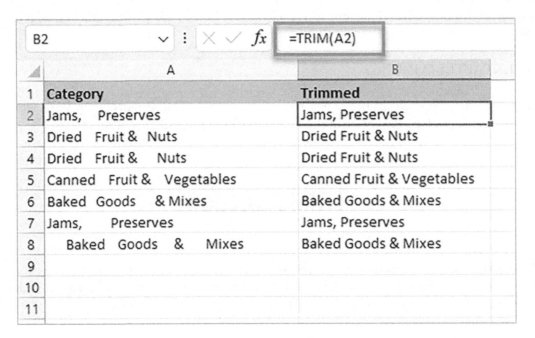

LEN Function

The LEN function returns the number of characters in a text string. The LEN function is useful when combined with other Excel functions like RIGHT, LEFT, and MID, where you can use LEN as an argument to return the length of the string from which you want to extract a portion.

Syntax

=LEN(text)

Argument	Description
Text	Required. A text string or a cell reference containing the text for which you want to find the length. Spaces are counted as characters.

Example

In the following example, we use the LEN function to count the number of characters in an item code. The example also demonstrates how the LEN function can be combined with the MID function to return part of a string.

	A	B	C	D
1	Text	Result	Formula text	Description
2	NWTCFV-88	9	=LEN(A2)	Length of item code
3	NWTCFV-90	90	=MID(A3,8,LEN(A3)-7)	MID (used with LEN) extracts only the numbers in the item code
4	NWTCFV-91	NWTCFV	=MID(A4,1,LEN(A4)-3)	MID (used with LEN) extracts only the letters in the item code
5				
6				
7				

FIND Function

The FIND function is used to locate the starting position of one text string within another. It returns the position of the first character of the text you're searching for within the second text. The search is case-sensitive.

Syntax

=FIND(find_text, within_text, [start_num])

Arguments

Argument	Description
find_text	Required. The text you want to find.
within_text	Required. The text string in which you want to find text.
start_num	Optional. Specifies the point from which you want to start the search in within_text. The first character in within_text is 1; the second is 2, etc.
	If you omit this argument, it will start from the first character in within_text.

Example 1

This example uses the FIND function to return the position of different characters in the string "United States." As shown in the results below, the FIND function is case-sensitive.

▲	A	B	C	D
1	Data			
2	United States			
3				
4	Search term	Result	Formula text	Explanation
5	Position of S	8	=FIND("S",$A$2)	Returns the position of uppercase S in United States
6	Position of s	13	=FIND("s",$A$2)	Returns the position of lowercase s in United States
7	Position of first t	4	=FIND("t",$A$2)	Returns the position of the first lowercase t in United States
8				
9				
10				
11				

Example 2

The FIND function is most useful when used as an argument in another function. In the following example, we combine FIND with RIGHT, LEFT, and LEN to perform different string extractions. The formulas use FIND to identify the divider's position, then LEFT/RIGHT extracts the portion of the required string.

G	H	I
Text	Result	Formula text
California - CA	California	=LEFT(G2,FIND("-",G2)-1)
Colorado - CO	Colorado	=LEFT(G3,FIND("-",G3)-1)
Connecticut - CT	Connecticut	=LEFT(G4,FIND("-",G4)-1)
Delaware - DE	DE	=RIGHT(G5,LEN(G5)-(FIND("-",G5)+1))
Florida - FL	FL	=RIGHT(G6,LEN(G6)-(FIND("-",G6)+1))
Georgia - GA	GA	=RIGHT(G7,LEN(G7)-(FIND("-",G7)+1))

=LEFT(G2,FIND("-",G2)-1)

FIND returns the position of "-", which is 12 in this case. We need to subtract 1 from this number to remove the divider from the part of the string we want to extract. The LEFT function then uses 10 as the starting point to return the characters in the string, starting from right to left. See the section **LEFT, RIGHT Functions** for more on the LEFT function.

LEFT and RIGHT Functions

The LEFT function returns the leftmost characters in a text string based on the number of characters you specify in one of its arguments. The RIGHT function returns the rightmost characters in a text string starting from the position you specify.

-$\bigcirc$-**Tip**   You can now use the new TEXTBEFORE and TEXTAFTER functions to extract text more easily than you could with the LEFT and RIGHT functions.

Syntax

=LEFT(text, [num_chars])

=RIGHT(text,[num_chars])

Arguments

Argument	Description
text	Required. This argument represents the text string with the characters you want to extract.
num_chars	Optional. An integer that specifies the number of characters you want to extract from the text. The count starts from the left for the LEFT function and the right for the RIGHT function.

Remarks

- If *num_chars* is larger than the length of *text*, the functions will return all characters in *text*.

- If *num_chars* is omitted, the functions return only the first character for the LEFT function and only the last character for the RIGHT function.

Example

In the example below, we use the LEFT and RIGHT functions to extract portions of text in different ways.

	A	B	C
1	Text	Result	Formula text
2	Alabama - AL	A	=LEFT(A2)
3	Alaska - AK	K	=RIGHT(A3)
4	Arizona - AZ	Arizona	=LEFT(A4,7)
5	Arkansas - AR	AR	=RIGHT(A5,2)
6	California - CA	California	=LEFT(A6,FIND("-",A6)-1)
7	Colorado - CO	Colorado	=LEFT(A7,FIND("-",A7)-1)
8	Connecticut - CT	Connecticut	=LEFT(A8,FIND("-",A8)-1)
9	Delaware - DE	DE	=RIGHT(A9,LEN(A9)-(FIND("-",A9)+1))
10	Florida - FL	FL	=RIGHT(A10,LEN(A10)-(FIND("-",A10)+1))
11	Georgia - GA	GA	=RIGHT(A11,LEN(A11)-(FIND("-",A11)+1))
12	Quanta Builders	Quanta	=LEFT(A12, FIND(" ",A12)-1)
13			
14			

Formula explanations

=LEFT(A2)

In the formula above, cell A2 is the text argument. There is no num_chars argument. Thus, LEFT returns the first character on the left of the string.

=RIGHT(A3)

This formula has cell A3 as the text argument, and there is no num_chars argument. Hence, RIGHT returns the last character in the string.

=LEFT(A4,7)

This formula has cell A4 as the text argument and 7 as the num_chars argument. It returns **Arizona**, 7 characters from the left of the string.

=RIGHT(A5,2)

This formula takes cell A4 as the text argument and 7 as the num_chars argument. It returns **AR**, 2 characters from the right of the string.

=LEFT(A6,FIND("-",A6)-1)

This formula takes cell A6 as the text argument. We calculate the num_chars argument using the FIND function to find and return the position of the hyphen character (-) in the text.

We then subtract 1 from the result to return the number of characters in the text before the hyphen. Hence **FIND("-",A6)-1** will return 10. The result is California. This formula will work for any piece of text separated by a hyphen where we want to extract the left portion.

=RIGHT(A9,LEN(A9)-(FIND("-",A9)+1))

This formula takes cell A9 as the text argument. We calculate the num_chars argument by using FIND to return the position of the hyphen character (-) in the text. We then add 1 to move to the position of the first character after the hyphen (on the right).

The LEN function is used to get the length of the string as we want to subtract the number of characters returned by FIND to give us the number of characters after the hyphen, which is 2 in this case.

This formula will work for a piece of text of any length separated by a hyphen, regardless of the position of the hyphen.

=LEFT(A12, FIND(" ",A12)-1)

This formula uses LEFT to return the string before the first space. A12 is the cell containing the string from which we want to extract text. **FIND(" ",A12)-1** returns the number of characters before the first space.

LEFTB, RIGHTB Functions

LEFTB and RIGHTB are variants of the LEFT and RIGHT functions that return characters in a text string based on the number of bytes you specify.

RIGHTB/LEFTB are for systems set to a default language that supports the double-byte character set (DBCS). The languages that support DBCS include Japanese, Traditional Chinese, Simplified Chinese, and Korean. If your system has a default language that supports DBCS, you would have LEFTB and RIGHTB in place of LEFT and RIGHT.

If your system has a default language that supports the single-byte character set (SBCS), LEFTB/RIGHTB will behave the same as LEFT/RIGHT, counting 1 byte per character.

MID Function

The MID function extracts a portion of a text from another text based on a specified starting position and the number of characters to be extracted.

-💡-**Tip**   For more complex text extractions, use the new TEXTBEFORE or TEXTAFTER functions. They're easier to use, offer more options, and can do most tasks you can do with MID.

Syntax

=MID(text, start_num, num_chars)

Arguments

Argument	Description
text	Required. A text string or a cell reference containing the characters you want to extract.
start_num	Required. A number that represents the starting point of the first character to extract from the value in *text*. The first character in *text* starts with 1. The second is 2, and so on.
num_chars	Required. A number specifying the number of characters you want to extract from *text*.

Remarks

- If the start_num argument is larger than the length of the string in the text argument, MID will return an empty text ("").

- MID will return the #VALUE! error if start_num is less than 1.

- MID returns the #VALUE! error if num_chars is a negative value.

Examples

The examples use the MID function to extract characters from several text values.

	A	B	C
1	**Text**	**Result**	**Formula text**
2	NWTCFV-91	NWTCFV	=MID(A2,1,LEN(A2)-3)
3	NWTCFV-90	90	=MID(A3,FIND("-",A3)+1,2)
4	NWT-100-CFV	100	=MID(A4,FIND("-",A4)+1,3)
5	01-345-4000	345	=MID(A5,4,3)
6	Andrew Steven James	Steven	=MID(A6,FIND(" ",A6)+1,FIND(" ",A6,FIND(" ",A6)+1)-FIND(" ",A6))
7	Minnesota(MN)	MN	=MID(A7,FIND("(",A7)+1,2)
8			
9			

Formula descriptions

=MID(A2,1,LEN(A2)-3)

Removes the last 3 characters in the text and returns the rest.

For this formula, A2 is the cell reference containing the string from which we want to extract text. We're starting from the first character, so start_num is 1. We want to return the length of the text except for the last 3 characters. We can use LEN to return this number for the num_chars argument.

=MID(A3,FIND("-",A3)+1,2)

Finds the hyphen in the text and returns the two characters after.

For this formula, A3 is the cell containing the string from which we want to extract text. We're starting from the first character after the hyphen "-", which we can identify with FIND("-",A3)+1. We want to return two characters, so 2 is the *num_chars* argument.

=MID(A5,4,3)

For this formula, A5 is the cell containing the string from which we want to extract characters. The first character to extract is 3, which starts at the fourth position, so we have 4 as our start_num. We want to return three characters, so we have 3 as the num_chars.

=MID(A6,FIND(" ",A6)+1,FIND(" ",A6,FIND(" ",A6)+1)-FIND(" ",A6))

This formula extracts the middle name from the full name.

The **text** argument is A6.

The **start_num** argument is FIND(" ",A6)+1. This nested formula identifies the position of the first character after the first space, which is 8.

The **num_chars** argument is FIND(" ",A6,FIND(" ",A6)+1)-FIND(" ",A6).

FIND(" ",A6,FIND(" ",A6)+1) finds the position of the second space, which is 14, and **FIND(" ",A6)** finds the position of the first space, which is 7.

We then subtract the position of the first space from the position of the second space like this **FIND(" ",A6,FIND(" ",A6)+1)-FIND(" ",A6)**, which is 14-7.

=MID(A7,FIND("(",A7)+1,2)

This formula finds the opening bracket in a string and returns the two characters after the bracket.

A7 is the cell containing the string from which we want to extract two characters. Our start_num is the position of the first character after the opening bracket "(", which we can identify with FIND("-",A3)+1. We want to return two characters, so 2 is the num_chars argument.

Split or Concatenate Text

The functions in this subcategory enable you to create formulas that can split a text into different columns or combine text from different columns into one cell.

TEXTSPLIT Function

The TEXTSPLIT function enables you to split text strings into different columns or rows. TEXTSPLIT is a dynamic array function that can take in one value and return multiple values. You can use the Text-to-Columns wizard in Excel for splitting text into columns, but TEXTSPLIT is easier to use and offers more splitting options.

Note This function is currently only available in Excel for Microsoft 365.

Syntax

=TEXTSPLIT(text,col_delimiter,[row_delimiter],[ignore_empty],   [match_mode], [pad_with])

Arguments

Argument	Description
text	Required. A value or cell reference representing the text you want to split.
col_delimiter	Required. The delimiter used to split the text into different columns.
row_delimiter	Optional. The delimiter used to split the text into different rows.
ignore_empty	Optional. Enter TRUE to ignore empty values, i.e., two or more consecutive delimiters without a value in-between them. Enter FALSE to create empty cells for empty values. FALSE is the default if this argument is omitted.

match_mode	Optional. Determines if case sensitivity is used to match the delimiter. Case sensitivity is used by default. 0 = case-sensitive (default). 1 = case-insensitive.
pad_with	Optional. A value to use for missing values in two-dimensional arrays. The default is #N/A.

Remarks:

If you set ignore_empty to TRUE, ensure there are no spaces between the consecutive delimiters. Otherwise, the feature to ignore empty values does not work.

Example 1 – Splitting into columns

The table below has examples of text being split into different columns using different delimiters.

Notice that you have to enter the delimiter precisely. For example, if there is a gap (or space) after a delimiter, you must enter that space after the delimiter in your formula to ensure blank spaces are not added to the split values. You can also use the TRIM function in your formula to remove any blank spaces from the result if the original text contains irregular spacing.

C2			fx	=TEXTSPLIT(A2,",")			

	A	B	C	D	E	F	G
1	Text		Split text result			Formula text	
2	Cary,Illinois(IL),60013		Cary	Illinois(IL)	60013	=TEXTSPLIT(A2,",")	
3	Mineola, Texas(TX), 75773		Mineola	Texas(TX)	75773	=TEXTSPLIT(A3,", ")	Delimiter has a space after
4	Vidalia, Georgia(GA) , 30474		Vidalia	Georgia(GA)	30474	=TRIM(TEXTSPLIT(A4,","))	TRIM used to remove blank spaces
5	L = 15;W = 14;H = 10		L = 15	W = 14	H = 10	=TEXTSPLIT(A5,";")	
6	Andrew Steven James		Andrew	Steven	James	=TEXTSPLIT(A6," ")	
7	Paul Coleman		Paul	Coleman		=TEXTSPLIT(A7," ")	
8	600 x 400		600	400		=TEXTSPLIT(A8," x ")	Delimiter has a space before and after
9							
10							
11							

Example 2 – Splitting into rows

The example below splits the text in A13 into rows rather than columns. To split the text into rows, leave the col_delimiter argument empty, and enter the delimiter for the row_delimiter argument.

=TEXTSPLIT(A13,,", ")

C13				fx	=TEXTSPLIT(A13,,", ")		
	A		B	C		D	
11	**Splitting into rows**						
12	Text			Split text			
13	Mineola, Texas(TX), 75773			Mineola		Spill	
14				Texas(TX)			
15				75773			
16							
17							

Example 3 – Splitting text with different delimiters

If the text values to be split have more than one delimiter type, you can use curly brackets to specify more than one delimiter for the col_delimiter argument. See the example below.

=TEXTSPLIT(A2,{",",";"})

C2			fx	=TEXTSPLIT(A2,{",",";"})			
	A	B	C	D	E	F	G
1	Text		Split text result				Formula text
2	NWTB-1,Chai,Beverages;18.00		NWTB-1	Chai	Beverages	18.00	=TEXTSPLIT(A2,{",",";"})
3							
4							
5							
6							

Example 4 – Two-dimensional splits

TEXTSPLIT allows you to split a text string into rows and columns simultaneously, where you specify delimiters for both the col_delimiter and row_delimiter arguments.

The example below splits the text in A2 into columns and rows by providing the following:

- The **col_delimiter** - an equal sign ("=")

- The **row_delimiter** - a semi-colon, and space "; "

The formula looks like this:

=TEXTSPLIT(A2,"=",";")

The formula creates a 2D array made up of 2 columns and 3 rows:

C2		⋮ ✕ ✓ *fx*	=TEXTSPLIT(A2,"=","; ")		
⬜	A	B	C		D
1	**Text**		**Split text**		
2	Chai=18.00; Syrup=10.00; Cajun Seasoning=22.00		Chai	18.00	
3			Syrup	10.00	
4			Cajun Seasoning	22.00	
5					
6					
7					

Example 5 – Handling empty values

In the example below, the text string to be split has empty values indicated by two or more consecutive delimiters. The formula below has been wrapped in TRIM to fix any inconsistent spacing.

By default, TEXTSPLIT will create empty cells for the missing values, as shown in the image below. You can also set the ignore_empty argument to FALSE to get the same result.

=TRIM(TEXTSPLIT(A2,",",))

C2	⌄ : ✕ ✓ *fx*	=TRIM(TEXTSPLIT(A2,",",,,FALSE))			
▲	A	B	C	D	E	F
1	Text		Split text - ignore_empty = FALSE			
2	817 Short St, , Texas(TX), 75773		817 Short St		Texas(TX)	75773
3	127 Lake Shore Dr, Cary, Illinois(IL), 60013		127 Lake Shore Dr	Cary	Illinois(IL)	60013
4	1008 Roosevelt St, Vidalia, Georgia(GA), 30474		1008 Roosevelt St	Vidalia	Georgia(GA)	30474
5	11 Locust Ave, , New York(NY), 12180		11 Locust Ave		New York(NY)	12180
6	6820 Spaatz Dr, Edwards, California(CA), 93523		6820 Spaatz Dr	Edwards	California(CA)	93523
7	Hc 36, , West Virginia(WV), 26201		Hc 36		West Virginia(WV)	26201
8	32 Cherubina Ln, , New York(NY), 11703		32 Cherubina Ln		New York(NY)	11703
9						
10						

To ignore empty values, set the ignore_empty argument to TRUE, as shown in the formula below.

=TEXTSPLIT(A14,", ",,TRUE)

C14	⌄ : ✕ ✓ *fx*	=TEXTSPLIT(A14,", ",,TRUE)			
▲	A	B	C	D	E	F
13	Text		Split text - ignore_empty = TRUE			
14	817 Short St, , Texas(TX), 75773		817 Short St	Texas(TX)	75773	
15	127 Lake Shore Dr, Cary, Illinois(IL), 60013		127 Lake Shore Dr	Cary	Illinois(IL)	60013
16	1008 Roosevelt St, Vidalia, Georgia(GA), 30474		1008 Roosevelt St	Vidalia	Georgia(GA)	30474
17	11 Locust Ave, , New York(NY), 12180		11 Locust Ave	New York(NY)	12180	
18	6820 Spaatz Dr, Edwards, California(CA), 93523		6820 Spaatz Dr	Edwards	California(CA)	93523
19	Hc 36, , West Virginia(WV), 26201		Hc 36	West Virginia(WV)	26201	
20	32 Cherubina Ln, , New York(NY), 11703		32 Cherubina Ln	New York(NY)	11703	
21						
22						
23						

TEXTJOIN Function

TEXTJOIN is the opposite of TEXTSPLIT, as it enables you to combine text values from multiple cells into one string. The difference between TEXTJOIN and the CONCAT function is that TEXTJOIN has extra arguments that allow you to specify a delimiter as a separator. If your delimiter is a blank space, this function concatenates the ranges like CONCAT. This function also has options that allow you to ignore empty cells.

Syntax

=TEXTJOIN(delimiter, ignore_empty, text1, [text2], …)

Arguments

Argument	Description
delimiter	Required. The character you want to use to separate text items in your string. The delimiter can be a string, one or more characters enclosed in double quotes, or a cell reference containing a text string. If this argument is a number, it will be treated as text.
ignore_empty	Required. Enter TRUE or FALSE. If the value is TRUE, Excel ignores empty cells.
text1	Required. The first text item to be joined. It can be a string, a cell reference, or a range with several cells.
[text2, ...]	Optional. Additional text items you want to join. You can have up to 252 arguments for the text items, including text1. Each can be a string, a cell reference, or a range with several cells.

Remarks

TEXTJOIN will return the #VALUE! error if the resulting string exceeds the cell limit of 32767 characters.

Example

In the following example, we use TEXTJOIN in C2:C7 to combine the First and Last name values from A2:A7 and B2:B7. The flexibility provided by TEXTJOIN enables us to swap the order of the names and separate them with a comma.

	A	B	C	D
1	First name	Last name	Combined	Formula text
2	Bruce	Henderson	Henderson, Bruce	=TEXTJOIN(", ", TRUE,B2,A2)
3	Louis	Anderson	Anderson, Louis	=TEXTJOIN(", ", TRUE,B3,A3)
4	Earl	Foster	Foster, Earl	=TEXTJOIN(", ", TRUE,B4,A4)
5	Sean	Hill	Hill, Sean	=TEXTJOIN(", ", TRUE,B5,A5)
6	Benjamin	Martinez	Martinez, Benjamin	=TEXTJOIN(", ", TRUE,B6,A6)
7	Joe	Perez	Perez, Joe	=TEXTJOIN(", ", TRUE,B7,A7)
8				
9	Name			
10	Bruce Henderson			
11	Louis Anderson			
12	Earl Foster			
13	Sean Hill			
14				
15	Combined			
16	Bruce Henderson, Louis Anderson, Earl Foster, Sean Hill			=TEXTJOIN(", ",TRUE,A10:A13)
17				

Explanation of formula

=TEXTJOIN(", ", TRUE,B2,A2)

The *delimiter* argument is a comma enclosed in quotes. The *ignore_empty* argument is TRUE because we want to ignore empty cells. The *text1* and *text2* arguments are cell references B2 and A2, representing the first and last names. The formula is copied to the other cells to populate the other results in the column.

=TEXTJOIN(", ",TRUE,A10:A13)

The second example uses the TEXTJOIN function to concatenate names in a range of cells (A10:A13) into a single string with a comma used as a separator.

CONCAT Function

The CONCAT function enables you to combine the text from multiple ranges or strings into one string. The function does not provide a delimiter, so you must add that manually in your formula. For example, =CONCAT("Hello"," ","world") will return *Hello world*. If you want to specify a delimiter, see the TEXTJOIN function.

Note This function was introduced as a replacement for the CONCATENATE function. CONCATENATE is still available in Excel for backward compatibility, but it is recommended that you use CONCAT going forward.

Syntax

=CONCAT(text1, [text2],…)

Arguments

Argument	Description
text1	Required. This argument represents a text item to be joined. It could be a string or a range of cells with text.
[text2, ...]	Optional. Additional text to be joined. You can have up to 253 arguments of text items to be joined. Each can be a string or a range of cells with text.

Remarks

- If the resulting string exceeds the cell limit of 32767 characters, CONCAT returns the #VALUE! error.

- You can use the TEXTJOIN function to include delimiters like spacing and/or commas between the texts you want to combine.

Example

In the example below, we used the CONCAT function differently to concatenate text from different cells.

	A	B	C	D	E
1	First name	Lastname		Result	Formula text
2	Bruce	Henderson		Bruce Henderson	=CONCAT(A2," ",B2)
3	Louis	Anderson		Bruce & Louis	=CONCAT(A2, " & ", A3)
4	Earl	Foster		Bruce and Louis did a good job.	=CONCAT(A2, " and ", A3, " did a good job.")
5				Anderson, Louis	=CONCAT(B3,", ",A3)
6				Anderson, Louis	=B3 & ", " & A3
7					
8					
9					

Explanation of formulas

=CONCAT(A2," ",B2)

This formula concatenates the text in A2 and B2 with an empty string in between, represented by the empty string in the formula.

=CONCAT(A2, " & ", A3)

This formula concatenates the text in cells A2 and A3 with an ampersand character (&) in the middle representing two first names.

=CONCAT(A2, " and ", A3, "did a good job.")

This formula uses the text in cells A2 and A3 to form part of a larger sentence.

=CONCAT(B3,", ",A3)

This formula concatenates the text in cells B3 and A3 with a comma in-between, representing the Last name and First name.

=B3 & ", " & A3

The formula above is for comparisons. It doesn't use CONCAT but achieves the same result using ampersands (Excel's concatenation operator).

Change the Case of Text Values

The functions in this category enable you to change the case of text values using formulas.

UPPER, LOWER, and PROPER Functions

The UPPER, LOWER, and PROPER functions are similar and take only one argument. UPPER converts all characters to uppercase, while LOWER converts all characters to lowercase. PROPER capitalizes the first character of every word in a string and converts all other characters to lowercase. A text string is a continuous stream of characters without spaces. Every letter after a space or punctuation character is capitalized.

Syntax

=UPPER(text)

=LOWER(text)

=PROPER(text)

Argument	Description
Text	Required. The text for which you want to change the case. This argument can be a cell reference or text string.

Example

In the example below, we use the UPPER, LOWER, and PROPER functions to change the case of the text values in column A. The results are in column B, and column C displays the formulas in column B.

	A	B	C
1	**Text**	**Result**	**Formula text**
2	NWTB-1	nwtb-1	=LOWER(A2)
3	NWTCO-3	nwtco-3	=LOWER(A3)
4	Beverages	BEVERAGES	=UPPER(A4)
5	Condiments	CONDIMENTS	=UPPER(A5)
6	Oil	OIL	=UPPER(A6)
7	Jams, Preserves	JAMS, PRESERVES	=UPPER(A7)
8	tesTinG capitalization now	Testing Capitalization Now	=PROPER(A8)
9	this is a TITLE	This Is A Title	=PROPER(A9)
10	bruce henderson	Bruce Henderson	=PROPER(A10)
11	louis anderson	Louis Anderson	=PROPER(A11)
12	Earl foster	Earl Foster	=PROPER(A12)
13	sean hiLL	Sean Hill	=PROPER(A13)
14	benjamiN MartineZ	Benjamin Martinez	=PROPER(A14)
15			

Chapter 8

Financial Functions

This chapter covers functions used to calculate the following:

- Present Value of an investment or a loan.

- Future Value of an investment.

- Net Present Value of an investment taking cash flows into account.

- Monthly payments for a loan over a given period.

- Straight-line depreciation of an asset over a period.

- Sum-of-years' digits depreciation of an asset over a period.

- Fixed-declining balance depreciation of an asset over a given period.

- Double-declining balance depreciation of an asset over a given period.

Y ou can access financial functions in Excel by clicking the Financial button, in the Function Library group, on the Formulas tab. Most of the financial functions in Excel are specialized functions used for financial accounting.

Definitions

Most of the financial functions in Excel have arguments that are acronyms for financial terms. For example, terms like PV (Present Value), FV (Future Value), PMT (Payment), and IPMT (interest payment) show up as arguments in many functions. It is important to understand the terminology to better understand these functions. The following section covers some key terms used.

Annuity

An annuity is a series of regular cash payments over a certain period. For example, a mortgage or a car loan is an annuity. An investment that pays regular dividends is also an annuity. Most of the functions covered in this chapter are known as annuity functions.

PV (Present Value)

PV is the present value of an investment based on a constant growth rate. It is the lump-sum amount that a series of future payments is worth right now.

FV (Future Value)

FV is the future value of an investment based on a constant rate of growth. Imagine a scenario where you need to save $25,000 to pay for a project in 20 years. In that case, $25,000 is the future value. To calculate how much you need to save monthly, you'll also need to factor in an assumed interest rate over the period.

PMT (Payment)

PMT is the payment made for each period in the annuity. Usually, the payment includes the principal plus interest (without any other fees) set over the life of the annuity. For example, a $100,000 mortgage over 25 years at 3% interest would have monthly payments of $474. You would enter -474 into the formula as the *pmt*.

RATE

RATE is the interest rate per period. For example, a loan at a 6% annual interest rate will have an interest rate of 6%/12 per month.

NPER (Number of periods)

NPER is the number of payment periods for a loan or investment based on constant periodic payments and a constant interest rate. For example, a three-year loan with monthly payments will have 36 periods (3 x 12). Hence, the *nper* argument would be 3*12 for such a scenario.

Note The FV, PV, and PMT arguments can be positive or negative, depending on whether you are paying or receiving money. The values will be negative if you're paying out money and positive if you're receiving money.

Calculating Investments and Loans

The functions in this category enable you to build formulas that calculate annuities like the value of investments and loans.

PV Function

The PV function calculates the present value of an investment (or a loan), assuming a constant interest rate. The present value is the amount a series of future payments is currently worth. You can use PV with regular payments (such as a mortgage or other loan), periodic payments, or the future value of a lump sum paid now.

Syntax

=PV(rate, nper, pmt, [fv], [type])

Arguments

See the Definitions section above for a more detailed description of these arguments.

Arguments	Description
rate	Required. The interest rate per period.
nper	Required. The total number of payment periods in an annuity.
pmt	Required. The payment made for each period in the annuity.
	If you omit *pmt*, you must include the *fv* argument.
fv	Optional. This argument is the future value of an investment based on an assumed rate of growth.
	If you omit fv, it is assumed to be 0 (zero). For example, the future value of a loan is 0. If you omit fv, then you must include the pmt argument.
type	Optional. This argument is 0 or 1 and indicates when payments are due.
	0 or omitted = at the end of the period.
	1 = at the beginning of the period.

Remarks

- You must always specify the rate argument in the same units as the nper argument. For example, say you have monthly payments on a three-year loan at 5% annual interest. If you use 5%/12 for *rate*, you must use 3*12 for *nper*. If the payments on the same loan are being made annually, then you would use 5% for rate and 3 for nper.

- In annuity functions, the cash paid out (like a payment to savings) is represented by a negative number. The cash received (like a dividend payment) is represented by a positive number. For example, a $500 deposit would be represented by -500 for the depositor and by 500 for the bank.

Example

In the example below, we use the PV formula to calculate:

1. The present value of a $500 monthly payment over 25 years at a rate of 1.5% interest.

2. The present value of the lump sum that is needed now to create $20,000 in 10 years at a rate of 3.5% interest.

E4			fx	=PV(A4/12,B4*12,C4)	
	A	B	C	D	E	F
1	Present Value (PV)					
2						
3	Annual Interest Rate	Term (years)	Payment	Future Value	Present Value	Formula text
4	1.50%	25	($500.00)		$125,019.90	=PV(A4/12,B4*12,C4)
5	3.50%	10		$20,000.00	($14,100.94)	=PV(A5/12,B5*12,,D5)
6						
7						
8						
9						
10						
11						

Explanation of Formulas:

=PV(A4/12,B4*12,C4)

As you've probably noticed, the units for *rate* and *nper* have been kept consistent by specifying them in monthly terms, A4/12 and B4*12. The payment (pmt) has been entered in the worksheet as a negative value as this is money being paid out.

=PV(A5/12,B5*12,,D5)

The present value is a negative number as it shows the amount of cash that needs to be invested today (paid out) to generate the future value of $20,000 in 10 years at a rate of 3.5% interest.

FV Function

The FV function calculates an investment's future value (at a specified date in the future) based on a constant interest rate. You can use FV to calculate the future value of regular, periodic, or a single lump-sum payment.

Syntax

=FV(rate,nper,pmt,[pv],[type])

Arguments

Arguments	Description
rate	Required. The interest rate per period.
nper	Required. The total number of payment periods.
pmt	Required. The payment made for each period in the annuity. If you omit pmt, you must include pv.
pv	Optional. The present value of an investment based on a constant growth rate. If you omit pv, it is assumed to be 0 (zero), and you must include pmt.
type	Optional. The *type* is 0 or 1, indicating when payments are due. 0 (or omitted) = at the end of the period. 1 = at the beginning of the period.

Remarks

- You must always specify the rate argument in the same units as the nper argument. For example, say you have monthly payments on a three-year loan at 5% annual interest. If you use 5%/12 for *rate*, you must use 3*12 for *nper*. If the payments on the same loan are being made annually, then you would use 5% for rate and 3 for nper.

- In annuity functions, the cash paid out (like a payment to savings) is represented by a negative number. The cash received (like a dividend payment) is represented by a positive number. For example, a $500 deposit would be represented by -500 for the depositor and by 500 for the bank.

Example

The example below uses the FV function to calculate:

1. The future value of a monthly payment of $200 over 10 months at an interest of 6% per annum.

2. The future value of a lump sum of $1,000 plus 12 monthly payments of $100 at an interest rate of 6%.

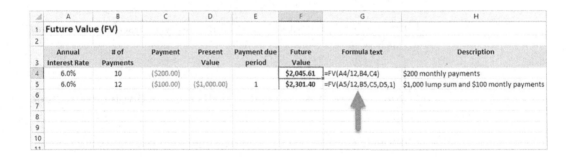

	A	B	C	D	E	F	G	H
1	Future Value (FV)							
2								
3	Annual Interest Rate	# of Payments	Payment	Present Value	Payment due period	Future Value	Formula text	Description
4	6.0%	10	($200.00)			$2,045.61	=FV(A4/12,B4,C4)	$200 monthly payments
5	6.0%	12	($100.00)	($1,000.00)	1	$2,301.40	=FV(A5/12,B5,C5,D5,1)	$1,000 lump sum and $100 montly payments
6								
7								
8								
9								
10								

Explanation of Formulas:

=FV(A4/12,B4,C4)

Note that the *rate* argument has been divided by 12 to represent monthly payments. The *pmt* argument is a negative value (C4) as this is money being paid out.

=FV(A5/12,B5,C5,D5,1)

This formula has the pmt argument and the optional pv argument, which represents the present value of the investment. The payment due period is 1, which means the payment starts at the beginning of the period.

NPV Function

The NPV function calculates the net present value, which is the present value of cash inflows and cash outflows over a period. It calculates the present value of an investment by applying a discount rate and a series of future payments that may be income (positive values) or payments/losses (negative values).

Syntax

=NPV(rate,value1,[value2],...)

Arguments

Argument	Description
Rate	Required. This argument is the percentage rate of discount over the length of the investment.
Value1	Required. This argument represents either a payment/loss (negative value) or income (positive value).
value2, ...	Optional. You can have additional values representing payments and income up to 254 value arguments. The length of time between these payments must be equally spaced and occur at the end of each period.

Remarks

- The rate argument in the function might represent the rate of inflation or the interest rate you might get from an alternative form of investment, such as a high-yield savings account.

- The value arguments represent the projected income (or loss) values over the period of the investment.

- Ensure you enter the payment and income values in the correct order because NPV uses the order of the value arguments to interpret the order of cash flows.

- The NPV investment begins one period before the date of the first cash flow (value1) and ends with the last cash flow (valueN) in the list of value arguments. If the first cash flow happens at the beginning of the period, you must add it to the result of the NPV function and not include it as one of its value arguments.

- The main difference between NPV and PV is that with PV, the cash flows can start at the beginning or end of the period, while for NPV, the cash flows start at the beginning of the period. Also, PV has the same cash flow amount throughout the investment, while NPV can have different cash flow amounts.

- Arguments that are not numbers are ignored.

Example

The example below calculates the net present value of an initial investment of $50,000 over five years, considering an annual discount rate of 2.5 percent.

A4			fx	=NPV(I4,C4:G4)+B4					
	A	B	C	D	E	F	G	H	I
1	Net Present Value - 5 Year Investment								
2									
3	NPV	Initial cost of investment	Year 1 Return	Year 2 Return	Year 3 Return	Year 4 Return	Year 5 Return		Annual discount rate
4	$46,727.78	($50,000.00)	($1,000.00)	$15,000.00	$22,500.00	$30,000.00	$40,000.00		2.50%
5									
6									
7									
8									
9									

Formula explanation

=NPV(I4,C4:G4)+B4

In the figure above, Year 1 of the investment shows a loss of $1,000. Hence, Year 1 has been entered as a negative value. The other years of the investment (years two to five) returned profits, which were entered as positive values.

The function uses two arguments, the *rate* and *value1*, which references cells C4:G4. The initial investment is added to the result returned by the function rather than being an argument in the function.

The result shows the investment's net present value over five years is $46,727.78.

PMT Function

The PMT function calculates the payment of a loan on regular payments and a constant interest rate over a period. The PMT function is often used to calculate the repayment of a mortgage with a fixed interest rate.

Syntax

=PMT(rate, nper, pv, [fv], [type])

Arguments

Arguments	Description
rate	Required. The interest rate per period.
nper	Required. The total number of payment periods.
pv	Required. This argument is the present value of a principal or a series of future payments.
fv	Optional. This argument is the future value of an investment based on an assumed growth rate.
	If you omit fv, it is assumed to be 0 (zero), i.e., the future value of a loan is 0.
type	Optional. This argument is 0 or 1 and indicates when payments are due.
	0 (or omitted) = at the end of the period.
	1 = at the beginning of the period.

Remarks

- The payment returned by PMT is for the principal and interest. It does not include taxes, reserve payments, or other loan fees.

- You must always specify the *rate* argument in the same units as the *nper* argument. For example, say you have monthly payments on a three-year loan at 5% annual interest. If you use 5%/12 for *rate*, you must use 3*12 for *nper*. If the payments on the same loan are being made annually, then you would use 5% for rate and 3 for nper.

-💡-**Tip** To calculate the total amount paid over the duration of the loan, simply multiply the value returned by PMT by the number of payments (nper).

Example

In the example below, we calculate the PMT for two loans:

- A $10,000 loan over 12 payments at 8.0 percent interest.

- A $10,000 loan over 60 payments at 4.9 percent interest.

	A	B	C	D	E
1	**Payment (PMT)**				
2					
3	**Annual Interest Rate**	**# of payments**	**Loan amount**	**PMT**	**Formula text**
4	8.0%	12	$10,000.00	($869.88)	=PMT(A4/12,B4,C4)
5	4.9%	60	$10,000.00	($188.25)	=PMT(A5/12,B5,C5)
6					
7					
8					
9					
10					

Formula explanation

−PMT(A4/12,B4,C4)

The rate argument is the value in cell A4 divided by 12 to represent the interest rate in monthly terms because nper (in cell B4) is also specified in monthly terms. The pv argument is C4, which is the present value of the loan, $10,000.

Result: A monthly payment of $869.88 pays the loan off in 12 months.

=PMT(A5/12,B5,C5)

This formula is also for a loan of $10,000. However, the nper is 60, and the rate is 4.9 percent.

Result: A monthly payment of $188.25 pays the loan off in 60 months (5 years).

Calculating Depreciation

The functions in this section enable you to create formulas that calculate the depreciation of an asset using various depreciation methods.

SLN Function

The SLN function is a depreciation function and calculates the straight-line depreciation of an asset over a period. It depreciates the asset by the same amount each year.

Syntax

=SLN(cost, salvage, life)

Arguments

Argument	Description
cost	Required. The initial cost of the depreciating asset.
salvage	Required. The value at the end of the depreciation (also referred to as the salvage value of the asset).
life	Required. The number of periods over which the asset is depreciating (also known as the useful life of the asset).

Example

In the example below, we have a report calculating the SLN depreciation of a couple of cars with a useful life of 10 years.

E4			⌄ ⋮ ✕ ✓	fx	=SLN(B4,D4,C4)	
	A	B	C	D	E	F
1	**Company car - straight-line depreciation (SLN)**					
2						
3	Car	Cost	Yrs of useful life	Salvage value	Yearly depreciation allowance	Formula text
4	Car 1	$20,000.00	10	$2,500.00	$1,750.00	=SLN(B4,D4,C4)
5	Car 2	$30,000.00	10	$7,500.00	$2,250.00	=SLN(B5,D5,C5)
6	Car 3	$45,000.00	10	$10,000.00	$3,500.00	=SLN(B6,D6,C6)
7						
8						
9						
10						
11						

Formula explanation

=SLN(B4,D4,C4)

In the formula above for **Car 1**, the cost references cell B4 ($20,000). The salvage value references cell D4 ($2,500). The life is C4 (10 years).

The formula returns $1,750, which is the yearly depreciation allowance to be made for the car. When listing this asset on the company's balance sheet, this value would be subtracted from the car's value.

The formula in E4 was copied down using the cell's fill handle to calculate the SLN value of the other cars on the list.

SYD Function

The SYD function (sum of years' digits) is a depreciation function that returns an asset's sum-of-years' digits depreciation over a specified period.

Syntax

=SYD(cost, salvage, life, per)

Arguments

Argument	Description
cost	Required. The initial cost of the asset you're depreciating.
salvage	Required. The value at the end of the depreciation (also referred to as the salvage value of the asset).
life	Required. The number of periods over which the asset is depreciated (also referred to as the useful life of the asset).
per	Required. The period for which to calculate the depreciation. It must be in the same units as life. For example, the period for the third year of an asset with a ten-year life will be 3.

Example

In the example below, we use the SYD function to calculate the depreciation of some office equipment over 10 years.

Function arguments:
- Cost = $40,000
- Life = 10 (years)
- Salvage = $1,000

| B9 | | ⌄ ⋮ ✕ ✓ *fx* | =SYD(InitialCost,SalvageValue,Life,A9) | | |

⊿	A	B	C	D	E	F
1	**Depreciation of office equipment - SYD**					
2						
3	Initial Cost	$40,000.00		*InitialCost = B3*		
4	Life (years)	10		*Life = B4*		
5	Salvage value	$1,000.00		*SalvageValue = B5*		
6						
7	Year	SYD	Asset value			
8	0	$0.00	$40,000.00			
9	1	$7,090.91	$32,909.09			
10	2	$6,381.82	$26,527.27			
11	3	$5,672.73	$20,854.55			
12	4	$4,963.64	$15,890.91			
13	5	$4,254.55	$11,636.36	Cumulative		
14	6	$3,545.45	$8,090.91	depreciation		
15	7	$2,836.36	$5,254.55			
16	8	$2,127.27	$3,127.27			
17	9	$1,418.18	$1,709.09			
18	10	$709.09	$1,000.00			
19						

Formula explanation

=SYD(InitialCost,SalvageValue,Life,A9)

The formula in cell B9 uses the following range names for the cost, salvage, and life arguments:

- InitialCost = B3
- Life = B4
- SalvageValue = B5

The values in the cells above remain the same over the 10-year depreciation period, so using range names makes it easier to copy the formula for the other years. The *per* argument is a relative reference, cell A9, which changes with the year being calculated.

As depicted in the image above, with the SYD function, the depreciation amount gets progressively smaller compared to an SLN depreciation, for example, which is constant over the period.

=C8-SYD(InitialCost,SalvageValue,Life,A9)

The formulas in the **Asset value** column (C9:C18) subtract each year's depreciation from the previous year's calculated asset value. Hence, this column shows a progressive decrease in the asset's value over the 10-year period until it reaches the salvage value.

DB Function

The DB function is a depreciation function that uses the fixed-declining balance method to return the depreciation of an asset over a specified period. The fixed-declining balance method calculates the depreciation at a fixed rate.

Syntax

=DB(cost, salvage, life, period, [month])

Arguments

Arguments	Descriptions
cost	Required. The initial cost of the depreciating asset.
salvage	Required. The value at the end of the depreciation (also referred to as the salvage value of the asset).
life	Required. The number of periods over which the asset is depreciating (also referred to as the useful life of the asset).
period	Required. The period in the asset's life for which to calculate the depreciation. The period must be in the same units as life.
month	Optional. The number of months in the first year of the depreciation if it is not 12. If this argument is omitted, the default is 12.

Remarks

- The following formulas are used to calculate depreciation for a period:

```
(cost - total depreciation from prior periods) * rate
```

```
Where:
```

```
rate = 1 - ((salvage / cost) ^ (1 / life))
```

- DB uses different formulas to calculate the depreciation for the first and last periods.

First period:

```
cost * rate * month / 12
```

Last period:

```
((cost - total depreciation from prior periods) * rate * (12 -
month)) / 12
```

Example 1

In the following example, we're calculating the depreciation of an asset over 5 years using the following data:

Argument	Value
Costs	$10,000
Salvage value	$2,000
Life	5 years

The first year has 12 months, so we can omit the month argument.

The formula for the **first year** will be thus:

=DB(10000, 2000, 5, 1)

Result: $2,750.00

Example 2

The following example calculates the depreciation of an asset with the following parameters:

Parameter	Value
Costs	$10,000
Salvage value	$2,000
Life (years)	5
Period (year)	5th year
First year (months)	8

The depreciation is calculated for the fifth year, and there are 8 months in the first year:

=DB(10000, 2000, 5, 5, 8)

Result: $855.84

Example 3

In this example, we use the SYD function to calculate the depreciation of office equipment with a useful life of 10 years. The initial cost is $40,000, and the salvage value is $1,000.

The first year has only 7 months, so we need to specify that in the *month* argument.

B9			fx	=DB(InitialCost,Salvage,Life,A9,FirstYr)	
	A	B	C	D	E
1	Depreciation of office equipment - (DB)				
2					
3	Initial Cost	$40,000.00		InitialCost = B3	
4	Life (years)	10		Life = B4	
5	Salvage value	$1,000.00		Salvage = B5	
6	First Yr (# of months)	7		FirstYr = B6	
7					
8	Year	DB	Asset value		
9	1	$7,186.67	$32,813.33		
10	2	$10,106.51	$22,706.83		
11	3	$6,993.70	$15,713.12		
12	4	$4,839.64	$10,873.48		
13	5	$3,349.03	$7,524.45		
14	6	$2,317.53	$5,206.92		
15	7	$1,603.73	$3,603.19		
16	8	$1,109.78	$2,493.41		
17	9	$767.97	$1,725.44		
18	10	$531.43	$1,194.00		
19					

Formula explanation

=DB(InitialCost,Salvage,Life,A9,FirstYr)

The formula in cell B9 uses the following range names:

- InitialCost = B3
- Salvage = B4
- Life = B5
- FirstYr = B6

The range names correspond to the *cost*, *salvage*, *life*, and *month* arguments, as these remain the same over the 10-year depreciation period. The *per* argument is a relative reference, which changes in column A according to the year being calculated.

The *month* argument, FirstYr, holds a value of 7. This value specifies that the first year of the depreciation is 7 months rather than 12. This argument could have been omitted if the first year was 12 months.

From the image above, we can see that apart from the first year (7 months), the depreciation progresses linearly as the asset value reduces.

DDB Function

This DDB function returns the depreciation of an asset for a specified period using the double-declining balance method. The double-declining balance method calculates depreciation at an accelerated rate, with the depreciation highest in the first period and decreasing in successive periods.

This function is flexible, as you can change the *factor* argument if you don't want to use the double-declining balance method.

Syntax

=DDB(cost, salvage, life, period, [factor])

Arguments

Argument	Description
cost	Required. The initial cost of the depreciating asset.
salvage	Required. The value at the end of the depreciation (also referred to as the salvage value of the asset).
life	Required. The number of periods over which the asset is depreciating (also referred to as the useful life of the asset).
period	Required. The period in the asset's life for which to calculate the depreciation. It must be in the same units as life.
factor	Optional. The rate at which the balance declines.
	If omitted, the factor is assumed to be 2, which is the double-declining balance method.

Remarks

- The five arguments must be positive numbers.

- The DDB function uses the following formula to calculate depreciation for a period:

```
Min( (cost - total depreciation from prior periods) *
(factor/life), (cost - salvage - total depreciation from prior
periods) )
```

Example

In the following example, we use different DDB formulas to return results for the depreciation of a car.

Data:
- Initial Cost: $25,000.00
- Salvage value: $2,500.00
- Life (in years): 10

	A	B	C	D
1	**Depreciation of car - DDB**			
2				
3	Initial Cost	$25,000.00		
4	Salvage value	$2,500.00		
5	Life (in years)	10		
6				
7	**Period**	**Depreciation**	**Formula text**	
8	First day	$13.70	=DDB(Cost,Salvage,LifeInYrs*365,1)	*Factor 2 (default)*
9	First month	$416.67	=DDB(Cost,Salvage,LifeInYrs*12,1)	
10	First year	$5,000.00	=DDB(Cost,Salvage,LifeInYrs,1)	
11	First year (factor of 1.5)	$3,750.00	=DDB(Cost,Salvage,LifeInYrs,1,1.5)	*For comparisons*
12	Tenth year	$671.09	=DDB(Cost,Salvage,LifeInYrs,10)	
13				
14	*Cost = B3*			
15	*Salvage = B4*			
16	*LifeInYrs = B5*			
17				

Explanation of formulas

=DDB(Cost,Salvage,LifeInYrs*365,1)

The above formula uses range names for cell references:
- Cost = B3
- Salvage = B4
- LifeInYrs = B5

These range names relate to the *cost, salvage,* and *life* arguments in the formula.

Life is (10 * 365) because we want to calculate the depreciation in daily units rather than months or years. The period is 1, representing the first day of the item's life. The factor argument is omitted, so it defaults to 2, using the double-declining balance method.

=DDB(Cost,Salvage,LifeInYrs*12,1,2)

The formula above calculates the first month's depreciation. The factor argument was included in this case to specify the double-declining balance method. However, omitting the factor defaults to 2.

=DDB(Cost,Salvage,LifeInYrs,1)

The first year's depreciation. Notice that the *life* argument LifeInYrs has not been multiplied by 12, so the formula will return a result for year 1 as specified in the period argument.

=DDB(Cost,Salvage,LifeInYrs,1,1.5)

This formula is the first year's depreciation using a factor of 1.5 instead of the double-declining balance method.

=DDB(Cost,Salvage,LifeInYrs,10)

The above formula returns the tenth year's depreciation calculation. Factor has been omitted, so it defaults to 2.

Installing the Analysis ToolPak

The Excel Analysis ToolPak is an add-on that you can install that enables you to carry out complex statistical or engineering analyses. You can save a lot of time as you simply provide the data and parameters, and the tool uses the appropriate engineering or statistical functions to calculate and display the results in output tables. Some of the tools even generate charts in addition to output tables.

You can only use the data analysis functions on one worksheet at a time. When you carry out data analysis on a group of worksheets at the same time, results will appear on the first worksheet, and empty tables will appear on the remaining worksheets. To carry out the data analysis on the rest of the worksheets, you'll need to recalculate the analysis tool for each worksheet.

Follow these steps to install the Analysis ToolPak:

1. Select **File** > **Excel Options** (or press Alt+FT to directly open the Excel Options dialog box), and then click **Add-Ins**.

    The Add-Ins tab lists all the names, locations, and types of the add-ins currently available to you in Excel.

2. In the **Manage box** (at the bottom of the Add-ins tab), select **Excel Add-ins** and then click **Go**.

    If you're on a Mac, in the file menu, go to **Tools** > **Excel Add-ins**.

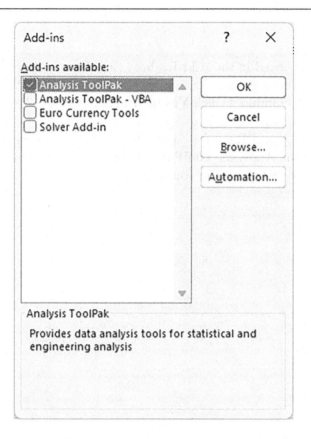

3. In the **Add-Ins** dialog box, select the **Analysis ToolPak** check box, and then click **OK**.

4. To access the Analysis ToolPak tools on the Excel ribbon, click the **Data** tab, then in the **Analysis** group, click the **Data Analysis** button.

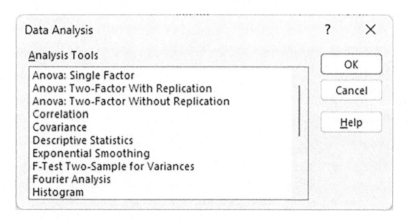

Remarks:

- If Analysis ToolPak is not listed in the Add-Ins box, click **Browse** to find it on your computer. You may get a prompt saying that the Analysis ToolPak is not currently installed on your computer. Click **Yes** to install it.

- (Optional) To include the Visual Basic for Application (VBA) functions for the Analysis ToolPak, select the **Analysis ToolPak - VBA** check box. This is only required if you intend to use VBA code in your data analysis.

Appendix A: More Help with Excel

For more help with Excel, you can visit Excel's official online help site.

https://support.office.com/en-gb/excel

This website is a comprehensive help center for Excel. Although not an organized tutorial like this book, it is useful when you're looking for help on a specific topic. You'll also find resources like Excel templates that you can download and use as the starting basis for your worksheets.

You can also visit our website for many free Excel tips and techniques.

https://www.excelbytes.com

Appendix B: Keyboard Shortcuts (Excel for Windows)

The Excel Ribbon comes with new shortcuts called Key Tips. Press the **Alt** key when Excel is the active window to see Key Tips.

The following table lists the most frequently used shortcuts in Excel.

Keystroke	Action
F1	Opens Excel's Help window
Ctrl+O	Open a workbook
Ctrl+W	Close a workbook
Ctrl+C	Copy
Ctrl+V	Paste
Ctrl+X	Cut

Ctrl+Z	Undo
Ctrl+B	Bold
Ctrl+S	Save a workbook
Ctrl+F1	Displays or hides the Ribbon
Delete key	Remove cell contents
Alt+H	Go to the Home tab
Alt+H, H	Choose a fill color
Alt+N	Go to the Insert tab
Alt+A	Go to the Data tab
Alt+P	Go to the Page Layout tab
Alt+H, A, then C	Center align cell contents
Alt+W	Go to the View tab
Shift+F10, or Context key	Open context menu
Alt+H, B	Add borders
Alt+H,D, then C	Delete column
Alt+M	Go to the Formula tab
Ctrl+9	Hide the selected rows
Ctrl+0	Hide the selected columns

Keyboard Shortcuts for Functions and Formulas

The table below covers some of the most useful Excel for Windows shortcut keys when working with functions, formulas, and the formula bar.

Keystroke	Action
F2	Moves the insertion point to the end of the contents of the active cell.
Ctrl+Shift+U	Expands or reduces the size of the formula bar.
Esc	Cancels an entry in the formula bar or a cell.
Enter	Confirms an entry in the formula bar and moves to the cell below.
Ctrl+End	Moves the cursor to the end of the contents in the formula bar.
Ctrl+Shift+End	Selects everything in the formula bar from the current position of the cursor to the end.
F9	Calculates all worksheets in all open workbooks.
Shift+F9	Calculates the active worksheet.
Ctrl+Alt+F9	Calculates all worksheets in all open workbooks, even if they have not changed since the last calculation.
Ctrl+Alt+Shift+F9	Checks all dependent formulas and then calculates all cells in all open workbooks.
Ctrl+A	Opens the Function Arguments dialog box when the insertion point is to the right of a function name in a formula bar.
Ctrl+Shift+A	Inserts the argument names and parentheses for a function when the insertion point is to the right of a function name in the formula bar.

Ctrl+E	Executes the Flash Fill command to fill down the current column if Excel recognizes patterns in the values in adjacent columns.
F4	Changes the selected cell reference or range in the formula bar to absolute references. Further presses will cycle through all combinations of absolute and relative references for the selected cell reference or range.
Shift+F3	Opens the Insert Function dialog box.
Ctrl+Shift+Quotation mark (")	Copies the value from the cell directly above the active cell into the active cell or formula bar.
Alt+F1	Automatically inserts an embedded chart of the data in the selected range.
F11	Automatically inserts a chart of the data in the selected range in a different worksheet.
Alt+M, M, D	Opens the New Name dialog box for creating a named range.
F3	Opens the Paste Name dialog box if a range name has been defined in the workbook.
Alt+F8	Opens the Macro dialog box where you can run, edit, or delete a macro.
Alt+F11	Opens the Visual Basic for Applications editor.

Access Keys for Ribbon Tabs

To go directly to a tab on the Excel Ribbon, press one of the following access keys.

Action	Keystroke
Activate the Search box.	Alt+Q
Open the File page, i.e., the Backstage view.	Alt+F
Open the Home tab.	Alt+H
Open the Insert tab.	Alt+N
Open the Page Layout tab.	Alt+P
Open the Formulas tab.	Alt+M
Open the Data.	Alt+A
Open the Review.	Alt+R
Open the View.	Alt+W

To get a more comprehensive list of Excel for Windows shortcuts, press **F1** to open Excel Help and type in "Keyboard shortcuts" in the search bar.

Glossary

Absolute reference
This is a cell reference that doesn't change when you copy a formula containing the reference to another cell. For example, $A$3 means the row and column have been set to absolute.

Add-in
A different application you can add to extend the functionality of Excel. It could be from Microsoft or a third-party vendor.

Active cell
The cell that is currently selected and open for editing.

Alignment
The way a cell's contents are arranged within that cell. The alignment could be left, centered, or right.

Argument
The input values a function requires to carry out a calculation or evaluation.

Array
An array can be seen as a row of values, a column of values, or a combination of both.

AutoCalculate

An Excel feature that automatically calculates and displays the summary of a selected range of numbers on the status bar.

AutoComplete

This is an Excel feature that completes data entry for a range of cells based on values in other cells in the same column or row.

Backstage view

The screen you see when you click the File tab on the ribbon. It has menu options for managing your workbook and configuring global settings in Excel.

Boolean array

A Boolean array is an array of TRUE/FALSE Boolean values or (0 and 1). You can create such an array in Excel by applying logical tests to the values in a column or row.

Cell reference

The letter and number combination that represents the intersection of a column and row. For example, B10 means column B, row 10.

Chart

A visual representation of summarized worksheet data.

Conditional format

This is a format that applies only when certain criteria are met by the cell content.

Conditional formula

A conditional formula calculates a value from one of two expressions based on whether a third expression evaluates to true or false.

Delimiter

A character in a text file that is used to separate the values into columns.

Dependent

A cell with a formula that references other cells, so its value is dependent on other cells.

Dialog box launcher

In the lower-right corner of some groups on the Excel ribbon, you'll see a diagonal down-pointing arrow. When you click the arrow, it opens a dialog box containing several additional options for that group.

Digital certificate

A file with a unique string of characters that can be combined with an Excel workbook to create a verifiable signature.

Digital signature

A mathematical construct that combines a file and a digital certificate to verify the authorship of the file.

Dynamic array formula

Dynamic array formulas are a set of formulas in Excel that can return multiple values to a range of cells called the *spill range*.

Excel table

This is a cell range that has been defined as a table in Excel. Excel adds certain attributes to the range to make it easier to manipulate the data as a table.

Fill handle

A small square on the lower right of the cell pointer. You can drag this handle to AutoFill values for other cells.

Fill series

This is the Excel functionality that allows you to create a series of values based on a starting value and any rules or intervals included.

Formula

An expression used to calculate a value.

Formula bar

This is the area just above the worksheet grid that displays the value of the active cell. This is where you enter a formula in Excel.

Function

A function is a predefined formula in Excel that just requires input values (arguments) to calculate and return a value.

Goal Seek
An analysis tool that can be used to create projections by setting the goal, and the tool calculates the input values required to meet the goals from a set number of variables.

Graph
A representation of summarized worksheet data, also known as a chart.

Live Preview
A preview of whatever task you want to perform based on your actual data. So, you get to see how your data will look if you carry out the command.

Locked cell
A locked cell cannot be modified if the worksheet is protected.

Macro
A series of instructions created from recording Excel tasks that automate Excel when replayed.

Named range
A group of cells in your worksheet given one name that can then be used as a reference.

OneDrive
This is a cloud storage service provided by Microsoft which automatically syncs your files to a remote drive, hence providing instant backups.

PivotChart
A specific kind of Excel chart related to a PivotTable. A PivotChart can be dynamically reorganized to show different views of your data, just like a PivotTable.

PivotTable
This is an Excel summary table that allows you to dynamically summarise data from different perspectives. PivotTables are highly flexible, and you can quickly adjust them depending on how you need to display your results.

Precedent
A cell that is used as a cell reference in a formula in another cell. Also, see Dependent.

Quick Access Toolbar
This is a customizable toolbar with a set of commands independent of the tab and ribbon commands currently on display.

Relative reference
Excel cell references are relative references by default. This means when copied across multiple cells, they change based on the relative position of columns and rows.

Ribbon
This is the top part of the Excel screen that contains the tabs and commands.

Scenario
An alternative set of data that you can use the compare the impact of changes in your data. This is useful when creating projections and forecasts.

Slicer
A graphical tool for filtering the data in your Excel table, list, or PivotTable. A Slicer gives you a visual indication of which items are displayed or hidden in your PivotTable.

Solver
An Excel add-in that enables you to create scenarios for more complex data models.

Sort
A sort means to reorder the data in a worksheet in ascending or descending order by one or more columns.

Sparkline
A small chart that visually represents data in a single worksheet cell.

Spill Range
This is the range of cells that contains the results returned from an array formula. A spill range can be multiple rows and/or columns.

Tracer arrows
Graphical arrows that are used to indicate dependent or precedent cells.

Validation rule
A test that data must pass to be a valid entry in a cell.

Watch
The watch window can be used to display the contents of a cell in a separate window even when the cell is not visible on the screen.

What-If Analysis

A series of methods that can be used to determine the impact of changes on your data. This could include projections and forecasts.

Workbook

This is the Excel document itself, and it can contain one or more worksheets.

Worksheet

A worksheet is like a page in an Excel workbook.

x-axis

The horizontal axis of a chart where you could have time intervals etc.

y-axis

This is the vertical axis of a chart, which usually depicts value data.

Index

About the Author

Nathan George is a computer science graduate with several years of experience in the IT services industry in different roles, which included Excel VBA programming, Access development, Excel training, and providing end-user support to Excel power users. One of his main interests is using computers to automate tasks and increase productivity. As an author, he has written several technical and non-technical books.

Leave a Review

If you found this book helpful, I would be very grateful if you could spend just 5 minutes leaving a customer review. You can go to the link below to leave a customer review.

https://www.excelbytes.com/mastering-excel-365-review

Thank you very much!

Other Books by Author

Mastering Access 365

An Easy Guide to Building Efficient Databases for Managing Your Data

Has your data become too large and complex for Excel?

If so, then Access may just be the tool you need. Whether you're new to Access or looking to refresh your skills on this popular database application, you'll find everything you need to create efficient and flexible database solutions for your data in this book.

Mastering Access 365 offers straightforward step-by-step explanations using real-world examples.

This book comes with downloadable sample databases for hands-on learning.

Available at Amazon:

https://www.amazon.com/dp/1916211399

Excel 2019 Macros and VBA

An Introduction to Excel Programming

Take your Excel skills to the next level with macros and Visual Basic for Applications (VBA)!

Create solutions that would have otherwise been too cumbersome or impossible to create with standard Excel commands and functions. Automate Excel for repetitive tasks and save yourself time and tedium.

With *Excel 2019 Macros and VBA,* you'll learn how to automate Excel using quick macros as well as writing VBA code. You'll learn all the VBA fundamentals to enable you to start creating your own code from scratch.

Available at Amazon:

https://www.amazon.com/dp/1916211348

For more Excel books visit:

https://www.excelbytes.com/excel-books/